The Best
Mid-Atlantic Colleges

The Best
Mid-Atlantic Colleges

98 Great Schools
to Consider

By Robert Franek,
Tom Meltzer, Roy Opochinski,
Tara Bray, Christopher Maier, Carson Brown,
Julie Doherty, K. Nadine Kavanaugh,
Catherine Monaco, and Dinaw Mengestu

Random House, Inc.

New York

www.PrincetonReview.com

Princeton Review Publishing, L. L. C.
2315 Broadway
New York, NY 10024
E-mail: bookeditor@review.com

ISBN 0-375-76341-4

Editorial Director: Robert Franek
Editors: Robert Franek, Erik Olson, and Erica Magrey
Designer: Scott Harris
Production Editor: Julieanna Lambert
Production Coordinator: Scott Harris

Manufactured in the United States of America.

9 8 7 6 5 4 3 2 1

FOREWORD

Every year, about three million high school graduates go to college. To make sure they end up at the *right* school, they spend several billion dollars on the admissions process. This money pays for countless admissions officers and counselors, a bunch of standardized tests (and preparation for them), and many books similar to—but not as good as—this one.

It's so expensive because most admissions professionals have a thing about being in control. As a group, colleges resist almost every attempt to standardize or otherwise simplify the process. Admissions officers want you to believe that every admissions decision that they render occurs within systems of weights, measures, and deliberations that are far too complex for you to comprehend. They shudder at the notion of having to respond to students and their parents in down-to-earth language that might reveal the arbitrary nature of a huge percentage of the admissions and denials that they issue during each cycle. That would be admitting that good luck and circumstance play a major part in many successful applications. So, in flight from public accountability, they make the process a lot more mysterious than it needs to be.

Even the most straightforward colleges hide the information you would want to know about the way they'll evaluate your application: What grades and SATs are they looking for? Do their reported SAT averages include minority students, athletes, and legacies (kids whose parents went to their school)? Exactly how much do extracurricular activities count? What percentage of the aid that they give out is in loans and what percentage is in grants?

We couldn't get answers to these questions from many colleges. In fact, we couldn't get answers to *any* questions from some schools. Others who supplied this information to us for earlier editions of this guide have since decided that they never should have in the first place. After all, knowledge is power.

Colleges seem to have the time and money to create beautiful brochures that generally show that all college classes are held under a tree on a beautiful day. Why not just tell you what sort of students they're looking for, and what factors they'll use to consider your application?

Until the schools demystify the admissions process, this book is your best bet. It's not a phone book containing every fact about every college in the country. And it's not a memoir written by a few graduates describing their favorite dining halls or professors. We've given you the facts you'll need to apply to the few hundred best schools in the country. And enough information about them—which we gathered from hundreds of counselors and admissions officers and more than 100,000 college students—to help you make a smart decision about which school to attend.

One note: We don't talk a lot about majors. This is because most high school students really don't know what they want to major in—and the ones who do almost always change their minds by the beginning of junior year. Choosing a school because of the reputation of a single department is often a terrible idea.

If you're interested in learning about majors and the colleges that offer them, pick up our *Guide to College Majors* or visit our website, www.princetonreview.com, where we explain majors and list the colleges that offer them.

As complicated and difficult as the admissions process is, we think you'll love college itself—especially at the schools listed in this book.

Good luck in your search.

John Katzman

June 2003

ACKNOWLEDGMENTS

I am blessed year after year with a talented group of colleagues working together to produce our guidebooks. This book, part of our "building out" of the concept of our flagship college guide, *The Best 351 Colleges,* yields, like its predecessor, what prospective college students really want: the most honest, accessible, and pertinent information on colleges they are considering attending for the next four years of their lives. Collectively including profiles of more than 600 colleges and universities, our *Best Regional Colleges* series was an unprecedented undertaking, requiring well-coordinated student survey, editorial, and production efforts, and my sincere thanks go to the many who contributed to this tremendous project. I am proud to note here that we have again successfully provided an uncompromising look into the true nature of each profiled college or university, based on the opinions of each college's current students. I know our readers will benefit from our cumulative efforts.

A special thank you goes to our authors, Tom Meltzer, Tara Bray, Roy Opochinski, Christopher Maier, Carson Brown, Julie Doherty, Nadine Kavanaugh, Catherine Monaco, and Dinaw Mengestu for their dedication in sifting through thousands of surveys to produce the essence of each school in three paragraphs! Very special thanks go to two stellar producers from our editorial staff: Erik Olson and Erica Magrey. Erik, our Senior Editor, is an essential resource to our department and a clear driver of this series. I can always trust Erik to provide clear direction in both the voice and sensibilities of The Princeton Review; he has proven himself again here. Erica, in her freshman performance, took this trial by fire with grace and moxie. On a daily basis, Erica brought quiet competence to the student survey process, adhering meticulously to our standards and goals for each book's narrative profiles.

Sincere thanks go to Jillian Taylor, our Student Survey Manager. Jillian provided clear messaging on our survey methodology and editorial procedure, remaining evenhanded and approachable throughout the process. A special note goes to Amy Kinney, a veteran student surveyor, for her unwavering dedication to relaying our books' mission to the schools included in these pages. She provided sincere representation of the mission of The Princeton Review. Michael Palumbo also deserves praise for his indispensable contributions in the last days of production.

My continued thanks go to our data collection staff—David Soto, Ben Zelavansky, and Yojaira Cordero—for their successful efforts in collecting and accurately representing the statistical data that appear with each college profile. In turn, my gratitude goes to Chris Wujciak for his competence in all of our book pours.

The enormity of this project and its deadline constraints could not have been realized without the calm presence of our production team, Julieanna Lambert and Scott Harris. Their ability to remain focused throughout the production of this project inspires and impresses me. They deserve great thanks for their flexible schedules and uncompromising efficiency.

Special thanks go to Jeanne Krier, our Random House publicist, for the work she has done on this new series and the overall work she has done on our flagship book, *The Best 351 Colleges*, since its first edition. Jeanne continues to be my trusted colleague, media advisor, and friend. I would also like to make special mention of Tom Russell, our publisher, for his continuous investment in our new book ideas.

Lastly, I thank John Katzman and Mark Chernis for their steadfast confidence in both this series and our publishing department, and for always being the champions of student opinion. It is pleasure to work with you both.

Again, to all who contributed so much to these publications, thank you for your efforts; they do not go unnoticed.

Robert Franek

Editorial Director

Lead Author—The Best Regional Colleges

Contents

PART 1

INTRODUCTION

A P _ L I C _ T _ O _.

What's *that*?!?!

It's APPLICATION with P-A-I-N removed from the process.

We removed the paper, too.

With PrincetonReview.com's Online College Applications there are no endless piles to shuffle. No leaky pens, no hand cramps, no trying to figure out how many stamps to stick on that envelope.

The process is so painless, online applications practically submit themselves for you. Watch . . .

Type in your main contact information just once in our application profile and every subsequent application you file from our database— picking from hundreds of top schools—is automatically filled in with your information.

Not only are online applications:

- Faster to fill out

- Completely safe and secure

- Instantly trackable (check your application status online!)

- And . . . impossible to lose in the mail (they reach schools instantly)

But also: On PrincetonReview.com, there's no extra fee to submit your application online—our technology is totally FREE for you to use. In fact, some colleges even *waive* the application fee if you apply online.

Still have questions?

- Can I start an application now and finish it later?

- Are there easy-to-use instructions or someone I can call if I have a question? If I get stuck are there application instructions?

- Do schools *really* want to receive applications online?

Yes, yes, and yes!

It's easy to see the advantages of online applications. Almost as easy as actually applying.

Just log on and apply. It's that easy.

PrincetonReview.com—Applications without the pain.

How We Produce This Book

Welcome to the first edition of *The Best Mid-Atlantic Colleges*, one-fifth of our *Best* regional guidebook series. Our decision to produce this series was fueled by a desire to raise awareness of academically excellent but lesser-known regional colleges for those looking to study within a specific geographic area. Many of the schools within these pages are nationally competitive institutions of higher learning; we therefore also include their profiles in the 2004 edition of our best-selling *The Best 351 Colleges*. In fact, for these regional guides, we employ the same methodology for collecting student surveys and distilling them into college profiles as we do for *The Best 351 Colleges*. An important difference between this series and *The Best 351 Colleges*, however, is that we do not include any ranking lists. The profiles in these regional guides also appear in a slightly different format than those in *The Best 351 Colleges*.

But why are some of the outstanding schools in this book *not* included in *Best 351*? For one or both of two possible reasons. First, it may be because—at this time—they have a regional, rather than a national, focus. That is, they draw their students primarily from the state in which they are located, or from bordering states. A second possible reason is that—again, at this time—they have not met the rather rigorous standards for inclusion in *The Best 351 Colleges*. Is that meant as a snub to the schools that didn't make it into *Best 351*? Absolutely not. There are more than 3,000 institutions of higher learning in the United States, and *The Best 351 Colleges* profiles the top 10 percent, academically, of those schools. These regional guides, on the other hand, offer student opinion–driven information on all of those top colleges as well as the colleges just outside of that highest 10 percent.

For each school, we provide both in-depth statistical data (on admissions, financial aid, student body demographics, and academics) and narrative descriptions of academic and social life based on the opinions of the very students who attend them. Although we have expanded the scope of schools profiled from *Best 351*, we have also narrowed our focus to aid students for whom location is a key consideration.

We avoided using any sort of mathematical calculations or formulas to determine which colleges and universities to include in the regional guides. For each region, we aim to provide an inclusive cross-section of colleges: large and small, public and private, all-male and all-female, historically black colleges and universities, science and technology–focused institutions, nontraditional colleges, highly selective and virtually open-door admissions, great buys and the wildly expensive. Like the other schools in these guides, all are institutions well worth considering. Though not every college included will appeal to every student, this guide represents the top 98 colleges in the Mid-Atlantic states. We've surveyed students at 604 colleges across the nation and sorted their profiles into five regional guides. The following books complete the series:

The Best Midwestern Colleges

The Best Northeastern Colleges

The Best Southeastern Colleges

The Best Western Colleges

Each college we surveyed this year had to meet two criteria: first, they had to meet our standards for academic excellence within their region, and second, we had to be able to survey their students anonymously, either through our online survey (http://survey.review.com) or through our paper survey, which we distribute and collect during an on-campus visit.

Surveying thousands of students on hundreds of campuses is a mammoth undertaking, but the launch of our online student survey, available 24/7, has made it possible for students to complete a survey anytime and anywhere an Internet-enabled computer can be found. We've surveyed anywhere from all twenty-odd men at Deep Springs College in the California desert to thousands of collegians at places like Clemson University and Utah State University.

So how do we do it? All colleges and universities we plan to visit are notified through established campus contacts that we wish to arrange a survey; we depend on these contacts for assistance in identifying common, high-traffic areas on campus in which to distribute our paper survey and to help us make any necessary arrangements as required by campus policies. When possible, and when the college is willing, our contacts will arrange for an e-mail to be sent to the entire student body encouraging them to fill out our online survey. (In recent years, many schools have chosen to send an e-mail to the entire student body, which in some cases yielded astonishing results.) At colleges in the New York metropolitan area (we call it home), we most often send our own team to conduct the typically half-day surveys; at colleges that are further afield, we typically either send Princeton Review people from our field offices or hire current students at the college to conduct the surveys. Some of the colleges also included in *The Best 351 Colleges* series were surveyed this past year, but not *all*; each is surveyed *at least* once every three years. The reality is that, unless there's been some grand upheaval at a campus, we've found that there's little change in student opinion from one year to the next. Colleges that wish to be resurveyed prior to their turn in the regular survey cycle are accommodated with an earlier visit if at all possible.

The survey itself is extensive, divided into four fundamental sections—"About Yourself," "Your School's Academics/Administration," "Students," and "Life at Your School"—that collectively include more than 70 questions. We ask about everything imaginable, from "How many out-of-class hours do you spend studying each day?" to "How widely used is beer?" Most questions are multiple-response in nature, but several offer students the opportunity to expand on their answers with narrative responses. These narrative responses are the source of the student quotes that appear throughout each college profile in *The Best Mid-Atlantic Colleges*.

Once the surveys have been completed and the responses stored in our database, each college is given a grade point average (GPA) for its students' answers to each multiple-response question. It is these GPAs that enable us to compare student opinions from college to college, and to gauge which aspects of the complete experience at each college rate highest and lowest according to the institution's own students. (They are also the basis for three of the ratings—Quality of Life, Financial Aid, and Academic—that appear at the top of each college profile.) Once we have this information in hand, we write the individual college profiles. Student quotes within the profiles are not chosen for their extreme nature, humor, or singular perspective—in all cases the intention is that they represent closely the sentiments expressed by the majority of survey respondents from the college or that they illustrate one side or another of a mixed bag of student opinion (in which case the counterpoint will also appear within the text). And of course, if a student's quote accomplishes this *and* is noteworthy for it's wittiness, it'll definitely make it into the guide.

The profiles in general seek to accomplish that which a college admissions viewbook by its very nature can never really hope to achieve—to provide a (relatively) uncensored view of life at a particular college, and acknowledge that even the best colleges have their shortcomings. Though some college administrators find this book hard to accept, most have come to recognize that college officials no longer enjoy the luxury of controlling every word that students hear or read about their institutions and that the age of consumerism in the college search process is here to stay.

Our survey is qualitative and anecdotal. While this approach sometimes means we blow a result—such as when we surveyed at Stephens College during the week the administration was debating the abolition of women's studies as a major at that small women's college and *(surprise!)* the survey results indicated an unhappy student body— most of our results are confirmed by feedback we get from alums, current students, counselors, and prospective students who visit the campuses. In order to help guard against the likelihood that we produce an entry that's way off the mark, we send administrators at each school a copy of the entry we intend to publish prior to its actual publication date, with ample opportunity to respond with corrections, comments, and/or outright objections. In every case in which we receive a reply, we take careful steps to ensure that we review their suggestions and make appropriate changes when warranted.

Far more important than what college administrators think is what *you* think. Take our information on colleges as you should take information from all sources—as input that reflects the values and opinions of others, which may be helpful to you as you *form your own opinions*. This guide is not an end point from which you should cull your list of possible colleges but rather a starting point, a tool that can help you to probe the surface and get a sense of the college experience. You must do your own investigation, refer to other sources, visit the campuses, and develop your own list of best colleges. Only then will this book be the useful tool that it is intended to be.

HOW THIS BOOK IS ORGANIZED

Each of the colleges and universities listed in this book has its own two-page spread. To make it easier to find information about the schools of your choice, we've used the same format for every school. Look at the sample pages below:

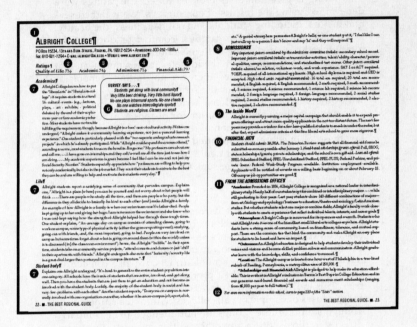

Each spread has several components. First, at the very top of the spread you will see the school's address, telephone and fax numbers for the admissions office, the telephone number for the financial aid office, and the school's website and/or e-mail address. Next, you will find the school's ratings in four categories: Quality of Life, Academics, Admissions, and Financial Aid, which are described further below. Then you will see our "Survey Says . . ." bubble and the first three sections—"Academics," "Life," and "Student Body"—which are drawn primarily from student survey responses for that particular college. Then comes the "Admissions" section with information on how the admissions office weighs the different components of your application; followed by the "Inside Word" on admissions, academics, life, or demographics at that school; "Financial Aid" application pointers; and an institution-authored message under the title "From the Admissions Office." Finally, at the end of the profile is the page number on which the school's statistical data appears. Here's an explanation of each part:

1. Contact Information

Includes school address, admissions phone and fax numbers, financial aid phone number, admissions e-mail address, and school website.

2. Quality of Life Rating

How happy students are with their lives outside the classroom. This rating is given on a scale of 60 to 99. The ratings were determined using the results of our surveys. We weighed several factors, including students' overall happiness; the beauty, safety, and location of the campus; comfort of dorms; food quality; and ease in dealing with the administration. Note that even if a school's rating is in the low 60s, it does not mean that the quality of life is horrible—there are no "failing" schools. A low ranking just means that the school placed low compared with others in our *Best* regional series. This individual rating places each college on a continuum for purposes of comparing all colleges within this edition of the series only. Though similar, these ratings are not intended to be compared directly to those within any subsequent edition, as our ratings computations are refined and change somewhat annually.

3. Academic Rating

On a scale of 60 to 99, how hard students work at the school and how much they get back for their efforts. The ratings are based on results of our surveys of students and administrators. Factors weighed included how many hours students study and the quality of students the school attracts; we also considered students' assessments of their professors' abilities and helpfulness. This individual rating places each college on a continuum for purposes of comparing all colleges within this edition only. Though similar, these ratings are not intended to be compared directly to those within any other edition, as our ratings computations are refined and change somewhat annually.

4. Admissions Rating

How competitive admission is at the school, on a scale of 60 to 99. This rating is determined by several factors, including the class rank of entering freshmen, their test scores, and the percentage of applicants accepted. By incorporating all these factors, our competitiveness rating adjusts for "self-selecting" applicant pools. University of Chicago, for example, has a very high competitiveness rating, even though it admits a surprisingly large proportion of its applicants. Chicago's applicant pool is self-selecting; that is, nearly all the school's applicants are exceptional students. This individual rating places each college on a continuum for purposes of comparing all colleges within this edition only. Though similar, these ratings are not intended to be compared directly to those within any other edition, as our ratings computations are refined and change somewhat annually.

5. Financial Aid Rating

Based on school-reported data on financial aid awards to students and students' satisfaction, as collected on our survey, with the financial aid they receive. Again, this is on a scale of 60 to 99. This individual rating places each college on a continuum for purposes of comparing all colleges within this edition only. Though similar, these ratings are not intended to be compared directly to those within any other edition, as our ratings computations are refined and change somewhat annually.

6. Survey Says . . .

Our "Survey Says" list, located under the ratings on each school's two-page spread, is based entirely on the results of our student surveys. In other words, the items on this list are based on the opinions of the students we surveyed at those schools (*not* on any numerical analysis of library size, endowment, etc.). Items listed are those that are unusually popular or unpopular on that campus. Some of the terms that appear on the list are not entirely self-explanatory; these terms are defined below.

Diverse students interact: We asked whether students from different class and ethnic backgrounds interacted frequently and easily. When students' collective response is "yes," the heading "Diverse students interact" appears on the list. When student response indicates there are not many interactions between students from different class and ethnic backgrounds, the heading "Students are cliquish" appears on the list.

Cheating: We asked students how prevalent cheating is at their school. If students reported cheating to be rare, "No one cheats" shows up on the list.

Students are happy: This category reflects student responses to the question "Overall, how happy are you with your school?"

TAs teach upper-level classes: At some large universities, you'll continue to be taught by teaching assistants even in your upper-level courses. It is safe to assume that when "Lots of TAs teach upper-level courses" appears on the list, TAs also teach a disproportionate number of intro courses as well.

Students are very religious or **Students aren't religious:** We asked students how religious they are. Their responses are reflected in this category.

Diverse student body: We asked students whether their student body is made up of a variety of ethnic groups. This category reflects their answers, and shows up as "Diversity lacking on campus" or "Ethnic diversity on campus."

Town-gown relations: We asked students whether they got along with local residents; their answers are reflected by this category.

7. Academics, Life, and Student Body

The first three sections summarize the results of the surveys we distributed to students at the school. The "Academics" section reports how hard students work and how satisfied they are with the education they are getting. It also often tells you which academic departments our respondents rated favorably. Student opinion regarding administrative departments often works its way into this section, as well. The "Life" section describes life outside the classroom and addresses questions ranging from "How nice is the campus?" and "How comfortable are the dorms?" to "How popular are fraternities and sororities?" The "Student Body" section tells you about what type of student the school usually attracts and how the students view the level of interaction between various groups, including those of different ethnic origins. All quotes in these three sections are from students' essay responses to our surveys. We choose quotes based on the accuracy with which they reflect our overall survey results for that school.

8. Admissions

This section tells you what aspects of your application are most important to the school's admissions officers. It also lists the high school curricular prerequisites for applicants, which standardized tests (if any) are required, and special information about the school's admissions process (e.g., Do minority students and legacies, for example, receive special consideration? Are there any unusual application requirements for applicants to special programs?).

9. The Inside Word

This section contains our own insights into each school's admissions process, student-body demographics, life on campus, or unique academic attributes.

10. Financial Aid

This section summarizes the financial aid process at the school—what forms you need and what types of aid and loans are available. (More information about need-based aid is listed under "Financial Facts" in the school's statistical profile at the back of the book.) While this section includes specific deadline dates as reported by the colleges, we strongly encourage students seeking financial aid to file all forms—federal, state, and institutional—as soon as they become available. In the world of financial aid, the early birds almost always get the best worms (provided, of course, that they're eligible for a meal!).

11. From the Admissions Office

This section contains text supplied by the colleges in response to our invitation that they use this space to "speak directly to the readers of our guide."

12. For More Information

We refer you to the page number in our school statistics section where you can find detailed statistical information for the particular school you're reading about.

SCHOOL STATISTICS

This section, located in the back of the book, contains various statistics culled from our student surveys and from questionnaires school administrators fill out. Keep in mind that not every category will appear for every school, since in some cases the information is not reported or not applicable. Please note that ratings for Quality of Life, Academics, Admissions, and Financial Aid are explained on pages 10-11.

If a school has completed each and every data field, the headings will appear in the following order:

Type of school: Whether the school is public or private.

Affiliation: Any religious order with which the school is affiliated.

Environment: Whether the campus is located in an urban, suburban, or rural setting.

Total undergrad enrollment: The total number of undergraduates who attend the school.

% male/female through **# countries represented:** The demographic breakdown of the full-time undergraduate student body, a listing of what percentage of the student body lives on campus, the percentage belonging to Greek organizations, and finally, the number of countries represented by the student body.

Calendar: The school's schedule of academic terms. A "semester" schedule has two long terms, usually starting in September and January. A "trimester" schedule has three terms, one usually beginning before Christmas and two after. A "quarterly" schedule has four terms, which go by very quickly: the entire term, including exams, usually lasts only nine or ten weeks. A "4-1-4" schedule is like a semester schedule, but with a month-long term in between the fall and spring semesters. (Similarly, a "4-4-1" has a short term following two longer semesters.) When a school's academic calendar doesn't match any of these traditional schedules we note that by saying "other." For schools that have "other" as their calendar, it is best to call the admissions office for details.

Student/faculty ratio: The ratio of full-time undergraduate instructional faculty members to all undergraduates.

Profs interesting rating: Based on the answers given by students to the survey question, "In general, how good are your instructors as teachers?"

Profs accessible rating: Based on the answers given by students to the survey question, "In general, how accessible are your instructors outside the classroom?"

% profs teaching UG courses: Largely self-explanatory; this category shows the percentage of professors who teach undergraduates and doesn't include any faculty whose focus is solely on research.

% classes taught by TAs: Many universities that offer graduate programs use graduate students as teaching assistants (TAs). They teach undergraduate courses, primarily at the introductory level. This category reports on the percentage of classes that are taught by TAs instead of regular faculty.

Avg lab size; Avg reg class size: College-reported figures on class size averages for regular courses and for labs/discussion sections.

Most Popular Majors: The three most popular majors at the school.

% of applicants accepted: The percentage of applicants to which the school offered admission.

% of acceptees attending: The percentage of those who were accepted who eventually enrolled.

 # accepting a place on wait list: The number of students who decided to take a place on the wait list when offered this option.

% admitted from wait list: The percentage of applicants who opted to take a place on the wait list and were subsequently offered admission. These figures will vary tremendously from college to college and should be a consideration when deciding whether to accept a place on a college's wait list.

# of early decision applicants: The number of students who applied under the college's early decision or early action plan.

% accepted early decision: The percentage of early decision or early action applicants who were admitted under this plan. By the nature of these plans, the vast majority who are admitted wind up enrolling. (See the early decision/action description on the next page for more detail.)

Range/Average SAT Verbal, Range/Average SAT Math, Range/Average ACT Composite: The average and the middle 50 percent range of test scores for entering freshmen. Don't be discouraged from applying to the school of your choice even if your combined SAT scores are 80 or even 120 points below the average, because you may still have a chance of getting in. Remember that many schools emphasize other aspects of your application (e.g., your grades, how good a match you make with the school) more heavily than test scores.

Minimum TOEFL: The minimum test score necessary for entering freshmen who are required to take the TOEFL (Test of English as a Foreign Language). Most schools will require all international students or non-native English speakers to take the TOEFL in order to be considered for admission.

Average HS GPA: We report this on a scale of 0 to 4.0 (occasionally colleges report averages on a 100 scale, in which case we report those figures). This is one of the key factors in college admissions. Be sure to keep your GPA as high as possible straight through until graduation from high school.

% graduated top 10%, top 25%, top 50% of class: Of those students for whom class rank was reported, the percentage of entering freshmen who ranked in the top tenth, quarter, and half of their high school classes.

Early decision/action deadlines: The deadline for submission of application materials under the early decision or early action plan. Early decision is generally for students for whom the school is a first choice. The applicant commits to attending the school if admitted; in return, the school renders an early decision, usually in December or January. If accepted, the applicant doesn't have to spend the time and money applying to other schools. In most cases, students may apply for early decision to only one school. Early action is similar to early decision, but less binding; applicants need not commit to attending the school and in some cases may apply early action to more than one school. The school, in turn, may not render a decision, choosing to defer the applicant to the regular admissions pool. Each school's guidelines are a little different, and the policies of a few of the most selective colleges in the country have changed quite dramatically recently. Some colleges offer more than one early decision cycle, so it's a good idea to call and get full details if you plan to pursue one of these options.

Early decision, early action, priority, and regular admission deadlines: The dates by which all materials must be postmarked (we'd suggest "received in the office") in order to be considered for admission under each particular admissions option/cycle for admission for the fall term.

Early decision, early action, priority, and regular admission notification: The dates by which you can expect a decision on your application under each admissions option/cycle.

Nonfall registration: Some schools will allow applicants or transfers to matriculate at times other than the fall term—the traditional beginning of the academic calendar year. Other schools will only allow you to register for classes if you can begin in the fall term. A simple "yes" or "no" in this category indicates the school's policy on nonfall registration.

Tuition, In-state tuition: The tuition at the school, or for public colleges, for a resident of the school's state. In-state tuition is usually much lower than out-of-state tuition for state-supported public schools.

Out-of-state tuition: For public colleges, the tuition for a nonresident of the school's state. This entry appears only for public colleges, since tuition at private colleges is generally the same regardless of state of residence.

Room and board: Estimated room and board costs.

Books and supplies: Estimated annual cost of necessary textbooks and/or supplies.

% frosh receiving aid: According to the school's financial aid department, the percentage of all freshmen who received need-based aid.

% undergrads receiving aid: According to the school's financial aid department, the percentage of all undergrads who receive need-based financial aid.

Avg frosh grant: The average grant or scholarship amount awarded to freshmen.

Avg frosh loan: The average amount of loans disbursed to freshmen.

If you have any questions, comments, or suggestions, please contact us at Princeton Review Publishing, 2315 Broadway, New York, NY 10024, or e-mail us at bookeditor@review.com. We appreciate your input and want to make our books as useful to you as they can be.

GLOSSARY

ACT: Like the SAT I but less tricky. Many schools accept either SAT or ACT scores; if you consistently get blown away by the SAT, you might want to consider taking the ACT instead.

College-prep curriculum: 16 to 18 academic credits (each credit equals a full year of a high school course), usually including 4 years of English, 3 to 4 years of social studies, and at least 2 years each of science, mathematics, and foreign language.

Core curriculum: Students at schools with core curricula must take a number of required courses, usually in such subjects as world history and/or western civilization, writing skills, and fundamental math and science.

CSS/Financial Aid PROFILE: The College Scholarship Service PROFILE, an optional financial aid form required by some colleges in addition to the FAFSA.

Distribution requirements: Students at schools with distribution requirements must take a number of courses in various subject areas, such as foreign language, humanities, natural science, and social science. Distribution requirements do not specify which courses you must take, only which types of courses.

FAFSA: The Free Application for Federal Student Aid. Schools are required by law to accept the FAFSA; some require that applicants complete at least one other form (usually a CSS/Financial Aid PROFILE or the college's own form) to be considered for financial aid.

4-1-4: A type of academic schedule. It's like a semester schedule, but with a short semester (usually one month long) between the two semesters. Most schools offer internship programs or nontraditional studies during the short semester. A 4-4-1 schedule is similar to this one, except the short semester comes after the second long semester, usually in the late spring or early summer.

GDI: "Goddamned independent," a term frequently used by students in fraternities and sororities to describe those not in fraternities and sororities.

Greek system, Greeks: Fraternities and sororities and their members.

Humanities: These include such disciplines as art history, drama, English, foreign languages, music, philosophy, and religion.

Merit-based grant: A scholarship (not necessarily full) given to students because of some special talent or attribute. Artists, athletes, community leaders, and geniuses are typical recipients.

Natural sciences: These include such disciplines as astronomy, biology, chemistry, genetics, geology, mathematics, physics, and zoology.

Need-based grant: A scholarship (not necessarily full) given to students because they would otherwise be unable to afford college. Student need is determined on the basis of the FAFSA. Some schools also require the CSS PROFILE and/or institutional applications.

Priority deadline: Some schools will list a deadline for admission and/or financial aid as a "priority deadline," meaning that while they will accept applications after that date, all applications received prior to the deadline are assured of getting the most thorough, and in some instances potentially more generous, appraisal possible.

RA: Residence assistant (or residential advisor). Someone, usually an upperclassman or graduate student, who supervises a floor or section of a dorm, usually in return for free room and board. RAs are responsible for enforcing the drinking and noise rules.

SAT I: A college entrance exam required by many schools.

SAT II: Subject Tests: Subject-specific exams administered by the Educational Testing Service (the SAT people). These tests are required by some, but not all, admissions offices. English Writing and Math Level I or IIC are the tests most frequently required.

Social sciences: These include such disciplines as anthropology, economics, geography, history, international studies, political science, psychology, and sociology.

TA: Teaching assistant. Most often a graduate student, a TA will often teach discussion sections of large lectures. At some schools, TAs and graduate students teach a large number of introductory-level and even some upper-level courses. At smaller schools, professors generally do all the teaching.

Work-study: A government-funded financial aid program that provides assistance to financial aid recipients in return for work in the school's library, labs, etc.

PART 2

THE SCHOOLS

ALBRIGHT COLLEGE

PO BOX 15234, 13TH AND BERN STREETS, READING, PA 19612-5234 • ADMISSIONS: 800-252-1856
FAX: 610-921-7294 • E-MAIL: ALBRIGHT@ALB.EDU • WEBSITE: WWW.ALBRIGHT.EDU

Ratings
Quality of Life: 73   **Academic:** 74   **Admissions:** 71   **Financial Aid:** 79

Academics

Albright College knows how to put the "liberal arts" in "liberal arts college": it requires students to attend 16 cultural events (e.g., lectures, plays, art exhibits, political debates) by the end of their sophomore year or face academic probation. Most students have no trouble

> **SURVEY SAYS . . .**
> *Students get along with local community*
> *Very little beer drinking, Very little hard liquor*
> *No one plays intramural sports, No one cheats*
> *No one watches intercollegiate sports*
> *Students are religious, Classes are small*

fulfilling the requirement, though, because Albright is a bees' nest of cultural activity. Writes one undergrad, "Albright makes it a community learning experience, not just a personal learning experience." One student is particularly pleased with the "two seperate undergraduate research projects" in which he's already participated. While "Albright could expand the courses offered," according to some, most students focus on the benefits. Brags one: "My professors care about me and call me. . . . I have gone on internships and they call/e-mail me all the time just to see how I am doing. . . . My academic experience is great because I feel like I can be me and not just my Social Security number." Students especially appreciate how "professors are willing to help you not only academically, but also in the job market. They want their students to strive to be the best they can be and are willing to help and motivate their students every day."

Life

Albright students report a satisfying sense of community that pervades campus. Explains one, "Albright is a place [where] you can be yourself and not worry about what people will think . . . . There are people who study all the time, and there are people who party, but the difference is they all decide to basically be kind to each other [and] make Albright a family. An example of how Albright is a family is when our swim team coach's father died. People kept going up to her and giving her hugs. I am not even on the swim team and she knew who I was and kept saying how the strength of Albright helped her through these tough times. One student explains, "An average day on campus consists of attending classes, going to work on campus, some type of physical activity (either the gym or sporting event), studying, going out with friends, and, the most important, going to bed. People are very involved on campus but sometimes forget about what is going on around them (within the world) unless it is discussed [in] the classroom environment"; hence, the Albright "bubble." In their spare time, students take on community service projects, "attend concerts and dances or just 'chill' in their apartments with friends." Albright undergrads also note that "fraternity/sorority life is a great deal larger than portrayed in the campus literature."

Student Body

Explains one Albright undergrad, "It's hard to generalize the entire student population into one category. All schools have their mix of students that are active, involved, and get along well. Then you have the students that are just there to get an education and not become as involved with the student body. Luckily, the majority of the student body is social and has very few problems with each other." Another student reports, "Everyone on campus is normally involved with one organization or another, whether it be an on-campus job, sport, club, etc." A genial atmosphere permeates Albright's halls; as one student put it, "I feel like I can just walk up to a person I don't know and say 'hi' and they will respond."

ADMISSIONS

Very important factors considered by the admissions committee include: secondary school record. *Important factors considered include:* extracurricular activities, talent/ability, character/personal qualities, essays, recommendations, and standardized test scores. *Other factors considered include:* alumni/ae relation, volunteer work, and work experience. SAT I or ACT required. TOEFL required of all international applicants. High school diploma is required and GED is accepted. *High school units required/recommended:* 16 total are required; 20 total are recommended; 4 English required, 4 English recommended, 2 math required, 3 math recommended, 3 science required, 4 science recommended, 1 science lab required, 2 science lab recommended, 2 foreign language required, 3 foreign language recommended, 2 social studies required, 2 social studies recommended, 1 history required, 2 history recommended, 2 elective required, 2 elective recommended.

The Inside Word

Albright is currently pursuing a major capital campaign that should enable it to expand program offerings and attract more quality applicants in the not-too-distant future. The next few years may provide a window for a few less-qualified students to sneak in under the radar, but after that, expect admissions criteria at this fine liberal arts school to grow more rigorous.

FINANCIAL AID

Students should submit: FAFSA. The Princeton Review suggests that all financial aid forms be submitted as soon as possible after January 1. *Need-based scholarships/grants offered:* Pell, SEOG, state scholarships/grants, private scholarships, and the school's own gift aid. *Loan aid offered:* FFEL Subsidized Stafford, FFEL Unsubsidized Stafford, FFEL PLUS, Federal Perkins, and private loans. Federal Work-Study Program available. Institution employment available. Applicants will be notified of awards on a rolling basis beginning on or about February 15. Off-campus job opportunities are good.

FROM THE ADMISSIONS OFFICE

"**Academics:** Founded in 1856, Albright College is recognized as a national leader in interdisciplinary study. Nearly half of our students opt for combined or interdisciplinary majors . . . . while still graduating in four years. Last year, students chose 143 different combinations of majors—from art/biology and psychology/business to education/theatre and sociology/Latin American studies. But whether students select one major or combine fields, Albright's faculty work closely with students to create experiences that reflect individual talents, interests, and career goals.

"**Atmosphere**: Albright College is renowned for its openness and warmth. Students who visit Albright rate it as one of the friendliest small liberal arts colleges anywhere. Albright students have a strong sense of community, based on friendliness, tolerance, and mutual support. These are the common ties that bind the community and make Albright an easy place for students to be heard and have an impact.

"**Outcomes:** An Albright education is designed to help students develop their individual voices and visions and become skilled problem solvers and communicators. Albright graduates leave with the knowledge, skills, and confidence to succeed.

"**Location:** The Albright campus is located one hour west of Philadelphia in a tree-lined suburb of Reading, Pennsylvania, a metropolitan area of 250,000.

"**Scholarships and Financial Aid:** Albright is pledged to help make its education affordable. This is evident in Albright's inclusion in Barron's Best Buys in College Education and in our generous need-based financial aid awards and numerous merit scholarships (ranging from $5,000 per year to full tuition)."

For even more information on this school, turn to page 220 of the "Stats" section.

ALLEGHENY COLLEGE

Office of Admissions, Meadville, PA 16335 • Admissions: 800-521-5293
Fax: 814-337-0431 • Financial Aid: 800-835-7780 • E-mail: admiss@allegheny.edu
Website: www.allegheny.edu

Ratings
Quality of Life: 75   Academic: 83   Admissions: 87   Financial Aid: 85

Academics

A warm communal feeling pervades the Allegheny academic setting, according to the school's satisfied undergraduates. One writes, "I consider many administrators and faculty good friends outside the academic realm. Allegheny is about people, not numbers. It is a gold mine waiting to be tapped." Students also appreciate that Allegheny is "really strong in the sciences, which gives us great placement for graduate schools," and are even happier for the support they receive in pursuit of their degree: "The professors are always willing to give their time to help and do their best to accommodate their schedules for you." All the assistance comes in handy at this "very academically challenging" school; students warn that "this place is very competitive. Many people double major, and classes can get rough." Adds another, "The workload here is intense, but the classes prepare you well for life beyond Allegheny." Students greatly value their "experiential learning opportunities [offered] through ACCEL (the Allegheny College Center for Experiential Learning)," which provides leadership training and internships in places including New York; Washington, D.C.; and Boston as well as spring term study tours both in and outside the United States. Almost everyone agrees that ACCEL "distinguishes Allegheny from other, larger schools." Several students note that the school's curriculum requirements help students develop a valuable generalist's perspective; "Instead of knowing a lot about something, I now know something about everything. That is Allegheny summed up to me," concludes one student.

> **SURVEY SAYS . . .**
> *Athletic facilities are great*
> *Frats and sororities dominate social scene*
> *Classes are small*
> *Student publications are ignored*
> *Library needs improving*
> *Lousy food on campus*
> *Political activism is (almost) nonexistent*
> *Lousy off-campus food*
> *Diversity lacking on campus*

Life

Undergraduates overwhelmingly agree with the student who opines that "Academics are very important to Allegheny students, but I think there is a healthy balance between study and social activities." Elaborates a peer, "Life at Allegheny is stressful, but very rewarding. Everybody works hard during the week and plays hard on the weekends. There are plenty of parties, but there are also a lot of fun, school-sponsored events like movies, karaoke, and comedians." Because there is "not a whole lot to do in Meadville," students tend to find fun on and around campus. Some tell us that "people seem to have fun whatever they do. There is bowling, restaurants, ice skating, movies, and stuff on campus such as musicians, comedians, games, etc." An athletic type adds, "Depending on what the weather is like, we play football, go sledding, toss the Frisbee, that sort of thing. Most people here like sports." When the urge for big-city diversion takes them, Allegheny students drive to Pittsburgh or Cleveland, the two closest large cities, both about an hour and a half away.

Student Body

Allegheny undergrads generally concede that theirs "is a 'cliquey' school." Explains one student, "I would say the mainstream social scene of fraternities and athletic groups can be very segregated at times." The glass-half-empty types among them observe with scorn that "students here tend to be rich and snobby" and that "the campus is very homogeneous as to types of students, and sometimes it seems everyone just thinks and acts the same way." To the majority of students, however, Allegheny is home to a "friendly, comfortable campus. When you walk down the street, most everyone says 'hi' and smiles." Notes one student, "I really was attracted to Allegheny's small campus. It's always nice to see a familiar face when you walk down the street."

ADMISSIONS

Very important factors considered by the admissions committee include: class rank, secondary school record. *Important factors considered include:* character/personal qualities, extracurricular activities, interview, recommendations, standardized test scores. *Other factors considered include:* alumni/ae relation, essays, geographical residence, minority status, talent/ability, volunteer work, work experience. SAT I or ACT required; SAT II recommended. TOEFL required of all international applicants. High school diploma or GED is required. *High school units required/recommended:* 16 total required; 4 English required, 3 math required, 3 science required, 2 foreign language required, 3 social studies required, 1 elective required.

The Inside Word

Don't be deceived by the fairly high admit rate here—Allegheny draws a strong pool of academically well-qualified applicants, and candidate evaluation here is rigorous and personalized. The admissions staff strongly recommends campus visits and interviews; students who visit the campus prior to Allegheny's application deadline receive application fee waivers. Given the highly personalized nature of candidate evaluation here, we'd suggest both the visit and taking the most challenging courses in high school in order to be as competitive in the applicant pool as possible.

FINANCIAL AID

Students should submit: FAFSA. No deadline for regular filing. The Princeton Review suggests that all financial aid forms be submitted as soon as possible after January 1. *Need-based scholarships/grants offered:* Pell, SEOG, state scholarships/grants, private scholarships, the school's own gift aid. *Loan aid offered:* FFEL Subsidized Stafford, FFEL Unsubsidized Stafford, FFEL PLUS, Federal Perkins, state loans, private loans from commercial lenders. Federal Work-Study Program available. Institutional employment available. Applicants will be notified of awards on a rolling basis beginning on or about March 1. Off-campus job opportunities are excellent.

FROM THE ADMISSIONS OFFICE

"Allegheny, the nation's 32nd oldest college, is a nationally recognized college of the liberal arts and sciences. Allegheny's nearly 2,000 students are active in social, economic, and environmental issues and work collaboratively with faculty as part of the learning process. The College's nationally recognized programs, such as the Center for Political Participation, the Center for Experiential Learning, and the Center for Economic and Environmental Development offer powerful and engaging out-of-classroom experiences. With about 40 programs of study and a capstone comprehensive senior project, the College's rigorous education results in benefits that include acceptance rates to medical and law school that are twice the national average. And Allegheny's geographic setting is ideal for our active student population, who enjoy biking, rock climbing, canoeing, and kayaking."

For even more information on this school, turn to page 220 of the "Stats" section.

AMERICAN UNIVERSITY

4400 MASSACHUSETTS AVENUE, NW, WASHINGTON, DC 20016-8001 • ADMISSIONS: 202-885-6000
FAX: 202-885-1025 • FINANCIAL AID: 202-885-6100 • E-MAIL: AFA@AMERICAN.EDU
WEBSITE: WWW.AMERICAN.EDU

Ratings
Quality of Life: 80   **Academic:** 79   **Admissions:** 83   **Financial Aid:** 84

Academics

"So many academic and social opportunities" await one at American University, thanks in large part to its location in northwest Washington, D.C. Students have to be self-starters to take advantage of those opportunities, however; no one will hold your hand and accompany you to the threshold of learning here. "If you know what you want out of AU, you

> **SURVEY SAYS . . .**
> *Political activism is hot, Students are happy*
> *Students are religious*
> *Lots of classroom discussion*
> *Great food on campus, Dorms are like palaces*
> *Ethnic diversity on campus, Unattractive campus*
> *Lots of long lines and red tape*
> *Very little beer drinking*

will get it," explains one student. Professors here ("about half are brilliant, and half are just okay," reports one undergrad) often have multiple commitments beyond campus. "We have lots of adjuncts who have super professional experiences, but who are inaccessible outside class," warns one student. Students don't feel completely ignored on the matter of their instructors, though, as "the school really takes the students' feedback on the professors very seriously," which means bad teachers often quietly and mysteriously disappear. And the faculty has plenty of bright lights, dedicated teachers who "are really amicable and cordial and are willing to help students." Students generally dislike the administration, perceiving it as "much more concerned with the outward appearance of the school" than with current students' concerns. Some are willing to concede, however, "Although our president rules the school like a banana republic, he has brought about much-needed improvements in the community." The business department draws kudos, though science facilities reportedly need some TLC. The study abroad program and internship opportunities earn students' universal praise.

Life

"D.C. is a great city to go to school in," AU students agree. "The city is the school's most valuable asset; it's got a life of its own, in contrast to many college towns. It really makes going to school here exciting." Students love Dupont Circle and the nearby neighborhood of Adams Morgan ("a big attention drawer because there are so many restaurants, clubs, bars, and poetry places") but find plenty to do all over town. Another enthusiastic undergraduate adds, "It is not possible to go a single day without experiencing at least one aspect of a different culture." The city picks up the slack for the AU campus, which is often dormant: "Campus life itself isn't as exciting as a Big Ten school or something," concedes one student, "but that's because we're in a big city that actually has places to go [to] and hang out [in]." The campus is officially dry, a fact that further encourages this outwardly oriented student body to look for gathering places beyond the campus gates. With D.C. at the university's doorstep, partying away from school is a no-brainer.

Student Body

The "idealistic, smart, concerned" students at American University are "extremely politically involved. People here are passionate about various issues, due in no small part to our location."

Most are to the left end of the political spectrum; one disaffected undergrad writes, "The typical student is a liberal tree-hugger who thinks he/she has an open mind but actually doesn't." A large international population ("lots of diplomats' kids"), along with smaller minority populations, engenders a diversity that is "wonderful; it makes political science classes quite invigorating!" When we asked what the typical American student was like, we typically got one of two responses. Some balked at the request: "This school is way too diverse to pinpoint the typical student," while others described a white kid from the "middle to upper middle class, interested in international relations, likes trying new things, [and] interested in community service."

ADMISSIONS

Very important factors considered by the admissions committee include: secondary school record, standardized test scores. *Important factors considered include:* class rank, essays, extracurricular activities, recommendations, volunteer work. *Other factors considered include:* alumni/ae relation, character/personal qualities, interview, minority status, talent/ability, work experience. SAT I or ACT required; SAT II recommended. TOEFL required of all international applicants. High school diploma or GED is required. *High school units required/recommended:* 16 total required; 20 total recommended; 4 English required, 3 math required, 4 math recommended, 2 science required, 4 science recommended, 2 science lab required, 2 foreign language required, 3 foreign language recommended, 2 social studies required, 4 social studies recommended, 4 elective recommended.

The Inside Word

Washington, D.C., is indeed a tremendous attraction for students who aspire to careers in government, politics, and other areas of public service. Georgetown skims most of the cream of the crop off the top of this considerable pool of prospective students, but American does quite nicely. Because the university is nationally known it also has formidable competition outside its own backyard, and as a result its yield of admits who enroll is on the low side. This necessitates a higher admit rate than one might expect at a school with considerable academic strength and an impressively credentialed faculty. If you're an active leadership type with a strong academic record the admissions process should be fairly painless—American offers a great opportunity for a quality educational experience without having to plead for admission.

FINANCIAL AID

Students should submit: FAFSA, institution's own financial aid form. Regular filing deadline is March 1. The Princeton Review suggests that all financial aid forms be submitted as soon as possible after January 1. *Need-based scholarships/grants offered:* Pell, SEOG, state scholarships/grants, private scholarships, the school's own gift aid. *Loan aid offered:* Direct Subsidized Stafford, Direct Unsubsidized Stafford, Direct PLUS, Federal Perkins, college/university loans from institutional funds. Federal Work-Study Program available. Institutional employment available. Applicants will be notified of awards on or about April 1. Off-campus job opportunities are excellent.

FROM THE ADMISSIONS OFFICE

"Our students learn how to turn ideas into action and action into service by interacting regularly with decision makers and leaders in every profession and from every corner of the world. If you are looking to be academically challenged in a rich multicultural environment, then American University is the place you want to be. Our expert teaching faculty provide a well-rounded liberal arts education, characterized by small classes, the use of cutting-edge technology, and an interdisciplinary curriculum in the arts, education, humanities, social sciences, and sciences. Not just a political town, Washington, D.C., offers a variety of internship opportunities in every field. And AU's World Capitals Program, with locations in 16 nations, lets you expand your studies into international settings. Because of these resources, AU enables you to put your education to work as nowhere else in the country."

For even more information on this school, turn to page 221 of the "Stats" section.

ARCADIA UNIVERSITY

450 SOUTH EASTON ROAD, GLENSIDE, PA 19038 • ADMISSIONS: 215-572-2910 • FAX: 215-572-4049
E-MAIL: ADMISS@ARCADIA.EDU • WEBSITE: WWW.ARCADIA.EDU

Ratings
Quality of Life: 71   Academic: 73   Admissions: 71   Financial Aid: 84

Academics

Though they say they are "a little upset about the name change," students at the former Beaver College feel that their school continues to uphold its standards of excellence. Professors are "highly qualified and down to earth," "devoted to their job," and "personable," qualities that translate into a high level of

> **SURVEY SAYS . . .**
> *School is well run, Registration is a breeze*
> *Instructors are good teachers, Students are happy*
> *Lousy food on campus*
> *Lab facilities need improving*
> *No one plays intramural sports*
> *Ethnic diversity lacking on campus*

"accessibility" and "individual attention" for Arcadia students. Recounts one, "Professors are excellent, and a lot of them remember my name, even a year and a half after I took their class." Students praise the fact that classes are generally "small discussion groups" in which "participation is encouraged." Most agree that the "awesome," "down to earth, approachable" administration is more than willing to take "a moment (or hour) to talk to students. . . . The dean of students really DOES know all of the students' names." Arcadia University's extensive list of study abroad programs, which includes "lots of locations and schools to choose from," is so robust that Arcadia actually serves as a hub for overseas opportunity, connecting students at other universities across the United States with programs unavailable at their own institutions. In particular, many Arcadians note the London Preview Program, in which "every freshman has the opportunity to go to London over spring break for only $245, and honors program students go for free." There is, however, one caveat to the blissful host of options: some warn that you shouldn't choose Arcadia "unless you know what you want to do and are pretty sure you will stick with it," as the school offers a number of "specialized majors . . . (psychobiology, art therapy)" with "very few courses offered outside those majors."

Life

Life at Arcadia University is a "balance between academia, and good, old-fashioned college fun," as one student illustrates: "I spend a lot of time with friends, at the gym and partying, as well as doing my schoolwork." Students do "like to party"; one confesses, "Weekends are usually one long, intoxicated stretch," while another reassures, "If you are not a drinker, nobody is going to make you drink." Arcadia undergrads also like to "run around and play soccer, Frisbee, and football," "eat junk food a lot," and attend school-sponsored activities such as weekly "films, game shows, comedy hours, and coffeehouses with new musical acts." Despite the general praises for campus life, students agree Arcadia is somewhat of a "suitcase campus." One happy student testifies that packing your bag doesn't curb your capacity to contribute: "I am in a number of organizations where I am either the president or an active chair member," and yet, "I don't stay here on weekends." Other than heading home, students often "go into Philadelphia to go clubbing or shopping."

Student Body

Because Arcadia's student body is "mostly white, middle-class women," many students agree that "there needs to be more diversity on campus." The student body is, in fact, nearly 70 percent white, but some stress the diversity in students' "backgrounds, personal morals, and standings on issues"; adds one, "We have more types of students than Ben & Jerry's [has] flavors." There are complaints that "the gay organization on campus is very strong and supportive, but outside of that circle, most gays are forced to remain closeted." One gay student warns, "I wouldn't recommend this school to any homosexual male." In fact, students generally say they "all get along very well" and describe their classmates as "intelligent, caring, and mature." In general, students perceive Arcadia to be "relaxed and comfortable," "a very friendly atmosphere where holding doors and saying 'hi' to strangers is not uncommon!"

ADMISSIONS

Very important factors considered by the admissions committee include: secondary school record. *Important factors considered include:* class rank, essays, extracurricular activities, recommendations, and standardized test scores. *Other factors considered include:* alumni/ae relation, character/personal qualities, interview, talent/ability, volunteer work, and work experience. SAT I or ACT required. TOEFL required of all international applicants. High school diploma or GED is required. *High school units required/recommended:* 4 English recommended, 3 math recommended, 3 science recommended, 3 science lab recommended, 2 foreign language recommended, 2 social studies recommended, 2 history recommended.

The Inside Word

Changing the name of the school from Beaver College to Arcadia University has already paid handsome dividends: enrollment has increased by 20 percent since the switch. Expect admissions to grow more competitive here in the next few years as more high school seniors hear about this "new school."

FINANCIAL AID

Students should submit: FAFSA and institution's own financial aid form. The Princeton Review suggests that all financial aid forms be submitted as soon as possible after January 1. *Need-based scholarships/grants offered:* Pell, SEOG, state scholarships/grants, private scholarships, and the school's own gift aid. *Loan aid offered:* FFEL Subsidized Stafford, FFEL Unsubsidized Stafford, FFEL PLUS, Federal Perkins, and college/university loans from institutional funds. Federal Work-Study Program available. Institutional employment available. Applicants will be notified of awards on a rolling basis beginning on or about February 1. Off-campus job opportunities are good.

FROM THE ADMISSIONS OFFICE

"Arcadia University is a coeducational, private, comprehensive university founded in 1853 and located on a 60-acre private estate in Glenside, Pennsylvania, just 25 minutes from Center City Philadelphia. As a student at Arcadia University, your education expands beyond the classroom. Our study abroad programs, international faculty, and global vision of education combine to create an environment that affords you a world of opportunities. Our Center for Education Abroad is currently ranked second nationally, and students have the opportunity to study in England, Equatorial Guinea, Scotland, Wales, Ireland, Northern Ireland, Australia, Greece, Korea, Italy, Spain, Mexico, and New Zealand. Freshmen at Arcadia have the unique opportunity to spend spring break in London for only $245. The London Preview Program introduces students to overseas study and travel. Students may choose from more than 30 different undergraduate programs and 12 graduate degrees. Our 12:1 student/faculty ratio enables students to work closely with faculty for academic advising, research, and publication activities.

"This year, Arcadia University will celebrate its 150-year anniversary. The year will be marked with many celebrations and activities on campus. We will also complete our library expansion project in the fall of 200, doubling the current library size. So many exciting things are happening on campus. Come and take a look for yourself."

For even more information on this school, turn to page 222 of the "Stats" section.

BLOOMSBURG UNIVERSITY OF PENNSYLVANIA

104 STUDENT SERVICES CENTER, 400 EAST SECOND STREET, BLOOMSBURG, PA 17815 ADMISSIONS: 570-389-4316
FAX: 570-389-4741 • E-MAIL: BUADMISS@BLOOMU.EDU • WEBSITE: WWW.BLOOMU.EDU

Ratings
Quality of Life: 76   Academic: 70   Admissions: 66   Financial Aid: 77

Academics

Bloomsburg University has earned a regional reputation for its education programs. Incoming students are particularly drawn to the dual degree in elementary and early-childhood education and the deaf education programs. (The deaf education degree is one

> **SURVEY SAYS . . .**
> *No one watches intercollegiate sports*
> *Students get along with local community*
> *Classes are small*
> *Lousy food on campus*
> *School is well run*

of only a few offered in the state of Pennsylvania.) Students also point approvingly to the speech pathology and business programs. Overall, though, academics at Bloomsburg receive mixed reviews. Undergrads here complain that uninspiring instructors teach many general education classes, which each student must take to fulfill core-curriculum requirements. Students were particularly critical of professors who were long in the tooth and short on technology savvy: "I had a CIS prof who didn't know how to use a computer—terrible!" moaned one. But since Bloomsburg's offers nearly 70 majors and hundreds of classes from which to choose, undergrads should be able to avoid lackluster profs. Students may also apply to join the well-respected honors program. Regarding the administration, students often sing the common refrain sounded at most public institutions of higher learning: too much bureaucracy. But overall, Bloomsburg's undergrads look fondly on their administration. "Our university brings to the forefront problems that other schools just hide. Our president addresses problems such as alcohol, fire safety, etc., and works out solutions to benefit everyone."

Life

Students at Bloomsburg claim, "This is the best social school in the state of Pennsylvania. From campus activities (dances, movies, athletic events) to a great party scene, you can't ask for anything more." While according to some students here, "you can choose from multiple parties going on," a number of upperclassmen tell us that the party scene at Bloomsburg isn't what it used to be, thanks largely to the recent imposition of "much stricter rules on drinking and behavior following consumption." Students here also enjoy investing their free time in intramural sports. And with a list of 160 extracurricular activities to pick from, nonpartiers and nonathletes needn't worry—they'll find something that piques their interest. The town of Bloomsburg is a quiet, rural community of about 12,000 and, as you might expect, doesn't offer the adventurous student many options. But what you'll find in town are "really cute shops," some bars and restaurants, and a handful of nice parks and recreation areas. Oh, and there's a Wal-Mart nearby—"the college hangout worldwide in small towns." Aside from intramurals, Bloomsburg has 18 intercollegiate sports teams (9 male and 9 female). Outdoor enthusiasts can head to any of four major state parks within an hour's drive of campus. And city slickers can reach New York City or Philadelphia in less than three hours. But students need to be cautious about leaving campus too often; they may end up missing the party of the century.

Student Body

You'll know Bloomsburg students by their down-to-earth attitudes. "We are real people who, on Friday morning at 8:00, will wear sweatpants and sweatshirts [to] class." It's also a school where apparent social barriers don't get in the way of civil interaction. Sure, you have "the Greeks and the athletes and [the] hippies," but everyone seems to get along just swell. And students feel at ease to flourish in several capacities: "It's not uncommon to find a frat brother in the honor society or a football player as a member of the physics club." Part of the reason that everyone gets along so well is that they come from "similar backgrounds." Around 90 percent of Bloomsburg's student body is native to Pennsylvania and many have middle-class upbringings in common. But regardless of race, religion, or economic status, if you're "very socially oriented" you'll get along fine at Bloomsburg. "As long as you enjoy going out, you will love it here!"

ADMISSIONS

Very important factors considered by the admissions committee include: class rank, secondary school record, and standardized test scores. *Important factors considered include:* recommendations. *Other factors considered include:* character/personal qualities, essays, extracurricular activities, geographical residence, interview, state residency, talent/ability, volunteer work, and work experience. SAT I or ACT required. TOEFL required of all international applicants. High school diploma is required and GED is accepted. *High school units required/recommended:* 16 total required; 20 total recommended; 4 English required, 3 math required, 3 science required, 2 science lab required, 2 foreign language recommended, 2 social studies required, 2 history required.

The Inside Word

Bloomsburg begins reviewing applications on a rolling basis in September. The school uses generous admissions criteria but warns that some majors fill quickly; contact the admissions office to find out which departments require an application by December 15. Notification of admissions decisions are usually sent out two to three weeks after the school receives an application.

FINANCIAL AID

Students should submit: FAFSA and state aid form. The Princeton Review suggests that all financial aid forms be submitted as soon as possible after January 1. *Need-based scholarships/grants offered:* Pell, SEOG, state scholarships/grants, private scholarships, and the school's own gift aid. *Loan aid offered:* FFEL Subsidized Stafford, FFEL Unsubsidized Stafford, FFEL PLUS, Federal Perkins, state loans, college/university loans from institutional funds, and alternative loans. Federal Work-Study Program available. Institution employment available. Applicants will be notified of awards on a rolling basis beginning on or about April 1. Off-campus job opportunities are fair.

For even more information on this school, turn to page 222 of the "Stats" section.

BRYN MAWR COLLEGE

101 NORTH MERION AVENUE, BRYN MAWR, PA 19010-2899 • ADMISSIONS: 610-526-5152
FAX: 610-526-7471 • FINANCIAL AID: 610-526-5245 • E-MAIL: ADMISSIONS@BRYNMAWR.EDU
WEBSITE: WWW.BRYNMAWR.EDU

Ratings
Quality of Life: 87   Academic: 96   Admissions: 93   Financial Aid: 80

Academics

You'll find few colleges where more than a handful of overly exuberant students would refer to their professors as "gods and goddesses," but such overwhelming praise is precisely the case at Bryn Mawr. A small and very elite woman's college located just outside of Philadelphia, Bryn Mawr is known not only for challenging and difficult academics, but also for

> **SURVEY SAYS . . .**
> *Theater is hot, No one cheats*
> *Great food on campus, Dorms are like palaces*
> *Campus feels safe, Very little beer drinking*
> *No one plays intramural sports*
> *Very little hard liquor*
> *Intercollegiate sports are*
> *unpopular or nonexistent*

its commitment to its approximately 1,300 undergraduates. "The courses that are offered are extremely challenging and interesting," declares one student. And "the professors are dedicated individuals who always make themselves available." It's not just easy access, though, that makes the faculty and the academics here so inspiring for so many students. Perhaps more than anything else it's the level of instruction gauged to each student's abilities. As one student notes, "The profs at Bryn Mawr take everything to the next level. If you think you can get a B, they don't give you one until you have an A." And professors trust their students. The revered honor code allows undergraduates the freedom to schedule their own exams and ensure the integrity of their work. The college's close proximity to three other excellent schools (Haverford, Swarthmore, and the University of Pennsylvania) also provides students with the opportunity to enroll in classes not offered at Bryn Mawr. New freshmen should come prepared because "there is A LOT of work," and the competition and debates in class are intense, leaving little room for students who aren't interested in taking class seriously.

Life

Bryn Mawr is known as a "quiet campus," where everyone is too busy studying or thinking about studying to go out and party. Students are not, however, hermits cloistered in their ivory towers. They do have a host of odd traditions like "lantern night" where students carry lanterns, don robes, and have a sing-along in the campus cloister. Sound strange? As any student here will tell you, you have to experience it to understand it. When the students at Bryn Mawr aren't walking around in the dark and singing, however, they are pretty much having a good time. Campus groups play a large and active role here, and freshman customs groups are a vital way of forming lifelong bonds between students. The city of Philadelphia is only a train ride away and offers a great and active getaway from the campus, as do the neighboring campuses of Haverford and U Penn. Most students wouldn't mind seeing campus life given a B-12 injection, but fortunately, as one student notes, "I think the campus activities have improved a lot in my time here."

Student Body

Bryn Mawr may enroll only women, but it's definitely not lacking in diversity. The students at Bryn Mawr come from varied backgrounds, and if they share any common traits, it's probably a genuine "warmth," "openness," and liberalism. Many of the students here are just as in love with their peers as they are with their college and often describe the tenor of their campus as that of "one big sorority." They consider one another "brilliant," and for good reason, since almost all of them aren't afraid to roll up their sleeves and work out the challenges their professors lay before them (there's a reason why they call themselves "Mawrtyrs"). The women of Bryn Mawr may be open-minded and liberal and could care less about your sexuality or race, but conservative politics are a different story, and as one student notes, some of her classmates "are extremely close-minded to any views (particularly conservative or religious ones) and deride anything not related to the typical 'liberal' collegiate view."

ADMISSIONS

Very important factors considered by the admissions committee include: essays, recommendations, secondary school record. *Important factors considered include:* character/personal qualities, extracurricular activities. *Other factors considered include:* class rank, interview, standardized test scores, talent/ability, volunteer work, work experience. TOEFL required of all international applicants. High school diploma or GED is required. *High school units required/recommended:* 16 total recommended; 4 English recommended, 3 math recommended, 2 science recommended, 1 science lab recommended, 3 foreign language recommended, 2 social studies recommended, 2 history recommended, 2 elective required.

The Inside Word

Do not be deceived by Bryn Mawr's admit rate; its student body is among the best in the nation academically. Outstanding preparation for graduate study draws an applicant pool that is well prepared and intellectually curious. The admissions committee includes eight faculty members and four seniors. Each applicant is reviewed by four readers, including at least one faculty member and one student.

FINANCIAL AID

Students should submit: FAFSA, CSS/Financial Aid PROFILE, noncustodial (divorced/separated) parent's statement, business/farm supplement. Regular filing deadline is January 15. The Princeton Review suggests that all financial aid forms be submitted as soon as possible after January 1. *Need-based scholarships/grants offered:* Pell, SEOG, state scholarships/grants, the school's own gift aid. *Loan aid offered:* FFEL Subsidized Stafford, FFEL Unsubsidized Stafford, FFEL PLUS, Federal Perkins, college/university loans from institutional funds. Federal Work-Study Program available. Institutional employment available. Applicants will be notified of awards on or about April 1. Off-campus job opportunities are good.

FROM THE ADMISSIONS OFFICE

"One wouldn't ordinarily assume that a small institution could offer as diverse a range of opportunities as many large universities, or that a campus that looks like the English countryside could exist within 20 minutes of downtown Philadelphia, but Bryn Mawr is far from ordinary. Prepare to be surprised. Innovative, creative, and purposeful, the students at Bryn Mawr inspire their peers as much and as often as any faculty member. Spirited intellectual inquiry, a commitment to academic excellence, and a desire to impact the world in a meaningful way are the hallmarks of this community of equals. Students at Bryn Mawr learn by doing and lead by example. They take full advantage of all that Bryn Mawr has to offer, including internship opportunities, an active Alumnae Association, a lively Community Service office and a consortium of schools that includes Haverford, Swarthmore, and the University of Pennsylvania. Bryn Mawr's Student Government Association is the oldest in the country and students participate in every aspect of the College's decision-making process, serving as representatives to Admissions, The Honor Board, The Curriculum Committee, and even The Board of Trustees. Bryn Mawr is a demanding and caring place where both ideas and individuals matter."

For even more information on this school, turn to page 223 of the "Stats" section.

BUCKNELL UNIVERSITY

FREAS HALL, LEWISBURG, PA 17837 • ADMISSIONS: 570-577-1101 • FAX: 570-577-3538
FINANCIAL AID: 570-577-1331 • E-MAIL: ADMISSIONS@BUCKNELL.EDU • WEBSITE: WWW.BUCKNELL.EDU

Ratings
Quality of Life: 91   Academic: 91   Admissions: 91   Financial Aid: 82

Academics

Engineering, science, and business are among the top drawing cards at Bucknell University, where tomorrow's leaders (and the sons and daughters of today's leaders) enjoy a great faculty, up-to-date facilities, and—perhaps most important to students—"a

> **SURVEY SAYS . . .**
> *Frats and sororities dominate social scene*
> *Great food on campus*
> *Great library*
> *Low cost of living*
> *Diversity lacking on campus*

great reputation. Everyone that goes here has worked hard in their life to actually make it here, so you know that they are smart." Professors here "are unbelievably enthusiastic and genuinely care about their students." Administrators receive similarly high praise. Reports one student, "I have eaten meals with school administrators. They are very accessible. If I ever need to speak with a dean, I never have to wait more than a couple of minutes even if I show up without an appointment." All of these institutional assets help students handle the "challenging" academic environment at Bucknell, which is definitely not for the faint at heart. "The workload is tough," warns one student, and competition for good grades is stiff.

Life

On Bucknell's "gorgeous" campus, most agree that "the Greek system is everything." This helps make up for the fact that "there is not much to do in this area." Some warn that "the Greek stuff makes our school cliquey. It also makes dating a rare thing. Sororities are usually fun, except during rush, which is miserable. You are basically judged based on a short first impression." For those adverse to Greek life, "Bucknell is really good at having events on the weekends that people who do not want to participate in Greek life can attend. There are always movies being shown or comedians or musical entertainment." Adds one student, "Bucknell really tries to bring in programs that would be attractive for students to participate in," including the construction of "Uptown," a student nightclub. As far as hometown Lewisburg is concerned, "it's a quaint Victorian-style town, but it's rather lacking as far as activities go. There aren't really any stores of interest in town other than the CVS and grocery store. This makes it hard on freshman, since no cars are permitted first year. There is a mall, a Wal-Mart, and a K-mart in the area, but none are within walking distance." Reports one student, "The school needs to improve the relations between students and the town; there have been problems with off-campus houses and parties disrupting" members of the community.

Student Body

A homogeneous, upper-crust student body has always been part of Bucknell's reputation. According to students, that reputation is justified. Writes one student, "Everyone here is pretty much the same. You wear J.Crew and Abercrombie, you join a frat or sorority, you have a stylish and conservative haircut. It sounds scary, but it really isn't." Jokes one undergrad, "It's kind of irritating that everyone here is so incredibly attractive, although you get used to it. Actually, I'm not complaining. It's weird to go home, though, and realize that in the real world not every girl is a size two and has long, blonde hair." Students are comfortable with their classmates, reporting that "most of the kids at Bucknell are nice. It's not the most intellectual school on the face of the planet, but the kids are friendly, 'good kids.' "

ADMISSIONS

Very important factors considered by the admissions committee include: character/personal qualities, recommendations, secondary school record, standardized test scores, talent/ability. *Important factors considered include:* class rank, extracurricular activities, minority status, volunteer work. *Other factors considered include:* alumni/ae relation, essays, geographical residence, interview, work experience. SAT I or ACT required, SAT I preferred. TOEFL required of all international applicants. High school diploma or GED is required. *High school units required/recommended:* 16 total required; 20 total recommended; 4 English required, 3 math required, 4 math recommended, 2 science required, 3 science recommended, 2 foreign language required, 4 foreign language recommended, 2 social studies required, 2 history required, 1 elective required.

The Inside Word

Each application is read by two admissions officers. If you are serious about attending Bucknell as well as strong grades and test scores, you'll need to take the most competetive courses available at your high school. Still, overconfidence or a so-so match can throw a wrench in the plans of some; recent trends show larger numbers on the university's wait list and a track record of increased competitiveness for admission.

FINANCIAL AID

Students should submit: FAFSA, CSS/Financial Aid PROFILE, noncustodial (divorced/separated) parent's statement, business/farm supplement. Regular filing deadline is January 1. The Princeton Review suggests that all financial aid forms be submitted as soon as possible after January 1. *Need-based scholarships/grants offered:* Pell, SEOG, state scholarships/grants, private scholarships, the school's own gift aid. *Loan aid offered:* FFEL Subsidized Stafford, FFEL Unsubsidized Stafford, FFEL PLUS, Federal Perkins. Federal Work-Study Program available. Institutional employment available. Applicants will be notified of awards on or about April 10. Off-campus job opportunities are poor.

FROM THE ADMISSIONS OFFICE

"Bucknell offers a unique learning environment and is one of a few primarily undergraduate colleges that offers the opportunity to investigate both the human and technical aspects of life in the 21st century. A major curricular revision was implemented by the faculty in 1993. All students enrolling in the College of Arts and Sciences will complete a first-year foundation seminar; distributional requirements which include four humanities courses, two social science courses, and three courses in natural science and mathematics; broadened perspectives for the 21st century consisting of one course each in natural and fabricated worlds and on human diversity; departmental, college, or interdepartmental majors; and a capstone seminar or experience during the senior year. Bucknell also requires all students to complete three writing emphasis courses."

For even more information on this school, turn to page 224 of the "Stats" section.

CARNEGIE MELLON UNIVERSITY

5000 FORBES AVENUE, PITTSBURGH, PA 15213 • ADMISSIONS: 412-268-2082 • FAX: 412-268-7838
FINANCIAL AID: 412-268-2068 • E-MAIL: UNDERGRADUATE-ADMISSIONS@ANDREW.CMU.EDU
WEBSITE: WWW.CMU.EDU

Ratings

Quality of Life: 81   **Academic:** 94   **Admissions:** 92   **Financial Aid:** 84

Academics

The students of Carnegie Mellon University proudly report that their school fulfills the fundamental mission of the university: to offer excellent instruction in a wide variety of fields while also promoting cutting-edge research. "Of all the schools I've seen, no other is as well-known in so many different fields: architecture, engineering, drama, science, design, music, and business, just to name a few," is how one undergrad put

> **SURVEY SAYS . . .**
> *Great computer facilities*
> *Ethnic diversity on campus*
> *Campus easy to get around*
> *Registration is a breeze*
> *Lots of beer drinking*
> *Campus feels safe*
> *(Almost) everyone smokes*
> *Great off-campus food*
> *Hard liquor is popular*
> *Students are happy*

it, adding, "If you couldn't decide what path to take in life, you could still come to Carnegie Mellon and have a world-class education in almost any interest." Students warn, "Academically, this school will push you to your limit." As one put it, "CMU is a very research-oriented university. . . . It has truly opened doors for me that I did not know were available. The professors are actively involved in the topics in which they teach. . . . There is no such thing as a 'basic' course at CMU." The school does a good job of recognizing the demands it makes, however, and "in many departments, professors actually coordinate their tests and papers so that there is very little overlap in workloads between classes." It's just such little touches that so endear CMU to its students. Another example: "The Business School's administration loves to send us notes about various types of opportunities for internships, jobs, and lectures through email." Students are also unanimous in their praise for online services: "You can register online, check your grades online, often get assignments online, and even check what movie is playing at school online," reports an undergrad.

Life

Because of CMU's intense academic demands, "people here think about school 90 percent of the time. The other 10 percent is divided among when they're going to sleep next [and] how they're going to blow off some stress." Fortunately, there are lots of options for that scant 10 percent. Hometown Pittsburgh "is a great city if you let it be. There are many theaters, museums, and sporting events. Shops and great restaurants are all really close, and we get bus passes as students, so you can get anywhere." There are also many nearby bars, "most of which don't card." On campus, "people go to the fraternities on weekends." Also popular are one-dollar movies ("shown from Thursday to Sunday, which are a real great getaway from work, and they get good, recent movies") and student-produced plays. Student clubs and organizations also have their boosters; writes one student, "CMU has a lot of really fun, quirky organizations. . . . My two favorites are the Kiltie Band and KGB. The Kiltie Band is our band for nonmajors. As The Band Without Pants, we wear our kilts proudly, cheer giddily, click our heels, and beep when we back up. Talent for music and/or marching is not a requirement. . . . KGB stands for Keeping Geeks Busy. . . . Each semester, they host Capture the Flag with Stuff, a game that always attracts a large crowd." Although "there are sports games going on, no one ever knows when or cares to go."

Student Body

"There are a few types that are typical," at CMU; identifiable factions include: "a large number of tech, math, and computer geeks . . . strange art students, loud drama students, and many Asian student groups." Most are "hardworking, bright, ambitious," and shy. Reports one undergrad, "Students here would be considered very friendly if they weren't so reserved. You'll find that the person who sits next to you in lecture is always really nice if either of you ever overcomes your shyness enough to say hello." Politically "there is a large minority of very left-wing, extremely active students who are responsible for most of what occurs on campus. Most students, however, are apathetic and very absorbed in their studies."

ADMISSIONS

Very important factors considered by the admissions committee include: secondary school record, standardized test scores. *Important factors considered include:* alumni/ae relation, character/personal qualities, class rank, extracurricular activities, recommendations, talent/ability, volunteer work, work experience. *Other factors considered include:* essays, interview, minority status. SAT I or ACT required, SAT II also required. TOEFL required of all international applicants. High school diploma or GED is required. *High school units required/recommended:* 4 English required, 4 math required, 3 science required, 3 science lab required, 2 foreign language required, 1 social studies required, 2 history required, 3 elective required, 4 elective recommended.

The Inside Word

The Office of Admission reports that it uses "no cutoffs, no formulas" in assessing its applicant pool. Don't get too excited—that doesn't necessarily mean that applicants are looked at in a more personal fashion. Applications have seesawed here over the past couple of years, and to temper the effects of a decline in application totals on selectivity CMU maintains a huge wait list. A very low yield of admits who enroll keeps selectivity moderate, but you've got to have strong numbers to gain admission.

FINANCIAL AID

Students should submit: FAFSA, institution's own financial aid form, parent and student federal tax returns, parent W-2 forms. Regular filing deadline is May 1. The Princeton Review suggests that all financial aid forms be submitted as soon as possible after January 1. *Need-based scholarships/grants offered:* Pell, SEOG, state scholarships/grants, private scholarships, the school's own gift aid. *Loan aid offered:* FFEL Subsidized Stafford, FFEL Unsubsidized Stafford, FFEL PLUS, Federal Perkins, GATE Loans. Federal Work-Study Program available. Institutional employment available. Applicants will be notified of awards on a rolling basis. Off-campus job opportunities are good.

FROM THE ADMISSIONS OFFICE

"Carnegie Mellon is a private, coeducational university with approximately 5,100 undergraduates, 3,300 graduate students, and 778 full-time faculty members. The University's 103-acre campus is located in the Oakland area of Pittsburgh, five miles from downtown. The University is composed of seven colleges: the Carnegie Institute of Technology (engineering); the College of Fine Arts; the College of Humanities and Social Sciences (combining liberal arts education with professional specializations); the Graduate School of Industrial Administration (undergraduate business and industrial management); the Mellon College of Science; the School of Computer Science; and the H. Hohn Heina III School of Public Policy and Management."

For even more information on this school, turn to page 224 of the "Stats" section.

CATHOLIC UNIVERSITY OF AMERICA

CARDINAL STATION, WASHINGTON, DC 20064 • ADMISSIONS: 202-319-5305 • FAX: 202-319-6533
FINANCIAL AID: 202-319-5307 • E-MAIL: CUA-ADMISSIONS@CUA.EDU • WEBSITE: WWW.CUA.EDU

Ratings

Quality of Life: 80   **Academic:** 82   **Admissions:** 86   **Financial Aid:** 85

Academics

In Washington, D.C., a city known for its prestigious academic institutions, students seeking a quality education sometimes overlook The Catholic University of America. Some might be discouraged by the fact that the university is—surprise!—overwhelmingly populated by students who have Catholic backgrounds and are

> **SURVEY SAYS . . .**
> *Very little drug use, Classes are small*
> *Diversity lacking on campus*
> *Registration is a breeze*
> *Very small frat/sorority scene*
> *Library needs improving, Lousy food on campus*
> *No one plays intramural sports*
> *Dorms are like dungeons*

politically conservative to boot. Those who eliminate Catholic from their list of potential schools might miss out on a place where "professors know [students] by name" and the "faculty is extremely accessible." Catholic students praise the "great and available professors truly committed to a student's learning." The only university in the United States with a papal charter, it isn't surprising that the religion department earns high marks from many students, one senior writing, "My experience as a religion major has convinced me that this department is the best in the country. Where else can students have [this kind of] access to faculty members . . . even for an e-mail discussion at 3 a.m.?" The theater, nursing, and biology departments are touted by undergraduates, and many cite the quality of the music department as the primary reason they decided to attend Catholic. Meanwhile, the modern language departments need improvement, and many students wish that more classes were offered each semester and complain that the library could stand some improvement. Also, students are just plain unhappy with the university's administrators. One junior grumbles that "the administration treats us as if we cannot think for ourselves. Unless our parents call or are people of the cloth, we are not taken seriously." Despite students' dislike of the administration, most describe Catholic in a very positive light. "An education at Catholic University will last a lifetime," writes one student. "The doors opened by the professors here are amazing."

Life

Though they cite Catholic as having "perhaps the most boring campus life this side of a veterans' hospital," most students agree that the university's proximity to the center of town (eight minutes by Metro) was a deciding factor in their decision to attend Catholic because "D.C. is full of things to do." The world-famous museums, shops, and clubs easily counterbalanced a "slow" campus life. One student explains, "The city offers a great club scene, and there's always something going on downtown." The school's strict alcohol policies cause most students to "depend on the city for night fun." One student points out that age is rarely a factor for those looking for a good time in the immediate neighborhood surrounding Catholic: "If you have a good fake ID, your weekends will be rockin'." Undergrads also mention that the food, housing, and athletic facilities need significant improvement. "We're working out on ancient machines," writes one student. Though many students point out that there are not enough on-campus activities, most agree that Catholic's campus ministry, which sponsors some events, is "very strong and growing," and "provides great support." Overall, the unique opportunities provided by living in Washington, D.C., and the "beautiful" campus more than outweigh the concerns that most students have about the lack of on-campus social activities.

Student Body

Most students agree that homogeny in the student body is Catholic's biggest weakness. However, most say that while "the lack of diversity here is very disappointing," the majority of the students are "friendly and approachable." Many also point to a lack of school spirit as another shortcoming." Despite the religious affiliation of the university, students do not feel smothered by religion. While many students speak of an abundance of cliques, most say "people here generally get along. There is a fairly friendly atmosphere on campus."

ADMISSIONS

Very important factors considered by the admissions committee include: character/personal qualities, essays, recommendations, secondary school record, standardized test scores, volunteer work. *Important factors considered include:* extracurricular activities, interview, talent/ability. *Other factors considered include:* alumni/ae relation, class rank, minority status, work experience. SAT I or ACT required. TOEFL required of all international applicants. High school diploma or GED is required. *High school units required/recommended:* 17 total recommended; 4 English recommended, 3 math recommended, 3 science recommended, 1 science lab recommended, 2 foreign language recommended, 4 social studies recommended, 1 history recommended.

The Inside Word

This is not the place to try radical approaches to completing your admissions application: smooth sailing for solid students and even friendlier for candidates from distant states or unique high schools.

FINANCIAL AID

Students should submit: FAFSA. Regular filing deadline is February 1. The Princeton Review suggests that all financial aid forms be submitted as soon as possible after January 1. *Need-based scholarships/grants offered:* Pell, SEOG, state scholarships/grants, private scholarships, the school's own gift aid, Federal Nursing. *Loan aid offered:* FFEL Subsidized Stafford, FFEL Unsubsidized Stafford, FFEL PLUS, Federal Perkins, Federal Nursing. Federal Work-Study Program available. Institutional employment available. Applicants will be notified of awards on a rolling basis beginning on or about April 1. Off-campus job opportunities are excellent.

FROM THE ADMISSIONS OFFICE

"The Catholic University of America's friendly atmosphere, rigorous academic programs, and emphasis on time-honored values attract students from most states and more than 100 foreign countries. Its 144-acre, tree-lined campus is only 10 minutes from the nation's capital. Distinguished as the national university of the Catholic Church in the United States, CUA is the only institution of higher education established by the U.S. Catholic bishops; however, students from all religious traditions are welcome. CUA offers undergraduate degrees in more than 60 major areas in 6 schools of study. Students enroll into the School of Arts and Sciences, Architecture, Nursing, Engineering, Music, or Philosophy. Additionally, CUA students can concentrate in areas of pre-professional study including law, dental, medicine, or veterinary. With Capitol Hill, the Smithsonian Institution, NASA, the Kennedy Center, and the National Institutes of Health among the places students obtain internships, first-hand experience is a valuable piece of the experience that CUA offers. Numerous students also take the opportunity in their junior year to study abroad at one of Catholic's 17 country program sites. Political science majors even have the opportunity to do a Parliamentary Internship in either England or Ireland. With the campus just minutes away from downtown via the Metrorail rapid transit system, students enjoy a residential campus in an exciting city of historical monuments, theaters, festivals, ethnic restaurants, and parks."

For even more information on this school, turn to page 225 of the "Stats" section.

CHATHAM COLLEGE

WOODLAND ROAD, PITTSBURGH, PA 15232 • ADMISSIONS: 412-365-1290 • FAX: 412-365-1609
E-MAIL: ADMISSIONS@CHATHAM.EDU • WEBSITE: WWW.CHATHAM.EDU

Ratings
Quality of Life: 80   Academic: 67   Admissions: 64   Financial Aid: 79

Academics

Students at Chatham College love their school's overseas study program. Reports one undergrad, "My favorite activity is the sophomore interim abroad. All sophomores have the chance to take a class in another country. I went to Ireland and made new friends and learned a lot, while getting to enjoy

> **SURVEY SAYS . . .**
> *Students are cliquish*
> *Students get along with local community*
> *Students are happy, Campus is beautiful*
> *Dorms are like palaces, Lousy food on campus*
> *Athletic facilities need improving*
> *No one watches intercollegiate sports*

another country. I also went and lived in Japan for three months. It was fantastic. I got credit for all my classes and learned a new language." Back in the states, Chatham students enjoy the quintessential small-school experience, replete with professors who "have an 'open-door' policy and are very welcoming even when a student does not have an appointment. They are open to suggestions for the course and want to help you as much as they can. Most professors want to know what you are planning on doing when you graduate, summer plans, or just how your semester is going." On the downside, due to the school's small size, "there are very limited classes offered each semester. There is the option of cross-registration at some other area schools, but only one class per semester can be taken at another institution." Students also warn that, due to budgetary constraints, "we have a lot of adjunct professors. While our full-time faculty is excellent, the adjuncts are hit-and-miss." Students may complain about athletics at Chatham, but a $16 million sports center due in 2004 should boost spirits in this regard. Chatham students also note its "great master's programs in physical therapy, occupational therapy, physician assistant training, teaching, business, and counseling psychology"; in only 5 years, students can complete integrated BA/Master's degrees in these areas.

Life

The Chatham community is small and single sex, so it should come as no surprise that campus extracurricular life presents limited options. Students involve themselves in "very time-consuming campus organizations" but otherwise characterize life at Chatham as "boring, especially on the weekends because a lot of students go home." The neighborhood surrounding the school, Shadyside, offers little help. Fortunately, hometown Pittsburgh is full of fun activities, as well as several larger coed campuses. Reports one student, "Since there aren't any guys, you have to go to Pitt or Carnegie-Mellon to find them. The easiest way to do that is to go to frat parties. That's also where all the girls who drink go to get alcohol, since the policy here is very strict. If you even have unopened or empty containers of alcohol [on campus], you will suffer the consequences." Students see benefits to the small-campus atmosphere: "Life on campus is like living in a small town" where "everyone knows everyone else, it seems; everyone says 'hi,'" explains one satisfied undergrad.

Student Body

Chatham women are "leaders and innovators," according to their peers. As for the diversity of the student body, it all depends on whether you see the glass as half-empty or half-full. In terms of percentages, minority populations here are large; in terms of absolute numbers, however, they are tiny. This explains the many contradictory comments we received from students. "Chatham students are diverse and dynamic. My friends are Muslim, Latina, Indonesian, Jewish, African American, gay and straight, and range in age from 17 to 65," writes one student. "This is a predominantly white campus," counters an African American undergrad. Students warn that "it is all girls, so you have to deal with the same sh*t [as] in high school. Everyone talks, and everyone knows everyone else's business."

ADMISSIONS

Very important factors considered by the admissions committee include: secondary school record. *Important factors considered include:* standardized test scores. *Other factors considered include:* character/personal qualities, class rank, essays, extracurricular activities, interview, recommendations, talent/ability, volunteer work, and work experience. SAT I or ACT required. TOEFL required of all international applicants. High school diploma or GED is required. *High school units required/recommended:* 12 total required; 16 total recommended; 4 English required, 2 math required, 3 math recommended, 2 science required, 3 science recommended, 2 social studies required, 2 social studies recommended, 2 history required, 3 history recommended.

The Inside Word

Chatham's single-sex demographic turns off some potential undergraduates. As a result, Chatham presents underachieving women a unique opportunity for admittance to a fine liberal arts college. Cooperative learning programs provide some access to UPitt and Carnegie Mellon.

FINANCIAL AID

Students should submit: FAFSA. No deadline for regular filing. The Princeton Review suggests that all financial aid forms be submitted as soon as possible after January 1. *Need-based scholarships/grants offered:* Pell, SEOG, state scholarships/grants, private scholarships, and the school's own gift aid. *Loan aid offered:* FFEL Subsidized Stafford, FFEL Unsubsidized Stafford, FFEL PLUS, and Federal Perkins. Federal Work-Study Program available. Applicants will be notified of awards on a rolling basis beginning on or about February 15. Off-campus job opportunities are good.

FROM THE ADMISSIONS OFFICE

"Chatham College's World-Ready Women are excited about learning—about themselves and about their place in this world. More important, they are ready to make their mark on this world. Grounded in the liberal arts and focused on preparing students for the future, a Chatham College education emphasizes the environment, global issues, and women's leadership.

"Chatham is the college for independent women who have a desire to succeed. Each year members of the senior class complete a yearlong independent research project known as the Senior Tutorial. Eighty-five percent of Chatham students take advantage of the countless internship opportunities available to them, with most students participating in at least two. In addition, almost three-quarters of the senior class participated in service learning last year, with more than 32,000 total hours completed by Chatham students.

"Chatham students may also participate in the Rachel Carson Institute, where the focus is on global environmental issues. Established to honor the legacy of Chatham alumna Rachel Carson '29, the center's concentration is on the impact of environmental degradation on women's health and societal roles and the promotion of women's leadership in the environmental movement. Likewise, the Center for Women in Politics in Pennsylvania exposes students to the world of politics, public policy, and civic engagement. Students meet and work with top-level practitioners in public policy and related fields.

"Finally, the Global Focus Program brings a region of the world—the politics, geography, cultures, and perceptions—to campus each year. Recent Global Focus topics include Ireland and the Communities of Islam."

For even more information on this school, turn to page 226 of the "Stats" section.

CHRISTOPHER NEWPORT UNIVERSITY

ONE UNIVERSITY PLACE, NEWPORT NEWS, VA 23608 • ADMISSIONS: 757-594-7015 • FAX: 757-594-7333
E-MAIL: ADMIT@CNU.EDU • WEBSITE: WWW.CNU.EDU

Ratings
Quality of Life: 78   Academic: 65   Admissions: 78   Financial Aid: 75

Academics

A relatively young university in Virginia, Christopher Newport University is building a student body on the foundation of its motto, "Students First." So far, it seems to ring true: "The president and other administrators are VERY available and anxious to help students. In fact, I know most of them by face and name." Some of the biggest accolades are

> **SURVEY SAYS . . .**
> *Athletic facilities are great*
> *Dorms are like dungeons*
> *Class discussions encouraged*
> *Classes are small*
> *Very little drug use*
> *Lousy food on campus*
> *Campus feels safe*
> *Very little hard liquor*

reserved for Paul Trible, president of the university, who "goes out of his way to meet, greet, and get to know as many students as he possibly can. He invites all freshman students to his home at the beginning of the school year for dinner." Trible also "eats in the dining hall with us, he goes to basketball games, football games, and he even cheers our soccer team on when it's snowing outside." The faculty is also generally well received: "Professors are always pushing me to accomplish bigger and better things," says one satisfied student. Another beams, "What I really love about CNU is the fact that most of the professors are really approachable, even if you are not in that particular major." Not all students as pleased as pie, though; as one puts it, "The professors at my university are wonderful; however, they've become complacent in the face of apathetic students." Others find discrepancies with what's sold and what's bought: "Though they claim to put students first, that is really only directed toward 'prospective students first.'" One topic you won't hear trashed at CNU is the cost, because, as one CNU tour guide boasts, "it's like a private school at a public school cost!"

Life

If you're keen on keg stands, think twice before sending your deposit to CNU, where "people generally respect the rules because they know that the rules and consequences of breaking them are enforced, not merely threatened. As a result, there are no keg parties in the residence halls (CNU is a dry campus), drugs are a rarity (I have yet to come across any), and the campus is very safe." Students who are of legal age can drink off the premises, but social life here is not dampened by the rules. "Everyone enjoys life here," says one. "There is not a day that passes that something is not going on. Concerts, lip-sync contests, talent shows, pageants, meetings, and various other events" keep everyone busy in addition to the 30 new clubs this year and brand new football team. "In the absence of the alcohol party scene, students will often go out to movies . . . go bowling, go for walks on nearby nature trails, go to the beach," or take weekend trips to Washington, D.C., Nag's Head, or Virginia Beach. "Many of us spend time volunteering, raising money for charities, and working on other social issues," shares one student. The SGA, the Captain's Log (student paper), and the Campus Activities Board "put in long hours and are dedicated to making CNU a great university."

Student Body

According to one student, "My fellow students are some of the most friendly, outgoing, and involved people that I have ever met. I find that they all love CNU and want to be here." Others concur: "It's very easy to meet people at CNU, whether in class, in the gym, at work or just hanging around the student center." Although one student claims that "everyone here is generally the same: conservative, religious, and Virginian," another shares the feeling of brotherhood: "We all have the same vision, to leave a legacy behind us, to make an impression on this young campus. We are driven to start new traditions." There is still some separation between boarders and nonboarders at CNU, which used to be more of a commuter school; "it's an up-and-coming liberal arts university still stuck in the commuter-based frame of mind," explains an undergrad. But this attitude "is changing since we are a growing school and more and more people are living on campus each year," adds an optimistic student.

ADMISSIONS

Very important factors considered by the admissions committee include: secondary school record and standardized test scores. *Important factors considered include:* class rank. *Other factors considered include:* alumni/ae relation, essays, extracurricular activities, interview, recommendations, talent/ability, volunteer work, and work experience. SAT I or ACT required. TOEFL required of all international applicants. High school diploma or GED is required. *High school units required/recommended:* 4 English required, 4 math required, 3 science required, 6 foreign language required, 3 social studies required, 2 elective recommended.

The Inside Word

CNU was once an easy school to get into. But those days are over; the school's applicant pool has more than tripled in the last five years, and the average SAT score has increased by 160 points. The admissions office looks closely at individual applications and considers candidates' leadership experience and community service when making its decisions.

FINANCIAL AID

Students should submit: FAFSA. No deadline for regular filing. The Princeton Review suggests that all financial aid forms be submitted as soon as possible after January 1. *Need-based scholarships/grants offered:* Pell, SEOG, state scholarships/grants, private scholarships, and the school's own gift aid. *Loan aid offered:* FFEL Subsidized Stafford, FFEL Unsubsidized Stafford, FFEL PLUS, state loans, college/university loans from institutional funds, and alternative education loans. Federal Work-Study Program available. Institutional employment available. Applicants will be notified of awards on a rolling basis beginning on or about February 15. Off-campus job opportunities are excellent.

For even more information on this school, turn to page 226 of the "Stats" section.

COLLEGE OF NOTRE DAME OF MARYLAND

4701 NORTH CHARLES STREET, BALTIMORE, MD 21210 • ADMISSIONS: 410-532-5330 • FAX: 410-532-6287
E-MAIL: ADMISS@NDM.EDU • WEBSITE: WWW.NDM.EDU

Ratings

Quality of Life: 79   Academic: 80   Admissions: 73   Financial Aid: 73

Academics

Students at the College of Notre Dame of Maryland, a Catholic women's school in Baltimore, are proud of their school's rich academic heritage. The school's mission, students tell us, "is all about 'educating women to transform the world.' By coming here, I feel that I will be able to experience a liberal education that will help me [grow] into a well-rounded intel-

> **SURVEY SAYS . . .**
> School is well run
> (Almost) everyone plays intramural sports
> Students are religious
> No one watches intercollegiate sports
> Lots of beer drinking
> Classes are small
> Hard liquor is popular
> Popular college radio

lectual." Liberal arts, education, business, and psychology are among the top academic offerings. One sanguine student opines, "The academics at my school are unbelievable. There is no place on Earth where professors, deans, and other administrators . . . care so much about students. I am consistently impressed with the quality of learning that takes place at Notre Dame." Many feel that "the size of the school is [its] greatest strength. Having a small school allows students to know each other better." This sense of community is enhanced by "the best faculty and administration. . . . They all genuinely care about the students and empowering women." Adds one student, "The professors are very nice and concerned. . . . When you're sick they send you e-mails, and most of them give you their home phone number." Students here have few complaints, the only major one being that "technology on campus needs a huge improvement. Students do not have Internet access to their records, grades, or schedules. It's like we are still living in the 19th century!"

Life

If a bustling campus life is among your goals, Notre Dame may not be the school for you. As one student put it, "Life at the college is boring. There aren't any fun activities to go to, no parties, no special fun events. On campus, other than class, there is nothing much to do." Agreed another undergrad, "Academically the college is good. The only bad thing is the college campus life is extremely dull. Other than coming to take your class, there is nothing on campus that a student can do for fun." Most here don't mind, however, because hometown Baltimore offers students all the entertainment they want. Writes one student, "Because the college is located in Baltimore there are many opportunities to learn new things. There are over 100,000 college students in the area, so there is always something to do. The colleges and universities have recognized this and are working together to promote intercollegiate events." (Nearby undergrad institutions include Johns Hopkins, the Peabody Conservatory, Morgan State, Goucher, Loyola, and the Maryland Institute of Art.) Baltimore offers a variety of nightlife; writes one student, "The weekends are spent at the malls, bars, and clubs downtown, in Canton, Fells Point, and Towson. People generally go out in groups, and those of us who stay on campus over the weekend (which can be a small number at times) bond for life." However, "during the week, we often are a pretty studious bunch, although [we] do have fun during study breaks being silly and discussing life. Intelligence is prized here, and we enjoy our education." Some students "complain about the number of people who go home on the weekend."

Student Body

The women of Notre Dame enjoy "a very supportive campus. It is like one big extended family. Sure, there are smaller groups, but the whole campus does unite when needed." Reports one student, "This school is a wonderful place to live, work, and study. There is an unwritten rule that people hold doors for one another. Guests and visitors are easily identified because they are the ones who do not hold doors and smile." Notre Dame draws nearly all its students from the Baltimore area. African Americans make up one-fifth of the student body, lending support to the school's claim that it recruits "students who have special talents, a variety of interests, and diverse backgrounds."

ADMISSIONS

Very important factors considered by the admissions committee include: essays, interview, recommendations, secondary school record, and standardized test scores. *Important factors considered include:* extracurricular activities, talent/ability, and volunteer work. *Other factors considered include:* alumni/ae relation, class rank, and work experience. SAT I or ACT required, SAT I preferred. TOEFL required of all international applicants. High school diploma is required and GED is accepted. *High school units required/recommended:* 18 total are required; 4 English required, 3 math required, 2 science required, 2 science lab required, 3 foreign language required, 2 history required, 4 elective required.

The Inside Word

Expect a close review of all your application materials from the admissions counselors at Notre Dame. Evidence of leadership, creativity, special talents, compassion, and community service will all be seen as positive indicators that may offset the occasional bad grade or low standardized test score.

FINANCIAL AID

Students should submit: FAFSA and institution's own financial aid form. The Princeton Review suggests that all financial aid forms be submitted as soon as possible after January 1. *Need-based scholarships/grants offered:* Pell, SEOG, and state scholarships/grants. *Loan aid offered:* Direct Subsidized Stafford, Direct Unsubsidized Stafford, Direct PLUS, and Federal Perkins. Federal Work-Study Program available. Institution employment available. Applicants will be notified of awards on a rolling basis beginning on or about March 1. Off-campus job opportunities are good.

For even more information on this school, turn to page 227 of the "Stats" section.

COLLEGE OF WILLIAM AND MARY

PO Box 8795, WILLIAMSBURG, VA 23187-8795 • ADMISSIONS: 757-221-4223 • FAX: 757-221-1242
FINANCIAL AID: 757-221-2420 EXT. 4290 • E-MAIL: ADMISS@FACSTAFF.WM.EDU • WEBSITE: WWW.WM.EDU

Ratings

Quality of Life: 84   Academic: 92   Admissions: 94   Financial Aid: 81

Academics

Looking for a small public university with a big reputation (considered by some to be the most "prestigious" and "competitive" in the country), excellent location, and a down-to-earth attitude? William and Mary might just be your answer. Its students are certainly aware of this traditional liberal arts college's strengths and express

> **SURVEY SAYS . . .**
> *Frats and sororities dominate social scene*
> *Beautiful campus, No one cheats*
> *(Almost) everyone plays intramural sports*
> *Campus feels safe, Students are very religious*
> *Musical organizations are hot*
> *(Almost) no one listens to college radio*
> *Students get along with local community*

them with intelligence and ease: "William and Mary is an undiscovered gem," writes one student. "It is an excellent undergraduate institution: small, but big enough to not limit you." Adds another, "At William and Mary, you get out of a class exactly what you put in. It's called self-determination. So, really, the school itself doesn't set the standards; we do." Listing the honor code, small class size, and rigorous academic standards as being among the college's greatest assets, students also appreciate its accessible, student-focused faculty, noting that at William and Mary, "we have professors who can make classes of 50 and more feel personal." One sophomore likes the fact that teachers "reward excellence and not competency with A's," while another appreciates "the option of being able to get to know the professors on a personal level." And though "the administration is a tad clueless," they also "listen to students the best that they can"—which presumably includes the issues surrounding financial aid, a popular gripe among William and Mary undergrads. "It's the best school for the money," comments a junior—with one caveat: You have to be a Virginia resident to take advantage of its state-school price tag. Basically, it comes down to one's feeling about a place, and the zeitgeist at William and Mary seems to be summed up best by a freshman: "Good times, guys. Good times."

Life

"Intimate," "warm," and "tightly knit" are words often used to describe William and Mary's fairly well-developed social scene. According to a sophomore, it's the "size of the school" that "permits students to get involved in campus life." Writes another, "There is always something going on at William and Mary. It's easy to make friends and easy to be involved in activities. You can be as active as you want—there are a lot of opportunities." Some students might say that social life is somewhat skewed toward "fraternity parties and the brotherhood," however. There are lots of parties on weekends, and "delis [basically bars across the street from campus] are very fun to go to and hang out at." Williamsburg doesn't receive rave reviews. Writes one student, "Being far-ish from any major metropolitan area, cultural activities (concerts, museums, etc.) are rather rare." Still, while Williamsburg "doesn't have much," a trip to D.C. is worth the drive. Athletics are also a big draw; by one student's reckoning, "About 80 percent of the students participate in some kind of sport." Alas, "the meal plan is a rip-off," and while the colonial-style campus is scenic and lovely, parking seems to be a huge hassle (and impossible for first and second years). But hey—when the biggest complaint about a school is "more parking, better food, more hot boys," it can't be that bad.

Student Body

In keeping with William and Mary's down-to-earth vibe, students at the school characterize their peers as "real" and "friendly," with "no fake attitudes and phoniness." Writes a sophomore, "Most everyone is approachable and genuinely concerned for others." Adds another, "Students are interesting and have neat stories—basically the same socioeconomic status but different life experiences." Of course not everyone is down with the group thing; a sophomore points out that "most students come from middle-class white backgrounds so the student body is too homogenous in attitudes/perspectives. Many are therefore unoriginal and boring." Still, a strong sense of community seems to be one of W&M's greatest strengths, even if it means getting through the hard times together. Jokes a junior, "Though half of the students are probably depressed, there exists an undeniable spirit of solidarity among them."

ADMISSIONS

Very important factors considered by the admissions committee include: secondary school record, state residency. *Important factors considered include:* alumni/ae relation, class rank, essays, extracurricular activities, standardized test scores. *Other factors considered include:* character/personal qualities, geographical residence, minority status, recommendations, talent/ability, volunteer work, work experience. SAT I or ACT required; SAT II optional. TOEFL required of all international applicants. *High school units required/recommended:* 4 English recommended, 4 math recommended, 4 science recommended, 3 science lab recommended, 4 foreign language recommended, 4 social studies recommended.

The Inside Word

The volume of applications at William and Mary is extremely high; thus admission is ultra-competitive. Only very strong students from out of state should apply. The large applicant pool necessitates a rapid-fire candidate evaluation process; each admissions officer reads roughly 100 application folders per day during the peak review season. But this is one admissions committee that moves fast without sacrificing a thorough review. There probably isn't a tougher public college admissions committee in the country.

FINANCIAL AID

Students should submit: FAFSA. Regular filing deadline is March 15. The Princeton Review suggests that all financial aid forms be submitted as soon as possible after January 1. *Need-based scholarships/grants offered:* Pell, SEOG, state scholarships/grants, private scholarships, the school's own gift aid. *Loan aid offered:* FFEL Subsidized Stafford, FFEL Unsubsidized Stafford, FFEL PLUS, Federal Perkins. Federal Work-Study Program available. Institutional employment available. Applicants will be notified of awards on or about April 1. Off-campus job opportunities are good.

FROM THE ADMISSIONS OFFICE

"If you are an academicaly strong, involved student looking for a challenge in a great campus community, William and Mary may well be the place for you. Every year, students are drawn from all parts of the United States and dozens of foreign countries by the excellence of the undergraduate experience, the beauty of the campus and its surroundings, the size and residential character of the student body, and the history and traditions of the country's second oldest college."

For even more information on this school, turn to page 228 of the "Stats" section.

DELAWARE VALLEY COLLEGE

700 East Butler Avenue, Doylestown, PA 18901-2697 • Admissions: 215-489-2211
Fax: 215-230-2968 • E-mail: admitme@devalcol.edu • Website: www.devalcol.edu

Ratings

Quality of Life: 72 **Academic:** 77 **Admissions:** 75 **Financial Aid:** 73

Academics

Delaware Valley College, students agree, "is a great agricultural school" as well as "a good school for people who want to get involved with animals or education." Writes one animal science major, "I have thoroughly enjoyed the majority of academic courses that I have enrolled in while at Del Val; they have provided me with excellent hands-on experience with

> **SURVEY SAYS . . .**
> *Campus is beautiful*
> *Lousy food on campus*
> *Students are happy*
> *Classes are small*
> *Campus feels safe*
> *Diverse students interact*
> *Dorms are like dungeons*

both large and small animals that I would not have attained at a larger university." Students here appreciate the fact that "the classes are small enough that you get a lot of one-on-one attention if you need it" and that "the majority of the professors here are so open-minded and willing to discuss things that the students want to talk about as well as general lecture topics." Students praise professors for "knowing what they are talking about and not being too caught-up in their degree. They are down to earth and treat you like a friend." Writes one undergrad, "Professors are frequently available to the students outside of the classroom setting for help with class work, exam reviews, job searches, or personal matters." Some students feel that "less popular majors (e.g., criminal justice) do not get any support from the school, while there is loads of funding and support for the agricultural-based majors."

Life

Students on the "beautiful campus" of Delaware Valley College tell us that life at their school is "all about friends—hanging out, going out, even studying in groups makes everything better. If you're not out with someone or doing something, there's not much else to be doing!" Commenting both on campus life and the surrounding town of Doylestown, a typical student told us that "it is pretty boring because there really isn't much to do [other than] taking a 45-minute drive to Philadelphia." As a result, students say, "Parties are the nightly thing, especially if you're in a frat/sorority. Drugs are very popular, and security really doesn't care to deal with them." Writes one student, "I think the student population as a whole is a normal college-age group who are experiencing freedom for the first time. The school does not stress responsibility for actions, and I do not feel they assist with the maturity of the students. Del Val is quite a party school, and [the administration] lets a lot of mischief go on." Undergrads also note that "Del Val is basically a suitcase college. The weekends are generally small groups of friends hanging out. The big night on campus is Thursdays."

Student Body

Undergrads report that "most people at Del Val are very 'upper class' or 'farmers.' These two groups clash slightly, but most often they get along." There are points of tension: writes one 'upper class' student, "I was extremely offended at the fact that many students wave their Confederate flags with pride, not taking into consideration that it may be offensive to other students. On the other hand, if I waved a flag that said 'All Ag students are hicks,' I would get into an unbelievable amount of trouble." Others tell us that "the worst things here are the cliques. We have the sorority sisters, the agricultural science people, the equine science girls, the frat brothers, and then everybody else. For the most part we all get along, but I wish there was more 'crossing over the lines' between groups."

ADMISSIONS

Very important factors considered by the admissions committee include: secondary school record. *Important factors considered include:* character/personal qualities, class rank, interview, and standardized test scores. *Other factors considered include:* alumni/ae relation, essays, extracurricular activities, recommendations, talent/ability, volunteer work, and work experience. SAT I or ACT required. TOEFL required of all international applicants. High school diploma or GED is required. *High school units required/recommended:* 15 total required; 3 English required, 2 math required, 2 science required, 1 science lab required, 2 social studies required, 6 elective required.

The Inside Word

Delaware Valley admits students on a rolling basis. Apply early for the popular agricultural programs, as they can fill quickly. Candidates with weak academic records may be admitted through the CHOICES program; this program accepts freshman conditionally, pending completion of a required introductory curriculum.

FINANCIAL AID

Students should submit: FAFSA. The Princeton Review suggests that all financial aid forms be submitted as soon as possible after January 1. *Need-based scholarships/grants offered:* Pell, SEOG, state scholarships/grants, private scholarships, and the school's own gift aid. *Loan aid offered:* FFEL Subsidized Stafford, FFEL Unsubsidized Stafford, FFEL PLUS, and Federal Perkins. Federal Work-Study Program available. Institutional employment available. Applicants will be notified of awards on a rolling basis beginning on or about February 1. Off-campus job opportunities are excellent.

For even more information on this school, turn to page 228 of the "Stats" section.

DICKINSON COLLEGE

PO Box 1773, Carlisle, PA 17013-2896 • Admissions: 717-245-1231 • Fax: 717-245-1442
Financial Aid: 717-245-1308 • E-mail: admit@dickinson.edu • Website: www.dickinson.edu

Ratings
Quality of Life: 83   Academic: 88   Admissions: 82   Financial Aid: 87

Academics

Dickinson College is a small school with about one professor for every 12 students. And while this has its benefits, one students jokes, "Be careful . . . if you skip or slack off, your professors will see you at the hockey game or the local bars and give you a piece of their minds." Students have plenty of opportunity to interact with the "well-read, super intelligent"

> **SURVEY SAYS . . .**
> *Frats and sororities dominate social scene*
> *Great food on campus*
> *Diversity lacking on campus*
> *Students don't get along with local community*
> *Campus easy to get around*
> *Students don't like Carlisle, PA*
> *Low cost of living*
> *Class discussions encouraged*

profs in class, too, because "all courses are taught by professors," rather than TAs. Administrators are also easily accessible. In fact, around suppertime you're likely to "see the president and his wife eating in the cafeteria." Plenty of distribution requirements ensure that students get a broad taste of the academic spectrum. Once in class, you'll find that you're "expected to read heavy amounts, do independent research . . . presentations, group work, and lead discussions." With the Trout Gallery, the national headquarters of the Oral History Association, a recently renovated library, and a new science building on campus, students have an abundance of resources to help them on their journey on the academic high road.

Life

Life "in a small town in central PA" isn't always exciting. According to one student, in hometown Carlisle, you'll find "a few bars, one movie theater, a handful of small parks, minimal shopping, lots of rednecks!" When students need a taste of city life, they "can get to Philly in under two hours, to Baltimore in an hour and a half, and to Harrisburg in about 20 minutes." But when they really want to get away, they go overseas. "Eighty-five percent of the student body studies abroad once in their four years, whether it be [for a] semester, year-long, summer, or winter program." Student sentiment about life on campus varies. While one complains that "there are not many things to do besides sit and drink in one's room," another counters that "there are lots of things to do socially here, 90 percent of them student-organized and run, but the students who complain can't see that." Aside from the fraternity or off-campus house parties, students can find "plays, intramural and intercollegiate sports to watch or play, movies, comedy clubs, dances, free food, Monday night football, lectures, and much, much more." Outdoorsy types enjoy "hiking, biking, caving, canoeing," or wandering around on the Appalachian Trail, which "runs pretty close to campus." Interestingly enough, some students would like to see a little more partying. "We still hear about 'Drinkinson,'" laments one student, referring to a nickname from several years ago, "but we're all wondering where the hell it went."

Student Body

Students are the first to acknowledge the rich kid stigma they bear. "Dickinson definitely has a J.Crew image," one student admits. "However, the socioeconomic backgrounds of all students that attend the school are as diverse as you'll find anywhere in America." In fact, in recent years, "more and more public-school graduates and middle or lower [income] students are coming here and getting involved." Dickinson's diversity is improving, but many students tell us that "Dickinson could be a lot more diverse than it is." Nevertheless, the student body doesn't lack in "friendliness." According to one upperclassman, "I like being able to walk from my apartment to class, to lunch, to class, to work, and back and see/say 'hi' to 50 people I know." It's also the place for you if you like to study, as students often spend many of their night and weekend hours in the library's study rooms. But they're not simply a herd of nerds: "The students at Dickinson are smart as hell and love to party like rock stars."

ADMISSIONS

Very important factors considered by the admissions committee include: extracurricular activities, minority status, secondary school record, talent/ability, volunteer work. *Important factors considered include:* alumni/ae relation, class rank, recommendations, standardized test scores, work experience. *Other factors considered include:* character/personal qualities, essays, geographical residence, interview, state residency. The SAT I recommended. TOEFL required of all international applicants. High school diploma or GED is required. *High school units required/recommended:* 16 total required; 4 English required, 3 math required, 3 science required, 2 science lab required, 2 foreign language required, 3 foreign language recommended, 2 social studies required, 2 elective required.

The Inside Word

Dickinson's admissions process is typical of most small liberal arts colleges. The best candidates for such a place are those with solid grades and broad extracurricular involvement—the stereotypical "well-rounded student." Admissions selectivity is kept in check by a strong group of competitor colleges that fight tooth and nail for their cross-applicants.

FINANCIAL AID

Students should submit: FAFSA, CSS/Financial Aid PROFILE, state aid form, noncustodial (divorced/separated) parent's statement, business/farm supplement. Regular filing deadline is February 1. The Princeton Review suggests that all financial aid forms be submitted as soon as possible after January 1. *Need-based scholarships/grants offered:* Pell, SEOG, state scholarships/grants, private scholarships, the school's own gift aid. *Loan aid offered:* FFEL Subsidized Stafford, FFEL Unsubsidized Stafford, FFEL PLUS, Federal Perkins, college/university loans from institutional funds. Federal Work-Study Program available. Institutional employment available. Applicants will be notified of awards on or about March 1. Off-campus job opportunities are good.

FROM THE ADMISSIONS OFFICE

"College is more than a collection of courses. It is about crossing traditional boundaries, about seeing the interrelationships among different subjects, about learning a paradigm for solving problems, about developing critical thinking and communication skills, and about speaking out on issues that matter. Dickinson was founded to be different from the 15 colleges that existed in our nation before it: to provide a 'useful' education, where students would learn by doing, through hands-on experiences and engagement with the community the region, the nation and the world. And this is truer today than ever, with workshop science courses replacing traditional lectures, fieldwork experiences in community studies where students take oral histories, and 12 study centers abroad in nontourist cities where students, under the guidance of a Dickinson faculty director, experience a true international culture. Almost 80 percent of the student body studies abroad, preparing them to compete and succeed in a complex global world."

For even more information on this school, turn to page 229 of the "Stats" section.

DREXEL UNIVERSITY

3141 CHESTNUT STREET, PHILADELPHIA, PA 19104 • ADMISSIONS: 215-895-2400 • FAX: 215-895-5939
FINANCIAL AID: 215-895-2535 • E-MAIL: ENROLL@DREXEL.EDU • WEBSITE: WWW.DREXEL.EDU

Ratings

Quality of Life: 68   Academic: 73   Admissions: 79   Financial Aid: 78

Academics

Drexel University is known for its co-op program, which adds an extra year to an undergraduate education, and provides three half-year internships with companies in and around the Philadelphia area. The co-op program "is the best part of Drexel." Some students complain that the course work is "unchallenging," and that while some of the profes-

> **SURVEY SAYS . . .**
> *Popular college radio*
> *Musical organizations aren't popular*
> *High cost of living, Students aren't religious*
> *Class discussions are rare*
> *Campus difficult to get around*
> *Ethnic diversity on campus*
> *Lots of long lines and red tape*
> *Political activism is (almost) nonexistent*

sors are good, others are not. The university employs some foreign professors, and students grumble about the difficulty understanding many of them. Classes often get canceled, and students find that it is difficult to get into required classes because not enough sections are offered. Students gush about the wireless system that enables a student anywhere on campus to connect to the Internet via a T1 connection. They note, however, that the $5 million system allows faculty to post "assignments, study guides, notes, and exam times and locations for each class." Many believe that the engineering and hotel management departments are among the university's best. While students have mixed feelings about the quality of a Drexel education, they agree that "the Drexel Shaft," perpetrated by the administration, "is running the school into the ground." Students believe that "they accept too many students, have no place to house them, and spend too much time recruiting new students and not enough time keeping current students satisfied." The prevailing attitude amongst the administration is that the students are "customers." Administrative offices "are not coordinated with each other, and if you want something done, you have to do it yourself." The administrative problems begin at the top levels; student issues are "only cared about . . . if they were going to do it anyway."

Life

Students love the fact that Drexel is located only five blocks away from Center City, Philadelphia. The City of Brotherly Love offers numerous cultural opportunities, from the museums and art galleries, to the city's four professional sports franchises, to the fantastic zoo. National music acts perform in town every night in venues of varying size. "It may be because we have an inner-city campus, but this whole East Coast urban feeling kind of creates this feeling of a hectic, nonstop lifestyle," writes one student. "Everyone is either working hard or playing hard. There's no such thing as relaxing and doing nothing." There are plenty of nightclubs and bars in the area, and students often attend frat parties and visit the neighboring University of Pennsylvania. Undergrads spend much of their time studying and praise the quality of the school newspaper. A significant number of students work off campus, and their prolonged absence diminishes school spirit.

Student Body

Drexel students describe their peers as "apathetic" but "friendly and diverse," claiming "everyone gets along because there is a common bitterness against the school's administration." International students are valued for the different views that they bring to the university. Though certain groups "tend to stick together, I don't think they try to discriminate." Still, the "Drexel Shaft" is a "bond that ties us together." Another student adds, "We bond in our utter hatred of the Drexel empire." The Greek system also brings students together.

ADMISSIONS

Very important factors considered by the admissions committee include: class rank, essays, secondary school record, standardized test scores. *Important factors considered include:* character/personal qualities, extracurricular activities, interview, recommendations, talent/ability. *Other factors considered include:* alumni/ae relation, minority status, volunteer work, work experience. SAT I or ACT required; SAT I preferred. TOEFL required of all international applicants. High school diploma or GED is required. *High school units required/recommended:* 3 math required, 1 science required, 1 science lab required, 1 foreign language recommended.

The Inside Word

Drexel's distinct nature creates a high level of self-selection in the applicant pool, and most decent students are admitted.

FINANCIAL AID

Students should submit: FAFSA. The Princeton Review suggests that all financial aid forms be submitted as soon as possible after January 1. *Need-based scholarships/grants offered:* Pell, SEOG, state scholarships/grants, private scholarships, the school's own gift aid, United Negro College Fund. *Loan aid offered:* FFEL Subsidized Stafford, FFEL Unsubsidized Stafford, FFEL PLUS, Federal Perkins, college/university loans from institutional funds. Federal Work-Study Program available. Institutional employment available. Applicants will be notified of awards on a rolling basis beginning on or about April 1. Off-campus job opportunities are excellent.

FROM THE ADMISSIONS OFFICE

"Since its inception in 1891, Drexel University has gained national recognition among colleges and universities for its academic excellence, experiential education program (Drexel Co-op), technological expertise, and curricular innovation. In 1998, Drexel began operating one of the Philadelphia region's premier medical and health sciences schools, MCP Hahnemann University. In April, Drexel's Board of Trustees unanimously voted to approve merging MCP Hahnemann into Drexel University.

"With the addition of the nation's largest private medical school, an outstanding college of nursing and health professions, and one of only two schools of public health in Pennsylvania, Drexel University now comprises 12 academic colleges and schools. By this summer, we will offer 175 degree programs to some 11,500 undergraduates and 4,200 graduate students. Alumni will number 90,000, and the size of the full-time faculty will exceed 1,000.

"The post-merger Drexel will join the fewer than 50 private universities classified by the Carnegie Foundation as Doctoral/Research Universities-Extensive, which include Carnegie Mellon, MIT, Caltech, and Penn. Drexel also joins the top 100 U.S. universities in federal research expenditures and market value of endowment. Another benefit of this merger is that qualified Drexel applicants can now pursue four new accelerated dual-degree programs in the health sciences: the Bachelor's/MD in Medicine; Bachelor's/Master's in Nursing; Bachelor's/Doctor of Physical Therapy; and Bachelor's/Master's for Physician Assistants.

"By combining our expertise in advanced technology and cooperative education with academic programs in medicine and health-related fields, we can now offer our students a unique set of skills with which to succeed in today's ever-changing world."

For even more information on this school, turn to page 230 of the "Stats" section.

DUQUESNE UNIVERSITY

600 FORBES AVENUE, PITTSBURGH, PA 15282 • ADMISSIONS: 412-396-5000 • FAX: 412-396-5644
FINANCIAL AID: 412-396-6607 • E-MAIL: ADMISSIONS@DUQ.EDU • WEBSITE: WWW.DUQ.EDU

Ratings
Quality of Life: 70   Academic: 72   Admissions: 76   Financial Aid: 82

Academics

Duquesne University students are satisfied with the education they receive. They are very career-oriented and believe that a Duquesne education prepares them for life after college. Students adore their instructors, and few classes—if any—are taught by TAs. A secondary education major writes, "I believe Duquesne University has an excellent staff who are always willing to assist the students as much

> **SURVEY SAYS . . .**
> *Students love Pittsburgh, PA*
> *Very little drug use*
> *Great off-campus food*
> *Student publications are ignored*
> *High cost of living*
> *Political activism is (almost) nonexistent*
> *Student government is unpopular*
> *Dorms are like dungeons*
> *Students get along with local community*

as they can." A sophomore accounting major adds, "All of [my professors] have been willing to help outside of class." Professors keep classes interesting, comments one psychology major. Another student declares, "When I first came to college, I thought everything was going to be up to me. I was very surprised at how much my professors at Duquesne University are willing to help me." The administration fares just as well with Duquesne's students. "This school's administration [is] very thoughtful and caring. They will always be there when you need them," an athletic training major says. The administration is "available at convenient times to help answer any questions we may have," a special education major says. This wouldn't be *The Best 351 Colleges* without at least one student gripe, and for Duquesne students it's that Duquesne is too expensive. Also, while the university "offers great learning and research opportunities, even for undergrads," students believe that the library and research centers need improvement.

Life

Duquesne is located in Pittsburgh, and students take advantage of the city's many cultural diversions. Students enjoy "both the benefits of a small campus and the opportunities of city life." Many of the university's students are commuters, and many residential students often go home on the weekend. Those who remain on campus tell us that campus life is only "satisfactory" because the place is a seeming ghostown from Friday through Sunday. Those who live on campus spend their weeknights studying and going to downtown clubs and enjoying late-night, on-campus movies on the weekends. "Life at school is fun. I feel very safe and comfortable on campus, despite the fact that we are located in the city," one biology major comments. Commuting students rave about the commuter center, where many activities go down. Parties at neighboring universities, such as the University of Pittsburgh and Carnegie Mellon, offer extra-campus amusement. The symphony is another popular distraction, as are the numerous coffee shops on the city's south side. Students say that the food and dorms need improvement ("fix the heating and cooling systems"), and they complain about the dorm policies that are "way too strict about visitors."

Student Body

Duquesne is a Roman Catholic institution, one where students are extremely committed to volunteer work and to helping their fellow students. "You can always find someone willing to lend a helping hand," writes one biology major. Though some students mention that the campus lacks diversity, most agree that "everyone here is friendly and they seem to get along." Students mention that cliques are prevalent on campus. Nevertheless, you'll hear many students say, "I've met the best friends of my life at this campus." Oh yeah, and "everyone smokes except about 5 percent of the students." Commuter students have little interaction with those who live on campus full-time.

ADMISSIONS

Very important factors considered by the admissions committee include: secondary school record. *Important factors considered include:* character/personal qualities, essays, extracurricular activities, recommendations, standardized test scores, talent/ability. *Other factors considered include:* alumni/ae relation, class rank, interview, volunteer work, work experience. SAT I or ACT required. High school diploma or GED is required. *High school units required/recommended:* 16 total recommended; 4 English recommended, 2 math recommended, 2 science recommended, 2 foreign language recommended, 2 social studies recommended.

The Inside Word

With such a high admit rate, the admissions process should create little anxiety in all but the weakest candidates.

FINANCIAL AID

Students should submit: FAFSA, institution's own financial aid form. Regular filing deadline is May 1. The Princeton Review suggests that all financial aid forms be submitted as soon as possible after January 1. *Need-based scholarships/grants offered:* Pell, SEOG, state scholarships/grants, private scholarships, the school's own gift aid. *Loan aid offered:* FFEL Subsidized Stafford, FFEL Unsubsidized Stafford, FFEL PLUS, Federal Perkins, Federal Nursing, college/university loans from institutional funds, health profession loans. Federal Work-Study Program available. Institutional employment available. Applicants will be notified of awards on a rolling basis beginning on or about March 15. Off-campus job opportunities are excellent.

FROM THE ADMISSIONS OFFICE

"Duquesne University was founded in 1878 by the Holy Ghost Fathers. Although it is a private, Roman Catholic institution, Duquesne is proud of its ecumenical reputation. The total University enrollment is 9,595. Duquesne University's attractive and secluded campus is set on a 43-acre hilltop ('the bluff') overlooking the large corporate metropolis of Pittsburgh's Golden Triangle. It offers a wide variety of educational opportunities, from the liberal arts to modern professional training. Duquesne is a medium-size university striving to offer personal attention to its students while having the versatility and opportunities of a true university. A deep sense of tradition is combined with innovation and flexibility to make the Duquesne experience both challenging and rewarding. The Palumbo Convocation/Recreation Complex features a 6,300-seat arena, home court to the University's Division I basketball teams; racquetball and handball courts; weight rooms; and saunas. Extracurricular activities are recognized as an essential part of college life, complementing academics in the process of total student development. Students are involved in nearly 100 university-sponsored activities, and Duquesne's location gives students the opportunity to enjoy sports and cultural events both on campus and citywide. There are five residence halls with the capacity to house 2,777 students."

For even more information on this school, turn to page 230 of the "Stats" section.

EASTERN MENNONITE UNIVERSITY

1200 PARK RD., HARRISONBURG, VA 22802 • ADMISSIONS: 540-432-4118 • FAX: 540-432-4444
E-MAIL: ADMISS@EMU.EDU • WEBSITE: WWW.EMU.EDU

Ratings
Quality of Life: 72   Academic: 73   Admissions: 70   Financial Aid: 74

Academics

With barely over 1,000 undergraduates, Eastern Mennonite
University provides students an
intimate, discussion-oriented education that they appreciate. Many
are aware of the benefits and
drawbacks of an academic experi-

> **SURVEY SAYS . . .**
> *Students are religious, Students are happy*
> *Diversity lacking on campus, Very little drug use*
> *Very little hard liquor, High cost of living*
> *Classes are small*

ence at a tiny institution; writes one: "The plus of a small school is having profs available a lot
of the time. The downside is having the quality of a department or a course hang on one person (and thus change dramatically if that person is not there)." EMU students tell us that their
school is "really strong in sciences, social work, and education." Travel plays an integral part in
students' education; through the school's cross-cultural program, all students have the opportunity to study away from EMU. Nearly three-quarters head outside the United States; writes
one student, "I think the greatest strength of the school is the cross-cultural programs. . . . Many
students have life-changing trips to other countries. . . . We are taught to not be tourists on these
trips but to immerse ourselves in the culture, get to know residents, and get a greater understanding of what their lives are like in comparison to ours." Because half, but not all, students
here are Mennonites, opinions about the proper relation between the church and the school
vary widely. The most orthodox among the students complain whenever a Bible teacher offers
a less-than-traditional reading of the text; the less spiritually inclined counter that because
EMU is an institution "of higher learning, I feel that the administration and the faculty need to
be more open to hearing and accepting different viewpoints and beliefs."

Life

Student life at EMU is somewhat more upright than at your typical American college.
Explains one student, "Alcohol, tobacco, and other drugs are not permitted on campus. When
admitted to EMU each student must sign a lifestyle agreement that says we will not use drugs
or alcohol on campus and that we will abstain from sexual intercourse." Students admit that
"we are not as much 'fun' as the big party schools my friends went to back home. But I think
I'm having more fun here than I ever would at a big school. If you like hanging out with well-
balanced, funny people who choose to engage in more sustainable recreational activities like
cards and climbing the water tower, not because they suck but because they have made a decision to live a wholesome life, then you'll have a blast here at EMU." Students report that
"there is usually something to do each night. Weekends have planned activities (movies, off-
campus activities, sport games, etc.), but there are also things to do that aren't planned (hanging with friends, watching movies, mall, etc.)." A few detractors complain that "truthfully, life
at EMU is very boring. During the week it is okay, because you have classes and work to do,
but on the weekends it's awful." Students appreciate the "beautiful location for a college
campus, with many outdoor activities (camping, caving, rock climbing . . .)" and EMU's
"great fitness center." They note that Washington, D.C., is only two hours away.

Student Body

EMU students think you should know that "this is a Mennonite school, and Mennonites have a culture beyond the religion. You can't really understand it unless you're Mennonite or until you live with a bunch of them for four years. However, there are a lot of non-Mennonites here. Some Catholics, Baptists, agnostics, even a Muslim or a Buddhist or two. And, though there aren't many international students, their presence on campus is definitely felt." While some laud this modicum of diversity, others complain that "not all students here are as Christian as I would like them to be." If Mennonite values don't figure prominently in your life, you might not feel at home within this "generally cool, somewhat conservative, and overall, anti-gay and anti-lesbian climate." Students also warn that because many students "are from four major Mennonite high schools, they already know each other." However, others express that "overall there is a lot of respect for other students."

ADMISSIONS

Very important factors considered by the admissions committee include: secondary school record and standardized test scores. *Important factors considered include:* recommendations and religious affiliation/commitment. *Other factors considered include:* character/personal qualities. SAT I or ACT required. TOEFL required of all international applicants. High school diploma or GED is required. *High school units required/recommended:* 21 total recommended; 4 English recommended, 3 math recommended, 3 science recommended, 3 science lab recommended, 2 foreign language recommended, 3 social studies recommended, 6 elective recommended.

The Inside Word

Admissions officers at EMU have a very good idea of who will and who won't fit comfortably into this devoutly religious community. Call or e-mail an admissions counselor if you have any questions about whether EMU is the right choice for you.

FINANCIAL AID

Students should submit: FAFSA and state aid form. The Princeton Review suggests that all financial aid forms be submitted as soon as possible after January 1. *Need-based scholarships/grants offered:* Pell, SEOG, state scholarships/grants, private scholarships, and the school's own gift aid. *Loan aid offered:* FFEL Subsidized Stafford, FFEL Unsubsidized Stafford, FFEL PLUS, Federal Perkins, Federal Nursing, and state loans. Federal Work-Study Program available. Institutional employment available. Applicants will be notified of awards on a rolling basis beginning on or about March 1. Off-campus job opportunities are excellent.

FROM THE ADMISSIONS OFFICE

"How will you be challenged at Eastern Mennonite University? By thought-provoking discussions . . . by classmates whose perspectives differ from your own . . . by faculty experts who know your potential and push you to achieve it. At EMU, you'll experience a change of scenery that can take you from our beautiful Virginia campus to any part of the world. Cross-cultural semesters and experiences immerse you in a way of life that differs from your own—whether you're in Central America, Northern Ireland, the Middle East, or urban Washington, D.C. And EMU prepares you for a life rich with choices. You'll find an EMU graduate (Dr. Joseph Martin) as dean of Harvard Medical School. Nine out of 10 graduates work in their fields within six month of graduation. Academic programs are top-notch. Our business program is in the top 10 percent of the nation's leading 300 business schools, and our teacher education, nursing, and social work programs carry special national accreditation. EMU will challenge you to grow spiritually, to own your faith, to serve and get involved in things you love. And you don't need to be a Mennonite to fit in. 'I've enjoyed the mix of students at EMU. I've been able to make more informed decisions about what I believe and why I believe it. It's my faith now,' says student Holly Miller. Create an exciting new future for yourself at EMU. A challenge. A change. A choice."

For even more information on this school, turn to page 231 of the "Stats" section.

ELIZABETHTOWN COLLEGE

LEFFLER HOUSE, ONE ALPHA DRIVE, ELIZABETHTOWN, PA 17022 • ADMISSIONS: 717-361-1400
FAX: 717-361-1365 • E-MAIL: ADMISSIONS@ETOWN.EDU • WEBSITE: WWW.ETOWN.EDU

Ratings
Quality of Life: 73   Academic: 79   Admissions: 75   Financial Aid: 77

Academics

Five-hundred-and-eighty is a number that the administrators at Elizabethtown College mention with pride. That's the average number of courses from which Etown students have to choose. Undergrads here also have the

> **SURVEY SAYS . . .**
> *Students are happy, Dorms are like dungeons*
> *Lousy food on campus, Very little drug use*
> *Students get along with local community*
> *Library needs improving, Classes are small*

chance to take their academic careers in any of 41 major directions. The classroom work is supplemented by "research and internship opportunities," that figure "very prominently into the college curriculum." Core requirements are hard to miss as well. Aside from completing a freshman seminar and a junior/senior colloquium, each student must take courses in nine "areas of understanding," as the college dubs them, ranging from foreign languages to physical health. While it seems that this string of requirements could be daunting, students tell us that the college's small size and attentive advisors allow students to "feel challenged, yet comfortable with this challenge." Inside the classrooms, small numbers give the undergrads every opportunity to ask questions when the challenge seems overwhelming. "My largest class may have been around 30 people," guesses one student. If a problem can't be addressed in the classroom, "both administration and professors have office hours," and they are even "willing to meet with students outside their office at a scheduled time." By setting this helping-hand example, the faculty and administration at Etown are upholding the school's motto, "Educate for Service."

Life

"We're out in the middle of nowhere, right smack in the middle of cow pastures." Well, that leaves plenty of open space for Frisbee. And if there's a car available, students can quickly leave "the middle of nowhere" and land in some place like Hershey, America's chocolate capital (not to mention home to a large amusement park, popular outlet stores, and well-known restaurants). Harrisburg is also just up the road, and Philadelphia, Baltimore, and Washington, D.C., are all under two hours away. Most undergrads live on campus, and they've discovered that "there is always something to do or get involved in." One student estimates that "over 80 percent of our students are involved in a club." This 1,900-strong student body has more than 80 clubs to choose from, as well as a string of intramural teams and 9 men's and 10 women's intercollegiate athletic programs. The school itself occasionally sponsors weekend events, "such as dances and concerts." Though "this is definitely not a party school," Fridays and Saturdays give interested students ample opportunity to imbibe at parties. Weekend nights find students donning their best duds and venturing into nearby cities such as "Lancaster, Harrisburg, or York" to hit the clubs. There's another place that students often visit on the weekends: home. Because many students hail from the area, they'll clear out for the weekend when Etown starts to wear on them.

Student Body

"There is a certain type of person that goes to Etown." And what kind of person is that? According to students, the "very friendly" kind. One student recalls, "When I first stepped on this campus for a tour during my junior year in high school, I was amazed at the friendliness of the students. Complete strangers would walk by our tour group and say 'hi'. This hasn't changed since I, myself, have become a student here. People say 'hi' to each other all the time, even if they don't know one another." Despite the "positive vibe" emitted by students here, there's also a homogenous vibe. About two-thirds of Etown's undergrads hail from Pennsylvania, with most others coming from states in the surrounding region. While one junior assures us that "everyone at the school is very friendly and open to different races and varieties of people," another student warns, "If you're someone who lives in a more culturally diverse area, you may find it difficult to adjust to the vanilla flavor of the school."

ADMISSIONS

Very important factors considered by the admissions committee include: secondary school record. *Important factors considered include:* class rank, interview, minority status, recommendations, standardized test scores, and volunteer work. *Other factors considered include:* alumni/ae relation, character/personal qualities, essays, extracurricular activities, geographical residence, religious affiliation/commitment, state residency, talent/ability, and work experience. SAT I or ACT required. TOEFL required of all international applicants. High school diploma or GED is required. *High school units required/recommended:* 15 total required; 20 total recommended; 4 English required, 3 math required, 4 math recommended, 2 science required, 4 science recommended, 2 science lab required, 2 foreign language recommended, 2 social studies required, 2 social studies recommended, 2 history required, 2 elective recommended.

The Inside Word

The admissions office at Elizabethtown strongly encourages you to tell "what experiences are uniquely yours and how [they] will distinguish you from other applicants." The popular occupational therapy and allied health programs fill quickly, so if you are interested in these options, apply early.

FINANCIAL AID

Students should submit: FAFSA, institution's own financial aid form, and federal tax records. The Princeton Review suggests that all financial aid forms be submitted as soon as possible after January 1. *Need-based scholarships/grants offered:* Pell, SEOG, state scholarships/grants, private scholarships, and the school's own gift aid. *Loan aid offered:* FFEL Subsidized Stafford, FFEL Unsubsidized Stafford, FFEL PLUS, Federal Perkins, and state loans. Federal Work-Study Program available. Institutional employment available. Applicants will be notified of awards on a rolling basis beginning on or about February 15. Off-campus job opportunities are good.

FROM THE ADMISSIONS OFFICE

"The most important aspect of the admissions program is to admit graduates of Elizabethtown College. The entire focus of the admissions process is determining if a student is a good fit for E-town and if E-town is a good fit for the student. We pride ourselves on our 'conversational interviews' as a way to set a student at ease so that we can discover their potential to contribute to our community. Applicants are assessed in three areas: academic fit, co-curricular fit, and social fit. Integrity, diversity, academic excellence, and a commitment to services are qualities that are highly valued.

"E-town distinguishes itself from its peers through its commitment to personal attention, experiential learning, and diverse curriculum and a historic commitment to human service. The college is also one of the few small, regional colleges to have recently graduated a Rhodes Scholar. The campus visit will set E-town apart from other places as you experience the beautiful campus and surrounding area. Campus visitors are welcomed year-around.

"E-town is likely one of the finest colleges that you don't know enough about."

For even more information on this school, turn to page 232 of the "Stats" section.

FRANKLIN & MARSHALL COLLEGE

PO Box 3003, Lancaster, PA 17604-3003 • Admissions: 717-291-3953 • Fax: 717-291-4381
Financial Aid: 717-291-3991 • E-mail: ADMISSION@FANDM.EDU • Website: WWW.FANDM.EDU

Ratings
Quality of Life: 80   **Academic:** 92   **Admissions:** 89   **Financial Aid:** 81

Academics

Academics at Franklin & Marshall are "very challenging no matter what your major. We don't get a good enough reputation for the amount of work we do. Expect to work long, hard hours for a B." Reason for disappointment? No, because "in the end, you end up getting a better education for it." Students appreciate professors who "are great, for the most part, and really like interaction with students in and out of class."

> **SURVEY SAYS . . .**
> *Popular college radio*
> *Frats and sororities dominate social scene*
> *Campus easy to get around*
> *Profs teach upper-levels*
> *Classes are small*
> *Students are cliquish*
> *Students don't like Lancaster, PA*
> *Lousy food on campus*
> *Very little drug use*
> *Student publications are ignored*

Explains one student, "The professors are always around to help with anything. I'm on a first-name basis with the professors in my major department, and I only just finished my first year. I hear most departments are like that." Similarly, the administration "is surely unique. The president and vice president of the college even co-teach a course. The president holds luncheons at which any student may eat and discuss issues. I was even invited to a dean's house for dinner on one occasion." So it's not too hard to see why so many students put up with the demands at Franklin & Marshall; most of them feel like they've got a good support group behind them. And with F&M's solid reputation, many students feel as if they are bound to succeed after graduation. As one student points out, "Not a liberal arts college, really, but a pre-professional school."

Life

Students caution prospects that F&M "is an extremely hard school." Many find the academic pressure stressful, which may help explain why "alcohol is a big part of campus life, whether it's beer in frat parties, or hard liquor in apartment parties, or just sitting in your room, watching TV and swigging Smirnoff." The Greeks "are the main social activity on weekends." Some feel that "there is nothing to do besides fraternity parties, which are very snobbish." Others disagree, reporting that "fraternities do dominate the social scene on Friday and Saturday nights. However, there has been an increase in late night activities, such as off-campus trips, comedians, and other forms of entertainment. The College Entertainment Committee is wonderful for setting up events both on and off campus. There are weekly movies that cost $1 for students, which are great. There have been trips to Philadelphia, Washington D.C., and New York City." Students particularly enjoy the Spring Arts Festival, "the craziest time of the year. It's a week of celebrating like you wouldn't believe. The administration sets up a beer tent for those who are 21, and the main street in town is closed so we can party in it. We bring in bands and chill with everyone."

Student Body

F&M students derive largely "from the same background: Mid-Atlantic state, white, suburban, and upper middle-class. It gets boring." Complains one city dweller, "I've only met two other people that actually live in a city. There are four black students in the class of 2005, and yet we're the 'most diverse class ever.' " "It's pretty much agreed among students that they "are rather conservative and conformist. Most people will be sporting new clothes from J.Crew or Abercrombie and Fitch." Some point out that "while we do have our stereotypical frat boys and sorority girls, there are certainly places where those for whom that is not the crowd can fit in. I have made friends [of students who hail] from France, Scotland, and England" and of students from "various economic and religious backgrounds, sexual orientations, and in academic years."

ADMISSIONS

Very important factors considered by the admissions committee include: character/personal qualities, class rank, secondary school record. *Important factors considered include:* essays, extracurricular activities, interview, minority status, recommendations, standardized test scores, talent/ability, volunteer work. *Other factors considered include:* alumni/ae relation, geographical residence, work experience. TOEFL required of all international applicants. High school diploma or GED is required. *High school units required/recommended:* 4 English required, 3 math required, 4 math recommended, 2 science required, 3 science recommended, 2 science lab required, 3 science lab recommended, 2 foreign language required, 4 foreign language recommended, 1 social studies required, 3 social studies recommended, 2 history required, 3 history recommended.

The Inside Word

Applicants who are serious about attending the college should definitely interview; it will also help to make it known that F & M is one of your top choices. The college loses a lot of its admits to competitor colleges and will take notice of a candidate who is likely to enroll.

FINANCIAL AID

Students should submit: FAFSA, CSS/Financial Aid PROFILE, state aid form, noncustodial (divorced/separated) parent's statement, business/farm supplement, previous year's federal taxes and W-2s. Regular filing deadline is February 1. The Princeton Review suggests that all financial aid forms be submitted as soon as possible after January 1. *Need-based scholarships/grants offered:* Pell, SEOG, state scholarships/grants, private scholarships, the school's own gift aid. *Loan aid offered:* FFEL Subsidized Stafford, FFEL Unsubsidized Stafford, FFEL PLUS, Federal Perkins, college/university loans from institutional funds. Federal Work-Study Program available. Institutional employment available. Applicants will be notified of awards on or about April 1. Off-campus job opportunities are excellent.

FROM THE ADMISSIONS OFFICE

"Franklin & Marshall students choose from a variety of fields of study, traditional and interdisciplinary, that typify liberal learning. Professors in all of these fields are committed to a common purpose, which is to teach students to think, speak, and write with clarity and confidence. Whether the course is in theater or in physics, the class will be small, engagement will be high, and discussion will dominate over lecture. Thus throughout his or her four years, beginning with the First Year Seminar, a student at Franklin & Marshall is repeatedly invited to active participation in intellectual play at a high level. Our graduates consistently testify to the high quality of an F&M education as a mental preparation for life."

For even more information on this school, turn to page 232 of the "Stats" section.

GANNON UNIVERSITY

University Square, Erie, PA 16541 • Admissions: 814-871-7240 • Fax: 814-871-5803
E-mail: admissions@gannon.edu • Website: www.gannon.edu

Ratings

Quality of Life: 74   **Academic: 79**   **Admissions: 70**   **Financial Aid: 73**

Academics

Students choose Gannon Uni-versity, a Roman Catholic school in northwestern Pennsylvania, for the stellar regional reputation its academic departments enjoy. As one undergrad told us, "The greatest strengths at my school are the academic programs. We excel in engineering, physical therapy, biol-

> **SURVEY SAYS . . .**
> *Classes are small*
> *No one plays intramural sports*
> *School is well run, Very little beer drinking*
> *Student publications are popular*
> *Very little hard liquor, Students are religious*
> *Students get along with local community*

ogy, and many other programs. Also, the school is well located for graduates seeking employment. We're only two to three hours from Cleveland, Buffalo, and Pittsburgh, and employers there know Gannon." At the root of Gannon's academic success is its faculty, which students praise highly. Writes one student, "I've had some really wonderful professors here. That is one thing that Gannon does well—it promotes the teacher-student relationship with small classes and a lot of interaction." Adds another, "The professors are more than willing to help a student out as long as the student puts the time and effort into the work required for the course." Administrators ease students' transition from high school to college life by being "very friendly and always willing to listen to your personal problems as well as academic problems. They are willing to do things to get problems resolved the best they can." Students warn that annoying administrative problems can occur, however, "due to poor communication between departments." Gannon currently offers mini-term study abroad options in Spain, France, Germany, and the Bahamas, as well as longer study opportunities in Ireland.

Life

Erie, Pennsylvania, hometown of Gannon University, is no bustling metropolis, students agree. "Erie is not the most exciting place to live," writes one student. For most, the party scene at local frats and off-campus apartments is the place to be. "Gannon tries to say that it is a dry campus," explains one undergrad, "but all the students know better than that. There are major parties every week; all you have to do is look for them." Adds another student, "Bars are huge in Erie. There's at least one on ever block, or so it seems. Students know which ones accept fakes and who can get in. Gannon is very alcohol-focused." Many here concede this point but add that "if you don't drink, there are lots of options, too. Our activities programming board does a pretty good job keeping activities like movies and special speakers and stuff going on all the time." Problem is, many of these events simply don't appeal to the majority of Gannon undergrads. "It is very hard to get students to actually come and participate in club activities," writes one frustrated student involved in extracurricular planning. Writes one who is not, "They don't offer much to do on weekend to prevent parties. There is little to do for fun." If it's any consolation, the situation has improved; notes one senior, "The only area that Gannon could improve is the weekend activity on campus. They should have more opportunities available for students. They have been working very hard to improve this, and in the three years that I have been here I have noticed an increase in these activities." Students warn that "the campus is in the middle of the city . . . and looks terrible."

Student Body

Gannon's overwhelmingly white, Catholic student body hails primarily from western Pennsylvania. The vibe among the students, many feel, closely approximates that of a prep school. Explains one student, "Gannon tends to attract a lot of snooty people for some reason, but everyone seems to tolerate each other pretty well. Student life around here involves a lot of cliques, and if you don't find yours, you can be left in the dust." Agrees another, "Students are somewhat arrogant. They are also very uninvolved, it is hard to get anybody to show up at campus events at this school. I think that school spirit is low here." On a positive note, many Gannon students are active in community service and social awareness programs.

ADMISSIONS

Very important factors considered by the admissions committee include: class rank, secondary school record, and standardized test scores. *Important factors considered include:* character/personal qualities, essays, interview, and recommendations. *Other factors considered include:* alumni/ae relation, extracurricular activities, volunteer work, and work experience. SAT I or ACT required. TOEFL required of all international applicants. High school diploma is required and GED is accepted. *High school units required/recommended:* 16 total are required; 4 English required, 4 math required, 2 science required.

The Inside Word

Admissions here focus heavily on curriculum, GPA, and standardized test scores. The school does not require recommendations, an essay, or a list of extracurricular activities, although you are welcome to provide them. Applications for the physician assistant and LECOM primary care programs are due by January 15; all others are processed on a rolling basis.

FINANCIAL AID

Students should submit: FAFSA and institution's own financial aid form. Regular filing deadline is May 1. The Princeton Review suggests that all financial aid forms be submitted as soon as possible after January 1. *Need-based scholarships/grants offered:* Pell, SEOG, state scholarships/grants, private scholarships, and the school's own gift aid. *Loan aid offered:* Direct Subsidized Stafford, Direct Unsubsidized Stafford, Direct PLUS, FFEL Subsidized Stafford, FFEL Unsubsidized Stafford, FFEL PLUS, Federal Perkins, Federal Nursing, and deferred payment. Federal Work-Study Program available. Institution employment available. Applicants will be notified of awards on a rolling basis beginning on or about October 30. Off-campus job opportunities are excellent.

FROM THE ADMISSIONS OFFICE

"Gannon University is a private, Catholic, Master's Comprehensive I university affiliated with the Roman Catholic Diocese of Erie, Pennsylvania. Gannon offers more than 70 associate's, bachelor's, and master's degrees as well as a doctoral program in counseling psychology. Founded in 1925, Gannon University has grown to become northwestern Pennsylvania's premier Catholic university, dedicated to a tradition of values-centered education. Cited as one of the top 15 'Great Schools at Great Prices' by *U.S. News & News Report*, Gannon enrolls approximately 3,400 students and maintains a low 13:1 student/faculty ratio, providing students with accessible faculty, a high level of individual attention, and greater opportunities for academic, personal, and professional growth. Gannon's campus is located in the heart of downtown Erie, giving students the benefit of internships and co-ops with businesses, healthcare facilities, industries, and social service organizations. Gannon is centrally located approximately 100 miles from Pittsburgh, Buffalo, and Cleveland. Students at Gannon explore internships, co-ops, and study abroad opportunities while developing a values-centered, liberal arts foundation. Students also have the opportunity to participate in 18 Division II athletic teams and become involved in more than 70 clubs and organizations."

For even more information on this school, turn to page 233 of the "Stats" section.

GEORGE MASON UNIVERSITY

UNDERGRADUATE ADMISSIONS OFFICE, 4400 UNIV. DRIVE MSN 3A4, FAIRFAX, VA 22030-4444
ADMISSIONS: 703-993-2400 • FAX: 703-993-2392 • FINANCIAL AID: 703-993-2353
E-MAIL: ADMISSIONS@GMU.EDU • WEBSITE: WWW.GMU.EDU

Ratings

Quality of Life: 74   Academic: 79   Admissions: 85   Financial Aid: 77

Academics

Despite its regular inclusion in this guide, "GMU has a reputation of almost being a joke university because it's mostly a commuter school. GMU deserves a lot more credit than it is given, and many people should not look at it as a 'back-up' school." We agree. At state university prices, GMU is a great bargain for Virginia residents, providing "an easygoing

> **SURVEY SAYS . . .**
> *Students love Fairfax, VA*
> *(Almost) everyone smokes*
> *Popular college radio*
> *Ethnic diversity on campus*
> *Large classes*
> *Athletic facilities need improving*
> *Campus difficult to get around*
> *Musical organizations aren't popular*

and helpful atmosphere and a spirit of innovation." Like many large schools, "Mason offers the best and the worst to its students. We have greatly talented administrators and professors who generally care about the students and are great educators. [Yet] there are also administrators and professors that should be teaching preschool." The most highly praised academic offerings include those of the School of Management ("getting in takes a lot of hard work") and the government studies department, which benefit from the proximity of Washington, D.C.; writes one student, "It's very cool to have a professor tell you about an encounter that he had with the secretary of defense or to hear another tell you that he will be on NPR later that evening discussing the Middle East peace process." Best of all is the Honors Program, which offers smaller classes and a strong emphasis on writing skills.

Life

Because so many of GMU's students commute, many here feel that "life at school ends at Thursday after class. Over the weekend this place is like a ghost town; even people who live on campus leave. Typical on-campus life is attending class, hanging out at Johnson [the student center], or playing pool at the game room. Anything else is done off campus." Off campus often means Washington, D.C., accessible by the D.C. Metro, which is itself accessible from campus via a school shuttle bus. "Being only about 45 minutes from Washington, D.C., there's plenty to do in regards to social activities if one is motivated enough. You can go to a club, get a really good dinner, see some great museums, and check out the government buildings." There is less to do in hometown Fairfax, "the richest county in the U.S. The average rent is WAY over $1,000 per month. It's ridiculous." The lack of off-campus housing has led to a severe shortage of dorm space. One student warns, "There is such a housing problem that all the two-, three- and four-person rooms are now three-, four-, and five- people . . . . Don't be the last man in on move-in day because then you are fighting with three people for the two available desks." On a positive note, "drama club performances are really popular," as are GMU men's basketball games. Students also report that "the school itself is extremely aesthetically pleasing."

Student Body

GMU is "a very diverse school, right near the heart of the nation's capital. There are students from all over the world, which really adds to the atmosphere." Some students write that "different groups do not usually interact"; more often, however, people complain that the lack of interaction is mostly caused by the fact that there are "lots of commuters" here, making students feel isolated from one another. Writes one student, "Unfortunately, the school is not very social at all. To get involved you pretty much need to go Greek. If you aren't in a fraternity or sorority you don't have the opportunity to meet many people outside of your classes." Academically, students feel there is an "excellent mix" here. "We have some of the most serious academic scholars and others who are more geared toward learning what they need to know to succeed in the real world, such as business or technology skills," writes one student.

ADMISSIONS

Very important factors considered by the admissions committee include: secondary school record. *Important factors considered include:* character/personal qualities, essays, recommendations, standardized test scores, talent/ability. *Other factors considered include:* alumni/ae relation, class rank, extracurricular activities, geographical residence, interview, minority status, state residency, volunteer work, work experience. SAT I or ACT required; SAT II recommended. TOEFL required of all international applicants. High school diploma or GED is required. *High school units required/recommended:* 18 total required; 24 total recommended; 4 English required, 3 math required, 4 math recommended, 3 science required, 4 science recommended, 3 science lab required, 4 science lab recommended, 2 foreign language required, 3 foreign language recommended, 3 social studies required, 4 social studies recommended, 3 elective required, 5 elective recommended.

The Inside Word

George Mason is a popular destination for college for two key reasons: its proximity to Washington, D.C., and the fact that it is not nearly as difficult to gain admission at Mason as it is at UVA or William and Mary, the two flagships of the Virginia state system. The university's quality faculty and impressive facilities make it worth taking a look if low-cost, solid programs in the D.C. area are high on your list.

FINANCIAL AID

Students should submit: FAFSA. The Princeton Review suggests that all financial aid forms be submitted as soon as possible after January 1. *Need-based scholarships/grants offered:* Pell, SEOG, state scholarships/grants, private scholarships, the school's own gift aid. *Loan aid offered:* Direct Subsidized Stafford, Direct Unsubsidized Stafford, Direct PLUS, Federal Perkins. Federal Work-Study Program available. Institutional employment available. Applicants will be notified of awards on a rolling basis beginning on or about April 1. Off-campus job opportunities are excellent.

FROM THE ADMISSIONS OFFICE

"Great minds don't think alike, and at George Mason University, we don't expect them to. From creative writing to systems engineering, Mason programs offer cutting-edge curricula and facilities along with the best that technology has to offer. Our visionary outlook has attracted a faculty of renowned scholars and teachers, while our business and community partnerships provide students with practical experience and career opportunities."

For even more information on this school, turn to page 234 of the "Stats" section.

GEORGE WASHINGTON UNIVERSITY

2121 I STREET NW, SUITE 201, WASHINGTON, DC 20052 • ADMISSIONS: 202-994-6040
FAX: 202-994-0325 • FINANCIAL AID: 202-994-6620 • E-MAIL: GWADM@GWIS2.CIRC.GWU.EDU
WEBSITE: WWW.GWU.EDU

Ratings

Quality of Life: 88   Academic: 88   Admissions: 91   Financial Aid: 84

Academics

Few schools exploit their location as fully as George Washington University, a school whose faculty and programs are deeply entrenched in the goings-on of Washington, D.C. "Being in D.C., GW takes advantage of the resources and personnel found here," notes one approving student. "Much of the faculty are experts in political science and criminal justice." Writes another, "It's all about location. Whatever teachers can't give you in the class-

> **SURVEY SAYS . . .**
> *Students love Washington, D.C.*
> *Political activism is hot*
> *Dorms are like palaces*
> *Students don't get along with local community*
> *High cost of living*
> *Unattractive campus*
> *Ethnic diversity on campus*
> *Lots of long lines and red tape*
> *Athletic facilities need improving*
> *No one plays intramural sports*

room, they send you out to get." A few caution that "GW's profs are part of D.C., not GW. That has benefits and drawbacks," but most agree that the pluses outweigh the minuses. Nearly one-quarter of the students here are engaged in international studies, and many others pursue such government-related majors as political science, political communication, and criminal justice. Other strong programs include biology, psychology, and English. Professors here "are what make or break the course. Some are excellent and some are horrible." Lecture courses, especially those at the intro level, "can be rather large," and some suggest that "there is never a need to attend large lecture classes. By attending only the discussion sections you gain all the information necessary for the course plus a couple of extra hours sleep." However, things improve with upper-level courses. GW's administration earns low marks, with students complaining that "there's a lot of administrative bureaucratic red tape to get through for certain things" and that "the administration tends not to listen to students until they raise a big public ruckus. Making appointments to meet with upper-level administrators can be very difficult." Students give props to the Honors Program and excellent marks to the library.

Life

GW, like New York University and Boston University, lacks a traditional campus, instead occupying buildings scattered throughout an urban neighborhood. As at other such schools, the sense of community here is weak and the social scene is fragmented. Fortunately, D.C. picks up the slack, offering students some of the nation's finest museums and monuments, beautiful public spaces, limitless shopping, a thriving nightlife, and a boatload of internship and networking opportunities. "D.C. rocks!" writes one student. "There is so much to do here, you literally could do something different every night of the week. A lot of bars and clubs turn into GW parties, which is cool." Also, "we do a lot of shopping because Georgetown is so close," explains another. On-campus activity centers on "over 300 student organizations on campus, so whatever your lifestyle is, there should be a group for you." Students complain that, due to an increase in admissions, classrooms and dining halls are growing uncomfortably overcrowded. Greek life is slight but students feel it "could be an important and positive part of this school except for the administration's vendetta against it."

Student Body

Students come to GW to be in the nation's capital, and accordingly "it's not a school for someone who isn't into politics. Everyone here is glued to CNN." On the political spectrum, "it's a very Democratic and liberal school," writes one student. "If you want to protest, this school's for you!" Students also tend to be reformed slackers. Explains one, "This school is for everyone who could have been accepted to an Ivy League school and could have afforded it, but never applied themselves to that extent." A huge international contingent contributes to "the diversity—ethnically, politically, geographically, and intellectually—that breeds so many wonderful relationships."

ADMISSIONS

Very important factors considered by the admissions committee include: secondary school record. *Important factors considered include:* class rank, essays, extracurricular activities, interview, recommendations, standardized test scores, talent/ability, volunteer work. *Other factors considered include:* alumni/ae relation, character/personal qualities, geographical residence, minority status, work experience. SAT I or ACT required; SAT I preferred. TOEFL required of all international applicants. High school diploma is required and GED is not accepted. *High school units required/recommended:* 4 English required, 2 math required, 4 math recommended, 2 science required, 4 science recommended, 1 science lab required, 2 foreign language required, 4 foreign language recommended, 2 social studies required, 4 social studies recommended.

The Inside Word

The low percentage of admitted students who enroll at GW works to keep the admit rate relatively high. For strong students, this is definitely a low-stress admissions process. The university's location and access to faculty with impressive credentials are the main reasons for GW's sound freshman profile.

FINANCIAL AID

Students should submit: FAFSA, CSS/Financial Aid PROFILE. The Princeton Review suggests that all financial aid forms be submitted as soon as possible after January 1. *Need-based scholarships/grants offered:* Pell, SEOG, state scholarships/grants, the school's own gift aid. *Loan aid offered:* FFEL Subsidized Stafford, FFEL Unsubsidized Stafford, FFEL PLUS, Federal Perkins. Federal Work-Study Program available. Institutional employment available. Applicants will be notified of awards on or about March 20. Off-campus job opportunities are excellent.

FROM THE ADMISSIONS OFFICE

"At GW, we welcome students who show a measure of impatience with the limitations of traditional education. At many universities, the edge of campus is the real world, but not at GW, where our campus and Washington, D.C., are seamless. We look for bold, bright students who are ambitious, energetic, and self-motivated. Here, where we are so close to the centers of thought and action in every field we offer, we easily integrate our outstanding academic tradition and faculty connections with the best internship and job opportunities of Washington, D.C. A generous scholarship and financial assistance program attracts top students from all parts of the country and the world."

For even more information on this school, turn to page 234 of the "Stats" section.

GEORGETOWN UNIVERSITY

37TH AND P STREETS, NW, WASHINGTON, DC 20057 • ADMISSIONS: 202-687-3600 • FAX: 202-687-5084
FINANCIAL AID: 202-687-4547 • WEBSITE: WWW.GEORGETOWN.EDU

Ratings
Quality of Life: 89   **Academic:** 96   **Admissions:** 99   **Financial Aid:** 84

Academics

Because of its location in the nation's capital, Georgetown University is uniquely positioned to offer advanced studies in government and foreign relations. The undergraduate student body is divided into four distinct schools: Arts and Sciences, Business Administration, Foreign Service, and Nursing and Health Studies.

SURVEY SAYS . . .
Students love Washington, DC
Everyone loves the Hoyas
Lots of classroom discussion
No one cheats, Campus feels safe
Classes are small, Political activism is hot
No one plays intramural sports
Very little beer drinking, Students are cliquish

Writes one student, "The schools are definitely divided: students in each have their own stereotype. E.g., 'Oh, you're in the SFS, you must be really smart,' or 'You're in the business school, so you're a slacker.' " In all schools, students report that "classes at Georgetown are qualitatively challenging, but the workload is very manageable" and that "professors pride themselves on making time for students outside of the classroom." The school is not without its administrative difficulties, though. Some undergrads complain that "you are a number at Georgetown" and that "the quality of academic assistance is not the best. As a School of Foreign Service student I don't even have an academic advisor until my junior year"—but most agree that the benefits of a Georgetown education make up for the drawbacks many times over. Students are particularly sanguine about the university's adjunct faculty, "highly respected professionals, often working in government (or in conjunction with the government) in Washington. Calling on their 'real life' experience, they make excellent teachers."

Life

Washington D.C., and the many career and social opportunities it presents, is one of the primary reasons students choose Georgetown. Few leave the city disappointed. "There is no better city than D.C. for internships and off-campus activities," explains one student. Points out another, "Because you are in Washington, there are countless other options if you don't feel like going to parties or don't drink (movies, theater, sports, sightseeing, every kind of restaurant imaginable . . .)." Because of the school's close connections with the government, undergrads "rub shoulders with senators and politicians. The White House is down the road, Madeline Albright lives a stone's throw away [she's also a professor], the Clintons just bought a house, there's constantly celebrities down here for filming. Students sometimes go down to the Capitol to be extras in *The West Wing*." On campus, students praise the absence of a Greek system and love the fact that "all clubs are student-run at GU, as are most other endeavors." They also love their men's basketball team, noting that "when there is a basketball game . . . we all stand together and celebrate." Their chief complaint concerns the university's neighbors, who have pressured the school to clamp down on rowdy off-campus activities. Offers one undergrad, "The silliest thing this year is that this man and his wife moved [into a house] a block away from the school years ago and now they are suing for TOO MUCH NOISE! Did they ever GO to college? I mean, what are they thinking?"

Student Body

Is there a 'typical' Georgetown undergrad? It depends who you ask. Writes one student, "I always hate the stereotype that Georgetown is a bunch of Roman Catholic prep students from Connecticut who work all day. That's BS. One of my best friends is a non-practicing Jew and an atheist, and another friend is Polish and Catholic, and another friend is British and Muslim. We all get along like a house on fire." Cautions another, "I am not Catholic and do, at times, feel overrun by all the Catholics. This has improved greatly since first semester though, as I am getting to know more people." All agree that Georgetown undergrads are "smart, driven, social, and vivacious. We are all from different parts of the country and the world, but we all have in common those characteristics." One student notes that "nowhere else have I heard so many different languages and met individuals from such diverse backgrounds."

ADMISSIONS

Very important factors considered by the admissions committee include: character/personal qualities, class rank, essays, recommendations, secondary school record, standardized test scores, talent/ability. *Important factors considered include:* extracurricular activities, interview, volunteer work. *Other factors considered include:* alumni/ae relation, geographical residence, minority status, state residency, work experience. SAT I or ACT required; SAT II recommended. TOEFL required of all international applicants. High school diploma or GED is required. *High school units required/recommended:* 4 English required, 2 math required, 4 math recommended, 2 science required, 4 science recommended, 1 science lab recommended, 2 foreign language required, 4 foreign language recommended, 2 social studies required, 4 social studies recommended.

The Inside Word

It was always tough to get admitted to Georgetown, but in the early 1980s Patrick Ewing and the Hoyas created a basketball sensation that catapulted the place into position as one of the most selective universities in the nation. There has been no turning back since. GU gets almost 10 applications for every space in the entering class, and the academic strength of the pool is impressive. Virtually 50 percent of the entire student body took AP courses in high school. Candidates who are wait-listed here should hold little hope for an offer of admission; over the past several years Georgetown has taken very few off their lists.

FINANCIAL AID

Students should submit: FAFSA, CSS/Financial Aid PROFILE, state aid form, noncustodial (divorced/separated) parent's statement, business/farm supplement. The Princeton Review suggests that all financial aid forms be submitted as soon as possible after January 1. *Need-based scholarships/grants offered:* Pell, SEOG, state scholarships/grants, private scholarships, the school's own gift aid, ROTC. *Loan aid offered:* FFEL Subsidized Stafford, FFEL Unsubsidized Stafford, FFEL PLUS, Federal Perkins, Federal Nursing. Federal Work-Study Program available. Institutional employment available. Applicants will be notified of awards on or about April 1. Off-campus job opportunities are excellent.

FROM THE ADMISSIONS OFFICE

"Georgetown was founded in 1789 by John Carroll, who concurred with his contemporaries Benjamin Franklin and Thomas Jefferson in believing that the success of the young democracy depended upon an educated and virtuous citizenry. Carroll founded the school with the dynamic, Jesuit tradition of education, characterized by humanism and committed to the assumption of responsibility and action. Georgetown is a national and international university, enrolling students from all 50 states and over 100 foreign countries. Undergraduate students are enrolled in one of four undergraduate schools: the College of Arts and Sciences, School of Foreign Service, Georgetown School of Business, and Georgetown School of Nursing and Health Studies. All students share a common liberal arts core and have access to the entire university curriculum."

For even more information on this school, turn to page 235 of the "Stats" section.

GETTYSBURG COLLEGE

ADMISSIONS OFFICE, EISENHOWER HOUSE, GETTYSBURG, PA 17325-1484
ADMISSIONS: 717-337-6100 • FAX: 717-337-6145 • FINANCIAL AID: 717-337-6611
E-MAIL: ADMISS@GETTYSBURG.EDU • WEBSITE: WWW.GETTYSBURG.EDU

Ratings

Quality of Life: 84   **Academic:** 90   **Admissions:** 87   **Financial Aid:** 87

Academics

At Gettysburg, "academics are challenging and stimulating without being overbearingly stressful," a situation appreciated by most undergraduates. "The work is difficult," warns one student, "but with concentration, balance, and help from a great faculty, any-

SURVEY SAYS . . .
Great food on campus
Frats and sororities dominate social scene
Diversity lacking on campus, Beautiful campus
Campus easy to get around
Theater is unpopular, Low cost of living

one can succeed." The small campus allows for plenty of personal attention. Writes one respondent, "At Gettysburg, I am pushed to do my best because professors will not let you slip through the cracks. We have to attend classes because they are so small. If you don't show up, you can expect a phone call." Faculty members earn high praise for being "friendly and acting as equals rather than authority figures" and for their helpfulness. They are "always willing to meet with students, [and] they offer help in obtaining internships and expose us to experiences outside the classroom." A "good advising system [that's] very personalized" helps students navigate curricular requirements, including a liberal arts core curriculum (really a set of distribution requirements covering the humanities, natural and social sciences, mathematics, foreign language, writing skills, and nonwestern civilization) geared toward introducing underclassmen to a broad spectrum of academics. Upperclassmen focus on their majors, among which history, political science, and the hard sciences are generally regarded as "top-notch." Students also applaud the computer facilities and the Honor Code, the latter "an undeniable part of campus. You're truly treated like an adult."

Life

Greek life, most undergrads concede, holds center court at Gettysburg College. Warns one student, "The administration wants prospectives to think that Greek life isn't essential, but don't let them fool you. A lot of people end up unhappy when they are left out." Says another, "Gettysburg does offer a lot of activities; it's just that so many of them are geared toward the Greek system. There's something for most people, but a lot of times the good events aren't publicized." Drinking, not surprisingly, is big here. Writes one student, "Beer is life. Even if you don't know what Natty Ice is before you get here, your fridge will be stocked by the second week." There are other options, among them intramural sports, community service, and events organized by the Student Activities Council and the Student Senate, but many still see the 'Burg as a one-horse town. As one student puts it, "Good luck if you aren't in Greek life. The frat doormen look you up and down and decide whether you are 'good enough' to enter their frat. If you are a girl in a skirt you can get in. If you're a guy, bring a girl in a skirt." Students speak highly of the Center for Public Service, which provides opportunities for "tutoring, clean-ups, and service-related trips all over the world." The campus is "beautiful and comfortable," and the food is "among the school's greatest strengths." Students give the "lame" town of Gettysburg a thumb's-down: "It's isolated, and there are no buses to other towns," gripes one. Students list a local diner, Wal-Mart, an outlet mall, and the tour of the famous local battlefield as the best off-campus attractions.

Student Body

Gettysburg undergrads are "very homogeneous, mostly upper- and middle-class white students." However, "although there is diversity lacking," reports one student, "the college has been doing better in recent years to change that." Politically, "many kids are very conservative. You have to search for liberals." The same goes for intellectuals; while kids here are bright, they are not bookish. Points out one frustrated egghead, "The classic term for girls here is 'eye candy,' and it goes for a lot of the guys too. They're fun to look at but don't talk about anything past next Friday night. My solution is to travel a lot and keep in touch with friends from home."

ADMISSIONS

Very important factors considered by the admissions committee include: class rank, recommendations, secondary school record. *Important factors considered include:* character/personal qualities, essays, extracurricular activities, interview, standardized test scores, talent/ability, volunteer work. *Other factors considered include:* alumni/ae relation, geographical residence, minority status, work experience. SAT I or ACT required. TOEFL required of all international applicants. High school diploma or GED is required. *High school units required/recommended:* 4 English required, 3 math required, 4 math recommended, 3 science required, 4 science recommended, 3 science lab required, 4 science lab recommended, 3 foreign language required, 4 foreign language recommended, 3 social studies required, 4 social studies recommended, 3 history required, 4 history recommended.

The Inside Word

Gettysburg's small size definitely allows for a more personal approach to admission. The admissions committee puts a lot of energy into matchmaking, and last year it paid off with its largest freshman class in its history. Most Gettysburg types are good students and also match up well with competitor colleges, which makes this accomplishment even more laudable. Look for a somewhat more selective profile as a result.

FINANCIAL AID

Students should submit: FAFSA, CSS/Financial Aid PROFILE, noncustodial (divorced/separated) parent's statement, business/farm supplement. Regular filing deadline is March 15. The Princeton Review suggests that all financial aid forms be submitted as soon as possible after January 1. *Need-based scholarships/grants offered:* Pell, SEOG, state scholarships/grants, private scholarships, the school's own gift aid. *Loan aid offered:* FFEL Subsidized Stafford, FFEL Unsubsidized Stafford, FFEL PLUS, Federal Perkins, college/university loans from institutional funds. Federal Work-Study Program available. Institutional employment available. Applicants will be notified of awards on or about March 30. Off-campus job opportunities are good.

FROM THE ADMISSIONS OFFICE

"Four major goals of Gettysburg College, to best prepare students to enter the 21st century, include: first, to accelerate the intellectual development of our first-year students by integrating them more quickly into the intellectual life of the campus; second, to use interdisciplinary courses combining the intellectual approaches of various fields; third, to encourage students to develop an international perspective through course work, study abroad, association with international faculty, and a variety of extracurricular activities; and fourth, to encourage students to develop (1) a capacity for independent study by ensuring that all students work closely with individual faculty members on an extensive project during their undergraduate years and (2) the ability to work with their peers by making the small group a central feature in college life."

For even more information on this school, turn to page 236 of the "Stats" section.

GOUCHER COLLEGE

1021 Dulaney Valley Road, Baltimore, MD 21204-2794 • Admissions: 410-337-6100
Fax: 410-337-6354 • Financial Aid: 410-337-6141 • E-mail: admissions@goucher.edu
Website: www.goucher.edu

Ratings
Quality of Life: 80   **Academic:** 81   **Admissions:** 80   **Financial Aid:** 88

Academics

"Many opportunities in a little school" makes the academically challenging Goucher College a popular choice for students looking for personal attention, top-quality professors, and a left-of-center social and political environment. With both a strong science program and a solid emphasis on writing proficiency, Goucher

> **SURVEY SAYS . . .**
> *Theater is hot*
> *Students love Baltimore, MD*
> *Great off-campus food*
> *(Almost) everyone smokes*
> *Student government is popular*
> *Class discussions encouraged*
> *Library needs improving*

manages to offer "creative and exceptional" classes in many disciplines, with professors who "go out of their way" to help students succeed. A first-year provides an example: "When teachers know what mode of transportation you use in coming to class (i.e., scooter), and they draw a 'scooter parking meter' on the board of the classroom, you know you're at a place where people care about your well-being and academic achievement." And though you wouldn't expect it from such a tiny school, it's Goucher's bureaucracy that gets the thumbs-down from students: "The administration process is lengthy and tedious at best," says a sophomore. Perhaps too much attention can be a bad thing? A junior notes that "student input is really used in the selection and hiring of professors. They're willing to do independent studies with you for whatever topic you want. Lots of paperwork, red tape, hoops to jump through, though." Still, with a "good reputation, great location, and generous scholarships" (the average frosh grant is about $13,500), a little paper pushing might not be such a bad thing. And though Goucher could "clean up their dorms," improve the library, and "get a T3," major renovation during the last few years should put Goucher back on track facilities-wise.

Life

Situated in an upscale suburb a few miles north of Baltimore, Goucher's "beautiful" campus is "close to D.C. and Baltimore but outside of the city"—important for students who consider themselves "politically aware" and "care about what's going on in the world," and also for those who like to go to Baltimore's "movies, concerts, clubs, and bars." Though Goucher's "warm environment," small size, and "active students" guarantee the "opportunity to get involved in the campus community," some students complain that "there needs to be more to do on campus. It's dead on the weekends." Some of it may have to do with Goucher's men-to-women ratio (about 70 percent of the former women's college are female). What does Goucher College need? A senior jokes, "cuter, smarter boys with better bodies who are sensitive to my needs." Or, as a first- year puts it, "The odds are good but the goods are odd." Baltimore, however, "is a 'college town,' so the lack of men is compensated by the large amount of Johns Hopkins boys." In terms of partying, although one sophomore claims that "we are all pot-smoking, fun-loving, intellectually curious, caring people," a been-there-done-that senior argues that "Goucher's once easy-going social atmosphere has been threatened by a heightened presence of policing/weekly pot busts and a new lockdown policy aimed to keep everyone in their respective houses." Maybe she's just tired of Goucher's "incredible one-on-one attention: professors, administration . . . even security."

Student Body

While "men are somewhat fishbowled at Goucher," notes a first-year, "everyone is really relaxed, and there is no real campus strife—except maybe the parking tickets." Adds a senior, "People here are politically aware, intelligent, and love class discussion. There are lots of weirdos but I love them anyway, and I know I'm one of them." Love—and lots of it—seems to be a theme at Goucher. Writes another freshman: "I love the majority of our students. They are very caring, loving, curious, optimistic, and out-to-get-the-world people, more conscious than most of our peers." And though there are your "superficial" types ("dancers & equestrians = snobs," writes a junior), a sophomore points out that "there are a lot of interesting people at Goucher. You just have to take the time to get to know them, which isn't hard at such a small school. I can't go anywhere on campus without seeing someone I can smile at."

ADMISSIONS

Very important factors considered by the admissions committee include: recommendations, secondary school record. *Important factors considered include:* essays, extracurricular activities, standardized test scores, talent/ability. *Other factors considered include:* alumni/ae relation, character/personal qualities, class rank, interview, volunteer work, work experience. SAT I or ACT required. TOEFL required of all international applicants. High school diploma is required and GED is not accepted. *High school units required/recommended:* 16 total required; 4 English required, 3 math required, 2 science required, 2 science lab required, 2 foreign language required, 2 social studies required, 3 social studies recommended.

The Inside Word

Goucher is in serious battle for the students to which it is best-suited, and often fills the role of safety to some of the region's strongest colleges. Though the College is a solid choice in its own right, its admissions profile reflects modest competitiveness as a result of these circumstances.

FINANCIAL AID

Students should submit: FAFSA, CSS/Financial Aid PROFILE. Regular filing deadline is February 15. The Princeton Review suggests that all financial aid forms be submitted as soon as possible after January 1. *Need-based scholarships/grants offered:* Pell, SEOG, state scholarships/grants, private scholarships, the school's own gift aid. *Loan aid offered:* Direct Subsidized Stafford, Direct Unsubsidized Stafford, Federal Perkins, state loans, college/university loans from institutional funds. Federal Work-Study Program available. Institutional employment available. Applicants will be notified of awards on or about April 1. Off-campus job opportunities are good.

FROM THE ADMISSIONS OFFICE

"A Goucher liberal arts education aims to prepare students for the real world. The college integrates thought and action, combining a strong liberal arts curriculum with hands-on learning in off-campus settings through internships, field work, study abroad, and independent projects. Students can choose majors in 18 departments and four interdisciplinary areas, or they may design their own individualized program of study. Small classes taught by skilled faculty, strong international studies programs, and research with faculty are other key characteristics. Goucher has impressive resources in technology, including a campus fully wired for access to the Internet and the World Wide Web. Goucher's merit scholarship program is one of the top programs in the nation, offering strong students awards ranging from partial tuition to full tuition plus room and board."

For even more information on this school, turn to page 237 of the "Stats" section.

GROVE CITY COLLEGE

100 CAMPUS DRIVE, GROVE CITY, PA 16127-2104 • ADMISSIONS: 724-458-2100 • FAX: 724-458-3395
FINANCIAL AID: 724-458-2163 • E-MAIL: ADMISSIONS@GCC.EDU • WEBSITE: WWW.GCC.EDU

Ratings

Quality of Life: 79   **Academic:** 86   **Admissions:** 91   **Financial Aid:** 88

Academics

The Grove City College environment allows students to be "continually challenged to learn more—more about my field of studies, more about the world around me, more about my faith, and more about myself." This "Ivy League school in disguise" runs according to a "Christian viewpoint that is refreshing and open-minded." Some students feel that the religious bent makes

> **SURVEY SAYS . . .**
> *Campus is beautiful*
> *Campus easy to get around*
> *Students are religious*
> *Campus feels safe*
> *(Almost) everyone plays intramural sports*
> *No one cheats*
> *Great computer facilities*
> *Students get along with local community*

"almost every course become in some way, shape, or form a theology course." One respondent feels that the school's "pride in a 'rigorous curriculum' translates into standards that sometimes border on the ridiculous." Amid the challenging course work, students work with professors who are "inconceivably intelligent and brilliant in their fields" and "not afraid to stand up for liberty and truth." Undergraduates feel personally supported by the faculty, noting that instructors "go out of their way to help students understand material without robbing them of the learning experience." Students embrace their core curriculum, eager to "dabble in everything from physics to Spanish to philosophy, no matter what your major." Several students think "it seems that faculty and students mesh well, while the administration isolates itself." Reportedly, students and professors alike "voice their displeasure concerning administrative direction." A common sentiment goes, "Administration needs to get with the times and realize we're big boys and big girls and we can handle ourselves." On the other hand, one student writes, "Where else can you watch the president of the college team up with faculty members for a basketball game against students?" In the end, the school succeeds in "giving support to students in many ways, which lightens the academic load."

Life

A defining factor of Grove is the "definite focus on God." That means "Calvin and Luther are generally on the tip of the tongue here" and "we do have parties, just minus the alcohol." Employing a well-used double negative, one student writes "the party scene isn't nonexistent," but typically, students partake in "snowball fights, movie nights, Bible study, IM bowling, ice cream socials, square dancing, lots of long conversations," and other activities that "don't involve breaking the law." Some students think that Greeks don't do much besides "wear matching sweatshirts," but others say, "Greek life gives variety, friendship, and fun that the campus does not offer." The anti-Greek faction goes so far as to say that fraternities and sororities are "the cause of all drinking and sex that goes on." "Intervisitation," that fated time when men and women are allowed to be in the same residences at the same time, means that "the freshmen dorms get loud, and stay loud until 12:45." That early collegiate bedtime hints at the "atmosphere bordering on repressive at times." All told, certain students remark suggestively, "Don't let the Norman Rockwell facade fool you."

Student Body

Students offer three basic descriptions of TGs, or "typical Grovers." The first camp, "the home-schooled, very sheltered kids who go home every weekend and are engaged by sophomore year," give the campus its reputation, but many students will tell you that students are not as marriage-obsessed as outsiders believe. These kids are the ones "who would ask, 'What are hallucinogens?'" one student explains. Another group comprises "the normal, Nalgene bottle–carrying, Christian summer camp–working, service-oriented students." The leftovers are those who "slack off, drink, and get off campus." In general, most undergrads are "white, suburban, Christian Republicans." Many students point out, "We're diverse in our Christian denominations, but not our ethnicities," to the degree that "there are more amputees than minorities on this campus." In this "homogenous group," "there are a few gays/lesbians, and they probably don't fit in well since this is a Christian school and the Bible is against homosexuality." Reportedly, atypical students are "acknowledged as individuals and accepted for [whom] they are." The cumulative effect is "so many people who enjoy being around each other so much."

ADMISSIONS

Very important factors considered by the admissions committee include: character/personal qualities, interview, secondary school record. *Important factors considered include:* essays, extracurricular activities, recommendations, standardized test scores, talent/ability. *Other factors considered include:* alumni/ae relation, class rank, geographical residence, minority status, religious affiliation/commitment, state residency, volunteer work, work experience. SAT I or ACT required. TOEFL required of all international applicants. High school diploma or GED is required. *High school units required/recommended:* 16 total recommended; 4 English recommended, 3 math recommended, 3 science recommended, 3 foreign language recommended, 2 social studies recommended, 1 history recommended.

The Inside Word

If you're looking for a northeastern college with a Christian orientation, Grove City is a pretty good choice, but it's getting tougher to get in as we speak. Applications and standards are on the rise, and the college is fast becoming the newest addition to the lofty realm of the highly selective. Minorities are in short supply, and will encounter a somewhat friendlier admissions process. All students should definitely follow the college's recommendation and interview.

FINANCIAL AID

Students should submit: institution's own financial aid form. Regular filing deadline is April 15. The Princeton Review suggests that all financial aid forms be submitted as soon as possible after January 1. *Need-based scholarships/grants offered:* private scholarships, the school's own gift aid. *Loan aid offered:* College Loan Program funded by PNC Bank. Institutional employment available. Applicants will be notified of awards on a rolling basis beginning on or about March 15. Off-campus job opportunities are good.

FROM THE ADMISSIONS OFFICE

"A good college education doesn't have to cost a fortune. For decades, Grove City College has offered a quality education at costs among the lowest nationally. Since the 1990s, increased national academic acclaim has come to Grove City College. Grove City College is a place where professors teach. You will not see graduate assistants or teacher's aides in the classroom. Our professors are also active in the total life of the campus. More than 100 student organizations on campus afford opportunity for a wide variety of co-curricular activities. Outstanding scholars and leaders in education, science, and international affairs visit the campus each year. The environment at GCC is friendly, secure, and dedicated to high standards. Character-building is emphasized and traditional Christian values are supported."

For even more information on this school, turn to page 237 of the "Stats" section.

HAMPDEN-SYDNEY COLLEGE

PO Box 667, HAMPDEN-SYDNEY, VA 23943 • ADMISSIONS: 804-223-6120 • FAX: 804-223-6346
FINANCIAL AID: 804-223-6119 • E-MAIL: HSAPP@TIGER.HSC.EDU • WEBSITE: WWW.HSC.EDU

Ratings

Quality of Life: 84   **Academic:** 85   **Admissions:** 78   **Financial Aid:** 87

Academics

Who says the Old South is dead? The students of Virginia's all-male Hampden-Sydney College, founded in 1775, continue the region's genteel traditions at an institution defined by its rigid honor code, a solid core curriculum emphasizing those things a gentleman needs to know, a great "'old boy' network' of alumni," and professors who "are more enjoyable than a glass of sweet ice tea and a plate of Mom's homestyle." For the

> **SURVEY SAYS . . .**
> Lots of conservatives on campus
> Students don't like , Hampden-Sydney, VA
> Diversity lacking on campus
> Frats dominate social scene, No one cheats
> Great library, Beautiful campus
> Musical organizations aren't popular
> Students get along with local community
> Class discussions encouraged
> Computer facilities need improving

right type of student—namely, one comfortable in so arguably archaic an atmosphere—H-SC is a slice of southern heaven on Earth. Students revere H-SC's age-old honor code, under which "no person who lies, cheats, [or] steals will be tolerated. There is a very strict honor code that all people should obey, not just inside the walls of Hampden-Sydney, but in society as a whole. A good system to live by." Work is hard and grades difficult to come by—"Don't expect an A in any class, even if you have the highest grade in the class, because H-SC doesn't have grade inflation," points out one student. Even so, students remain upbeat in assessing their academic experience. They brag that "small class sizes offer a great atmosphere for discussion among class members and faculty" and greatly appreciate how "everyone here at Hampden-Sydney is very accessible. All you have to do is ask for an appointment, and chances are you'll get one for the time requested." (It's even possible to "get a free meal or something like it out of the deal. Every effort is made to assure a good experience.") Many students think highly of the rhetoric requirement, which students feel "makes graduates competitive with grads from other schools. We may not have a diploma from one of the most recognized schools in the country, but thanks to Rhetoric, we can write and edit."

Life

Students report that "life at Hampden-Sydney is extremely academically oriented from Sunday through Thursday, but from Thursday night through Saturday night, the focus turns to social interaction." H-SC's all-male status is not a problem, most students agree, because there are "so many all-female schools around the area [that] the college basically turns coeducational on the weekends," which means that "a good time is had by all." Because of the school's rural setting, "some people have a hard time adjusting to life [here]. Hampden-Sydney is what you make of it, though. Social acceptance is sometimes hard to achieve at first, but once you start to meet people, it seems too easy. Fraternities are a very large part of the social scene." All students agree that "for fun, people go to fraternity parties and go out of town to the girls' schools." Otherwise, H-SC men love "play[ing] a lot of sports; hunting, fishing, and golf[ing] seem to be the most popular." Students note that "there are about 45 different student-operated clubs/societies/organizations that cater to just about every idea imaginable" and that "most of the student body is interested in politics and public service in [the] community."

Student Body

The student body at H-SC "is not very diverse, but everyone gets along amazingly well. People here don't care where you came from. This is because of the brotherhood at Hampden-Sydney. People, for the most part, are very friendly, and they are always willing to help you out." Undergraduates generally "come from upper-class, white backgrounds from throughout the South. . . . Many are the fraternity type. The remainder of the school, about 65 percent of us, fills in other groups on campus: football, basketball, lacrosse, rugby, rescue squad, stoners, and, of course, the dorks." Students are overwhelmingly "Christian in their beliefs" and generally quite conservative; warns one, "Only one group is isolated by the students: homosexuals. Not a good school for gay men at all."

ADMISSIONS

Very important factors considered by the admissions committee include: character/personal qualities, essays, recommendations, secondary school record, standardized test scores. *Important factors considered include:* class rank, extracurricular activities. *Other factors considered include:* alumni/ae relation, interview, minority status, talent/ability, volunteer work, work experience. SAT I or ACT required; SAT II recommended. TOEFL required of all international applicants. High school diploma or GED is required. *High school units required/recommended:* 16 total required; 4 English required, 3 math required, 4 math recommended, 2 science required, 3 science recommended, 1 science lab required, 2 foreign language required, 3 foreign language recommended, 1 social studies required, 3 elective required.

The Inside Word

Hampden-Sydney is one of the last of its kind. Understandably, the applicant pool is heavily self-selected, and a fairly significant percentage of those who are admitted choose to enroll. This enables the admissions committee to be more selective, which in turn requires candidates to take the process more seriously than might otherwise be necessary. Students with consistently sound academic records should have little to worry about nonetheless.

FINANCIAL AID

Students should submit: FAFSA, CSS/Financial Aid PROFILE, state aid form. Regular filing deadline is May 1. The Princeton Review suggests that all financial aid forms be submitted as soon as possible after January 1. *Need-based scholarships/grants offered:* Pell, SEOG, state scholarships/grants, private scholarships, the school's own gift aid. *Loan aid offered:* FFEL Subsidized Stafford, FFEL Unsubsidized Stafford, FFEL PLUS, Federal Perkins, college/university loans from institutional funds, private loans. Federal Work-Study Program available. Institutional employment available. Applicants will be notified of awards on or about March 1. Off-campus job opportunities are fair.

FROM THE ADMISSIONS OFFICE

"The spirit of Hampden-Sydney is its sense of community. As one of only 1,026 students, you will be in small classes and find it easy to get extra help or inspiration from professors when you want it. Many of our professors live on campus and enjoy being with students in the snack bar as well as in the classroom. They give you the best, most personal education as possible. A big bonus of small-college life is that everybody is invited to go out for everything, and you can be as much of a leader as you want to be. From athletics to debating to publications to fraternity life, this is part of the process that produces a well-rounded Hampden-Sydney graduate."

For even more information on this school, turn to page 238 of the "Stats" section.

HAMPTON UNIVERSITY

OFFICE OF ADMISSIONS, HAMPTON UNIVERSITY, HAMPTON, VA 23668 • ADMISSIONS: 804-727-5328
FAX: 757-727-5084 • FINANCIAL AID: 800-624-3341 • E-MAIL: ADMIT@HAMPTONU.EDU
WEBSITE: WWW.HAMPTONU.EDU

Ratings
Quality of Life: 69   **Academic:** 72   **Admissions:** 79   **Financial Aid:** 73

Academics

Hampton University, a historically black school founded in the wake of Reconstruction, makes no bones about its approach to undergraduate education. School promotional literature announces Hampton's commitment to "rigorous academics" that stress "scientific and professional [subjects] with a strong liberal arts undergirding" and an "emphasis on the development of character" through a strict code of

> **SURVEY SAYS . . .**
> *Very little drug use*
> *Frats and sororities dominate social scene*
> *Diversity lacking on campus*
> *Classes are small*
> *Students are cliquish*
> *Registration is a pain*
> *Library needs improving*
> *Lots of long lines and red tape*
> *Athletic facilities need improving*

conduct. In short: Get ready to work hard and toe the line if you choose Hampton. This approach yields ample benefits, according to students. Writes one, "Hampton University is a school of great educational opportunity. There is always room for academic, social, and personal growth. One must only take advantage of those opportunities." Adds a psychology/education double major, "Overall, the academic experience here is very fulfilling and educational. There are superior programs offered here at Hampton University." Professors "range from very articulate and understanding in their teachings to having a heavy accent and just lecturing the whole time, not answering students' questions." Students in business departments were most sanguine about their profs, while those in mathematics and computer science complained most about unintelligible instructors. Student opinion of the administration is more uniform—students agree it is "unorganized" because "the business office and administration do not communicate with each other."

Life

Life at Hampton involves conforming to an unusual number of rules, including an 11 p.m. curfew for freshmen, a schoolwide dress code, and strict visitation restrictions at dormitories, all of which are single-sex. Writes one student, "The school is very strict, too strict maybe. We are all adults, aren't we?" Freshmen and sophomores are not allowed to have cars, and "without a car or friends with cars you are stuck on campus, which sucks. There is nothing on campus, not to mention anything on or off campus open after 11 p.m." Sub-par dorms and dining services further undermine on-campus life. As a result, "Life at school can be boring. On weekends there are parties, but they are wack, and you get tired of seeing the same faces and the same parties ending at 2 a.m. Sororities and fraternities are stressed too much." Explains one student, "You must go off campus or to neighboring schools to find creative, stimulating, educational, and open-minded entertainment." Campus is not totally devoid of entertainment, though, as "Greeks are involved in a lot of fun yet educational opportunities. They provide a support group not only for themselves but for every student here." Furthermore, sports teams, especially the football team, provide a rallying point for most students. Despite the shortcomings of life here, students have a great deal of school spirit. Reports one, "Before freshmen even start class, they are taught a whole bunch of cheers and dances to do at sporting events. That's why I love Hampton: I can be the cheerleader I've always wanted to be."

Student Body

There is little racial diversity at Hampton, but there is a great deal of regional diversity. Explains one student, "We have students from all over the world. To attend a mostly black institution where I am able to learn alongside people who look and act like me is a very powerful experience." Students are generally "friendly but high maintenance." While they "always have smiles on their faces, and the upperclassmen are very helpful with orienting freshmen to campus," some complain that superficiality pervades the student body. One student comments, "My fellow students are sometimes shallow and pretentious. Although I enjoy fashion, too much emphasis is placed on it by students attending HU; there seems to be a judgment of one's character based on what one wears." Some see an upside, noting that "many of the students here are arrogant, but arrogance sparks competition and encourages students to do as well as they possibly can."

ADMISSIONS

Very important factors considered by the admissions committee include: character/personal qualities, essays, secondary school record, standardized test scores. *Important factors considered include:* class rank, recommendations. *Other factors considered include:* alumni/ae relation, extracurricular activities, talent/ability, volunteer work. SAT I or ACT required. TOEFL required of all international applicants. High school diploma or GED is required. *High school units required/recommended:* 17 total required; 4 English required, 3 math required, 2 science required, 2 science lab required, 2 foreign language recommended, 2 social studies required, 6 elective required.

The Inside Word

Hampton has less general visibility than such better-known historically black colleges as Morehouse, Spelman, and Howard, but it has just as much of a tradition of academic quality. In recent years the university's profile has been boosted by hosting national workshops on counseling minority students in the college admissions process. Candidates can expect a personal and caring experience in the admissions process.

FINANCIAL AID

Students should submit: FAFSA. The Princeton Review suggests that all financial aid forms be submitted as soon as possible after January 1. *Need-based scholarships/grants offered:* Pell, SEOG, state scholarships/grants, private scholarships, the school's own gift aid, Federal Nursing. *Loan aid offered:* Direct Subsidized Stafford, Direct Unsubsidized Stafford, Direct PLUS, Federal Perkins, alternative loans. Federal Work-Study Program available. Applicants will be notified of awards on a rolling basis beginning on or about April 1. Off-campus job opportunities are excellent.

FROM THE ADMISSIONS OFFICE

"Hampton attempts to provide the environment and structures most conducive to the intellectual, emotional, and aesthetic enlargement of the lives of its members. The university gives priority to effective teaching and scholarly research while placing the student at the center of its planning. Hampton will ask you to look inwardly at your own history and culture and examine your relationship to the aspirations and development of the world."

For even more information on this school, turn to page 239 of the "Stats" section.

HAVERFORD COLLEGE

370 LANCASTER AVENUE, HAVERFORD, PA 19041 • ADMISSIONS: 610-896-1350 • FAX: 610-896-1338
FINANCIAL AID: 610-896-1350 • E-MAIL: ADMITME@HAVERFORD.EDU • WEBSITE: WWW.HAVERFORD.EDU

Ratings
Quality of Life: 87   **Academic:** 98   **Admissions:** 98   **Financial Aid:** 86

Academics

Haverford College "is the quintessence of the liberal arts experience: superb academics with an emphasis on teacher/student interaction." Originally a Quaker school, Haverford has "never forgotten its Quaker roots" and accordingly "is a community committed to the ideals of taking responsibility for your actions." This is a "high-pressure academic environment" but

> **SURVEY SAYS . . .**
> *Campus is beautiful*
> *Campus easy to get around*
> *No one cheats*
> *Great library*
> *Campus feels safe*
> *Students are happy*
> *Registration is a breeze*
> *School is well run*

also "cooperative and nonthreatening." Students warn, "The sciences and math here are hard core; the humanities are somewhat less challenging," though "professors who are brilliant people and who truly care about their students" are there to ensure undergraduates' success. Haverford's Honor Code plays a prominent role in fostering a sense of unity; "the honor code here is amazing; it promotes a lot of trust and freedom in the community, which the students love," explains one undergrad. "Haverford knows how to take care of freshmen," explains one undergrad. "When you come here, you get Customs People (like RAs, except cooler), Honor Code Orienteers, an Upper Class Advisor, Peer Awareness Facilitators, a faculty advisor, and a dean. So there are a million people whom you can go to for help and advisement." For those students with wanderlust, "Our study abroad office is excellent! I'm studying at the London School of Economics this year thanks to my accessible, helpful and alarmingly organized study abroad dean." Students speak in similarly glowing terms about the rest of the administration. Explains one student, "In terms of the administrators, Haverford is mostly run by the students. We start our own organizations. We allocate where the Student Council funds go."

Life

Haverford's rigorous curriculum means that "during the week, work pretty much dominates everything." Students unwind on weekends, enjoying "a lot of activities, like dances, plays, concerts, and musicals. Last weekend, we had a play, a formal dance, a musical performance, and an improv group. It's pretty easy to find activities to keep you busy." While some here take advantage of nearby Philadelphia ("good history and culture, as well as a club scene and places like South Street to hang out at"), most tend to stick close to campus, which is "so beautiful that it's practically unbearable!" Parties here are generally low-key and usually involve alcohol and other substances; as with academics, the Honor Code applies. Reports one student, "I'm impressed by the leniency and respectfulness of Security and the administration vis-à-vis drinking and substance use. They definitely trust students to be responsible for themselves and for one another, and I think that for the most part, that trust is well placed." Students report an active intramural sports program, lots of clubs and organizations (with ample opportunities to start your own), and a fair amount of political activity, most of which leans leftward.

Student Body

As befits an elite liberal arts school, Haverford is home to a student body "good at more things than you can count on your fingers and toes, and interested in just about everything." More than one student confided that "the typical student is a cool dork: someone with really funky interests and life experiences who loves sharing and learning, even if s/he's not amazing at performing or shmoozing a crowd." Most "probably own a pair of Birkenstocks but aren't quite as leftist as they makes themselves out to be." Complains one conservative, "Haverford is accepting of anyone . . . except for non-left-wingers." While most feel that "there is a good amount of diversity here," especially for such a small, expensive school, many also report that the school needs to make an "effort to increase the diversity."

ADMISSIONS

Very important factors considered by the admissions committee include: character/personal qualities, recommendations, secondary school record, standardized test scores. *Important factors considered include:* class rank, essays, extracurricular activities, volunteer work. *Other factors considered include:* alumni/ae relation, geographical residence, interview, minority status, talent/ability, work experience. SAT I or ACT required; SAT II also required. High school diploma or GED is required. *High school units required/recommended:* 12 total required; 4 English required, 3 math required, 4 math recommended, 1 science required, 2 science recommended, 1 science lab required, 3 foreign language required, 1 social studies required.

The Inside Word

Candidate evaluation at Haverford is quite thorough, and the applicant pool is sizable and strong. Applicants who are successful through the initial academic review are then carefully considered for the match they make with the college. Students should definitely spend some time assessing the reasons for their interest in attending before responding to essays and interviewing. Interviewing is a must.

FINANCIAL AID

Students should submit: FAFSA, CSS/Financial Aid PROFILE, state aid form, noncustodial (divorced/separated) parent's statement, business/farm supplement. Regular filing deadline is January 31. The Princeton Review suggests that all financial aid forms be submitted as soon as possible after January 1. *Need-based scholarships/grants offered:* Pell, SEOG, state scholarships/grants, private scholarships, the school's own gift aid. *Loan aid offered:* FFEL Subsidized Stafford, FFEL Unsubsidized Stafford, FFEL PLUS, Federal Perkins. Federal Work-Study Program available. Institutional employment available. Applicants will be notified of awards on or about April 15. Off-campus job opportunities are good.

FROM THE ADMISSIONS OFFICE

"Haverford strives to be a college in which integrity, honesty, and concern for others are dominant forces. The college does not have many formal rules; rather, it offers an opportunity for students to govern their affairs and conduct themselves with respect and concern for others. Each student is expected to adhere to the Honor Code as it is adopted each year by the Students' Association. Haverford's Quaker roots show most clearly in the relationship of faculty and students, in the emphasis on integrity, in the interaction of the individual and the community, and through the college's concern for the uses to which its students put their expanding knowledge. Haverford's 1,100 students represent a wide diversity of interests, backgrounds, and talents. They come from public, parochial, and independent schools across the United States, Puerto Rico, and 27 foreign countries. Students of color are an important part of the Haverford community. The Minority Coalition, which includes Asian, black, and Hispanic students' associations, works with faculty and administration on matters directly concerned with the quality of life at the college."

For even more information on this school, turn to page 239 of the "Stats" section.

HOLLINS UNIVERSITY

PO BOX 9707, ROANOKE, VA 24020-1707 • ADMISSIONS: 540-362-6401 • FAX: 540-362-6218
FINANCIAL AID: 540-362-6332 • E-MAIL: HUADM@HOLLINS.EDU • WEBSITE: WWW.HOLLINS.EDU

Ratings
Quality of Life: 98   **Academic:** 90   **Admissions:** 79   **Financial Aid:** 95

Academics

Students agree that "the small size of the student body is the key factor in the greatness of academics at Hollins. The professors here are extremely accessible and get to know all their students personally, which is great motivation to work hard in classes and adds to the friendly, family atmosphere here at Hollins." This small, Virginian, all-women's school has "a great creative writing program" as well as a small but vibrant arts program that complement its more popular departments. In all areas, students proudly tell us, "The main focus of the professors is the student body. Classes are small and challenging, and the base of liberal arts is wonderful." Students also love the honor code, which allows them to take self-scheduled, unproctored exams, and the "amazing" study abroad opportunities, which send "two-thirds of the student body [to] spend at least a semester abroad. January term is well spent, too. January term is where we spend the month of January interning somewhere, or you can opt to travel with the school to other countries and learn [their] history." Students note that "while the administration tends to be more than a little clumsy and tangled in red tape at times, the friendliness and flexibility of the staff in all offices tends to make up for the mix-ups, confusion, and delays in administrative matters."

> **SURVEY SAYS . . .**
> *Dorms are like palaces*
> *Student government is popular*
> *Class discussions encouraged*
> *Classes are small*
> *No one cheats*
> *Campus feels safe*
> *Very small frat/sorority scene*
> *No one plays intramural sports*
> *(Almost) no one listens to college radio*

Life

Many students are pleasantly surprised that "for a women's college a good 20 to 40 minutes away from college-age males, this school does a pretty damn good job of keeping us entertained on campus. In addition to the many, many cultural events on campus, there are at least two school-sponsored popular concerts a month, visits by comedy troupes, and themed parties that people actually go to." Adds another student, "There are tons of organizations, and it is very easy to begin an organization if you are interested. The more you get involved, the more there is to do. Aside from the planned activities, there are often parties in the apartments or in NEFA (the fine arts house). There is also a small arcade and pool area in the snack bar, and it's pretty easy to find people around to play games." What's missing, of course, are boys; some students give this as the principal reason that Hollins "is pretty much a road trip/suitcase college. There is nothing to do here, especially on weekends." Typical weekend destinations include Washington and Lee University or all-male Hampden-Sydney. Students like Roanoke, "a medium-sized town with lots of things to do, good clubs and restaurants." The campus is conveniently located "very close to downtown Roanoke, and everything (grocery stores, malls, movie theatres, restaurants) is within a 10-minute drive from campus; still it would be nice if the school provided at least occasional transportation to popular destinations like the grocery store, for the unfortunate car-less students." Hollins' campus "is as beautiful as our publicity says" it is.

Student Body

As one student puts it, "Hollins has a reputation for being comprised of largely white upper-middle-class 'pearl girls,' and not without reason." Things are changing, though. As one undergraduate told us, "In the past, many of the students were rather wealthy, young, Southern women. Now it is composed generally of middle-class women. Most are easy to get along with, and traditions often bring us closer together." Explains another, "At our school, you're either A or you're B. We have the truly arty students who came to a liberal arts school to get a liberal arts education, and then we have these really sheltered, white, southern-belle types who sneer at anything the arts programs do." Most students agree that Hollins "could stand to improve on the diversity levels" by enrolling more "students of color and [varied] economic backgrounds." According to many we surveyed, the school's lesbian contingent has grown in number and volubility in recent years.

ADMISSIONS

Very important factors considered by the admissions committee include: recommendations, secondary school record, standardized test scores. *Important factors considered include:* class rank, essays, extracurricular activities, talent/ability. *Other factors considered include:* alumni/ae relation, character/personal qualities, interview, volunteer work, work experience. SAT I or ACT required; SAT II recommended. TOEFL required of all international applicants. High school diploma or GED is required. *High school units required/recommended:* 16 total required; 4 English recommended, 3 math recommended, 3 science recommended, 3 foreign language recommended, 3 social studies recommended.

The Inside Word

Only candidates who overtly display their lack of compatibility with the Hollins milieu are likely to encounter difficulty in gaining admission. A high level of self-selection and its weak, but improving, freshman profile allow most candidates to relax.

FINANCIAL AID

Students should submit: FAFSA, state aid form. Regular filing deadline is March 1. The Princeton Review suggests that all financial aid forms be submitted as soon as possible after January 1. *Need-based scholarships/grants offered:* Pell, SEOG, state scholarships/grants, private scholarships, the school's own gift aid, United Negro College Fund. *Loan aid offered:* Direct Subsidized Stafford, Direct Unsubsidized Stafford, Direct PLUS, Federal Perkins, state loans, Sallie Mae, OneChoice, GATE Loans, Plato. Federal Work-Study Program available. Institutional employment available. Applicants will be notified of awards on a rolling basis beginning on or about March 15. Off-campus job opportunities are good.

FROM THE ADMISSIONS OFFICE

"As a liberal arts college dedicated to high achievement for women, Hollins celebrates and encourages the success—whether in the classroom, in the laboratory, on stage, or on the athletic field—of each student. A spirit of independent inquiry, the free exchange of ideas, and a love for learning characterize life on campus. At Hollins, creativity and imaginative thinking are applauded with the same vigor that rewards academic achievement.

"Women who are going places start at Hollins."

For even more information on this school, turn to page 240 of the "Stats" section.

HOOD COLLEGE

401 ROSEMONT AVENUE, FREDRICK, MD 21701 • ADMISSIONS: 301-696-3400 • FAX: 301-696-3819
E-MAIL: ADMISSIONS@HOOD.EDU • WEBSITE: WWW.HOOD.EDU

Ratings
Quality of Life: 71   **Academic:** 78   **Admissions:** 73   **Financial Aid:** 82

Academics

Located in historic Frederick, Maryland, Hood College serves a quite content mostly female undergrad student body, as well as a sizeable coed grad population. The undergraduate gender dynamic is undergoing transformation, however, with the opening of coed resi-

> **SURVEY SAYS . . .**
> *Lots of classroom discussion, Classes are small*
> *Athletic facilities need improving*
> *Lousy food on campus, Students are happy*
> *Lab facilities need improving, Campus is beautiful*
> *Diverse students interact*

dence halls by fall 2003 The faculty receives rave reviews: "Most professors are wonderful," opines a student, and "most of my classes have been around 15 to 20 students, which is great for allowing discussions." Continues another, "They give you their home phone numbers . . . or you see them randomly in your dorm at midnight, or they respond to e-mails within five minutes of them being sent. They also love what they do—they love teaching, they love their discipline, and they love their students." "The administration is one of the low points of Hood," notes one undergrad, "but we just got a new president, and we are hopeful that things will improve." Dean White, the dean of students, "knows all of us by name and face" and will "bend over backwards to help out," while President Volpe "goes to more student activities than some students that I know." He dropped by the "Chemistry Club's Movie Night to watch *Men in Black*" and has been seen "playing football with the commuter boys" on the quad. A unique Hood tradition is the "honor code": professors are not present for any exam, test, or quiz, but every student must pledge that she has "neither given nor received any unauthorized aid on this assignment."

Life

"We make our own fun at school" writes one proud Hood student. "For instance, we can be found ice-skating on Pledge (the spray for dusting) in the hallway or dressing up in some wild costumes." Another adds, "We also do some crazy stuff like shopping-cart races and ticker-tape parades. Lets just say that as long as you're creative, there is NEVER a dull moment at Hood." Students venturing out into Hood's nightlife will find that "we are not a dry campus, and there are parties with free beer nearly every weekend." Community is key at Hood, from the patented "Hood Hello" greeting to the Honor Code, which carries over to residential life. (Any person can ask others to be quiet, move, close doors, etc., and the other is expected to comply.) Sans sororities or fraternities, "each dorm has its own identity, and the students all feel a strong loyalty to where they live." Many students go home for the weekend, but campuswide events are not lacking, from the annual Spring Parties Weekend to Messiah Weekend, featuring a choir performance with the Naval Academy. When students need a getaway "it's not too hard to find someone who wants to hit up a club in D.C. or Baltimore," so "if you have a car, you are GOD!" In Frederick, you will find "some really bizarre museums . . . like the Museum of Civil War Medicine, not to mention Baker Park, which puts on a fantastic Fourth of July celebration, and all the coffee shops and thrift stores."

Student Body

Students all seem to agree on the "strong sense of community at Hood," fostered in part by the big sister/little sister program, which pairs juniors with new students to encourage friendships between classes. Hood's "dedication to diversity" is apparent in Hood's "mixture of ethnic backgrounds, religious beliefs, and cultures," and its many international students. "People tend to form cliques," shares one student, but "most of the students"—dubbed a "rare bunch of jewels" by one gal—"are friendly and outgoing." While plenty of women bemoan the difficulty of finding "a decent guy," the "lesbian community is active and well protected." The predominant political tone is liberal.

ADMISSIONS

Very important factors considered by the admissions committee include: secondary school record and standardized test scores. *Important factors considered include:* class rank, essays, and recommendations. *Other factors considered include:* alumni/ae relation, extracurricular activities, interview, minority status, talent/ability, volunteer work, and work experience. SAT I or ACT required; SAT II recommended. TOEFL required of all international applicants. High school diploma or GED is required. *High school units required:* 16 total required; 4 English required, 3 math required, 3 science required, 2 foreign language required, 3 social studies required, 1 fine arts required.

The Inside Word

Applications to Hood for 2002–2003 were up 40 percent from previous years. The school recently offered "legacies" (the daughters/granddaughters of alumnae) a great incentive to apply: get in and your freshman tuition will equal whatever your mom or grandmother paid her freshman year.

FINANCIAL AID

Students should submit: FAFSA. The Princeton Review suggests that all financial aid forms be submitted as soon as possible after January 1. Priority deadline for institutional scholarships is February 15. *Need-based scholarships/grants offered:* Pell, SEOG, state scholarships/grants, private scholarships, and the school's own gift aid. *Loan aid offered:* Direct Subsidized Stafford, Direct Unsubsidized Stafford, Direct PLUS, FFEL Subsidized Stafford, FFEL Unsubsidized Stafford, FFEL PLUS, and Federal Perkins. Federal Work-Study Program available. Institutional employment available. Applicants will be notified of awards on or about March 1. Off-campus job opportunities are good.

FROM THE ADMISSIONS OFFICE

"Many changes are happening at Hood College. For almost 110 years, Hood was a liberal arts college dedicated to the education of women. In the past 30 years, men have been attending Hood as commuters in both the graduate and undergraduate programs. Effective fall 2003, men will also be admitted to the residential program, making the college fully coeducational. The change in residential programming is producing changes elsewhere on campus. Hood will add five varsity sports for men (basketball, cross-country, golf, swimming, and tennis) and will make changes to the women's athletic program: cross-country and golf will become varsity sports for women. Changes are also occurring for Hood's facilities. The college dedicated the Hodson Center for Science and Technology, a $20 million state-of-the-art facility for teaching and research, in 2002. The Center contains sophisticated laboratories designed specifically for biology, biochemistry, chemistry, and environmental studies. Hood also performed extensive renovations on the former science building, which now houses extensive computer laboratories, faculty offices, and spaces for students to gather and study. What won't change at Hood is the emphasis on student learning and leadership. Both the classroom—where the average class size is 14—and the extracurricular environment focus on active student learning. Hood students learn to lead by being campus leaders, planning events, and taking charge on the athletic field. Hood students also develop and practice critical leadership skills in every class and every campus activity. These skills are enhanced by internships for credit in almost every major."

For even more information on this school, turn to page 241 of the "Stats" section.

HOWARD UNIVERSITY

2400 SIXTH STREET NW, WASHINGTON, DC 20059 • ADMISSIONS: 202-806-2700 • FAX: 202-806-4462
FINANCIAL AID: 202-806-2800 • E-MAIL: ADMISSION@HOWARD.EDU • WEBSITE: WWW.HOWARD.EDU

Ratings

Quality of Life: 77   **Academic:** 72   **Admissions:** 80   **Financial Aid:** 76

Academics

Students at Howard University appreciate the "great legacy and wonderful traditions" of their HBCU (historically black college/university). Explains one undergraduate, "Our rich history is not just history, but is relived every day. Marches, rallies, and political activism are things that stay strong and are supported by the Administration." Students

> **SURVEY SAYS . . .**
> Frats and sororities dominate social scene
> Political activism is hot
> Student government is popular
> Students don't get along with local community
> Registration is a pain, Theater is unpopular
> Very little beer drinking
> Lots of long lines and red tape
> Student publications are popular

here feel strong bonds not only to the school's rich past but also to minority communities around the world today. Notes one, "'Leadership for America and the Global Community' is our phrase, and we stick by it to the end. For the people of the African Diaspora and all other minorities, this is a place to appreciate your culture in every way." Many brag that "research is another strength of our university. Howard is the only HBCU ranked as a Level 1 research institution by the Carnegie Foundation, and it is very clear why. With our huge library system and Moorland-Spingarn Research Center there is no doubting Howard's greatness!" Students brag that "professors are willing to help with problems, both inside and outside of school. Many of the professors take you into their families. You become their children for the four or more years that you attend." All these assets help soften the blow of the demanding curriculum ("Not very forgiving—perform or you're out. Typical days are long and tiring.") and the hassle-filled bureaucracy that runs the school.

Life

Washington, D.C., Howard's hometown, looms large in the extracurricular activities of most students. "Clubbing is one of the biggest weekend activities," writes one undergrad, adding that "some clubs provide shuttles from the dorms straight to the clubs." Students involve themselves in community volunteer work, internships, and the big-league politics that permeate the city. Nearly all love D.C., although most are less positive about the neighborhood surrounding the school: "It is in the middle of the ghetto. There are a bunch of crack fiends in the surrounding areas," warns one student. On campus, "there are a lot of groups, clubs, and organizations to get into, such as state clubs and religious organizations." Students also enjoy "on-campus concerts and shows." As for the party scene, students report that "unlike at most white schools, keg parties are not cool. Howard students prefer liquor and weed. Every now and then, a Greek organization will have a party, but more than likely it will be at a local club, not at a frat house." For those less inclined to party, one student sums up other possibilities, "There . . . is always something mind-stimulating that you can get into. Go to a student play on campus or visit a Shakespeare play downtown. Join NABA, NSBE, a pan-Hellenic organization, or student council. Take a walk downtown and visit the monuments, or simply gaze at the gorgeous fountains."

Student Body

The predominantly African American student body of Howard "comes from diverse backgrounds socially and economically." Notes one student, "Coming from a small town, I would have never imagined interacting with so many people from so many places and meshing so well with all of them. Students from Howard come from all 50 states, the two U.S. territories, and over 104 countries abroad! On top of that, they don't just stick to their own; everyone is in the mix with common goals." Some students complain that their classmates are too materialistic ("Prepare to enter the fashion zone. Students at HU spend lots of money on clothing and looking good. Most women wear full makeup and high-heeled boots to strut around campus.") and are overly focused on career goals ("The pre-professionalism at this place kills me," gripes one student. "If you're one of those rare breeds who's interested in learning for the sake of learning, go to Swarthmore or Bard or somewhere and deal with their respective low levels of melanin. Howard is NOT the place for you.").

ADMISSIONS

Very important factors considered by the admissions committee include: class rank, secondary school record, standardized test scores. *Important factors considered include:* character/personal qualities, recommendations. *Other factors considered include:* alumni/ae relation, essays, extracurricular activities, talent/ability, volunteer work, work experience. SAT I or ACT required. TOEFL required of all international applicants. High school diploma or GED is required. *High school units required/recommended:* 14 total required; 4 English required, 2 math required, 2 science required, 2 foreign language required, 2 social studies required, 2 history required.

The Inside Word

A large applicant pool and solid yield of acceptees who enroll is a combination that adds up to selectivity for Howard. Pay strict attention to the formula.

FINANCIAL AID

Students should submit: FAFSA, institution's own financial aid form. Regular filing deadline is April 1. The Princeton Review suggests that all financial aid forms be submitted as soon as possible after January 1. *Need-based scholarships/grants offered:* Pell, SEOG, private scholarships, the school's own gift aid, Federal Nursing. *Loan aid offered:* FFEL Subsidized Stafford, FFEL PLUS, Federal Perkins, Federal Nursing, college/university loans from institutional funds. Federal Work-Study Program available. Institutional employment available. Applicants will be notified of awards on a rolling basis. Off-campus job opportunities are excellent.

FROM THE ADMISSIONS OFFICE

"Since its founding, Howard has stood among the few institutions of higher learning where African Americans and other minorities have participated freely in a truly comprehensive university experience. Thus, Howard has assumed a special responsibility to prepare its students to exercise leadership wherever their interest and commitments take them. Howard has issued approximately 97,214 degrees, diplomas, and certificates to men and women in the professions, the arts and sciences, and the humanities. The university has produced and continues to produce a high percentage of the nation's African American professionals in the fields of medicine, dentistry, pharmacy, engineering, nursing, architecture, religion, law, music, social work, education, and business. There are more than 8,830 students from across the nation and approximately 104 countries and territories attending the university. Their varied customs, cultures, ideas, and interests contribute to Howard's international character and vitality. More than 1,360 faculty members represent the largest concentration of African American scholars in any single institution of higher education."

For even more information on this school, turn to page 241 of the "Stats" section.

INDIANA UNIVERSITY OF PENNSYLVANIA

216 PRATT HALL, INDIANA, PA 15705 • ADMISSIONS: 724-357-2230 • FAX: 724-357-6281
FINANCIAL AID: 415-357-2218 • E-MAIL: ADMISSIONS_INQUIRY@GROVE.IUP.EDU • WEBSITE: WWW.IUP.EDU

Ratings
Quality of Life: 80   **Academic:** 81   **Admissions:** 78   **Financial Aid:** 82

Academics

The Robert E. Cook Honors College is what distinguishes Indiana University of Pennsylvania from your typical big-box state university. Reports one honors student, "The Honors College allows students to take interesting discussion-based classes instead of the standard liberal studies freshman classes. These honor classes are never lecture-based, and have made me a much better

> **SURVEY SAYS . . .**
> *Lots of beer drinking*
> *(Almost) everyone smokes*
> *Hard liquor is popular*
> *Frats and sororities dominate social scene*
> *Registration is a breeze*
> *Student newspaper is popular*
> *Great off-campus food*
> *Students are happy*

writer and thinker." Students' only complaint about the honors program concerns its limited scope; as one student told us, "My academic experience has been pretty good; however, there needs to be more honors courses and an honors program in each academic college." Beyond the Honors College, "the rest of the university is pretty much only concerned with partying." While profs "are easily accessible and encouraging," they face "a huge obstacle: a student body with too much laziness." Since the Honors College covers only some of students' course work, all students must take at least some courses outside the college. Reports one student, "Required classes are large, freakishly easy, and completely made up of lecture time. . . . My honors classes are absolutely excellent, with discussion 60 percent of the time." Even so, IUP offers plenty of challenges to those willing to step up to the plate. Sums up one undergrad, "IUP might not have ten sets of all the newest equipment, but it does train me in everything I need to know and gives me additional chances to learn outside of the school through its numerous internship and study abroad programs."

Life

Hometown Indiana, students at IUP tell us, "is not the place for city people who like a lot of excitement and nightclubs." The town "offers a myriad of bars but very little else." it is the birthplace of film legend Jimmy Stewart, and many here feel "it could very well be named 'Jimmy Stewart–ville' for all the paraphernalia: the Jimmy Stewart Museum, the sign coming into town proclaiming that Indiana, Pennsylvania, is the birthplace of Jimmy Stewart, and the showings of It's a Wonderful Life during the holidays at the local theater." Irreverent IUP undergrads occasionally "steal away in the middle of the night to put a dress and hat on the Jimmy Stewart statue, which proudly stands in front of the courthouse," giving you some idea of how little else there is to do here. Students tell us IUP was once a big party school but that "life in general at IUP is changing. They have increased the police force in order to better enforce drug and alcohol laws." To fill the void, "IUP offers many student organizations and musical events . . . from an anime club to equestrian team to dance squad to sororities and fraternities. If you have an interest, IUP is a good place to pursue it." Otherwise, students seek quiet entertainment of their own devising or, more often, pack up and go home when their last class ends. Pittsburgh is only an hour's drive.

Student Body

With over 11,000 undergraduates, "there are students from all walks of life here at IUP.... The majority are related by the fact that they come from a middling-income family . . . and are here to get the best education they can for their dollar." Many "are from within a 60-mile radius of the school," an area that is "very conservative Christian and not generally accepting of liberal viewpoints." IUP also has "a large population of African Americans and foreign students from all around the world, like Asia, Africa, and Europe." Students warn, however, "There is a visual segregation between the African American community and the rest of the campus." Most here "are more concerned with getting a job and money than being educated," according to their critics.

ADMISSIONS

Very important factors considered by the admissions committee include: secondary school record, talent/ability. *Important factors considered include:* class rank, standardized test scores. *Other factors considered include:* alumni/ae relation, character/personal qualities, essays, extracurricular activities, geographical residence, interview, recommendations, state residency, volunteer work, work experience. SAT I or ACT required; SAT I preferred. TOEFL required of all international applicants. High school diploma or GED is required. *High school units required/recommended:* 16 total recommended; 4 English recommended, 3 math recommended, 3 science recommended, 2 foreign language recommended, 2 social studies recommended, 1 history recommended, 1 elective recommended.

The Inside Word

IUP is impressive in many ways and should command more attention than it does. As a state school, it provides Pennsylvania residents with a great education at a rock-bottom price. Students applying to IUP with an average academic record will have little trouble getting admitted. Once on campus, students will find an unexpectedly diverse population hailing from many states and countries.

FINANCIAL AID

Students should submit: FAFSA. Regular filing deadline is April 15. The Princeton Review suggests that all financial aid forms be submitted as soon as possible after January 1. *Need-based scholarships/grants offered:* Pell, SEOG, state scholarships/grants, private scholarships, the school's own gift aid. *Loan aid offered:* FFEL Subsidized Stafford, FFEL Unsubsidized Stafford, FFEL PLUS, Federal Perkins, private alternative loans. Federal Work-Study Program available. Institutional employment available. Applicants will be notified of awards on a rolling basis beginning on or about April 15. Off-campus job opportunities are fair.

For even more information on this school, turn to page 242 of the "Stats" section.

JAMES MADISON UNIVERSITY

Undergraduate Admissions, Sonner Hall MSC 0101, Harrisonburg, VA 22807
Admissions: 540-568-5681 • Fax: 540-568-3332 • Financial Aid: 540-568-7820
E-mail: gotojmu@jmu.edu • Website: www.jmu.edu

Ratings

Quality of Life: 85   **Academic:** 81   **Admissions:** 84   **Financial Aid:** 82

Academics

With "topnotch facilities," afford-able tuition for both in-state and out-of-state students, and standout programs in music and business, James Madison University has a lot going for it. JMU also boasts an "innovative" Integrated Science and Technology (ISAT) program that offers degree programs in health sciences, computer science, and other technology-based fields. Writes one student, "The new ISAT buildings are equipped with excel-lent computers, and every ISAT major

> **SURVEY SAYS . . .**
> *Campus feels safe, Lots of beer drinking*
> *Very little drug use*
> *Everyone loves the Dukes*
> *Student publications are popular*
> *Great food on campus, Beautiful campus*
> *Campus easy to get around*
> *Students are cliquish*
> *Students don't like Harrisonburg, VA*
> *Student government is unpopular*
> *Students are not very happy*

that I know has really liked the facilities." Not all students praise ISAT, however; many feel that "some areas of the university, such as the College of Integrated Science and Technology (ISAT), eat up (what seems like) more than their share of the school budget while the College of Arts and Letters remains underfunded." Students also gripe about core requirements, called General Education here; notes one, "Students don't really care about those classes and neither do pro-fessors." Making matters worse is the perception that "Gen Ed classes are hard to get into, which can be frustrating because they're required and a lot of teachers won't give overrides into their classes." Fortunately, things get better for upperclassmen. Writes one typical student, "The first two years were pretty bad. Classes were huge; teachers couldn't put faces with names unless you contacted them on a regular basis. This past year has been a totally different story. I'm final-ly taking classes for my major. The teachers are great. They listen to the students, are easy to find outside of the classroom, and really seem invested in helping us to learn."

Life

JMU's undergrads "are generally geared towards making their four years at school the most beneficial and most fun of their lives." Reports one, "For a good four days of every week the school is studious, the library is packed, and students read for pleasure on the quad and debate on picnic tables outside of the on-campus restaurants; but come Thursday night, JMU students know how to party!" Weekends here "pretty much give way to the party scene. Lots of drink-ing goes on. There aren't too many bars, so there are always tons of apartment parties and house parties." There are Greek organizations here, but "Greek life is not the center of the social [scene]." Student organizations are popular; writes one student, "There are a lot of kids in reli-gious groups (Inter Varsity, YL, etc.). There are tons of clubs (sports, ethnic, academic, religious, etc.)." Also, the "University Program Board sets out to attract large-name bands, comedians, or shows to campus. Although the school is mid-sized we've had names such as Vertical Horizon, Wyclef, Third Eye Blind, Foo Fighters, and the Indigo Girls." Beyond campus lies the "boring" town of Harrisonburg, but beyond that lies the Shenandoah Valley; brags one student, "Since

JMU is situated in the mountains, camping is a pretty popular activity. Tents, sleeping bags, and other gear can be rented from the rec center on campus for little money. Biking and hiking are also popular."

Student Body

The "active, open, and friendly" students of JMU strike newcomers with an "overwhelming feeling of niceness. Everyone smiles at you and everyone holds doors. Even the cafeteria ladies seem to brighten your day a little." Students report that "it is not cutthroat competitive like other schools. People compete, but it is not at the expense of others." Since "most everyone in the student body is from Virginia," "a southern gentility" pervades the campus. Students admit that "different races and ethnicities are very separate. It's not that they don't get along with each other or hate each other—there just isn't a lot of interaction."

ADMISSIONS

Very important factors considered by the admissions committee include: secondary school record, class rank, standardized test scores. *Important factors considered include:* essays, extracurricular activities. *Other factors considered include:* alumni/ae relation, character/personal qualities, geographical residence, minority status, recommendations, state residency, talent/ability, volunteer work, work experience. SAT I or ACT required. TOEFL required of all international applicants. High school diploma or GED is required. *High school units required/recommended:* 19 total required; 22 total recommended; 4 years in each core area: English, math, lab science, social science/history; 3 years of some foreign language.

The Inside Word

James Madison has prospered from the applications of students faced with severe competition for admission to UVA and William and Mary. Third place on the Virginia public university totem pole is not a bad spot to be, as JMU's admissions committee will attest. Pay attention when they stress that your high school schedule should be chock-full of challenging academic courses.

FINANCIAL AID

Students should submit: FAFSA. The Princeton Review suggests that all financial aid forms be submitted as soon as possible after January 1. *Need-based scholarships/grants offered:* Pell, SEOG, state scholarships/grants, private scholarships. *Loan aid offered:* FFEL Subsidized Stafford, FFEL Unsubsidized Stafford, FFEL PLUS, Federal Perkins. Federal Work-Study Program available. Institutional employment available. Applicants will be notified of awards on a rolling basis beginning on or about April 1. Off-campus job opportunities are excellent.

FROM THE ADMISSIONS OFFICE

"James Madison University's philosophy of inclusiveness—known as 'all together one'—means that students become a part of a real community that nurtures its own to learn, grow, and succeed. Our professors, many of whom have a wealth of real-world experience, pride themselves on making teaching their top priority. We take seriously the responsibility to maintain an environment that fosters learning and encourages students to excel in and out of the classroom. Our rich variety of educational, social, and extracurricular activities include more than 100 innovative and traditional undergraduate majors and programs, a well-established study abroad program, a cutting-edge information security program, more than 280 student clubs and organizations, and a 147,000-square-foot, state-of-the-art recreation center. The university's picturesque, self-contained campus is located in the heart of the Shenandoah Valley, a four-season area that's easy to call home. Great food, fun times, exciting intercollegiate athletics, and rigorous academics all combine to create the unique James Madison experience. From the library to the residence halls and from our outstanding honors program to our highly successful career placement program, the university is committed to equipping our students with the tools they need to achieve their dreams."

For even more information on this school, turn to page 243 of the "Stats" section.

JOHNS HOPKINS UNIVERSITY

3400 NORTH CHARLES STREET/140 GARLAND, BALTIMORE, MD 21218 • ADMISSIONS: 410-516-8171
FAX: 410-516-6025 • FINANCIAL AID: 410-516-8028 • E-MAIL: GOTOJHU@JHU.EDU • WEBSITE: WWW.JHU.EDU

Ratings
Quality of Life: 85   **Academic:** 96   **Admissions:** 99   **Financial Aid:** 86

Academics

Johns Hopkins has earned a top reputation as an "excellent and challenging" university, with students who believe their school is "second to none." They value the "contacts you can make" with top professionals in a wide variety of fields. Professors, known to be "experts in their respective areas," take the time to "learn names, talk with students, and give them great

> **SURVEY SAYS . . .**
> *Popular college radio*
> *Political activism is hot*
> *Students are religious*
> *Athletic facilities are great*
> *(Almost) everyone plays intramural sports*
> *Student publications are popular*
> *Unattractive campus*
> *Library needs improving*

advice," according to a student in the political science department, who adds, "Get to know them—it's worthwhile." Another student gushes, "I love the way instructors care about us," making themselves "generally available to offer help outside of class." One student in the "phenomenal" accelerated nursing program calls the course load "highly intense," which leaves "barely any time for social life." The most common complaint logged at Johns Hopkins concerns the perception that professors and administration alike prioritize research over teaching, leading some students to moan that professors think "undergraduates are peons who don't matter much." Students want to see more support for the arts at the school and say that professors in the humanities focus more on their role as teachers than their counterparts in the sciences. The administration, which "needs to be more helpful and understanding," in the words of a few respondents, "prioritizes engineering and medical research" over the needs of undergraduates. Current students remind prospective attendees that they will have to be "proactive to get the best education," but the rewards include the "immense amount of opportunity available for students with good ideas."

Life

In the "highly educational environment" of Johns Hopkins, it may seem that "there's not a lot to do besides fraternity parties and homework." Students report, "You have to find your own fun, but it isn't hard to do." Those who have a difficult time entertaining themselves can always fall back on the "instant social life that erupts when you join a fraternity." One undergrad writes, "We generally don't go out more than once or twice a week, but when we do, we live it up." A freshman majoring in international relations appreciates that "there's enough that you can find stuff to do but not so much that it is a distraction." Though one student whines that "Baltimore is a ghetto," many students head downtown when "there isn't much to do on campus." An upperclassman reassures students, "Once you are old enough for bars, it gets better," especially for those with wheels. Many surveys note the brand-spanking-new athletic center, which entices students to play sports and attend to their cardiovascular systems during study breaks. Some students say the school could improve in terms of "clubs and anything school supported," but others offer, "If you want to build a new social outlet, the money [from the school] is available."

Student Body

A typical student who chooses Johns Hopkins might be described as "overly ambitious," "introverted," and "hardworking." To some people, the assortment of "too many weirdos" that makes up the student body displays "little personality." A few students accuse their group of peers, in general, of being "ruled too much by their parents' wishes." On the other hand, one student tells us, "People surprise me (in a good way) every day." Even if "kids could be cooler," respondents agree that "most are good people" and "everyone tends to work together." Accusations of blandness aren't universal; some students boast that "everyone here has done interesting things." While many students say, "We all get along," the population seems to "lack of a sense of unified community," and at times "cultural barriers are very hard to break through."

ADMISSIONS

Very important factors considered by the admissions committee include: character/personal qualities, essays, recommendations, rigor of secondary school course load. *Important factors considered include:* class rank, extracurricular activities, standardized test scores, talent/ability, volunteer work. *Other factors considered include:* alumni/ae relation, geographical residence, interview, minority status, work experience. TOEFL required of all international applicants. *High school units required/recommended:* 20 total recommended; 4 English, 4 math, 2–3 lab science, 3–4 foreign language, 2–3 history and social science.

The Inside Word

The admissions process at Hopkins demands to be taken seriously. Competition with the best colleges and universities in the country keeps the acceptance rate artificially high. Make certain that your personal credentials—essays, recommendations, and extracurricular activities—are impressive.

FINANCIAL AID

Students should submit: FAFSA, institution's own financial aid form, noncustodial (divorced/separated) parent's statement, business/farm supplement, prior and current year's federal tax returns. Regular filing deadline is February 15. The Princeton Review suggests that all financial aid forms be submitted as soon as possible after January 1. *Need-based scholarships/grants offered:* Pell, SEOG, state scholarships/grants, private scholarships, the school's own gift aid. *Loan aid offered:* Direct Subsidized Stafford, Direct Unsubsidized Stafford, FFEL PLUS, Federal Perkins, college/university loans from institutional funds. Federal Work-Study Program available. Institutional employment available. Applicants will be notified of awards on or about April 1. Off-campus job opportunities are excellent.

FROM THE ADMISSIONS OFFICE

"The Hopkins tradition of preeminent academic excellence naturally attracts the very best students in the nation and from around the world. The Admissions Committee carefully examines each application for evidence of compelling intellectual interest and academic performance as well as strong personal recommendations and meaningful extracurricular contributions. Every applicant who matriculates to Johns Hopkins University was found qualified by the Admissions Committee through a 'whole person' assessment, and every applicant accepted for admission is fully expected to graduate. The Admissions Committee determines whom they believe will take full advantage of the exceptional opportunities offered at Hopkins, contribute the most to the educational process of the institution, and be the most successful in using what they have learned and experienced for the benefit of society."

For even more information on this school, turn to page 243 of the "Stats" section.

Juniata College

ENROLLMENT OFFICE, 1700 MOORE ST., HUNTINGDON, PA 16652 • ADMISSIONS: 877-586-4282
FAX: 814-641-3100 • FINANCIAL AID: 814-641-3142 • E-MAIL: ADMISSION@JUNIATA.EDU
WEBSITE: WWW.JUNIATA.EDU

Ratings

Quality of Life: 79   **Academic:** 81   **Admissions:** 76   **Financial Aid:** 83

Academics

Located in rural Pennsylvania, Juniata College wouldn't seem to be the place to offer stellar science and competitive pre-med programs. But the rural looks can be deceiving. "If you want to be a doctor, Juniata can show you how," states one student. Indeed,

> **SURVEY SAYS . . .**
> *Classes are small, Great computer facilities*
> *Dorms are like palaces, Very little drug use*
> *Campus easy to get around, Registration is a pain*
> *Students don't get along with local community*

Juniata prides itself on a relatively intense academic program, pre-med or not. One student warns, "Don't come here if you want to be lazy and do nothing but party. . . . The professors will challenge you until you think you can't take it anymore." The intensity may seem overwhelming, especially for incoming freshmen, but students at JC are pleased with the level of education and the caliber of their professors, who are "all very involved in their students' education." Each student at Juniata is assigned two advisors who "truly care about you and how you are doing. They help the students in any way that they can." One pleased student marvels that she's "developed excellent relationships with professors who respect, challenge, and inspire me, inside and outside of the formal classroom."

Life

Although students at Juniata readily admit that the small town of Huntingdon isn't the entertainment capital of the world, there's enough to do on campus that boredom is rarely an issue. JAB, "the activities board at Juniata, does a good job [in] bringing acts [like] comedians and other performers" to campus. With more than 90 organizations to choose from, "a lot of students here are in clubs involving their academic or career interests." Students can join socially active groups like "Model U.N., Peace and Conflict, or Habitat for Humanity," or simply partake in the hiking and hanging that goes on at nearby Raystown Lake. One student loves JC "traditions [like] Lobsterfest (where everyone gets together and eats lobster and hangs out on the lawn), Mountain Day (a surprise cancellation of classes for a day [when] everyone goes and has a picnic instead), Madrigal Dinner, All Class Night, Storming of the Arch, and Pig Roast." And while partying is another JC tradition, there is a strong contingent of students that doesn't feel the need to imbibe every weekend, but "the students that are not into nightlife are not frowned upon by the other students." For those who need a little break from the small town life of Huntingdon, or from the campus itself, students hop in a car and head to State College and Altoona.

Student Body

"Amicable but homogenous" is one student's description of the undergrads at Juniata, with many other students describing themselves as "white and middle class." But what JC might be lacking in diversity, it more than makes up for in an abundance of good cheer: "Everyone here is overly nice. Many feel that "students are anxious to meet new people and make as many friends as they can in the short time they're all here." Such a small campus also allows "everyone to know everyone else," which could be the reason why "cliques are not very dominant on this campus." Juniata is also host to many foreign exchange students who "are fun to hang out with and make daily life interesting." Some grumble that their peers "are narrow minded when it comes to sexual orientation." For the most part, though, "everyone is compatible, and if they're not, the campus isn't SO small that you can't avoid people."

ADMISSIONS

Very important factors considered by the admissions committee include: character/personal qualities, essays, extracurricular activities, recommendations, secondary school record, standardized test scores. *Important factors considered include:* alumni/ae relation, interview, talent/ability, volunteer work, minority status. *Other factors considered include:* class rank, work experience. SAT I or ACT required. TOEFL required of all international applicants. High school diploma or GED is required. *High school units required/recommended:* 16 total required; 4 English required, 3 math required, 3 science required, 2 foreign language required, 1 social studies required, 3 history required.

The Inside Word

Like at many traditional liberal arts schools, the admissions process at Juniata is a personal one. The school wants students who will decide to attend Juniata, and stay for the next fours years. Among Juniata's bragging rights are that a staggering 40 percent of students graduate with a degree in science, 60 percent of undergrads design their own major, and 70 percent participate in internships.

FINANCIAL AID

Students should submit: FAFSA. The Princeton Review suggests that all financial aid forms be submitted as soon as possible after January 1. *Need-based scholarships/grants offered:* Pell, SEOG, state scholarships/grants, private scholarships, the school's own gift aid. *Loan aid offered:* FFEL Subsidized Stafford, FFEL Unsubsidized Stafford, FFEL PLUS, Federal Perkins. Federal Work-Study Program available. Institutional employment available. Applicants will be notified of awards on a rolling basis beginning on or about December 1. Off-campus job opportunities are fair.

FROM THE ADMISSIONS OFFICE

"This is a great time to be a part of the Juniata community. There is intellectual engagement and opportunity at every turn. Our museum studies program is one of only 12 in the country. Our new information technology program is producing 'fearless learners' with the support of a $4 million endowment. The just-completed von Liebig Center for Science provides increased opportunities for student/faculty research surpassing those available even at large universities. The college's expanded Environmental Studies Field Station on nearby Raystown Lake provides 365 acres for exclusive college use and a full 29,000 acres for additional study. The future Halbritter Center will be an exceptional facility to house the performing arts. More importantly, we believe the ultimate measure of quality is found in the success of our graduates. Just a few include Dr. William Phillips '70, Nobel Prize winner in Physics; Rebecca McClaine '00, USA Today Academic All American; Robert Rose '61, Nevada supreme court justice; Casey Craig '97, director of special events, Boston Celtics; Dr. Robert Biter '92, playwright and AMA Outstanding Young Medical Professional Award recipient; Tonya Grimes '90, Sallie Mae Award (100 best teachers nationally); William Boswell '83, chief technology officer, E-Markets Inc.; Dr. James Madara '71, dean, University of Chicago Medical School; Peter Marzio '65, executive director, Houston Museum of Fine Arts; Timothy Statton '72, president, Bechtel Energy; Bruce Davis '65, executive director, Academy Motion Picture Arts and Sciences; Mary White '73, CEO, Swedish Medical Center; and Sammy Buo '73, deputy director, African Division, United Nations. At Juniata you will work harder and learn more than you ever have in your life, and we will provide the supportive faculty and staff to be certain that you have every opportunity to succeed."

For even more information on this school, turn to page 244 of the "Stats" section.

KUTZTOWN UNIVERSITY OF PENNSYLVANIA

ADMISSIONS OFFICE, 15200 KUTZTOWN ROAD, KUTZTOWN, PA 19530-0730 • ADMISSIONS: 610-683-4060
FAX: 610-683-1375 • E-MAIL: ADMISSION@KUTZTOWN.EDU • WEBSITE: WWW.KUTZTOWN.EDU

Ratings
Quality of Life: 76   **Academic:** 66   **Admissions:** 63   **Financial Aid:** 71

Academics

The undergraduate offerings at Kutztown University of Pennsylvania stem from four sources: the colleges of Visual and Performing Arts, Business, Education, and Liberal Arts and Sciences. "There are so many different academic programs," raves

> **SURVEY SAYS . . .**
> *Great library, Classes are small*
> *Campus is beautiful, Students are happy*
> *Athletic facilities need improving*
> *Students get along with local community*
> *Ethnic diversity lacking on campus*

an undergrad. The sciences here have earned particular praise from students; since Kutztown is "small" as far as universities go, students have "the opportunity to do many types of experiments on equipment that is used only for demonstration at larger schools." Lab or lecture, "classes are relatively small" at Kutztown—a trait that grants professors the room to be "concerned about their students" without detracting from the classroom progress. Overall, Kutztown's undergrads have been pleased to discover that the faculty members here, in the words of one student, "have been a great help in getting me organized and prepared for the future." But all of its virtues aside, Kutztown is still a state institution, mired in red tape and sometimes hampered by its need to locate more funds. "This school is a business first, then an institution of higher learning," moans a student, but administrative shortcomings are usually shrugged off. The biggest complaint from Kutztown students is the fact that the university does not receive the credit it deserves. "Kutztown is highly unknown," gripes a student. "It's a good school with great profs. People need to give it a chance."

Life

Wedged in the pastoralia of central Pennsylvania, about twenty miles from Reading and Allentown, the city of Kutztown is a rural, Pennsylvania Dutch community of about 4,500. Not sure what the Pennsylvania Dutch culture is all about? Don't worry. The Pennsylvania German Cultural Heritage Center on Kutztown U's campus can give you an in-depth education in the region's cultural color. Activities offered by the Association of Campus Events include occasions like "Casino Night, dance parties, and formals," and "they always have movies on Friday nights in the Multi-Cultural Center." To let loose, students also attend "many parties both on campus and off" on weekends, as well as Wednesdays and Thursdays. But for the non-partiers here, there's little trouble keeping the calendar full. One student gives us a sketch of a typical day at KU: "I wake up at about 7 and get showered and work in the history department, and then I go to class, then lunch, then two more classes, and then I go back to my room and study or hang out. We play ping pong a lot in the basement of our hall. We also like to just watch movies and talk. There really isn't much to do off campus [except] walk down Main Street and watch all these drunk people all over the place." Still, this student adds confidently, "We find things to do." Getaways are doable by car to Philadelphia, under an hour and a half from campus; or New York City, less than two hours away.

Student Body

Kutztown University is the temporary home of a "friendly and warm" student body. "Students are . . . easy to get along with." While some students here boast that they are able to "make new friends from all different backgrounds," others warn diversity is lacking at Kutztown. "Someone along the line told me that college would be great because of how open-minded people are," an art student says, adding, "This college has mostly middle- to upper-middle-class people—and for the most part, they are very narrow-minded and conservative." Though it may be true that students here cling to more conservative principles than students at other universities, there are rarely disturbances within this student body between the conservative majority and the visible liberal minority.

ADMISSIONS

Very important factors considered by the admissions committee include: class rank, secondary school record, and standardized test scores. *Other factors considered include:* character/personal qualities, essays, extracurricular activities, geographical residence, interview, minority status, recommendations, state residency, talent/ability, volunteer work, and work experience. SAT I or ACT required, SAT I preferred. TOEFL required of all international applicants. High school diploma or GED is required. *High school units required/recommended:* 16 total recommended; 4 English recommended, 3 math recommended, 3 science recommended, 2 foreign language recommended, 4 social studies recommended.

The Inside Word

Kutztown makes the vast majority of its admissions decisions based solely on GPA and standardized test scores. Candidates who think they may be on the cusp can, and should, include a personal essay, a list of extracurricular activities, and letters of recommendation with their applications.

FINANCIAL AID

Students should submit: FAFSA. Deadline for regular filing is February 15. The Princeton Review suggests that all financial aid forms be submitted as soon as possible after January 1. *Need-based scholarships/grants offered:* Pell, SEOG, state scholarships/grants, and the school's own gift aid. *Loan aid offered:* FFEL Subsidized Stafford, FFEL Unsubsidized Stafford, FFEL PLUS, and Federal Perkins. Federal Work-Study Program available. Institutional employment available. Applicants will be notified of awards on a rolling basis beginning on or about March 30. Off-campus job opportunities are excellent.

FROM THE ADMISSIONS OFFICE

"In a recent independent survey, 93 percent of students and recent alumni rated their education at Kutztown University as excellent or good in regard to their overall college experience, the quality of instruction they received, and the quality of the faculty. Kutztown offers excellent academic programs through its undergraduate Colleges of Liberal Arts and Sciences, Visual and Performing Arts, Business, and Education and through its graduate studies program. A wide range of student support services complements the high-quality classroom instruction.

"In addition, Kutztown students have the advantage of a well-rounded program of athletic, cultural, and social events. At Kutztown, there are clubs, organizations, and activities to satisfy nearly every taste. Currently, 8,524 full-time and part-time students are enrolled at the university. About half of the full-time undergraduates live in residence halls; the rest live at home or in apartments in nearby communities.

"Kutztown University's attractive 325-acre campus includes a mix of old and new buildings, including stately Old Main, the historic building known to generations of Kutztown's students; Golden Bear Village West, a modern townhouse complex; and the Student Union Building. A new state-of-the-art science facility is set to open in fall 2003.

"The university's graduate program awards the Master of Science, Master of Art, Master of Education, Master of Business Administration, Master of Library Science, Master of Public Administration, and Master of Social Work degrees."

For even more information on this school, turn to page 245 of the "Stats" section.

LAFAYETTE COLLEGE

118 MARKLE HALL, EASTON, PA 18042 • ADMISSIONS: 610-330-5100 • FAX: 610-330-5355
FINANCIAL AID: 610-330-5055 • E-MAIL: ADMISSIONS@LAFAYETTE.EDU • WEBSITE: WWW.LAFAYETTE.EDU

Ratings
Quality of Life: 80   Academic: 85   Admissions: 86   Financial Aid: 82

Academics

With "an engineering program that is top notch for a small liberal arts school," "opportunities for research" usually available only at larger schools, and "great accessibility to professors," Lafayette College of Pennsylvania presents a superlative academic package to

> **SURVEY SAYS . . .**
> *Frats and sororities dominate social scene*
> *Diversity lacking on campus*
> *Campus easy to get around, Classes are small*
> *Students don't like Easton, PA*
> *Theater is unpopular, Low cost of living*

those interested in engineering, business, pre-law, and pre-medical studies. Students warn that "Lafayette's academic standards are very high. The courses are extremely challenging but rewarding as well. The topics are covered in detail, and the examinations require you to know the material in detail and be able to apply what you have learned, not just memorize it." The intimate atmosphere helps ease the burden of Lafayette's workload; as one student puts it, "The size is a big strength. I was amazed at the availability and enthusiasm of my professors and have had a fulfilling and challenging academic life. I wish I could afford to stay longer just so I could take all the classes that I am interested in taking. The selection is excellent." Professors here receive high marks; students report that profs "are always willing to spend extra time with you, helping you sift through schedule changes around registration time, attempting to understand what you want from Lafayette, and helping with any problems you may have with homework, tests, etc." The administration receives mixed reviews, with students complaining about the school's drinking policies and also about various administrative chores.

Life

Undergrads report that "Lafayette's professors are demanding, so for the most part students study on weekdays and party during the weekend. Aside from academics, we spend time participating in sports, playing videogames, watching movies, and of course, partying." Students enjoy partying Wednesday through Saturday nights at the "huge" frats ("everyone goes to them and so many people join them") as well as at local bars on and around College Hill. Students report that "the administration is cracking down on the Greek system in general, and the alcohol policy has definitely affected the social life," so things may be changing here. Then again, maybe not; students here have complained of administration crackdowns in every edition of this guidebook, yet just as consistently report that drinking is big on campus. Students tell us that "LAF (Lafayette Activities Forum) brings a lot of great programs to campus," that "there are performances in the Williams Center quite frequently," and that "many students are involved in intramural sports, the choir has doubled in size in one year, and attendance at varsity sports events is a decent amount." In other words, the "absolutely beautiful" campus is a happening place. Not so for hometown Easton, which is "awful except the Crayola Factory, which is a neat place to visit." Students like to escape Easton and head to New York City, Philadelphia, or the New Jersey shore, all within reasonable driving distance.

Student Body

Students admit that "Lafayette has the reputation of being Prep School Part II with the high percentage of upper-middle-class white students, and there are a lot of people who fit in this stereotype. If you are seeking diversity in the traditional sense of the word then Lafayette will probably disappoint you." Observes one undergrad, "We all wear our newest Abercrombie outfits and drive around in our SUVs and BMWs. I know Lafayette College is in Easton, Pennsylvania, but the area code should be 90210." Diversity has recently received a boost: "This year there were many more international students, which a lot of the student population was happy to see," writes one undergrad. Students "have great school spirit (especially against Lehigh) and are genuinely nice to one another," but also form "a lot of different cliques . . . that don't mix as much as you'd like." They are a conservative lot who are "very homophobic," according to some.

ADMISSIONS

Very important factors considered by the admissions committee include: secondary school record. *Important factors considered include:* alumni/ae relation, character/personal qualities, class rank, essays, extracurricular activities, minority status, recommendations, standardized test scores, talent/ability, volunteer work. *Other factors considered include:* geographical residence, interview, work experience. SAT I or ACT required; SAT II recommended. TOEFL required of all international applicants. *High school units required/recommended:* 16 total recommended; 4 English recommended, 3 math recommended, 2 science recommended, 2 science lab recommended, 2 foreign language recommended, 5 elective recommended.

The Inside Word

Applications are reviewed three to five times and evaluated by as many as nine different committee members. In all cases, students who continually seek challenges and are willing to take risks academically win out over those who play it safe in order to maintain a high GPA.

FINANCIAL AID

Students should submit: FAFSA, CSS/Financial Aid PROFILE, noncustodial (divorced/separated) parent's statement, business/farm supplement. Regular filing deadline is February 1. The Princeton Review suggests that all financial aid forms be submitted as soon as possible after January 1. *Need-based scholarships/grants offered:* Pell, SEOG, state scholarships/grants, private scholarships. *Loan aid offered:* FFEL Subsidized Stafford, FFEL Unsubsidized Stafford, FFEL PLUS, Federal Perkins, state loans, college/university loans from institutional funds, HELP loans to parents. Federal Work-Study Program available. Institutional employment available. Applicants will be notified of awards on or about April 1. Off-campus job opportunities are good.

FROM THE ADMISSIONS OFFICE

"We choose students individually, one by one, and we hope that the ones we choose will approach their education the same way, as a highly individual enterprise. Our first-year seminars have enrollments limited to 15 or 16 students each in order to introduce the concept of learning not as passive receipt of information but as an active, participatory process. Our low average class size and 11:1 student/teacher ratio reflect that same philosophy. We also devote substantial resources to our Marquis Scholars Program, to one-on-one faculty-student mentoring relationships, and to other programs in engineering within a liberal arts context, giving Lafayette its distinctive character, articulated in our second-year seminars exploring values in science and technology. Lafayette provides an environment in which its students can discover their own personal capacity for learning, personal growth, and leadership."

For even more information on this school, turn to page 245 of the "Stats" section.

LEBANON VALLEY COLLEGE

101 NORTH COLLEGE AVENUE, ANNVILLE, PA 17003-6100 • ADMISSIONS: 717-867-6181
FAX: 717-867-6026 • E-MAIL: ADMISSION@LVC.EDU • WEBSITE: WWW.LVC.EDU

Ratings
Quality of Life: 77   Academic: 77   Admissions: 75   Financial Aid: 74

Academics

"The greatest strengths of LVC are: 1) the strong relationship between students and faculty; 2) the diverse courses that can be taken; 3) the excellent laboratory facilities." This list, compiled by a science student, highlights what many students tell us—that Lebanon Valley College is a small school that also boasts the virtues of a large school. For example, says one student, "I can pursue my own academic interests" but under the close guidance "of a gifted faculty." With an average class size of 20, students study under professors who are always available "to lend an ear or help out if needed." But some students wish their professors would up the ante, bringing greater challenges and expectations into the classrooms. A satisfied philosophy major concedes, "From talking to other students, it seems that not all departments are like my major, and in some, the faculty leaves much to be desired." Of the 33 majors here, those that garner the most praise from students are music, business, teacher education, psychology, and the sciences."

> **SURVEY SAYS . . .**
> *Classes are small, Students are happy*
> *Students are religious, Profs teach upper levels*
> *Diversity lacking on campus*

Life

Student life at Lebanon Valley College differs depending on your vantage point, the two main perspectives coming from commuters and residents. These days, commuters hang tough in "the local coffeehouse or the local bowling alley." Residents, on the other hand, find many more options at their fingertips. "There are a lot of organizations to become involved with and plenty of opportunities on campus for employment." The few dozen clubs on campus include the rarely mentioned Juggling Club and a group called Role Players and Wargamers. The college itself "plans activities, but they aren't widely attended," except for those that are musical in nature; regionally, "the school is well known for music," explains a student. When students with jobs manage to save some cash, they can wander over to Hershey, just 10 minutes away, where there's everything from roller coasters to strips of outlet stores—not to mention the omnipresent wafts of fresh chocolate. For something a little more urban, Harrisburg is only half an hour up the road. And for the true roadtrippers, Baltimore and Philadelphia can be reached in two hours, Washington, D.C., and New York City in three.

Student Body

At LVC, the Great Divide, so to speak, is the invisible line that separates the campus' commuters from its residents. "Many of the resident students look down upon me and my fellow commuters," says an LVC undergrad. Another commuter admits that "there are some problems with resident students looking down on commuting students," but adds that "other than that, most people on campus get along rather well. Most people are friendly." Friendly or not, some young scholars would appreciate an increased number of classmates who are more "interested in academia" than they are in "partying." Others feel that diversity could be improved, mentioning a "generally white, conservative" population. Despite any complaints rendered, an undergrad assures, "LVC, overall, feels like a happy little community."

ADMISSIONS

Very important factors considered by the admissions committee include: class rank and secondary school record. *Important factors considered include:* character/personal qualities, extracurricular activities, interview, standardized test scores, and talent/ability. *Other factors considered include:* alumni/ae relation, essays, geographical residence, minority status, recommendations, state residency, volunteer work, and work experience. SAT I or ACT required. TOEFL required of all international applicants. High school diploma or GED is required. *High school units required/recommended:* 16 total required; 4 English required, 2 math required, 3 math recommended, 1 science required, 3 science recommended, 2 science lab recommended, 2 foreign language required, 3 foreign language recommended, 1 social studies required.

The Inside Word

Lebanon Valley looks primarily at high school grades and curriculum. If you're a B student in the top half of your class, the school's website reports, you have a very good chance of gaining admittance. Students in the top 30 percent of their graduating class are eligible for generous scholarships.

FINANCIAL AID

Students should submit: FAFSA and institution's own financial aid form. The Princeton Review suggests that all financial aid forms be submitted as soon as possible after January 1. *Need-based scholarships/grants offered:* Pell, SEOG, state scholarships/grants, private scholarships, and the school's own gift aid. *Loan aid offered:* FFEL Subsidized Stafford, FFEL Unsubsidized Stafford, FFEL PLUS, and Federal Perkins. Federal Work-Study Program available. Institutional employment available. Applicants will be notified of awards on a rolling basis beginning on or about March 1. Off-campus job opportunities are good.

FROM THE ADMISSIONS OFFICE

"Lebanon Valley College encourages applications from students who have taken a challenging college-prep program in high school and performed well. Typical successful applicants have had 3 years of science, 3 of math, and 2 of a foreign language, in addition to English and social studies. While high school grading systems vary widely, we look for applicants to have at least a B average and rank in the top half of their class. Our outstanding, nationally recognized scholarship program complements this process. The College offers scholarships worth up to 50 percent of the value of tuition to students accepted for admission who ranked in the top 30 percent of their high school class. The scholarships are based on the class rank decile, with awards of one-quarter tuition going to those in the third decile, one-third to those in the second decile, and one-half to those in the top 10 percent of their class. Standardized test scores give students from high schools that do not provide a class rank access to the scholarships; during the interview process, the college provides an opportunity for students with a minimum combined SAT score of 1100 to apply for these scholarships. Admissions decisions for each class are made on a rolling basis beginning in mid-October. Students offered admission are also informed of their scholarship award based on class rank information received on the high school transcript. Students whose class rank improves during their senior year will be considered for an increased award."

For even more information on this school, turn to page 246 of the "Stats" section.

LEHIGH UNIVERSITY

27 MEMORIAL DRIVE WEST, BETHLEHEM, PA 18015 • ADMISSIONS: 610-758-3100 • FAX: 610-758-4361
FINANCIAL AID: 610-758-3181 • E-MAIL: ADMISSIONS@LEHIGH.EDU • WEBSITE: WWW.LEHIGH.EDU

Ratings
Quality of Life: 85   **Academic:** 87   **Admissions:** 88   **Financial Aid:** 85

Academics

Lehigh is well known for its P.C. Rossin College of Engineering and Applied Science and College of Business and Economics. But with about 45 percent of its undergrads enrolled in the College of Arts and Sciences, the university has made recent attempts to bolster the quality of its liberal arts program. Regardless of what col-

> **SURVEY SAYS . . .**
> *Beautiful campus, Great library*
> *Great computer facilities*
> *Athletic facilities are great*
> *Frats and sororities dominate social scene*
> *Students don't like Bethlehem, PA*
> *Political activism is (almost) nonexistent*
> *Lousy off-campus food*

lege the students settle into, most of them say that they've found "wonderful professors" who teach "very challenging" classes. Students are less enthusiastic about the "pretty bad" TAs and the regularity of visiting professors. As students progress, they often find that their classes become smaller. And "smaller classes are better," states an upperclassman. Opinions about the administration vary from "annoying in the way they get things done" to "superb." Regardless of dissent as to how the administration responds to them, students agree that they are "free to have an open and honest opinion" that'll be heard—in class or elsewhere.

Life

A few students have told us that Lehigh no longer deserves its reputation as a party school, but this is a minority opinion. "There's no denying it," report most students, "drinking is huge." "Work Hard, Drink Harder," is a common refrain heard from Lehigh undergrads. While "a decent amount of off-campus parties" provide bibulous opportunities, most of the guzzling takes place on "The Hill," where the university's 23 fraternity houses lie. "Hotels" are favorite frat events, where a "different mixed drink [waits] in every room of a frat." These sorts of bacchanalian fêtes are less common today than they were a few years ago, however, thanks largely to campus initiatives for a healthier and safer living and learning environment. "It's not all drinking and smoking" at Lehigh. There's often a good turnout "at on-campus events like theatre shows, magicians, psychics, comedians, and sports events." A student group called University Productions works hard to make sure that the entertainment options keep coming. As for the surrounding town of Bethlehem, students complain about its "dull nature" and the fact that it's "not a very inviting town for the students." If upperclassmen have cars (freshmen aren't allowed to have them), they'll often take day trips to Philadelphia or New York, each about an hour away.

Student Body

Clinging to the side of Bethlehem, Pennsylvania's "Old South Mountain," Lehigh's campus is an ivy-covered spread of "pretty buildings and steps." "Getting around is a chore—unless you are a mountain goat," jokes one student. Perhaps as a result of the hardy physiques students develop walking to and from class, "almost everyone participates in sports of some kind." Students here have other things in common, as well. Most of them "are from New York, New Jersey, or Pennsylvania," and many "are white, upper-middle class." While students will admit the campus' homogeneity, they tell us that it remains an open and tolerant community. "I am Asian and have found no problems as far as discrimination goes," assures a satisfied student. Overall, "friendliness" is the glue that holds together this undergraduate body of 4,700 students. Another thing that envelops undergrads is Greek life. About 37 percent of Lehigh students are members of fraternities or sororities.

ADMISSIONS

Very important factors considered by the admissions committee include: secondary school record. *Important factors considered include:* character/personal qualities, essays, extracurricular activities, recommendations, standardized test scores, talent/ability, volunteer work. *Other factors considered include:* alumni/ae relation, class rank, geographical residence, minority status, state residency, work experience. SAT I or ACT required. TOEFL required of all international applicants. High school diploma or GED is required. *High school units required/recommended:* 16 total required; 4 English required, 3 math required, 2 science required, 2 foreign language required, 2 social studies required, 3 elective required.

The Inside Word

Lots of work at bolstering Lehigh's public recognition for overall academic quality has paid off—liberal arts candidates will now find the admissions process to be highly selective. Students without solidly impressive academic credentials will have a rough time getting in regardless of their choice of programs. So will unenthusiastic but academically strong candidates who have clearly chosen Lehigh as a safety.

FINANCIAL AID

Students should submit: FAFSA, CSS/Financial Aid PROFILE, noncustodial (divorced/separated) parent's statement, business/farm supplement. The Princeton Review suggests that all financial aid forms be submitted as soon as possible after January 1. *Need-based scholarships/grants offered:* Pell, SEOG, state scholarships/grants, private scholarships, the school's own gift aid. *Loan aid offered:* FFEL Subsidized Stafford, FFEL Unsubsidized Stafford, FFEL PLUS, Federal Perkins, college/university loans from institutional funds. Federal Work-Study Program available. Institutional employment available. Applicants will be notified of awards on or about March 30. Off-campus job opportunities are fair. Merit scholarships offered.

FROM THE ADMISSIONS OFFICE

"Lehigh University is located 50 miles north of Philadelphia and 90 miles southwest of New York City in Bethlehem, Pennsylvania, where a cultural renaissance has taken place with the opening of more than a dozen ethnic restaurants, the addition of several boutiques and galleries, and Lehigh's new Campus Square residential/retail complex.

"Lehigh combines learning opportunities of a large research university with the personal attention of a small, private college, by offering an education that integrates courses from four colleges and dozens of fields of study. Students customize their experience to their interests by tailoring majors and academic programs from more than 2,000 courses, changing majors, carrying a double major, or taking courses outside their college or major field of study. Lehigh offers unique learning opportunities through interdisciplinary programs such as music and engineering and computer science and business (www.lehigh.edu/specialprograms). The arts are essential to the learning experience and are integrated throughout the curriculum. Students develop their imagination and creativity while acquiring skills that will complement their professional development.

"Students have access to world-class faculty who offer their time and personal attention to help students learn and succeed. Students gain hands-on, real-world experience and take part in activities that build confidence and help them develop as leaders.

"Lehigh's vibrant campus life offers many social and extracurricular activities. Choose from 130 clubs and social organizations or 24 intercollegiate sports teams or become one of the 3,500 students (75 percent) who participate in intramural and club programs."

For even more information on this school, turn to page 247 of the "Stats" section.

LONGWOOD UNIVERSITY

ADMISSIONS OFFICE, 201 HIGH STREET, FARMVILLE, VA 23909 • ADMISSIONS: 434-395-2060
FAX: 434-395-2332 • E-MAIL: ADMIT@LONGWOOD.EDU • WEBSITE: WWW.LONGWOOD.EDU

Ratings
Quality of Life: 73   **Academic:** 67   **Admissions:** 64   **Financial Aid:** 73

Academics

Located in the college town of Farmville, Virginia, Longwood University continues to implement new features to accommodate an ever-growing student body. The fact that Longwood "is attempting

> **SURVEY SAYS . . .**
> *Lots of classroom discussion*
> *Classes are small, Profs teach upper levels*
> *Instructors are good teachers*

to expand rapidly" alarms some students; one undergrad suggests that the faculty "reevaluate the original intentions and advantages that a small liberal arts college in a rural town in the middle of nowhere is supposed to provide to the students," then concedes, "Expansion is good, I guess. Perhaps, my degree will be worth more as Longwood's size and name increase." At the present, many students choose Longwood for its "really good education program," but under-grads assert that every department "has many great professors who are wonderful to work with." One student says Longwood is known as a "'Teacher College' [but] they have not let other programs go. They have excellent psychology, anthropology, business, and English departments, to name a few." Professors are reputedly "all very approachable and willing to work with you if you have any problems." "Generally the professors here love what they do," writes a student. "Why else would they live in Farmville?" As a result of individual attention from competent faculty, "Longwood students graduate with the academic knowledge and life skills to succeed in the real world." One student swears, "You WILL get a job."

Life

Though you might expect life to be boring in a town where "fun is going to Wal-Mart at 2 A.M.," students say college in Farmville is nothing short of "the best years of your life." Students can't agree whether the parties begin on Wednesday or Thursday, but some confess that "usually alcohol and drugs are the cornerstone for fun." Jokes one, "What else is there to do in a place called Farmville?" One student counters, "there is always something to do here even though it's in Farmville," and is backed up by another who claims the centrality of spending "time with friends, hanging out, watching movies, or listening to music." "Greek life is huge" on campus, and "generally the frats and sororities are cool," giving the school a nice "family atmosphere." However, even outside of the fraternities and sororities, Longwood life is boisterous. Students enthuse, "There is always something going on." Also, "There are also tons of activities on campus for nondrinkers," assures an undergrad. Nearby Hampden-Sydney College also provides entertainment for fun-seekers beyond on-campus options.

Student Body

At Longwood University, "the breakdown of archetypes is about the same as everywhere— sorority chicks, frat boys, geeks, weirdoes . . . but unlike high school, the lines are easier to cross." Indeed, students say that their classmates are generally "extremely nice and kind-hearted" and describe the campus as "a universal party school with love for all." Many point out, though, that "the student body is not very diverse although great effort has been made by the administration to correct this." Others claim that many people "are from small towns and have never experienced other minorities and cultures." Consequently, "a lot of the organizations are split along racial lines and there are not a lot of interracial friendship[s] amongst students on campus." In response to these problems, one student suggests that the school "put sexual orientation in the nondiscrimination clause in writing," while another thinks "activities should be planned so that various ethnicities can associate."

ADMISSIONS

Very important factors considered by the admissions committee include: secondary school record and standardized test scores. *Important factors considered include:* personal statements. *Other factors considered include:* alumni/ae relation, character/personal qualities, class rank, extracurricular activities, geographical residence, minority status, recommendations, talent/ability, volunteer work, and work experience. SAT I or ACT required, SAT I preferred. High school diploma or GED is required. *High school units required/recommended:* 18 total required; 23 total recommended; 4 English required, 3 math required, 4 math recommended, 3 science required, 4 science recommended, 2 science lab required, 3 or more foreign language recommended, 1 social studies recommended, 3 history required, 3 elective required, 4 elective recommended.

The Inside Word

The word is out on Longwood College, and as a result, admissions here are growing more competitive. Even with its largest incoming freshman class ever, Longwood admitted 10 percent fewer applicants for 2002–2003 than for the previous academic year.

FINANCIAL AID

Students should submit: FAFSA. The Princeton Review suggests that all financial aid forms be submitted as soon as possible after January 1. *Need-based scholarships/grants offered:* Pell, SEOG, state scholarships/grants, private scholarships, and the school's own gift aid. *Loan aid offered:* FFEL Subsidized Stafford, FFEL Unsubsidized Stafford, FFEL PLUS, Federal Perkins, state loans, and university loans from institutional funds. Federal Work-Study Program available. Institutional employment available. Applicants will be notified of awards on or about April 15. Off-campus job opportunities are fair.

FROM THE ADMISSIONS OFFICE

"Longwood University, founded in 1839, offers the opportunities, diversity, and affordability of a public university along with the warmth, spirit, and personal attention of a smaller college. To accommodate our planned growth to 5,000 students by 2007, we are building several academic facilities and enclosing the campus to create a park-like setting.

"Located in recreation-rich central Virginia, Farmville is a dynamic two-college town with a hometown appeal. Attending a play, cheering the Lancers to victory, meeting friends downtown, or listening to bands are typical choices students make every weekend. Additional activities, such as tubing down the James, sightseeing throughout historic Virginia, and hiking in the Blue Ridge Mountains, are available within a short driving distance.

"Students select from more than 100 majors, minors, and concentrations in our College of Arts and Sciences, our College of Business and Economics (AACSB accredited), or our College of Education and Human Services (NCATE accredited).

"Longwood is the only public institution in Virginia and one of only a few in the country to require internships or experiential learning of all graduates. Our wireless technology gives students access to the Internet and e-mail even while they study under a shade tree. But if they want to use their required laptops in the dorm, no problem—we provide a port per pillow.

"With our outstanding internship opportunities, integration of technology, study abroad programs, and accomplished faculty dedicated to teaching, it is no wonder that Longwood has the highest job placement rate among public institutions in Virginia."

For even more information on this school, turn to page 247 of the "Stats" section.

LOYOLA COLLEGE IN MARYLAND

4501 NORTH CHARLES STREET, BALTIMORE, MD 21210 • ADMISSIONS: 410-617-5012 • FAX: 410-617-2176
FINANCIAL AID: 410-617-2576 • WEBSITE: WWW.LOYOLA.EDU

Ratings
Quality of Life: 89   Academic: 84   Admissions: 83   Financial Aid: 90

Academics

"Extremely accessible teachers" who "really want to help students learn and grow into intelligent, mature, and enlightened adults" are "the strongest aspect of the academic component" at Loyola College in Maryland, a small Catholic, Jesuit school just north of downtown Baltimore. Explains one student, "The main reason I

> **SURVEY SAYS . . .**
> *Dorms are like palaces, Hard liquor is popular*
> *Lots of beer drinking*
> *Student government is popular*
> *Great off-campus food, Students are cliquish*
> *Very little drug use*
> *Student publications are ignored*
> *Musical organizations aren't popular*

chose [Loyola] was because it's a small school where professors get to know everybody by name. There aren't lectures and tutorials. There's more of a combined lecture/discussion group with no more than 25 to 30 students per class. Professors encourage classroom discussion." Psychology, communication, education, and especially business studies receive students' praise here. Students warn that academic demands—which include a rigorous core curriculum, the majority of which must be completed by the end of one's sophomore year—can be taxing. "If you are looking to coast through your classes without being challenged," writes one undergrad, "Loyola is not the place for you." Students also happily report that the variety of courses offered at Loyola is steadily increasing: "Although a great variety of new classes weren't available in the beginning," writes one senior, "the faculty is slowing expanding the course catalogue and introducing many new upcoming fields and subjects." Administrators receive low marks, with students complaining that "the red tape is ridiculous."

Life

Loyola College, according to many we surveyed, "is a bar school, no doubt about it. No sororities or fraternities, just a block full of bars dedicated to Loyola kids. You always know where you can find people if you want to go out." Notes one student, "Don't go here if you don't have or plan on getting a fake I.D. I know there are other options, but most people go to the bars" for entertainment. Warns another, "The school is very strict with on-campus drinking and even ventures its authority off campus to the local bars that most of the student body frequents." This policy irks many students who "understand that the college must enforce the drinking age; however, it must also understand that if we are prohibited from drinking on campus then we have no choice but to move off campus. What students do off campus should be their own business." Hometown Baltimore offers a lot more than bars: there's the Inner Harbor with its shops, restaurants, and a world-class aquarium; several exceptional art museums; a symphony; the opera; two major sports franchises; numerous college campuses that host parties, concerts, and the like; and much more. In addition, Washington, D.C., offering another universe of entertainment options, is less than an hour away by car or commuter train. Students report that "club and intramural sports are popular. The new fitness center is amazing and [provides] another option for something to do . . . . From the basketball courts to the field, most spaces are occupied with various sports at all times." Greyhound fans turn out in droves to support Loyola's excellent intercollegiate lacrosse and soccer teams.

Student Body

"Everyone looks exactly the same" at Loyola, complain many undergrads here. Some point out that "although there is undoubtedly a typical Loyola student (see any Abercrombie ad), individuals who don't fit this mold can find others like them. Overall, everyone is usually pretty friendly." Students hail primarily from "Long Island, New Jersey, and Maryland middle-upper-class backgrounds. We are all white, we all have money, and we all know it." Socially, "Loyola has the same cliques that your high school did, but all the groups interact on friendly terms. Walking across campus, you see a lot of smiles, and it seems as if students truly want to be here." There is a real commitment to public service at Loyola: "Community service is an integral part of my life and most students' lives."

ADMISSIONS

Very important factors considered by the admissions committee include: secondary school record. *Important factors considered include:* standardized test scores. *Other factors considered include:* alumni/ae relation, character/personal qualities, class rank, essays, extracurricular activities, minority status, recommendations, talent/ability, volunteer work, work experience. SAT I required. TOEFL required of all international applicants. High school diploma or GED is required. *High school units required/recommended:* 16 total required; 19 total recommended; 4 English required, 3 math required, 4 math recommended, 3 science required, 4 science recommended, 3 foreign language required, 4 foreign language recommended, 2 history required, 3 history recommended.

The Inside Word

Loyola is to be commended for notifying outstanding candidates of acceptance early in the applicant review cycle without demanding an early commitment in return. Traditional Early Decision plans are confusing, archaic, and unreasonable to students. A binding commitment is a huge price to pay to get a decision four months sooner. This is obviously one place that cares.

FINANCIAL AID

Students should submit: FAFSA, CSS/Financial Aid PROFILE application, noncustodial (divorced/separated) parent's statement, business/farm supplement. Regular filing deadline is February 10. The Princeton Review suggests that all financial aid forms be submitted as soon as possible after January 1. *Need-based scholarships/grants offered:* Pell, SEOG, state scholarships/grants, private scholarships, the school's own gift aid. *Loan aid offered:* Direct Subsidized Stafford, Direct Unsubsidized Stafford, FFEL PLUS, Federal Perkins, college/university loans from institutional funds. Federal Work-Study Program available. Institutional employment available. Academic scholarship recipients are notified by March 15. Applicants for need-based aid are notified of their eligibility by April 5. Off-campus job opportunities are good.

FROM THE ADMISSIONS OFFICE

"To make a wise choice about your college plans, you will need to find out more. We extend to you these invitations. Question-and-answer periods with an admissions counselor are helpful to prospective students. An appointment should be made in advance. Admissions office hours are 9 A.M. to 5 P.M., Monday through Friday. College day programs and Saturday information programs are scheduled during the academic year. These programs include a video about Loyola, a general information session, a discussion of various majors, a campus tour, and lunch. Summer information programs can help high school juniors to get a head start on investigating colleges. These programs feature an introductory presentation about the college and a campus tour."

For even more information on this school, turn to page 248 of the "Stats" section.

LYCOMING COLLEGE

700 COLLEGE PLACE, WILLIAMSPORT, PA 17701 • ADMISSIONS: 570-321-4026 • FAX: 570-321-4317
E-MAIL: ADMISSIONS@LYCOMING.EDU • WEBSITE: WWW.LYCOMING.EDU

Ratings
Quality of Life: 74   **Academic:** 77   **Admissions:** 75   **Financial Aid:** 80

Academics

One of the best things about Lycoming is the faculty, according to a seasoned junior. "We are a small enough school that professors know students and remember them from year to year." Some students even report that Lycoming is the kind of place "where teachers

> **SURVEY SAYS . . .**
> *Low cost of living*
> *Classes are small*
> *School is well run*
> *Students are religious*
> *Diversity lacking on campus*

give you their home phone numbers and want you to use it." This is the benefit of an institution, like Lycoming, that has a 13:1 student/faculty ratio. The full-time professors at Lycoming aren't simply nice, either. They're demanding. A sophomore notes, "This school makes you work hard but makes you realize that it is worth it." While the classes at Lycoming are enriching, "the amount of majors could be expanded" to give students more academic choices. And the library, which "doesn't have much," could use some attention. Overall, students here reflect positively on their liberal arts education. They even have nice things to say about the administration. According to one sophomore, "The school's response to my complaint about the bugs in my room was really good after I wrote a letter to the president."

Life

Don't be fooled into thinking that there's nothing to do at a small college in a small town in north-central Pennsylvania. "Lycoming offers many activities and Williamsport offers even more." Williamsport is a city of 35,000, home of the Little League World Series and a rich, intriguing history of American industry. While students say they enjoy heading out to restaurants, the mall, or the movie theatre, the most important social features in Williamsport are its bars. According to some, drinking occupies a central spot in the student life at Lycoming, and for some it seems that "if you don't go out to the bars, you're a nobody." Among the "many activities and organizations" on campus, Greek organizations are probably the most popular. "At Lyco, fraternity/sorority activities and large parties appear to dominate the social scene." This leads some people to utter, "Too much partying." But others assure that "if a student doesn't want to party, he may have to seek out nonparty activities, but once he finds them, he will have as active a social life as the partiers." Regardless of whether students end up at a large frat party or taking in a show at the Community Arts Center, students like to get out of their "old and crappy" dorms on the weekends.

Student Body

On this campus of about 1,500, students tend to "stay within their groups." The most problematic group of all, according to survey respondents, is the football players—unless you're a football player, of course. "I hate football players here," says a junior. "They're treated like gods." A senior says she finds athletes in general to be "arrogant and rude." Though students stick to the social groups they make in their dorms or on their sports teams, there remains an overall sense of friendliness here. "The attitude seems to be mainly, 'If you don't like someone or some group, you leave them alone and they leave you alone.' " Many students would like to see more diversity among their fellow students, which would combat the sense that "there is not enough culture on this campus." A senior describes Lycoming as "pretty much a white, upper-middle-class college." Because the campus is small and many of the students are alike, Lycoming can feel "like a big high school" at times. But opinions vary here. Students are "nice people," counters a junior. A senior adds, "We are very motivated, and many of us are leaders."

ADMISSIONS

Very important factors considered by the admissions committee include: secondary school record. *Important factors considered include:* class rank, interview, and standardized test scores. *Other factors considered include:* alumni/ae relation, character/personal qualities, essays, extracurricular activities, recommendations, talent/ability, volunteer work, and work experience. SAT I or ACT required. TOEFL required of all international applicants. High school diploma or GED is required. *High school units required/recommended:* 16 total required; 4 English required, 3 math required, 4 math recommended, 2 science required, 3 science recommended, 2 science lab required, 3 science lab recommended, 2 foreign language required, 3 foreign language recommended, 3 social studies required, 4 social studies recommended, 2 elective required.

The Inside Word

B students with above-average standardized test scores should clear all Lycoming admission hurdles without trouble. Those who don't meet these qualifications can improve their chances considerably by visiting the campus, interviewing, and expressing a strong interest in attending the college.

FINANCIAL AID

Students should submit: FAFSA and institution's own financial aid form. Regular filing deadline is May 1. The Princeton Review suggests that all financial aid forms be submitted as soon as possible after January 1. *Need-based scholarships/grants offered:* Pell, SEOG, state scholarships/grants, private scholarships, and the school's own gift aid. *Loan aid offered:* Direct Subsidized Stafford, Direct Unsubsidized Stafford, Direct PLUS, FFEL Subsidized Stafford, FFEL Unsubsidized Stafford, FFEL PLUS, Federal Perkins, and state loans. Federal Work-Study Program available. Applicants will be notified of awards on a rolling basis beginning on or about March 15. Off-campus job opportunities are good.

FROM THE ADMISSIONS OFFICE

"At a time when many colleges have tried to become all things to all people, Lycoming has chosen to remain a traditional, undergraduate, residential, liberal arts college. What makes Lycoming different is the way it chooses to deliver its curriculum—in small classes taught by highly credentialed, well-seasoned, full-time professors. 'It's how we teach, not what we teach that is special here,' says Professor Mel Zimmerman, chair of the faculty. 'It's the way we respond to questions, the comments we write on papers, and the way we interact with students outside the classroom that makes this school so appealing.' Staying true to who we are is the reason we've been in business since 1812."

For even more information on this school, turn to page 249 of the "Stats" section.

MARSHALL UNIVERSITY

One John Marshall Drive, Huntington, WV 25755 • Admissions: 304-696-3160 • Fax: 304-696-3135
E-mail: admissions@marshall.edu • Website: www.marshall.edu

Ratings
Quality of Life: 79   **Academic:** 64   **Admissions:** 60   **Financial Aid:** 76

Academics

Marshall University's campus in Huntington, West Virginia, is a patchwork of modern metallic architecture, old brick buildings, stodgy 1960s-style edifices, and faux Tudor designs, among other things. Similarly, Marshall's academics are a hodgepodge, as one

> **SURVEY SAYS . . .**
> *Everyone loves the Thundering Herd*
> *Lots of beer drinking*
> *Classes are small*
> *Athletic facilities are great*
> *Students are happy*

student puts it, of "some great teachers who have taught me a lot and . . . some bad teachers who may have not helped so much . . . .and bad teachers that have still taught me a lot." While there are plenty of profs here who "like to lecture," many others lean toward discussion, which helps give Marshall a small-school feel. On the whole, "professors and administrators are available and willing to help if needed," though a seasoned Marshall student says that the onus is on the student to arrange meetings with the instructors: "You get out of college what you put into it." If you're from West Virginia, one thing that you won't need to "put into" your education is a lot of money. Tuition and fees for in-state students land at under $3,000. Among the programs that students highlight as exemplary are journalism, business, medicine, and education. Overall, Marshall students can choose from 41 courses of study, and many of these proud students will tell you that their program of choice is among the best. A journalism student warns, "Watch out, Harvard, Marshall's coming your way!"

Life

On May 6, 1960, when John F. Kennedy was touring the nation as a presidential candidate, he stopped at Marshall College (it became a university a year later) in Huntsville, West Virginia, where he spoke from atop a car near the science building. Today, the city of Huntsville lists that event as one of the city's two most significant events in the 1960s. The other was Marshall becoming a university. As this quick portrait might suggest, "there is little to do" in the quiet town of Huntington—but students can "go to the movies, go out to eat, or go to a bar" in town if they so desire. Fortunately for these students, campus life is alive and well in the Marshall enclave. On campus, "all that is around for two to three miles is college kids," and they have "a wide selection of organizations" to keep them busy. Also, "there are usually activities on campus, sporting events, plays and theatre at the drama center, music at the jazz center, frat parties and events, and attractions at the civic center not far from campus." And "the library on campus is awesome—open 24 hours." One of this student body's great sources of pride is their nationally contending football team. "People live and breathe football here," assures one student; adds another, "In the winter basketball is popular, but not as popular as football." Football games are easy reasons for students to throw a bash—though it's not as if they really need an excuse. "There are a lot of Greek parties" and off-campus parties where you're sure to find "beer, jungle juice, and weed." If that sounds a little to indulgent for your tastes, you can always "go to the student union for some good clean fun."

Student Body

"Marshall is a small university that is made up mostly of small-town people who are all friendly and down to earth, which makes it a comfortable campus to be on." Because "most students are very social" here, they tend to get involved in a range of activities and intermingle social circles. "There isn't a whole lot of diversity" on campus, which these students readily admit. One student exaggerates, "97 percent Anglo." (In truth, Caucasians make up about 85 percent of the student body.) Increased ethnic diversity is on many students' wish list, but there is one brand of diversity at Marshall that many students aren't too keen on: range of intelligence. "The favorable tuition and fees attract many students who don't make it to the upper-level courses," sighs a student. But with "upwards of 17,000 students"—nearly 12,000 of those undergrads—there's sure to be many bright minds in the bunch.

ADMISSIONS

Very important factors considered by the admissions committee include: secondary school record and standardized test scores. SAT I or ACT required, ACT preferred. TOEFL required of all international applicants. High school diploma or GED is required. *High school units required/recommended:* 11 total required; 4 English required, 2 math required, 2 science required, 2 science lab required, 2 foreign language recommended, 3 social studies required.

The Inside Word

Marshall's admissions policies are cut-and-dried and also pretty generous: if you have at least a 2.0 GPA and a composite ACT of 19 or combined SAT I of 910, you're in. Candidates failing to meet these requirements will be admitted conditionally, space permitting.

FINANCIAL AID

Students should submit: FAFSA. No deadline for regular filing. The Princeton Review suggests that all financial aid forms be submitted as soon as possible after January 1. *Need-based scholarships/grants offered:* Pell, SEOG, state scholarships/grants, private scholarships, and the school's own gift aid. *Loan aid offered:* Direct Subsidized Stafford, Direct Unsubsidized Stafford, Direct PLUS, Federal Perkins, state loans, and college/university loans from institutional funds. Federal Work-Study Program available. Institutional employment available. Applicants will be notified of awards on a rolling basis beginning on or about May 1. Off-campus job opportunities are fair.

For even more information on this school, turn to page 249 of the "Stats" section.

MARY BALDWIN COLLEGE

PO BOX 1500, STAUNTON, VA 24402 • ADMISSIONS: 540-887-7019 • FAX: 540-886-6634
E-MAIL: ADMIT@MBC.EDU • WEBSITE: WWW.MBC.EDU

Ratings
Quality of Life: 75   Academic: 75   Admissions: 73   Financial Aid: 79

Academics

"Single sex education is truly an advantage" at Mary Baldwin College. Students at this small Virginia school are really "immersed in the teachings of women's lib" and benefit from "a wonderful support system" and true "personal attention" from

> **SURVEY SAYS . . .**
> *Students are happy*
> *Diverse students interact*
> *Students are religious*
> *Classes are small*
> *Very small frat/sorority scene*

teachers and staff. "I had lunch with the president of the college during my first semester!" a first-year student crows; another offers, "It's really easy to talk to the administration. They encourage students to talk to them actually." Students claim that administrators are on the up and up; they may "have their heads in the clouds a bit, but recently they have formed a commission that asks students how MBC is in the students' eyes." Students generally praise the academic caliber of the institution; one assures that "even though each academic department is small, the teachers are outstanding." "Like most schools, some of the professors are great and some are not so great," writes another student. "All of them, however, have excellent policies about being available for consultations with students." One student argues that certain professors are actually "not interested in teaching at a small, private, all-girls school" or are "too lenient" with students—a problem students claim originates from apathy within the student body. Reports one undergrad, "Academically, I've found that the professors are excellent teachers but that often the students are lacking in drive."

Life

Most students at MBC report that hometown Staunton is a bore, and while the campus hosts "mixers and bands," "comedy shows," and "campuswide parties like Fest o' Fools and Apple Day and Charm Jams, which bring in lots of guys from other colleges," the majority of students head off as soon as Friday rolls around. Writes one student, "We are, for the most part, a suitcase campus. Everyone goes home on the weekend or to some other college to party." "Many people enjoy hanging out at local coed colleges" and "finding different people to party with, i.e. guys." Nearby escapes include VCU, Virginia Military Institute, Virginia Tech, UVA, JMU, and Hampden-Sydney. When spending weekends on the sparsely populated campus, students "drink and party in their rooms." "Drinking is definitely a very popular thing on campus," one student confesses. "We have alcohol and drug policies, but they are extremely lenient." Another student adds that despite this propensity for leisurely alcohol consumption, "more than 90 percent of the people show up for the classes. I think students here are more focused on getting their academic degrees." During the week, "students here usually create our own fun, which can be anything from hanging out with friends in dorm rooms to going to the park to feed ducks to watching movies to going to parties."

Student Body

Students at Mary Baldwin College may get along like "one big sorority," but they admit that living on "an all-female campus creates a lot of unnecessary bickering" and "gossiping." One such bit of gossip involves "Lesbians Until Graduation ('LUGs')," students who "are just getting with other girls because it's more convenient and some think it's the 'cool' thing to do." Diversifying the student population has certainly become a priority at MBC, and "in the recent years, more racially diverse and more lesbian students seem to have been admitted." These changes have caused some growing pains in the campus community; "discrimination of homosexual students" is noted, as are students who are "hard to get along with, maybe because they have not been around different cultures before." Those who are prepared to learn from their peers might find their bliss at Mary Baldwin. "I have learned so much from the women who attend MBC," raves one student; a freshman writes, "This year has been a real eye-opener. Being at an all-women's college has made me more tolerant to gay/lesbian rights, which has been an incredible accomplishment." Another student sums it up, "In general, the school is a place to live, learn, and connect with other women there. It is only a strong, intelligent woman who can survive a women's college."

ADMISSIONS

Very important factors considered by the admissions committee include: secondary school record and standardized test scores. *Important factors considered include:* character/personal qualities, extracurricular activities, and interview. *Other factors considered include:* alumni/ae relation, class rank, essays, recommendations, talent/ability, volunteer work, and work experience. SAT I or ACT required. TOEFL required of all international applicants. High school diploma or GED is required. *High school units required/recommended:* 4 English required, 3 math required, 2 science required, 1 science lab required, 2 foreign language required, 3 foreign language recommended, 3 social studies required, 2 elective recommended.

The Inside Word

Candidates with solid high school grades and good standardized test scores should have no difficulties gaining admission to MBC. Others should stress their extracurricular commitments and, more importantly, their preference for single-sex education in general and attending MBC in particular. An interview is strongly recommended.

FINANCIAL AID

Students should submit: FAFSA and state aid form. The Princeton Review suggests that all financial aid forms be submitted as soon as possible after January 1. *Need-based scholarships/grants offered:* Pell, SEOG, state scholarships/grants, private scholarships, and the school's own gift aid. *Loan aid offered:* FFEL Subsidized Stafford, FFEL Unsubsidized Stafford, FFEL PLUS, Federal Perkins, and private alternative loans. Federal Work-Study Program available. Institutional employment available. Applicants will be notified of awards on a rolling basis beginning on or about January 1. Off-campus job opportunities are excellent.

FROM THE ADMISSIONS OFFICE

"Mary Baldwin is a private liberal arts college for women. Located in Staunton, Virginia, within the beautiful Shenandoah Valley, the college is steeped in the history that abounds throughout the area. Founded in 1842 by the Reverend Rufus W. Bailey as Augusta Female Seminary, the institution was renamed to honor Mary Julia Baldwin, pioneer educator and principal of the school from 1863–1897. Through Miss Baldwin's efforts, the seminary remained open during the Civil War when similar academies in the Valley were forced to shut their doors. Patterning her curriculum for young women after that used for young men at the nearby University of Virginia, the school's academic criteria became well known for its demanding program. In 1916 the institution was approved by the State of Virginia as a junior college, and by 1923 it had received full accreditation as a four-year institution. To this day, MBC remains committed to providing opportunities for academic excellence to young women."

For even more information on this school, turn to page 250 of the "Stats" section.

MARY WASHINGTON COLLEGE

1301 COLLEGE AVENUE, FREDERICKSBURG, VA 22401 • ADMISSIONS: 540-654-2000 • FAX: 540-654-1857
FINANCIAL AID: 800-468-5614 • E-MAIL: ADMIT@MWC.EDU • WEBSITE: WWW.MWC.EDU

Ratings
Quality of Life: 84   Academic: 80   Admissions: 91   Financial Aid: 83

Academics

If you manage to survive the oft-tedious class registration process at Mary Washington, you're in for an academic ride that'll leave you screaming, as this one senior did: "I hate every other college, but I love my college." At Mary Washington, the combination of rigorous courses and close student/faculty relationships chal-

> **SURVEY SAYS . . .**
> *Very little drug use*
> *Athletic facilities need improving*
> *Diversity lacking on campus*
> *No one cheats, Classes are small*
> *Campus is beautiful*
> *Very small frat/sorority scene*
> *Registration is a pain, Low cost of living*

lenges students without leaving them feeling as though they've been stranded at sea. While the "hard" classes are an important part of the college's academic landscape, the professors are the most outstanding feature of Mary Washington. "My professors are so rad!" exclaims one senior, mentioning that her professors have "hobbies that include skydiving and motor-cycle riding. And they know how to throw a great party, too!" Whether discussing a Keats poem in class or talking about the latest headlines at an "end-of-the-year dinner," professors at this liberal arts college seem to continually inspire their students. One freshman explains that she feels "like a person as well as student" in the faculty's eyes. And "they know their stuff," adds another. Most importantly, the professors are usually available to share the "stuff" they know. They "always make themselves available for extra help." So there is some hard work and some good help in Mary Washington's academic world. Or, as one freshman put it, "Mary Washington is a roller coaster ride of thrills and chills. I give it two thumbs up." Students are split on the administration, citing the increasing number of freshman it has admitted in recent years as the cause of a housing crunch.

Life

Not more than 50 miles south of Washington, D.C., and not more than 50 miles north of Richmond, Virginia, and not more than a few miles off of Interstate 95, you'll find the city of Fredericksburg and the "prestigious" and "beautiful campus" of Mary Washington College. Despite the campus' beauty, many students venture home or into the neighboring metro areas on the weekends. (Leaving campus is a tougher task for freshman, who "cannot have cars," which means they have to "ride public transportation to Wal-Mart or Target.") "It's a small school full of life," chirps one student who's happy to stick around on the weekends. But others complain that "life" is exactly what's lacking. "The social life is pretty weak unless you're into movies and small-party drinking," writes a senior. Without frats and sororities, students usually stumble upon parties "in people's rooms instead of houses." Another student laments, "Good parties are few and far between." OK, so Mary Washington is "NOT a party school," but that's not the end of the world. "Life here is great," declares a student. "You sometimes have to go out and look for the fun, but I have enjoyed my four years here thoroughly."

Student Body

About 30 years ago, if you took a look Mary Washington's student body, you'd notice that it was completely female. Today, that's not quite the case, with about two guys for every three girls. "A good gender ratio," comments a male student. Still, a student from New Jersey complains that Mary Washington, unlike his "ethnically diverse" hometown, seems full of "mostly white and female" students. While most students won't claim that diversity is one of the college's strong suits, few people will dispute that this is "a friendly campus." One freshman is pleased to report that "students get along, smile, and wave at each other across campus." "It's a small college so you know almost everyone," concurs another student. As in any small community, some students tend to be "cliquey"—"but there is still a lot of individuality."

ADMISSIONS

Very important factors considered by the admissions committee include: secondary school record. *Important factors considered include:* class rank, essays, standardized test scores. *Other factors considered include:* alumni/ae relation, character/personal qualities, extracurricular activities, geographical residence, minority status, recommendations, state residency, talent/ability, volunteer work, work experience. SAT I or ACT required; SAT II recommended. TOEFL required of all international applicants. High school diploma or GED is required. *High school units required/recommended:* 4 English required, 3 math required, 4 math recommended, 3 science required, 4 science recommended, 3 science lab required, 4 science lab recommended, 2 foreign language required, 4 foreign language recommended, 2 social studies required, 1 history required, 2 history recommended.

The Inside Word

It's hard to beat small, selective public colleges like Mary Washington for quality and cost, and more and more students are discovering this. The admissions process is very selective and, with the exception of preferential treatment for Virginia residents, functions in virtually the same manner as small private college admissions committees do. Students who are interested need to focus on putting their best into all aspects of the application.

FINANCIAL AID

Students should submit: FAFSA. The Princeton Review suggests that all financial aid forms be submitted as soon as possible after January 1. *Need-based scholarships/grants offered:* Pell, SEOG, state scholarships/grants, private scholarships, the school's own gift aid. *Loan aid offered:* FFEL Subsidized Stafford, FFEL Unsubsidized Stafford, FFEL PLUS, Federal Perkins. Federal Work-Study Program available. Institutional employment available. Applicants will be notified of awards on or about April 15. Off-campus job opportunities are excellent.

FROM THE ADMISSIONS OFFICE

"Among institutions of higher learning in Virginia, Mary Washington College stands alone. We have distinctive academic programs, a breathtakingly beautiful campus, a sharp and diverse student body, and a unique sense of friendship and camaraderie that make MWC very special. In fact, we have one of the best combinations of strong academics, personal attention, low cost, and impressive graduate school and job placement of any school in the country. Our students come from all over the country and the world, and are instructed by a faculty that considers teaching its primary objective—research and publishing come second. Committed to providing a well-rounded liberal arts and sciences education, MWC offers its students the opportunity to pursue individual or collaborative research projects. Supportive faculty and more than $60,000 in student research funds annually make ours one of the most ambitious undergraduate research programs in the country. Mary Washington College recently broke ground on a new student fitness center, and a new apartment-style housing community, which will both open in fall 2003."

For even more information on this school, turn to page 251 of the "Stats" section.

MERCYHURST COLLEGE

ADMISSIONS, 501 E. 38TH STREET, ERIE, PA 16546 • ADMISSIONS: 800-825-1926 • FAX: 814-824-2071
E-MAIL: ADMUG@MERCYHURST.EDU • WEBSITE: WWW.MERCYHURST.EDU

Ratings
Quality of Life: 74   Academic: 77   Admissions: 74   Financial Aid: 76

Academics

The classes at Mercyhurst are "challenging but not impossible." This probably has a great deal to do with Mercyhurst's "extremely excellent" professors, who seem to be able to bring even the most

> **SURVEY SAYS . . .**
> *Classes are small, Students are religious*
> *Instructors are good teachers*
> *Diversity lacking on campus*

mundane material to life. A student explains: "I have enjoyed the majority of my classes because of the teacher, not the subject matter." Teachers are "extremely understanding and accessible inside and outside of the classroom. They make extra time to help you with whatever you need." Mercyhurst runs classes on a trimester system, which means that students take three to four classes per term for ten weeks, so "as soon as you start to get sick of your classes, it's finals time and you get to start new classes." The social sciences and anthropology departments are particularly strong, and the Research Intelligence Analyst Program (RIAP)—("kinda like training for the CIA")—is the "only one of its kind." Plaudits rain upon the dance program as well. The administration has been cracking down on grade inflation recently, so students have to work much harder for that A. Opinion about the administration is split, with personal estimates ranging from "approachable," "very helpful," and "friendly" to "incompetent, rude, and uncaring." One student warns, "If papers need to be signed by more than one individual, start a month in advance." Students would especially like to see more sympathy in the financial aid office, and student accounts, reportedly, "is all messed up." These two offices also need to communicate better.

Life

"Erie doesn't offer a lot to do, but when you are surrounded by creative and wonderful people, they always have something going on," offers one student of the goings-on at Mercyhurst. Movies are apparently a popular time-killer for undergrads here ("I have never watched so many movies in my life"), and "if you're patient, most of the movies" make it to the Dollar Theatre in town. There are no fraternities or sororities at Mercyhurst, but students have no problem finding parties. The difficulty lies in keeping them going, as "security is really strict; almost every party gets busted." Mercyhurst maintains a strict alcohol policy, which some students appreciate, but others complain that "one of the purposes of going to college is being able to let loose on the weekends, and sometimes it's hard to do that here because you have to be so careful about not getting caught with beer or something." Begs another student, "They keep us so busy during the week. Just let us have some fun on the weekend!" Freshmen aren't allowed cars, and they live in designated dorms with regulated visitation hours for the opposite sex. Upperclassmen live in apartments, however, which do not have a curfew. Mercyhurst is going through a construction boom; the recreation center has been expanded, and there are new performing arts and academic centers. Students probably wouldn't mind if the school decided to throw some of the construction money instead into dining services; campus food could reportedly stand improvement.

Student Body

Attention eligible bachelors. The female/male ratio is around 60:40 at Mercyhurst. But behave yourself because "most of the guys are gentlemen here; they always open the doors for the girls." Some students do complain that "Mercyhurst is all upper-class, white kids," and a few students admit they have witnessed "instances of racism." As one student complained ironically, "There are about 25 nonwhite students on campus." As another evenhanded student explains, "Granted, Mercyhurst doesn't have an extremely diverse population, [but] I still find that my interaction with those few people have made my experience thus far a great one."

ADMISSIONS

Very important factors considered by the admissions committee include: class rank and secondary school record. *Important factors considered include:* character/personal qualities, standardized test scores, talent/ability, volunteer work, and work experience. *Other factors considered include:* alumni/ae relation, essays, extracurricular activities, geographical residence, interview, minority status, religious affiliation/commitment, and state residency. SAT I or ACT required. TOEFL required of all international applicants. High school diploma or GED is required. *High school units required/recommended:* 16 total recommended; 4 English recommended, 3 math recommended, 3 science recommended, 1 science lab recommended, 2 foreign language recommended, 1 social studies recommended, 2 history recommended.

The Inside Word

The trick at Mercyhurst is learning how to successfully navigate the administrative rigmarole necessary for achieving your academic goals. To gain entrée to this Catholic school with its recently added North East campus, impress upon the admissions committee your desire and ability to take advantage of the school's varied academic opportunities.

FINANCIAL AID

Students should submit: FAFSA and institution's own financial aid form. Regular filing deadline is August 1. The Princeton Review suggests that all financial aid forms be submitted as soon as possible after January 1. *Need-based scholarships/grants offered:* Pell, SEOG, state scholarships/grants, private scholarships, and the school's own gift aid. *Loan aid offered:* FFEL Subsidized Stafford, FFEL Unsubsidized Stafford, FFEL PLUS, and Federal Perkins. Federal Work-Study Program available. Institutional employment available. Applicants will be notified of awards on a rolling basis beginning on or about March 1. Off-campus job opportunities are good.

FROM THE ADMISSIONS OFFICE

"Mercyhurst College is a community of students who have come to expect a vibrant and challenging higher education experience. From its humble beginnings in 1926 to the current explosive growth in both size and reputation, Mercyhurst is a college full of tradition but not afraid of change.

"The motto *Carpe Diem* permeates throughout the college's history! The best illustration may be our collection of academic programs. In the last 20 years, Mercyhurst has had the foresight to add the cutting-edge fields of research intelligence, forensic science, and archaeology. We've also become home to very strong visual and performing arts programs such as dance, music, and art. Our 120 majors, both traditional and unique, have helped Mercyhurst draw students from 40 states and earn nationwide respect.

"Our campus is covered with beautiful buildings and landscaping, making it a comfortable place to spend your college years. After a year in one of four residence halls, upperclassmen live in one of the more than 300 college-owned apartments on the east side of campus. Living on campus has its perks. Students who venture out most any night on campus will find athletic events, concerts, and interesting guest speakers. An excellent recreation center, 25 varsity sports, and 50 student organizations offer other extra-curricular options for our active students.

"In selecting a student for admission, Mercyhurst looks for evidence of academic ability and readiness as demonstrated by high school course work, grades earned, performance on standardized tests, and personal characteristics that relate to a student's ability to succeed."

For even more information on this school, turn to page 251 of the "Stats" section.

MESSIAH COLLEGE

One College Avenue, Grantham, PA 17027 • Admissions: 717-691-6000 • Fax: 717-796-5374
E-mail: admiss@messiah.edu • Website: www.messiah.edu

Ratings
Quality of Life: 73   Academic: 76   Admissions: 73   Financial Aid: 75

Academics

At Messiah College, the professors "are people you not only want to know but are able to get to know! My overall academic experience has been fantastic at Messiah." Another student describes teach-

> **SURVEY SAYS . . .**
> *Profs teach upper levels, Classes are small*
> *Diversity lacking on campus*
> *Very small frat/sorority scene, Very little drug use*

ers as "wonderful models, always performing at their peak level." Religion and academics are both integral to Messiah's mission; as one student explains, "Unlike other Christian schools, we don't have legalistic tendencies making the religious aspect of our school a forced thing, and neither do we abandon academics to be a Christian school. It combines the two beautifully. It really is unapologetically Christian and rigorously academic!" "I have had a teacher pray with me on multiple occasions. I feel this shows that they really care," declares another enthusiastic student. One more adds, "We are equipped to balance our beliefs with the secular world." Classes are small, too, ensuring that "no one is overlooked." Opinions on the administration are split. While one student believes that "our administration is amazingly open and communicative with us," another suggests sarcastically that "they [administrators] should try communicating with the student body; last time I knew, we were the consumers."

Life

Due to Messiah's suburban setting, students warn, "We do have to kind of make our own fun, but that's the fun of it!" In keeping with this rule, it's apparently a birthday tradition to be "throw[n] in the creek" that runs through campus. Students occupy themselves with "deep thoughts and intellectual conversation—there's not a lot of wild partying going on here, but more low-key stuff like movies and concerts [and] sports." When the weather turns chilly, "Cemetery Hill is great for sled riding," and Messiah undergrads all know that they "get enough snow for that!" "For fun there is Powerhouse, a personal favorite of mine, which is student-led praise and worship," writes one student. Students also flock to Wilbur's Café, "a great meeting place on campus." "If you want a beautiful campus with good Christian people and not many distractions, this is a great place for you," sums up one student. "If you're looking for a fast-paced, loud, and wild campus, then this is the last place you will want to be." Messiah features a January term, known as "J-term," during which students take "just one class for three weeks. It's four hours a day, but getting a class you are dreading out of the way in three weeks is great. Or just taking a fun class like snowboarding for the three weeks gives [you] plenty of time to just have fun before the spring semester starts." In keeping with the Christian spirit of the school, there is no drinking or smoking on campus, and Messiah maintains strict dorm visitation rules.

Student Body

"There are many great Christians on this campus that are on track and on fire for God," is how one student describes his peers. However, another warns, "If you do not enjoy going to chapel (required) or do not appear at the optional praise sessions, you will not totally be accepted or fit in at this school." Still, comments a student even-handedly, "Of course we're not perfect, but Messiah College students are the nicest people you'll find anywhere." Adds another student, "Friendships can be made very easily because people care a lot about their peers." Those who dissent contend that "most of the students around here are cool as ice." Students do agree, however, that the school could improve by "attracting more minority students."

ADMISSIONS

Very important factors considered by the admissions committee include: character/personal qualities, class rank, extracurricular activities, recommendations, religious affiliation/commitment, secondary school record, standardized test scores, and talent/ability. *Important factors considered include:* essays and volunteer work. *Other factors considered include:* alumni/ae relation, interview, minority status, and work experience. TOEFL required of all international applicants. High school diploma or GED is required. *High school units required/recommended:* 16 total required; 23 total recommended; 4 English required, 2 math required, 3 math recommended, 2 science required, 3 science recommended, 2 science lab required, 3 science lab recommended, 2 foreign language required, 3 foreign language recommended, 2 social studies required, 2 social studies recommended, 2 history required, 2 elective required, 4 elective recommended.

The Inside Word

Admissions officers at Messiah are looking for students who are not only a good academic fit but who will also fit in well with the school's devoutly religious community. Those who embrace "the evangelical spirit rooted in the Anabaptist, Pietist, and Wesleyan traditions of the Christian Church" will be most comfortable here.

FINANCIAL AID

Students should submit: FAFSA. No deadline for regular filing. The Princeton Review suggests that all financial aid forms be submitted as soon as possible after January 1. *Need-based scholarships/grants offered:* Pell, SEOG, state scholarships/grants, private scholarships, and the school's own gift aid. *Loan aid offered:* Direct Subsidized Stafford, Direct Unsubsidized Stafford, Direct PLUS, Federal Perkins, and Federal Nursing. Federal Work-Study Program available. Institutional employment available. Applicants will be notified of awards on a rolling basis beginning on or about March 15. Off-campus job opportunities are good.

FROM THE ADMISSIONS OFFICE

"Messiah College is a place where education involves a student's intellect, character, and Christian faith. Students receive a superb higher education and also discover a higher calling as they prepare for lives of service, leadership, and reconciliation.

"As a community of learners, Messiah gives academics a high priority. More than 2,800 students from 38 states and 25 countries receive a thorough liberal arts foundation and pursue their choice of more than 50 liberal or applied majors.

"Messiah students learn in many settings. Whether they are involved in student government, a national championship–quality athletic tram, or a community service project, students apply what they have learned. Co-curricular activities and organizations provide a laboratory for testing values and convictions. These opportunities for character development at Messiah are as diverse as the students who bring their gifts and abilities. The 20 intercollegiate athletic teams, academic clubs, student publications, the radio station, music and theatre ensembles, and leadership development programs are just a few of the opportunities available.

"For the person of faith, rigorous intellectual study demands a similar response from the heart. Messiah College faculty and administration mentor students toward spiritual maturity. Students explore their faith while asking the difficult questions of life.

"Interested students should visit during their sophomore or junior year of high school either individually or during one of the various open house events. Applications for admission are considered for early decision (October 15), early action (November 15 and January 15), and regular admission (February 15 and thereafter)."

For even more information on this school, turn to page 252 of the "Stats" section.

MORAVIAN COLLEGE

1200 MAIN ST., BETHLEHEM, PA 18018 • ADMISSIONS: 800-441-3191 • FAX: 610-625-7930
FINANCIAL AID: 610-861-1330 • E-MAIL: ADMISSIONS@MORAVIAN.EDU • WEBSITE: WWW.MORAVIAN.EDU

Ratings
Quality of Life: 79   Academic: 76   Admissions: 78   Financial Aid: 83

Academics

Many students here agree that "the Moravian Experience is something definitely worthwhile." But what makes it truly distinctive? Maybe it's the "professors who really care about you,

> **SURVEY SAYS . . .**
> *Great computer facilities*
> *Student publications are popular*
> *Campus easy to get around*

whether or not it has to do with class." "Of course, there are a few bad apples, and a couple really rotten ones," but for the most part, you'd be hard pressed to find a Moravian student taking shots at the faculty or the administration at this college. Class sizes here are "small," the library is "excellent," and the music department is "very good for a small liberal arts college." (Actually, the 250-year-old department is housed on the college's slightly-set-apart Priscilla Payne Hurd Campus.) Still, when some students glance through the course booklet, they'd like to see "more choices for classes." At the head of this academic ship is a retired Air Force general, Dr. Ervin J. Rokke—and to the Moravian students he's both an icon and a best friend. "He holds regular fireside chats," explains a student, "which are open forums for students to ask questions and give suggestions to administrators." Of course, academics rarely cause complaint. More likely, students will bring up issues like the dining hall's habit of dishing out "the same thing for dinner that they serve for lunch."

Life

Here's a tidbit of info for all potential Moravian students: "Once you get involved there are worlds of things to do and explore." If you don't get involved, however, you may find that Moravian is "nothing out of the ordinary." Alcohol and drugs definitely have a place in the campus life, and as one student says, "It's party time every night." Some students consider Moravian a suitcase school. One student estimates that "about 60 percent of the students go home on the weekend because many live close to school." For those that stick around, IMPACT (Innovative Multi-Cultural Programming Activities for Campus Togetherness), a student organization, regularly offers well attended "concerts, trips, and events," among other diversions. And Greek life is alive and well on the Moravian campus—both "social and service" organizations. While nobody here will tell you that Bethlehem is a hopping metropolis, most have a secret affection for it. "The historic part of the town is within walking distance of campus," and there you'll find "quaint little stores and coffee shops and restaurants," as well as a few bars for the 21-and-overs. The town also has events like "a Celtic festival, Musikfest, and a Christmas festival." On the campus itself, sports are a favorite pastime, from collegiate competition to intramural recreation. If this isn't enough, there are other institutions in the neighborhood worth visiting, namely Lehigh University, also in Bethlehem, and Lafayette College in nearby Easton.

Student Body

"Friendliness" is the trademark of Moravian undergraduates. "It's like a disease," reports one student of his peers. "Generally there is an ease to the air" in Bethlehem, Pennsylvania, where Moravian has made its home since 1742. (In fact, it's the sixth oldest college in the nation.) But while Moravian has managed to survive the length of the nation's history, it hasn't quite managed to draw in the breadth of the nation's diversity. "We have barely any racial and ethnic diversity," grumbles a student. While the college reports that students hail from 25 U.S. states, many students complain that it seems like "everyone comes from the Lehigh Valley or somewhere within 30 to 40 minutes." Some cite that "the students are pretty religious" here. But as a rule, you should never stop with generalizations. "Individuals" with a range of interests can be found all over campus, and "everyone is respectful of everyone else."

ADMISSIONS

Very important factors considered by the admissions committee include: character/personal qualities, class rank, secondary school record. *Important factors considered include:* essays, extracurricular activities, recommendations, standardized test scores. *Other factors considered include:* alumni/ae relation, geographical residence, interview, minority status, talent/ability, volunteer work, work experience. SAT I or ACT required; SAT I preferred. TOEFL required of all international applicants. High school diploma or GED is required. *High school units required/recommended:* 15 total required; 17 total recommended; 4 English required, 3 math required, 4 math recommended, 2 science required, 2 science lab required, 2 foreign language required, 3 foreign language recommended, 4 social studies required.

The Inside Word

Moravian is a small liberal arts school with all the bells and whistles. Applicants will find a pretty straightforward admissions process—solid grades and test scores are required. Counselors will look closely to find the extras—community service, extracurricular activities—that make students stand out from the crowd. Moravian has many programs that should not be overlooked, including music, education, and the sciences.

FINANCIAL AID

Students should submit: FAFSA, CSS/Financial Aid PROFILE, state aid form, noncustodial (divorced/separated) parent's statement, business/farm supplement, copies of parent's and student's W-2s and 1040s. Regular filing deadline is March 15. The Princeton Review suggests that all financial aid forms be submitted as soon as possible after January 1. *Need-based scholarships/grants offered:* Pell, SEOG, state scholarships/grants, private scholarships, the school's own gift aid. *Loan aid offered:* FFEL Subsidized Stafford, FFEL Unsubsidized Stafford, FFEL PLUS, Federal Perkins, state loans. Federal Work-Study Program available. Institutional employment available. Applicants will be notified of awards on a rolling basis beginning on or about April 1. Off-campus job opportunities are good.

FROM THE ADMISSIONS OFFICE

"Founded in 1742, Moravian is proud of its history as one of America's oldest and most respected liberal arts colleges. The low student/faculty ratio allows for an immediate and unusually close bond. The Moravian family, comprising current students and faculty as well as alumni and emeritus professors, praises the College as a supportive environment for learning, personal exploration, and character development. The overarching emphasis of our curriculum is on scholarship enriched by self-discovery. In the last four years, Moravian has produced four Fulbright scholars, a Goldwater scholar, a Rhodes finalist, and three NCAA Postgraduate Scholars. Its robust varsity athletic program has produced All-American student athletes, Academic All-Americans, national champions, a national Player of the Year, and several Olympic hopefuls. The most important recent addition to the facilities is a $20 million academic building, completed in January 2003. At the heart of the central campus, it houses 15 new classrooms, four faculty departments, laboratories, research facilities, and 'smart' classrooms for easy technological interface. The College welcomes inquiries from students eager to participate in an environment of self-directed, life-long learning."

For even more information on this school, turn to page 253 of the "Stats" section.

MOUNT ST. MARY'S COLLEGE

16300 OLD EMMITSBURG ROAD, EMMITSBURG, MD 21727 • ADMISSIONS: 301-447-5214
FAX: 301-447-5860 • E-MAIL: ADMISSIONS@MSMARY.EDU • WEBSITE: WWW.MSMARY.EDU

Ratings

Quality of Life: 78   Academic: 72   Admissions: 67   Financial Aid: 72

Academics

"The Mount is a dynamic, independent, Catholic liberal arts college that has a wonderful, interactive core curriculum," avers one enthusiastic undergraduate. In fact, the core curriculum is one of the most popular aspects of a

> **SURVEY SAYS . . .**
> *School is well run, Classes are small*
> *Very small frat/sorority scene*
> *Students are religious, No one cheats*
> *Instructors are good teachers*

Mount St. Mary's education, unlike at many other institutions. Described by the college as the "cornerstone" of its academic structure, the core curriculum requires students to engage with a broad range of topics in the humanities and sciences, including a two-semester freshman seminar. Reflecting on the core curriculum, an upperclassman affirms, "I have been exposed to subjects and issues that I never would have taken an interest in independently." All students participate in a Freshman Seminar program that introduces them to the ideals and values of a Catholic liberal arts community. The small class sizes and close attention from professors makes learning at the college "a very personal experience." Students dub their professors "available," "knowledgeable," "understanding," and "friendly." This amity extends to the administration, which is led by a president who "takes every opportunity to talk to the students and assess how they are doing and what can be improved."

Life

Near the Maryland-Pennsylvania border stands a huge golden statue of the Virgin Mary atop the 80-foot-tall Pangborn Campanile on the side of St. Mary's Mountain. Pay heed: this is the beacon of Mount St. Mary's College. With this postcard-esque scene in mind, many students tell us that "the beauty of the campus" enhances student life. They also admit that just about everything around the campus adds nothing to student life: "One downside to the Mount is that it is located in an almost nonexistent town. The nearest Wal-Mart is 20 minutes away, and the nearest mall is about a half hour away. We are isolated and seem to live in our own little world." Whether students spend a hard night partying or a soft night in front a bag of chips and a flick, the majority of them try to work off those empty calories at "the very popular" gym or through the plentitude of intramural sports teams to be found traipsing across the fields of this bucolic campus. And, of course, there are also plenty of religious activities and groups on campus. So what if there is only "one real stop light" in the town of Emmitsburg; if you get bored on the Mount St. Mary's campus, you probably have only yourself to blame.

Student Body

At Mount St. Mary's, it's no secret that many of undergrads arrive holding many of the same religious beliefs. But the demographics are a little more complex than that. Just a little, one student tells us. "The students range from the hippy types to conservative [and] preppy." They can be "somewhat divided into groups according to the sports they play" but on the whole are "very friendly and welcoming," making the college community feel "like a family." There's certainly a shared desire to have a good time—hence the parties that light up the campus on weekends—but there's also an air of studiousness around here. As one student plainly states, Mount St. Mary's "is a fun school where most people take academics seriously."

ADMISSIONS

Very important factors considered by the admissions committee include: secondary school record. *Important factors considered include:* standardized test scores. *Other factors considered include:* alumni/ae relation, character/personal qualities, class rank, extracurricular activities, recommendations, talent/ability, volunteer work, and work experience. SAT I or ACT required. TOEFL required of all international applicants. High school diploma or GED is required. *High school units required/recommended:* 16 total required; 4 English required, 3 math required, 3 science required, 2 science lab required, 2 foreign language required, 3 social studies required, 1 elective required.

The Inside Word

The Mount is a place where an open-minded, curious, and committed individual will do well. The college's broad core curriculum grounded in a Catholic tradition gives students the tools—in the form of serious academics and social pursuits—to battle feelings of isolation in a rural setting.

FINANCIAL AID

Students should submit: FAFSA and CSS/Financial Aid PROFILE. Regular filing deadline is February 15. The Princeton Review suggests that all financial aid forms be submitted as soon as possible after January 1. *Need-based scholarships/grants offered:* Pell, SEOG, state scholarships/grants, private scholarships, and the school's own gift aid. *Loan aid offered:* FFEL Subsidized Stafford, FFEL Unsubsidized Stafford, FFEL PLUS, and Federal Perkins. Federal Work-Study Program available. Institutional employment available. Applicants will be notified of awards on a rolling basis beginning on or about January 1. Off-campus job opportunities are fair.

FROM THE ADMISSIONS OFFICE

"Mount St. Mary's College has a rich tradition as one of America's leading Catholic colleges. From our nationally recognized core curriculum and championship athletic achievements to international service and exchange projects, the Mount nourishes the whole student. Through a liberal arts education rooted in spiritual values, we encourage students to question and to search for truth and meaning.

"The Mount offers academic and athletic scholarships, grants, loans, and work-study jobs to help make this top-notch education affordable. Nearly 90 percent of Mount students receive financial aid. Freshmen were awarded an average of more than $15,000 in annual assistance.

"Mount St. Mary's strives to give students a worldview in their education. More than half of our students complete an internship and many more study abroad. They enjoy small classes taught by expert faculty who introduce them to different ideas and cultures. Students discover various talents and interests and learn how to use them in all endeavors of life.

"But is it all work and no play? Hardly. Mount students are extremely involved and engaged. More than 100 clubs and organizations are available for our 1,400 students. And our success is felt athletically, as well! Mount St. Mary's is one of the smallest yet most competitive NCAA Division I schools.

"You'll see as soon as you set foot on campus that there's something about Mount St. Mary's. Experience it for yourself!"

For even more information on this school, turn to page 253 of the "Stats" section.

MUHLENBERG COLLEGE

2400 WEST CHEW STREET, ALLENTOWN, PA 18104-5596 • ADMISSIONS: 484-664-3200 • FAX: 484-664-3234
FINANCIAL AID: 484-664-3175 • E-MAIL: ADMISSION@MUHLENBERG.EDU • WEBSITE: WWW.MUHLENBERG.EDU

Ratings
Quality of Life: 80   Academic: 82   Admissions: 82   Financial Aid: 82

Academics

Students praise the "amazing" theater and science departments at Muhlenberg College. Notes one undergrad here, "The single greatest strength [of this school] is the reputation of the science departments . . . . The rigor I have faced here as a biology major, although at times extremely tough, has been also very rewarding." Muhlenberg

SURVEY SAYS . . .
Students are religious
Political activism is hot
Popular college radio
Students don't get along with local community
Registration is a breeze
Very little beer drinking
Very little drug use

also boasts "excellent" departments of English and history; the business and philosophy departments here "aren't too shabby either." Indeed, Muhlenberg has a lot to offer for an institution with less than 3,000 students. Undergrads appreciate how "the small student body allows the professors to tailor the education for each student." As one student told us, "The best part about my school is its smallness—something I thought I would hate about Muhlenberg turned out to be what makes it so great." Another benefit of the school's small size: "Since we don't have a graduate school, we don't have any graduate students, so undergrads have opportunities to do research." Prospective students are forewarned that "this is a tough school to get into and to stay in, due to a heavy workload." While profs pile on the work, they are also "extremely approachable and welcome you to speak with them about anything, not just class work. They can help you succeed in school if you take the initiative to get to know them." Sums up one student here: "Muhlenberg is what you make of it; if you're ambitious, the school will be good to you; if you're not, most likely you'll get swept along for the ride."

Life

The "beautiful and safe" Muhlenberg campus provides a serene setting to counteract students' hectic academic schedules. "Life is very busy," notes one student. "The best days are the ones where you have a spare hour or two to sit out on the lawn and read or study with some friends when the weather is nice. The front lawn is great; it always gets crowded with kids just hanging out in the spring and fall or playing in the snow in the winter." An active social scene, however, is not part of what clutters most kids' calendars here. There are school-sponsored activities offered, but "most are lame," and as far as the Greek scene goes, the frats "are now either kicked off campus or on probation, so now we are becoming a bar and house party school." Hometown Allentown offers little. Explains one undergrad, "Allentown is technically a city, but don't expect it to be like Manhattan. The college is located in the middle of the suburbs, and most people don't go downtown." Adds another, "I wish they would just pick up the whole damn school and move it out of Allentown." Students enjoy "a few sporting events, mainly men's soccer and women's rugby." Even so, most who can do so seek entertainment elsewhere, often in Philadelphia or New York City. Unfortunately, "freshmen are not allowed to have cars on campus due to major lack of parking space and the rule is pretty strictly enforced," which is why they "tend to flock to the fraternities or hang out in their dorm rooms."

Student Body

Muhlenberg's student body is predominantly white and affluent, students here agree. Detractors describe their peers as people "who have never worked in their lives, drive BMWs and have exorbitant allowances." They "tend to be conservative" and cliquish; reports one, "I don't think anyone really goes out of their way to make new friends once they have found their clique. That's not to say people aren't friendly, though. Overall, the students all get along with each other." Theater majors tend to be the major exception to the preppy, conservative stereotype; their ranks include a disproportionate number of iconoclasts as well as gay students. Despite its Lutheran affiliation, "most kids here are Roman Catholic or Jewish."

ADMISSIONS

Very important factors considered by the admissions committee include: character/personal qualities, secondary school record, talent/ability. *Important factors considered include:* class rank, essays, extracurricular activities, interview, recommendations, standardized test scores, volunteer work. *Other factors considered include:* alumni/ae relation, geographical residence, minority status, work experience. TOEFL required of all international applicants. High school diploma or GED is required. *High school units required/recommended:* 16 total required; 4 English required, 3 math required, 2 science required, 3 science recommended, 2 science lab required, 2 foreign language required, 3 foreign language recommended, 2 history required, 1 elective required.

The Inside Word

Muhlenberg's inquiries and applications continue to increase, which serves to reinforce its selectivity. Competition for students among small Pennsylvania liberal arts colleges is quite heated, and the college is among the more competitive of the lot.

FINANCIAL AID

Students should submit: FAFSA, institution's own financial aid form, CSS/Financial Aid PROFILE, noncustodial (divorced/separated) parent's statement, business/farm supplement. Regular filing deadline is February 15. The Princeton Review suggests that all financial aid forms be submitted as soon as possible after January 1. *Need-based scholarships/grants offered:* Pell, SEOG, state scholarships/grants, private scholarships, the school's own gift aid. *Loan aid offered:* FFEL Subsidized Stafford, FFEL Unsubsidized Stafford, FFEL PLUS, Federal Perkins. Federal Work-Study Program available. Institutional employment available. Applicants will be notified of awards on or about April 1. Off-campus job opportunities are good.

FROM THE ADMISSIONS OFFICE

"Listening to our own students, we've learned that most picked Muhlenberg mainly because it has a long-standing reputation for being academically demanding on one hand, but personally supportive on the other. We expect a lot from our students, but we also expect a lot from ourselves in providing the challenge and support they need to stretch, grow, and succeed. It's not unusual for professors to put their home phone numbers on the course syllabus and encourage students to call them at home with questions. Upperclassmen are helpful to underclassmen. 'We really know about collegiality here,' says an alumna who now works at Muhlenberg. 'It's that kind of place.' The supportive atmosphere and strong work ethic produce lots of successes. The pre-med and pre-law programs are very strong, as are programs in theater arts, English, psychology, the sciences, business, and accounting. 'When I was a student here,' recalls Dr. Walter Loy, now a professor emeritus of physics, 'we were encouraged to live life to its fullest, to do our best, to be honest, to deal openly with others, and to treat everyone as an individual. Those are important things, and they haven't changed at Muhlenberg.'"

For even more information on this school, turn to page 254 of the "Stats" section.

NEUMANN COLLEGE

One Neumann Drive, Aston, PA 19014 • Admissions: 610-558-5616 • Fax: 610-558-5652
E-mail: neumann@neumann.edu • Website: www.neumann.edu

Ratings
Quality of Life: 82   **Academic:** 83   **Admissions:** 80   **Financial Aid:** 82

Academics

In Aston, Pennsylvania—just west of Philadelphia and north of Wilmington, Delaware—Neumann College contributes to the heavy concentration of colleges and universities in the Delaware Valley. While it is in the suburbs, it's not exactly "in the middle of nowhere," as one freshman claims. This "small catholic college" offers men and women the chance to study in nearly 20 fields—including tracks in pre-law and pre-med—and all students are required to complete a core of liberal arts courses. The most recent additions to the curriculum include majors in athletic training and criminal justice. One student refers to the faculty as "extraordinary . . . . Imagine your few favorite teachers from high school that really made an impact on you—now imagine a whole college full of them!" Adds a sophomore, "Their focus is entirely unselfish and they give 100 percent." And the accolades extend to the administration, as well. A junior asks, "Where else does the administration not only know your face and name, but also knows your favorite candy?" She's got us there.

> **SURVEY SAYS . . .**
> *Class discussions encouraged*
> *Diverse students interact*
> *School is well run*
> *Campus feels safe*
> *Lousy food on campus*
> *Classes are small*
> *Low cost of living*
> *Registration is a breeze*

Life

With a healthy population of commuting students from around the Delaware Valley, Neumann must cater to its resident and nonresident students. "There is not much to do at Neumann," says one commuter, echoing the impressions of other nonresidents. But, of course, the commuters aren't around campus at night or on weekends, and residents report that students who seek fun are able to find it. After all, Philadelphia and Wilmington are nearby. And on campus, friends are not tough to come by. "We are so small that you know most of the people," a sophomore says. Friends often venture to "parties or to the mall," as well as taking advantage of the "high number of activities" that the college offers. For instance, six arts groups are available for creative minds. And 15 NCAA teams cater to the athletes. (Athletes would be even happier if the college would "get a rugby team.") Most griping at Neumann is focused on three aspects of life: parking, food, and rules. Commuters and residents alike would be able to stave off their ulcers if the college would find more spots to park their cars. Students also report that on bad days, the cafeteria food is less than satisfactory. But the biggest point of contention is rules. "Be less strict," begs a nursing major, referring to the policies like the "dry campus" rule that drives many partiers to off-campus soirees.

Student Body

"Good people!" That's what you'll find at Neumann College. Most students here come from the Pennsylvania-Delaware-New Jersey tri-state area, and many choose to commute to school from their hometowns. But even good people can stand to grow up a little more. A seasoned senior explains, "The maturity level on this campus is lower than what I would expect from an institution of higher learning." This is partially because groups of friends transfer their cliquey attitudes directly from high school to this nearby college. But every group has its luster and its rust, its good days and its bad days. "It's like a big family," says a freshman.

ADMISSIONS

Very important factors considered by the admissions committee include: extracurricular activities, recommendations, secondary school record, and talent/ability. *Important factors considered include:* alumni/ae relation, character/personal qualities, class rank, interview, and standardized test scores. *Other factors considered include:* minority status, religious affiliation/commitment, and volunteer work. SAT I or ACT required. TOEFL required of all international applicants. High school diploma or GED is required. *High school units required/recommended:* 16 total required; 17 total recommended; 4 English required, 2 math required, 2 science required, 3 science recommended, 2 foreign language required, 2 social studies required, 4 elective required.

The Inside Word

Admission to Neumann College is not highly competitive. Admission to specific departments, which occurs during sophomore year, can be more competitive, depending on the popularity of the department. Check with the admissions office about the popularity of your intended major before applying if you already know what field you plan to enter.

FINANCIAL AID

Students should submit: FAFSA. No deadline for regular filing. The Princeton Review suggests that all financial aid forms be submitted as soon as possible after January 1. *Need-based scholarships/grants offered:* Pell, SEOG, state scholarships/grants, private scholarships, and the school's own gift aid. *Loan aid offered:* Direct Subsidized Stafford, Direct Unsubsidized Stafford, FFEL Subsidized Stafford, FFEL Unsubsidized Stafford, FFEL PLUS, and Federal Nursing. Federal Work-Study Program available. Institutional employment available. Applicants will be notified of awards on a rolling basis beginning on or about March 1. Off-campus job opportunities are excellent.

FROM THE ADMISSIONS OFFICE

"Neumann College offers the ideal educational setting. As a small college, it provides students with the personal attention and support they seek. Dedicated faculty teach and assist our students in developing their thinking, writing, communication, and technical skills. As a Catholic College in the Franciscan tradition, Neumann College supports the spiritual, social, and athletic development of students. Neumann College's academic majors most often include experiential components, allowing students to blend classroom study and real work experiences. Neumann College graduates are well on their way to career advancement, having benefited from a tailored curriculum, personal advisement, support, and field experiences that offer them the competitive edge. Freshmen begin career exploration right away through the Academic Resource and Career Counseling Center.

"Campus life is a real strength of Neumann College. Three new suite-style residence halls are home to almost 600 residents. Residence halls are totally wired. Designed to offer the advantage of living in a community while supporting privacy and independence, the Living Learning Centers combine academic space and recreational, health, and fitness facilities all under one roof. Two modern dining facilities offer a variety of meal plans including a late-night serving at 10 P.M.

"There's always plenty to do at Neumann. The advantages of nearby Philadelphia and a variety of on-campus activities and programs fill the student's schedule. Neumann College offers 15 intercollegiate sports (NCAA), 6 performing arts groups, and dozens of student clubs and organizations. Students planning for college are always invited to visit and see Neumann College first-hand."

For even more information on this school, turn to page 255 of the "Stats" section.

OLD DOMINION UNIVERSITY

108 ROLLINS HALL, 5215 HAMPTON BOULEVARD, NORFOLK, VA 23529-0050 • ADMISSIONS: 800-348-7926
FAX: 757-683-3255 • E-MAIL: ADMIT@ODU.EDU • WEBSITE: WWW.ODU.EDU

Ratings
Quality of Life: 79   **Academic: 71**   **Admissions: 63**   **Financial Aid: 68**

Academics

Students at Old Dominion University, a large commuter school in Norfolk, Virginia, say that theirs "is one of those universities that may not get all of the attention [of] a premier school," but they do have their share of "the best professors." Affirms one

> **SURVEY SAYS . . .**
> *Instructors are good teachers*
> *No one cheats*
> *Classes are small*
> *Very little drug use*
> *Diverse students interact*

student, "Name may be important, but if you want the opportunity to enhance your leadership and communication skills, along with challenging your intellectual capacity, come to Old Dominion." Another points out, "There are many professors from Brown, Cornell, Harvard, etc., who have migrated to ODU. It is not for money but because they have more freedom to make a difference and take ownership of their classroom." Old Dominion is particularly accommodating to older and working students, as the school has an "emphasis in distance learning" and most on-site upper level classes are offered at night. Though most students enjoy the diversity that nontraditional students bring to the classroom, some believe there are drawbacks: "The classes are usually full of students coming straight from the office or from the ship or from the bases . . . so most teachers tend to give a bit more slack than they normally would." This story only confirms, however, the general supportiveness for which ODU faculty is lauded. "All of my professors are always open to talk with me [about] any problems I have, whether in their classes or issues outside the classroom," remarks one student.

Life

"Basketball is a very popular sport" at Old Dominion University, but even if you don't make the team, "most people participate in some sort of campus activity, be it sports[-related] or academic." A prevalent complaint, however, is that "too many students commute," making the typical "college experience" elusive. One student bemoans, "There aren't that many on-campus activities because ODU is such a big commuter school, so I feel like I missed out on that part of college life." Confers another, "The only complaint I have about Old Dominion University is that most of the population of its student body are commuters, including myself. I find it very hard to create study groups and lasting relationships because everyone stays on their own." Nonetheless, students take advantage of the school's wonderful location, and do know how to have fun. A freshman confides, "Life on campus is all about studying or partying. If you don't find us studying, I guarantee you'll find us partying." And since their campus is "within miles to several malls, the beach, and a lot of popular hang outs," you can always, "go to bars in downtown Norfolk or Virginia Beach for fun on the weekends."

Student Body

Though there are 13,000 students at ODU, incoming freshman have no need for nerves: "There's never a worry of not fitting in because you're bound to find other people with your similar interests or background." Indeed, students praise the fact their student body comprises people of "different cultures and backgrounds." In the words of one, "ODU is a diverse campus, which in itself is educational." Quoth another, "There are people from all walks of life and they all bring something to the university." Though "the students at ODU are friendly, open to interacting with each other, and for the most part civil to one another," undergrads also warn that, "having a highly commuter-based campus, most students keep to themselves." On that note, students say, "There seems to be a wide array of ethnicities, but most students stick to their own kind."

ADMISSIONS

Very important factors considered by the admissions committee include: secondary school record. *Important factors considered include:* class rank and standardized test scores. *Other factors considered include:* extracurricular activities, recommendations, talent/ability, volunteer work, and work experience. SAT I or ACT required. TOEFL required of all international applicants. High school diploma or GED is required. *High school units required/recommended:* 16 total required; 4 English required, 4 math required, 4 science required, 1 science lab required, 2 foreign language required, 4 social studies required.

The Inside Word

Applicants to Old Dominion are lucky that the school's admission standards are not as high as the level of access students have to good professors. It can be an ideal choice if a job or military assignment puts you within commuting distance of campus and its fun surroundings.

FINANCIAL AID

Students should submit: FAFSA. Regular filing deadline is April 1. The Princeton Review suggests that all financial aid forms be submitted as soon as possible after January 1. *Need-based scholarships/grants offered:* Pell, SEOG, state scholarships/grants, private scholarships, and the school's own gift aid. *Loan aid offered:* Direct Subsidized Stafford, Direct Unsubsidized Stafford, Direct PLUS, and Federal Perkins. Federal Work-Study Program available. Institutional employment available. Applicants will be notified of awards on a rolling basis beginning on or about March 15. Off-campus job opportunities are excellent.

For even more information on this school, turn to page 255 of the "Stats" section.

PENNSYLVANIA STATE UNIVERSITY—UNIVERSITY PARK

201 SHIELDS BUILDING, UNIVERSITY PARK, PA 16802-3000 • ADMISSIONS: 814-865-5471
FAX: 814-863-7590 • FINANCIAL AID: 814-865-6301 • WEBSITE: WWW.PSU.EDU/ADMISSIONS

Ratings
Quality of Life: 78   **Academic:** 87   **Admissions:** 86   **Financial Aid:** 89

Academics

At a helluva big school like Pennsylvania State University, "you can find anything to do academically. If you want a school that will hold your hand, go to Swarthmore. If you're an independent, self-motivated person, come here." The school's main branch offers its students a mind-boggling array of majors, from turfgrass science to ancient

> **SURVEY SAYS . . .**
> *Everyone loves the Nittany Lions*
> *Lots of beer drinking*
> *Athletic facilities are great*
> *Great library*
> *Frats and sororities dominate social scene*
> *Student newspaper is popular*
> *Hard liquor is popular*
> *Campus is beautiful*

Mediterranean studies to aerospace engineering. Engineering at PSU "is a fantastic bargain, provided that you are willing to put in the work." Programs in business, education, and computer science are also excellent. Students warn that "in order to thrive within this gigantic university, you must be able to create your own little world in which to exist. Otherwise, you are not only liable but guaranteed to get lost in the crowd." Several survey respondents offer strategies for coping with PSU's vastness. Writes one, "The longer you are at PSU, the more tricks you learn, and the better and easier it becomes. Here's one: Schedule 24 credits at the beginning of the semester, then pick the five or six classes with the best professors and drop the rest." Offers another, "If you sit in front of classes, you can't tell that there are 150 people behind you." Professors "are very smart and know their stuff, but they are poor communicators." Notes one student, "How good professors are basically depends on two things: your interest in the subject and, more importantly, [whether] they can teach. You can tell some professors are here just to do research, while others can actually teach." While some feel that "TAs are depended on too much" here, others argue that "everyone has negative comments about TAs, but some are actually better, more down-to-earth, and easier to get in touch with than the professors." Administration of the school is unsurprisingly sluggish; recounts one student, "I'm in my fourth semester and I've had two classes cancelled for the semester and one class had a day/time shift. "

Life

With a student population the size of many American towns, Penn State can offer a wide variety of social options. "Anything you want to do on a weekend," explains one student, "you can find a group of people to do it with. It's not just about drinking. There are concerts, arts, club activities, everything." While it may not be just about drinking, most agree that "Penn State is a party school no matter what anyone says. We throw a party for any reason." Adds another student, "People drink a lot because all there [are] in this town are bars." When students tire of drinking in bars, they . . . drum roll please . . . drink at fraternities! The biggest thing on campus, however, is Nittany Lion football. Reports one student, "Kids go two or three hours early for front-row seats." Students approve of the "beautiful" campus but warn that "it is a pain in the ass to get around campus. Buses are always packed and the campus is huge." They appreciate the school's rural setting, however, which "allows easy access to lots of outdoors activities, like biking, hiking, skiing, canoeing, and boating." As an added bonus, University Park is a "good location for access to major cities (D.C., Baltimore, Philadelphia, Pittsburgh), all three to four hours away." The town itself, however, "is overpriced and pretentious."

Student Body

The 35,000-plus "very sociable, kind, and easy to talk to" undergraduates of Penn State represent a wide array of attitudes and backgrounds. Writes one student, "A wonderful thing about a large school is that you can find people and opinions from across the board." Geographically, though, "diversity is in short supply, with a large majority of students coming from Pennsylvania." Even though the minority population is proportionally small, they are still 3,000. Unfortunately, "races at PSU segregate themselves. There is no built-in racism; it's all by personal choice." The pragmatic, nonintellectual approach of the majority here doesn't appeal to everyone. To detractors, "the students are all right, but they're like high school students, just a little older."

ADMISSIONS

Very important factors considered by the admissions committee include: secondary school record, standardized test scores. *Other factors considered include:* alumni/ae relation, character/personal qualities, class rank, essays, extracurricular activities, recommendations, talent/ability, volunteer work, work experience. SAT I or ACT required. TOEFL required of all international applicants. High school diploma or GED is required. *High school units required/recommended:* 4 English required, 3 math required, 3 science required, 2 foreign language required, 3 social studies required.

The Inside Word

Penn State is deluged with applicants (they claim to receive more SAT score reports than any other college in the country), which makes it especially important for candidates to have better than average grades and test scores. Although a personal essay and information on extracurricular activities are requested, the university's formula focuses on the numbers. At schools this large it's hard for the admissions process to be more individualized.

FINANCIAL AID

Students should submit: FAFSA. No deadline for regular filing. The Princeton Review suggests that all financial aid forms be submitted as soon as possible after January 1. *Need-based scholarships/grants offered:* Pell, SEOG, state scholarships/grants, private scholarships, the school's own gift aid. *Loan aid offered:* FFEL Subsidized Stafford, FFEL Unsubsidized Stafford, FFEL PLUS, Federal Perkins, college/university loans from institutional funds, private loans. Federal Work-Study Program available. Applicants will be notified of awards on a rolling basis beginning on or about February 15. Off-campus job opportunities are good.

FROM THE ADMISSIONS OFFICE

"Unique among large public universities, Penn State combines the nearly 35,000-student setting of its University Park campus with 20 academically and administratively integrated undergraduate locations—small-college settings ranging in size from 600 to 3,400 students. Each year, more than 60 percent of incoming freshmen begin their studies at these residential and commuter campuses, while nearly 40 percent begin at the University Park Campus. The smaller locations focus on the needs of new students by offering the first two years of most Penn State baccalaureate degrees in settings that stress close interaction with faculty. Depending on the major selected, students may choose to complete their degree at University Park or one of the smaller locations. Your application to Penn State qualifies you for review for any of our campuses. Your two choices of location are reviewed in the order given. Entrance difficulty is based, in part, on the demand. Due to its popularity, the University Park campus is the most competitive for admission."

For even more information on this school, turn to page 256 of the "Stats" section.

RADFORD UNIVERSITY

PO Box 6903, RU Station, Radford, VA 24142-6903 • Admissions: 540-831-5371 • Fax: 540-831-5038
E-mail: RUADMISS@RADFORD.EDU • Website: WWW.RADFORD.EDU

Ratings
Quality of Life: 74   Academic: 68   Admissions: 61   Financial Aid: 73

Academics

When bragging about their school's academic strengths, Radford students will often mention the "nursing school, the criminal justice program, and the teaching program." Then they'll tell you about the 110 or so other

programs that undergrads can ensconce themselves in at this mid-sized public university in western Virginia. A cornerstone of the Radford curriculum is the general education program—anchored in the liberal arts principles that the university embraces—which requires undergrads to take 50 credit hours in a variety of foundational subjects, ranging from fine arts to mathematical sciences. Students here report that "professors have been very willing to spend as much time [as needed] outside of class to help every student understand the material" and that when they've gone to a prof's office to get extra help they've "never found a door shut." But some students would be satisfied if faculty doors were shut, as long as it meant that professors were figuring out how to make classes more challenging. On this tack, a "very dissatisfied" student complains, "I am frustrated with being forced to stay on a beginning level." And then there are the students, like this one, who take the middle road: academics are "good, not the best, but everything is definitely better than average." Another throws in a dose of wisdom, applicable to all college students everywhere: "School life is what you make of it."

Life

Radford is a small town of about 16,000 people in southwest Virginia. Ergo, "there is not much to do." If you look around town, however, you're sure to find a mall, some restaurants, a movie theatre, and those two primary indicators of that fact that you are approaching civilization: "Wal-Mart and a Waffle House." If you're outdoorsy, welcome to paradise: the surrounding Appalachians provide many a salubrious excursion for people of your ilk. But much of a Highlander's life revolves around the campus. "There are a lot of different organizations out there," including "music, theatre, art, sports, clubs, sororities/frats, student government, and the school newspaper." And what about the parties? "The reputation of Radford, as most people know, is that we are a party school. . . . The fact is [that] over the last two years there has been a lot [of] tightening up [of] the rules." Regardless of the label's validity, if you're looking to let loose once in a while, you'll have no problem. "There are always plenty of parties, from frat parties to private parties," assures one student. Speaking of classmates, another student adds, "Once Wednesday comes around, they go out to parties through Saturday night." The university is planning to increase the students' social options in coming years by erecting "a new student union building with cyber cafés, dining areas, a gymnasium, and other sponsored activities."

Student Body

If you had to choose one word to describe Radford students, "social" would probably be a good one. You'll find that the people "are available for anything from tutoring and study groups to pick-up basketball games and Friday-night parties." One Highlander believes that students "are focused on academics, but they do no let that interfere with their extracurricular activities." With such a genial atmosphere, "it is easy to meet people," particularly at parties. And incidentally, "there is a higher population of women on campus than men," one amused undergrad explains. "This makes for an interesting crowd at parties, considering you might see five girls fighting for one guy . . . and that one guy loving life!" While students here do tend to segregate into groups—often along the lines of Greek association, club participation, or dorm assignment—they assure us that "it's not as cliquey as high school was."

ADMISSIONS

Very important factors considered by the admissions committee include: secondary school record and standardized test scores. *Other factors considered include:* alumni/ae relation, character/personal qualities, class rank, essays, extracurricular activities, interview, recommendations, talent/ability, and work experience. SAT I or ACT required, SAT I preferred. TOEFL required of all international applicants. High school diploma or GED is required. *High school units required/recommended:* 13 total required; 21 total recommended; 4 English required, 3 math required, 2 science required, 2 science lab required, 2 foreign language required, 2 social studies required, 2 social studies recommended, 1 history recommended, 7 elective recommended.

The Inside Word

Echoes of its party reputation emanate from Radford's rural hideaway despite its sparse offerings as a college town. As the social infrastructure continues to improve, the question is left to you, the applicant: If you attend, will you choose to skate it or make it a challenge?

FINANCIAL AID

Students should submit: FAFSA. Regular filing deadline is March 1. The Princeton Review suggests that all financial aid forms be submitted as soon as possible after January 1. *Need-based scholarships/grants offered:* Pell, SEOG, state scholarships/grants, private scholarships, and the school's own gift aid. *Loan aid offered:* FFEL Subsidized Stafford, FFEL Unsubsidized Stafford, FFEL PLUS, Federal Perkins, Federal Nursing, state loans, and college/university loans from institutional funds. Federal Work-Study Program available. Institutional employment available. Applicants will be notified of awards on a rolling basis. Off-campus job opportunities are good.

For even more information on this school, turn to page 256 of the "Stats" section.

RANDOLPH-MACON COLLEGE

Box 5005-5505, Ashland, VA 23005 • Admissions: 804-752-7305 • Fax: 804-752-4707
Financial Aid: 804-752-7259 • E-mail: admissions@rmc.edu • Website: www.rmc.edu

Ratings
Quality of Life: 87   Academic: 79   Admissions: 77   Financial Aid: 91

Academics

If what you seek is a "great education to prepare you for the real world while still having a great, fun social life," then Randolph-Macon College just might be the undergraduate institution for you. The curriculum provides a solid liberal arts education to the pragmatic student body. Undergrads here are accomplished—one in four proceeds immediately to grad school upon graduation. As one student tells it, "Word is that R-MC is easy to get into but hard to stay [in], and I believe that's completely true; you really have to work to get what you want out of your experience." Support comes primarily from a dedicated faculty; explained one student, "Our slogan says it best: 'Believe in the Moment of Connection.' Our professors are very close to us. The administration tries to be." More than one undergraduate thinks "the greatest strength of my school has to be its size and the many benefits that come with that. We are only a little over 1,000 students, so classes are never over 25 students." On the downside, "the problem with such a small school is that only so many classes can be offered because there is not an excess of students to take them and not a lot of professors to teach them." Membership in the Seven College Consortium of Virginia mitigates this problem somewhat.

> **SURVEY SAYS . . .**
> *Frats and sororities dominate social scene*
> *Lots of beer drinking*
> *Campus easy to get around*
> *Hard liquor is popular*
> *(Almost) everyone smokes*
> *Campus is beautiful*
> *Athletic facilities are great*
> *Great computer facilities*

Life

"Greek life is a major part of campus life at our school," observes one R-MC student. Surprisingly few students here complain about the divisive effect Greek organizations often present, however, probably because "they provide so many student activities, even for those students who are not members." Notes one student approvingly, "Everyone gets along no matter what the differences may be (e.g., Greeks and non-Greeks are all friends). People look out for each other here. There is a real sense of community." This unity is obvious at every Yellow Jackets' home game; "sporting events such as men's basketball and football are popular, and they have a pretty big turnout for their games," writes one student. Outdoor enthusiasts speak highly of Macon Outdoors, a campus organization "dedicated to exploring the outdoors" through "rafting, skiing, hiking, kayaking, mountain biking, canoeing, and rock climbing" trips. Complains one student, "I have trouble finding things to do on the weekends because I don't drink." Some students commit to clubs, organizations, and public service. Those who don't usually frequent the Greek houses or "entertain themselves in downtown Richmond," just a half-hour to the south.

Student Body

Randolph Macon is "slowly becoming more diverse"; even so, the vast majority of undergraduates "come from a mid- to upper-socioeconomic-level background and tend to be Republican." The typical student is "from Virginia, Maryland, or Pennsylvania" and mostly "concerns him- or herself with the ongoing social aspects of campus, with little to no regard for what is going on in the outside world," writes one undergrad. Students here are sociable and easygoing about their academic commitments: "People . . . go out and party and still get their work done." Undergraduates are often "involved in many different aspects of college life . . . . [They are] active in sports (either competitive or intramural) and most likely also have a job somewhere on campus or in the nearby community."

ADMISSIONS

Very important factors considered by the admissions committee include: secondary school record. *Important factors considered include:* class rank, recommendations, standardized test scores. *Other factors considered include:* alumni/ae relation, character/personal qualities, essays, extracurricular activities, interview, minority status, talent/ability, volunteer work. SAT I or ACT required; SAT I preferred; SAT II also recommended. TOEFL required of all international applicants. High school diploma or GED is required. *High school units required/recommended:* 16 total required; 22 total recommended; 4 English required, 3 math required, 4 math recommended, 3 science required, 4 science recommended, 2 science lab required, 4 science lab recommended, 2 foreign language required, 4 foreign language recommended, 1 social studies required, 4 social studies recommended, 2 history required, 1 elective required.

The Inside Word

Candidates who are above-average students and testers are very likely to receive scholarships at Randolph-Macon. The college has a low yield of admits who enroll, and every strong student who signs on gives the freshman academic profile a boost. If the competition among Virginia colleges weren't so strong, admission to Randolph-Macon would be much tougher.

FINANCIAL AID

Students should submit: FAFSA, state aid form. The Princeton Review suggests that all financial aid forms be submitted as soon as possible after January 1. *Need-based scholarships/grants offered:* Pell, SEOG, state scholarships/grants, private scholarships, the school's own gift aid. *Loan aid offered:* FFEL Subsidized Stafford, FFEL Unsubsidized Stafford, FFEL PLUS, Federal Perkins, college/university loans from institutional funds. Federal Work-Study Program available. Institutional employment available. Applicants will be notified of awards on or about April 1. Off-campus job opportunities are good.

FROM THE ADMISSIONS OFFICE

"Randolph-Macon College, located in historic Ashland, just north of Richmond, is a co-educational, liberal arts and sciences college with a mission fulfilled through a combination of personal interaction and academic rigor. The student/faculty ratio is 11:1 and the average class size is 16 students. Enrollment is kept at approximately 1,150 to maintain this intimate atmosphere. Randolph-Macon College has an outstanding national reputation for its internships, study abroad, and undergraduate research. Founded in 1830, Randolph-Macon College is the oldest United Methodist Church–affiliated college in the nation, is a Phi Beta Kappa college, and is ranked as a Baccalaureate I college by the Carnegie Foundation. It offers the broadest liberal arts core curriculum of any college in Virginia.

"The College prepares students for any future, including success in securing a job or in gaining acceptance to graduate or professional school. The College offers a wide variety of social and recreational opportunities through more than 100 campus organizations. Forty percent of the students participate in one or more community service activities; 70 percent play intramural sports; 45 percent join a fraternity or sorority; and everyone has a voice in student government. A new $9.5 million sports and recreation center is very popular with students, and a new performing arts center opened this year. In addition, freshmen residence halls are now under extensive renovation and a new 'Peaks of Excellence' center is being constructed."

For even more information on this school, turn to page 257 of the "Stats" section.

RANDOLPH-MACON WOMAN'S COLLEGE

2500 RIVERMONT AVENUE, LYNCHBURG, VA 24503-1526 • ADMISSIONS: 800-745-7692 • FAX: 434-947-8996
FINANCIAL AID: 434-947-8128 • E-MAIL: ADMISSIONS@RMWC.EDU • WEBSITE: WWW.RMWC.EDU

Ratings
Quality of Life: 88   Academic: 93   Admissions: 80   Financial Aid: 92

Academics

Students at Randolph-Macon Woman's College love the small-school charm that imbues their academic experience. "This is NOT a finishing school," undergrads here say time and again. It's the kind of place where "many professors seem to take it upon themselves as a personal mission to not

> **SURVEY SAYS . . .**
> *Students are religious*
> *Political activism is hot*
> *Theater is hot*
> *(Almost) everyone plays intramural sports*
> *Unattractive campus*
> *Campus difficult to get around*

award high grades" and course work is "difficult. It is not too bad to get along if you took a few AP courses in high school, but if you just skated through easier classes, you may have trouble." Professors, the women here agree, are "without a doubt the best thing about R-MWC . . . . They care about the students, and actually interact with them." Students also love R-MWC's honor code, which they describe as "amazing. Self-scheduled exams, freedom in leaving belongings in public areas, and a general feeling of cooperation are wonderful things to have in a college environment." These assets help make up for Macon's shortcomings, which include "a student body so small that it leaves only a few options in terms of classes" and a registration system that "flows like a clogged toilet."

Life

Tradition is central to R-MWC extracurricular life. These traditions include the Even-Odd rivalry ("women that graduate in even years are even and women that graduate in odd years are odd; it helps create a bond based on graduation year"); Ring Week ("where juniors and [freshmen] are paired up to exchange little gifts and the first year decorates the junior's door and gives the junior her ring"); and Pumpkin Parade ("similar to Ring Week, but with sophomores and seniors, pumpkin carving, and a candlelight parade"). Students love these distinguishing touches, but wish the school could supplement them with a more active social calendar. Explained one student, "We are completely restricted by the school's visitation and alcohol policies. The school seems to still be stuck in an era when most schools in the area were single-sex and there was more incentive for men to come here." As a result, "many students feel they must go off-campus for fun," and so they do, road-tripping to "Charlottesville, home of UVA, which attracts a lot of live music," and Roanoke, which "has a decent nightlife, with three nightclubs and an all-night coffee shop." They rarely hang around hometown Lynchburg, which "is not a college town, despite having over 12,000 college students (combining our school, Liberty University, Lynchburg College, and Sweet Briar College)." As they do every time we survey them, the women of R-MWC brag that "we have the best dining service! They cook us real food (and I'm talking real chicken parmesan, steak, fried cod, shrimp) and if you can't find anything to eat (which is next to impossible), just go find Jeff, our head chef. He'll make you whatever you want!"

Student Body

"There is definitely a range" of women at R-MWC, "from the super-traditional girly girls who spend many a weekend at Hampden-Sydney or VMI looking for their future husbands to very liberal feminists who never look for guys; from girls who party and drink nearly every weekend to girls [who] think that a good time is a hot cup of tea and a Jane Austen novel." Students tell us that "everyone gets along pretty well. . . . Of course, on an all-female campus, there's always someone PMS-ing, but that's life." Many speak of a sense of sisterhood; as one student explained, "With so few students, all of them women, and nearly all living on campus, it is understandable that we would be a bit closer than many other colleges." Another benefit of attending an all-women's college: "It really decreases the emphasis on fashion, makeup, and the like."

ADMISSIONS

Very important factors considered by the admissions committee include: character/personal qualities, essays, recommendations, secondary school record. *Important factors considered include:* class rank, extracurricular activities, standardized test scores, talent/ability. *Other factors considered include:* alumni/ae relation, interview, minority status, volunteer work, work experience. SAT I or ACT required. TOEFL required of all international applicants. High school diploma or GED is required. *High school units required/recommended:* 16 total required; 4 English recommended, 3 math recommended, 2 science recommended, 2 science lab recommended, 4 foreign language recommended, 2 history recommended, 2 elective recommended.

The Inside Word

The admissions process at Randolph-Macon Woman's College works pretty much as it does at most small liberal arts colleges, with one worthwhile exception: Each candidate is assigned to an admissions staff member who functions as an advocate for the student throughout the process. It's nice to have somewhat regular contact with someone in the admissions office over the course of the cycle. This saves time restating problems, questions, and circumstances every time you call or write. It also helps the college make a strong positive impression on applicants.

FINANCIAL AID

Students should submit: FAFSA, state aid form. No deadline for regular filing. The Princeton Review suggests that all financial aid forms be submitted as soon as possible after January 1. *Need-based scholarships/grants offered:* Pell, SEOG, state scholarships/grants, private scholarships, the school's own gift aid. *Loan aid offered:* FFEL Subsidized Stafford, FFEL Unsubsidized Stafford, FFEL PLUS, Federal Perkins. Federal Work-Study Program available. Institutional employment available. Applicants will be notified of awards on a rolling basis beginning on or about March 1. Off-campus job opportunities are good.

FROM THE ADMISSIONS OFFICE

"Randolph-Macon Woman's College students appreciate the College's personalized approach to their educational program. Their individualized Macon Plan, which includes study abroad, internships, career guidance, leadership development, and one-on-one faculty advising, allows the student superior opportunities and direction in achieving their goals and dreams. The Honor System is a vital part of life at R-MWC, providing students with a living and learning environment based on integrity, trust, and mutual respect. A diverse student population from 43 states and 47 countries offers exceptional opportunities to learn about different cultures and perspectives. The College's solid academic reputation coupled with an impressive array of alumnae who are leaders in nearly every career field imaginable positions R-MWC as one of the finest liberal arts colleges in the nation.

"If you are bright, ambitious, and motivated, Randolph-Macon Woman's College is the place for you!"

For even more information on this school, turn to page 258 of the "Stats" section.

ROANOKE COLLEGE

221 COLLEGE LANE, SALEM, VA 24153-3794 • ADMISSIONS: 540-375-2270 • FAX: 540-375-2267
E-MAIL: ADMISSIONS@ROANOKE.EDU • WEBSITE: WWW.ROANOKE.EDU

Ratings

Quality of Life: 75   **Academic:** 79   **Admissions:** 75   **Financial Aid:** 73

Academics

Called a "New England school in the middle of southwest Virginia," Roanoke College makes it "clear that student satisfaction is the number one priority." With professors who "take a very per-

> **SURVEY SAYS . . .**
> *Lots of classroom discussion*
> *Classes are small*
> *Instructors are good teachers*

sonal interest in the success of every student" as well as enforced attendance policies, it is nearly "impossible to fall through the cracks." Though some students believe that the "academic experience is limited because this is a small school," others take advantage of the "warm learning environment" and "count some of [their] instructors as mentors and friends." Complaints arise stating that "lower-level courses taught by adjuncts are generally bad," but most classes "impart knowledge and convey enthusiasm." Undergraduates log mixed reviews regarding the administration: some call them "horribly distant" while others cite an "openness between administration and students." At minimum, "every single student has been given the chance to formally meet the president of the college." In terms of financial aid, a few students file complaints, but many have kind words for "the wonderful people at financial aid, who walk on water," as Roanoke is "able to offer tons of financial aid." Students generally lament sky-high tuition and fees, though, commenting, "Room and board prices are ridiculous." Says another student with a more moderate standpoint, "Tuition is a little steep but they are fairly generous with financial aid and they try to help as much as they can."

Life

Greek organizations form the foundation of Roanoke social life, to the point that some students dub the scene "overly predominant." Students comment that "going Greek is really, really important"; although some parties are "open to everyone," independents see the fraternities and sororities as "very exclusive." When they're not bolstering the college's archetypal "party school" reputation (the prevailing priority on campus is to "party and have a good time constantly"), Greeks also engage in "lip sync competitions, skits, scavenger hunts, and philanthropy." However, the active Campus Activity Board "plans events for students on a regular basis that promote fun and fellowship without alcohol." The "concerts and movies are pretty popular and usually really good," and "we even have bingo every once in a while on weekends." Gym rats and sports fans enjoy "great workout facilities and great athletic programs." Plus, outdoor enthusiasts find themselves in paradise, with "great places to hike." Though based in the "typical redneck town" of Salem, one student gushes, "Man, is it beautiful here, wedged in the middle of the Blue Ridge Mountains."

Student Body

The most evident lines between Roanoke students are those of latitude, with one student remarking, "Too many narrow-minded Yankees that come here and immediately start trashing the South." Other southerners feel more affinity for their northern cohorts, saying, "Hearing different accents is always a thrill." Racial diversity is called "more than lacking," with one minority student stating, "Many students here have never seen any minority students in their lives and make ignorant comments in classes and the cafeteria." Another reports, "While there is some mixing, the few black students usually hang out by themselves." However, progress is being made due to the school's "clear interest in working toward more ethnic diversity." Apparently the strongest factions develop "in terms of Greek affiliation, not gender or race or sexual orientation." Though some students characterize their college as "one of those rich-kid schools where everyone seems to be driving a Beemer with a Phi Mu sticker," most consider each other "well rounded and open to outside ideas and views." Overall, there exists an "undeniable sense of belonging" living among "Roanoke students that are genuinely nice, helpful, compassionate, and good-humored."

ADMISSIONS

Very important factors considered by the admissions committee include: character/personal qualities, class rank, secondary school record, and standardized test scores. *Important factors considered include:* extracurricular activities, interview, and recommendations. *Other factors considered include:* alumni/ae relation, essays, minority status, talent/ability, volunteer work, and work experience. SAT I or ACT required. TOEFL required of all international applicants. High school diploma or GED is required. *High school units required/recommended:* 18 total required; 4 English required, 3 math required, 2 science required, 2 science lab required, 4 foreign language recommended, 2 social studies required, 5 elective required.

The Inside Word

There's a lot to take advantage of both on and off the Salem campus of Roanoke College, but your decision to attend may come down to your comfort level with the school's diversity—more in terms of North/South origins than multiethnic. If you're smart and interesting, the school will probably be interested in you.

FINANCIAL AID

Students should submit: FAFSA and state aid form. No deadline for regular filing. The Princeton Review suggests that all financial aid forms be submitted as soon as possible after January 1. *Need-based scholarships/grants offered:* Pell, SEOG, state scholarships/grants, private scholarships, and the school's own gift aid. *Loan aid offered:* FFEL Subsidized Stafford, FFEL Unsubsidized Stafford, FFEL PLUS, Federal Perkins, and college/university loans from institutional funds. Federal Work-Study Program available. Institutional employment available. Applicants will be notified of awards on a rolling basis beginning on or about December 25. Off-campus job opportunities are excellent.

FROM THE ADMISSIONS OFFICE

"Roanoke College is dedicated to educating men and women in high standards of scholarship to prepare them for responsible lives of learning, service, and leadership. In pursuing this goal, the College is committed to an integrative approach to education that strives to balance intellectual, ethical, spiritual, and personal growth.

"The college pursues its mission through an innovative curriculum that includes a cohesive core of liberal arts as well as specialized, career-oriented programs of study. Students are encouraged to develop the habits of mind, aesthetic appreciation, and cultural awareness needed to thrive in a global society. Moreover, the college provides opportunities for students to take part in community service, to engage in ethical and social issues, to participate in religious life, and to further their physical and social well-being.

"The college supports its mission by ensuring excellent teaching, providing for communal activities and residential life, and maintaining a beautiful campus in the Blue Ridge Mountains. The college strives to be a diverse community, nationally and internationally, and is committed to seeking new ways to serve its students and community."

For even more information on this school, turn to page 259 of the "Stats" section.

ROSEMONT COLLEGE

1400 MONTGOMERY AVENUE, ROSEMONT, PA 19010 • ADMISSIONS: 610-526-2966 • FAX: 610-520-4399
E-MAIL: ADMISSIONS@ROSEMONT.EDU • WEBSITE: WWW.ROSEMONT.EDU

Ratings

Quality of Life: 74   **Academic:** 82   **Admissions:** 80   **Financial Aid:** 75

Academics

Described as a "quiet haven for study," Rosemont offers a program that "prepares young women to become critical thinkers while establishing a feeling of self-confidence." Professors here "not only inform the students in

> **SURVEY SAYS . . .**
> *Classes are small*
> *Profs teach upper levels*
> *Low cost of living*
> *Students are religious*

each subject, but also allow for discussion." One satisfied student writes, "The professors are easily accessible and will work to accommodate your goals. Whether that may be a specific country you would like to study in or an internship you want, they will help you make it happen." Despite this support, "an embarrassing percentage of the freshman class is on academic probation," and unfortunately, "class selection is small to say the least." On the administrative side, many call the situation decidedly "unstable." One student explains that the school is "going through a rough patch right now. We're looking for new administrators to revive the waning atmosphere of the college." This effort is off to a good start with the new president, who is "one of the kindest, most outgoing women I have ever met." According to some students, the school "lies to incoming students to increase enrollment," as they have been faced with decreasing applicant numbers. When suggestions are made, "I feel like administrators are smiling and nodding until I leave, then forget everything I said." In terms of financial aid, "I've got a great package, but not everyone does who needs it." A confident student adds her take on the Rosemont experience: "I feel that I have gained a well-rounded liberal arts education and also received the knowledge and know-how of my field of study. I feel ready to take the next step in my life."

Life

Social life is close to nonexistent on this small, "nominally Catholic" campus where students "are not allowed to drink in large groups." Thus, the "vast majority of students go home every weekend." For those primed to party, "there are more than five other colleges located in a 15-minute radius," and Villanova seems to be the campus of choice for a surrogate social life. The surrounding area is said to be "too haughty to admit it's a college town" and therefore doesn't cater to students, but fortunately, "The train station is right down the street," making access to Philadelphia easy. On campus, "the smoking lounge in my building is the center of activity. Girls go there to bitch about boyfriends, study together for history tests, play spades, or just hang out when there's nothing to do." One student observes, "You'd think that since there aren't parties there'd be more intellectual and activist organizations," but the school has trouble sustaining extracurriculars for lack of participation. One woman sums it up, writing, "Living among women gives you a chance to focus on yourself instead of being consumed [by] members of the opposite sex." She also adds that "there are LOTS of men about and plenty of things to do if you just look."

Student Body

Relations between "Rosemonsters" are described in the comment, "It isn't out-and-out harmony, nor is it war." A prevalent sentiment is that "the estrogen level is suffocating, and hair-pulling is common." One student tells us, "I feel more competition over the clothes I wear than the grades I receive in the classroom." Others complain that "when it comes down to getting involved and changing things, Rosemont students want no part of it." Another student adds, "There are many problems at Rosemont with race and class issues that have been swept under a bulging Rosemont welcome mat." While they claim to be a "diverse group in our interests and backgrounds," some say a "great deal of racism" exists, specifically surrounding underprivileged students from inner-city Philadelphia that attend the prevalently white, upper-class school. Still, students often characterize their peers as a "good group of girls" who are "always waving or smiling" and claim, "They are like my family." Amid the small community, an orientation volunteer says it's comforting to know "everyone's face and most people's names."

ADMISSIONS

Very important factors considered by the admissions committee include: class rank, interview, and secondary school record. *Important factors considered include:* essays, extracurricular activities, recommendations, standardized test scores, talent/ability, and volunteer work. *Other factors considered include:* alumni/ae relation, character/personal qualities, and work experience. SAT I or ACT required, SAT I preferred. TOEFL required of all international applicants. High school diploma or GED is required. *High school units required/recommended:* 18 total required; 4 English required, 2 math required, 2 science required, 2 science lab required, 2 foreign language required, 2 social studies required, 2 history required, 2 elective required.

The Inside Word

Rosemont is a choice that offers flexibility—a Catholic institution with off-campus alternatives in the Philly area if the campus scene isn't clicking for you. Its high academic standards offer its students distinct challenges.

FINANCIAL AID

Students should submit: FAFSA. Regular filing deadline is April 1. The Princeton Review suggests that all financial aid forms be submitted as soon as possible after January 1. *Need-based scholarships/grants offered:* Pell, SEOG, state scholarships/grants, private scholarships, and the school's own gift aid. *Loan aid offered:* FFEL Subsidized Stafford, FFEL Unsubsidized Stafford, FFEL PLUS, Federal Perkins, alternative loans, and payment plans. Federal Work-Study Program available. Institutional employment available. Applicants will be notified of awards on a rolling basis. Off-campus job opportunities are good.

For even more information on this school, turn to page 259 of the "Stats" section.

ST. JOHN'S COLLEGE

PO Box 2800, Annapolis, MD 21404 • Admissions: 410-626-2522 • Fax: 410-269-7916
Financial Aid: 410-626-2502 • E-mail: admissions@sjca.edu • Website: www.sjca.edu

Ratings
Quality of Life: 87   **Academic:** 92   **Admissions:** 85   **Financial Aid:** 91

Academics

St. John's gets back to basics with a classical education focused exclusively on 100 seminal texts of western civilization, concentrating on philosophy but also covering math, science, literature, and music. Rather than professors, "tutors" with a "passion for teaching" serve to "guide the discussion and keep it on track, but they are there to learn as much as we are." Considering that tutors are required to eventually teach every course, they are experts in cross-subject integration, a goal of the St. John's education. Students form close relationships with their tutors: "Without a doubt, there will be one who changes you forever." Seeing as the dean is simply a "tutor with a title," students say, "The administration? Well, I know all seven of them." Some undergrads find the set academic program "very limiting," but others point out, "I often have the freedom to concentrate on my interests because many essays have quite broad subject assignments." Students are "challenged to dive into our civilization's deepest texts, look into their soul, and really learn." They share the uncommon belief that "philosophy is self-evidently relevant and terribly important." A student tells us, "It felt like I had been asleep before I read these books." In summary, one student writes, "If you want to discover how math, language, and literature can be heartbreakingly beautiful, come to St. John's."

> **SURVEY SAYS . . .**
> *Theater is hot*
> *No one cheats*
> *Registration is a breeze*
> *Diversity lacking on campus*
> *(Almost) everyone plays intramural sports*
> *Class discussions encouraged*
> *Intercollegiate sports*
> *are unpopular or nonexistent*
> *Political activism is (almost) nonexistent*
> *Diverse students interact*

Life

Life and academics are virtually one and the same at St. John's. For example, one student says that he "sits in a diner and reads Dante" for fun. Others claim, "This is the place to sit up late at night with a bottle of wine talking about philosophy and the cosmos," and often, "students will still be debating metaphysics as they slip into drunken oblivion." All of this boozing is seen as an "escape from the gravity of the subject matter we face daily in class." The weekends begin early among Johnnies; Wednesday nights are known as "New Year's Eve" since the partying begins at midnight. Other than that, the "famous St. John's waltz parties" attract crowds, and for another break from mental acrobatics, "the intramural program here is extremely well-run and lots of fun. It's sports the way that they were meant to be played." Continuing the old-school flavor of the place, the only intercollegiate sports are fencing, crew, and croquet. Generally, students enjoy their "process of shared inquiry," adding "think hard" to the "work hard, play hard" equation.

Student Body

Amid the student body of 500 "Johnnies," the average student is described as "extremely pretentious, but highly intellectual." This "bright, self-confident, and neurotic" group sometimes displays an "almost complete lack of social graces," unless one counts being "both debauched and brilliant." Bringing the classroom into the interpersonal realm, often the "jokes and conversations center too much on philosophy and the program." The population shows evidence of the "general maturing effects of reading what we read" as they "learn to care for oneself in the transcendental sense." St. John's undergraduates may be regarded as "pretty strange" for their drive to "learn for the sake of learning." But at long last these high school misfits agree that they have "finally met other people like me." If the Annapolis crew gets too familiar, students have the option of transferring to the school's Santa Fe campus for a new crop of cohorts.

ADMISSIONS

Very important factors considered by the admissions committee include: essays. *Important factors considered include:* alumni/ae relation, character/personal qualities, interview, recommendations, secondary school record. *Other factors considered include:* class rank, extracurricular activities, minority status, standardized test scores, talent/ability, volunteer work, work experience. TOEFL required of all international applicants. High school diploma or GED is required. *High school units required/recommended:* 4 English recommended, 3 math required, 4 math recommended, 3 science recommended, 3 science lab recommended, 2 foreign language required, 4 foreign language recommended, 2 social studies recommended, 2 history recommended.

The Inside Word

St. John's has one of the most personal admissions processes in the country. The applicant pool is highly self-selected and extremely bright, so don't be fooled by the high acceptance rate—every student who is offered admission deserves to be here. Candidates who don't give serious thought to the kind of match they make with the college and devote serious energy to their essays are not likely to be successful.

FINANCIAL AID

Students should submit: FAFSA, CSS/Financial Aid PROFILE, noncustodial (divorced/separated) parent's statement, business/farm supplement. No deadline for regular filing. The Princeton Review suggests that all financial aid forms be submitted as soon as possible after January 1. *Need-based scholarships/grants offered:* Pell, SEOG, state scholarships/grants, the school's own gift aid. *Loan aid offered:* FFEL Subsidized Stafford, FFEL Unsubsidized Stafford, FFEL PLUS, Federal Perkins, college/university loans from institutional funds. Federal Work-Study Program available. Institutional employment available. Applicants will be notified of awards on a rolling basis beginning on or about November 1. Off-campus job opportunities are excellent.

FROM THE ADMISSIONS OFFICE

"The purpose of the admission process is to determine whether an applicant has the necessary preparation and ability to complete the St. John's program satisfactorily. The essays are designed to enable applicants to give a full account of themselves. They can tell the committee much more than statistical records reveal. Previous academic records show whether an applicant has the habits of study necessary at St. John's. Letters of reference, particularly those of teachers, are carefully read for indications that the applicant has the maturity, self-discipline, ability, energy, and initiative to succeed in the St. John's program. St. John's attaches little importance to 'objective' test scores, and no applicant is accepted or rejected because of such scores."

For even more information on this school, turn to page 260 of the "Stats" section.

St. Mary's College of Maryland

Admissions Office, 18952 East Fisher Road, St. Mary's City, MD 20686-3001
Admissions: 800-492-7181 • Fax: 240-895-5001 • Financial Aid: 240-895-3000
E-mail: admissions@smcm.edu • Website: www.smcm.edu

Ratings
Quality of Life: 81   **Academic:** 83   **Admissions:** 90   **Financial Aid:** 86

Academics

A small, private liberal arts school experience at state school prices: that's what regularly puts St. Mary's College in Maryland at or near the top of everyone's "Best Buys in Education" lists. Students here appreciate what the school offers, bragging about the "accessible and friendly" faculty, the availability of "lots of interdisciplinary courses and programs, basically lots of academic flexibility," and an administration that is "very open to student input and always willing to hold discussions and Q & A sessions." Students agree that "St. Mary's is well deserving of its 'Honors College' label. It makes you work for your degree with challenging classes that require a lot of work outside of class." Every student here may complete an extensive senior project, a "student-initiated, culminating experience" that is "the centerpiece of the honors college curriculum." Students are assisted in their endeavors by professors whom they "call by their first names and never hesitate to ask for private meetings when we have concerns or even just want to chat." Also, "another plus is that most of the profs are willing to take on freshmen to help with research if they want to do it. There are incredible opportunities here."

> **SURVEY SAYS . . .**
> *Classes are small, No one cheats*
> *Beautiful campus, Campus easy to get around*
> *Lab facilities need improving*
> *Great computer facilities*
> *Library needs improving*
> *Lousy off-campus food, Lousy food on campus*

Life

The secluded campus of St. Mary's College, students agree, "is absolutely breathtaking. It is right on the St. Mary's River, and the sunsets are magnificent! It is so calm and peaceful. There are these beautiful benches all over the campus, but the best ones are right on the water in a little garden. If you go and sit on those benches, all your troubles melt away. Also, the buildings are gorgeous." Not surprisingly, students "spend a lot of time on the river, either sailing, kayaking, or swimming." Many complain that there is little else to do. "It is rather isolated here," students tell us. "Town is 20 minutes away, even the closest McDonald's." ("Town," by the way, is historic St. Mary's City, the first capital of Maryland and host to many historical reenactments.) More than a few students, however, report having little trouble finding diversions: "There [are] always activities sponsored by the school, and there's always spontaneous fun" like "grabbing cafeteria trays, inflatable chairs, and garbage bags and sledding on this hill near my dorm. The whole school shows up, and everyone is laughing and having a great time." Some "chase the peacocks while drunk, watch movies, shop at Wal-Mart, drive an hour to get to a mall, go to lectures." Students also tell us that "community service is big here . . . . A majority of the college volunteers on a regular basis, and not only the students, but professors as well. I think that's pretty damn cool." Sports are popular; writes one undergrad, "My school is Division III, so the athletes aren't playing to be noticed, they're playing because they enjoy it. Our guys and girls lacrosse, sailing, and crew teams are very popular and ranked well."

Student Body

"The initial impression I got of SMCM was on my campus tour when random people walking by, said 'hello,' and told me to come here," explains one student. Sure, there are different cliques, like the athletes, the hippies, the administration-involved, etc., but everyone mixes and gets along." Most are hardworking and driven to succeed; notes one undergrad, "The students here are so motivated, both inside and outside the classroom. Students work hard at school, and they work hard in their extracurricular activities." The small student body means that "everyone here knows everyone else. Don't expect to come here and be anonymous." Racial diversity isn't as pronounced as most students would like it; reports one student, "Most people are white. There is a visible black population though. Most students are liberal (especially environmentally). There are many different groups here: the jocks, the 'nerds,' the preps, the hippies, etc. But everyone seems to get along pretty well. Everyone is nice."

ADMISSIONS

Very important factors considered by the admissions committee include: essays, secondary school record, standardized test scores. *Important factors considered include:* extracurricular activities, recommendations, talent/ability. *Other factors considered include:* alumni/ae relation, character/personal qualities, geographical residence, interview, minority status, state residency, volunteer work, work experience. SAT I or ACT required; SAT I preferred. TOEFL required of all international applicants. High school diploma or GED is required. *High school units required/recommended:* 20 total required; 22 total recommended; 4 English required, 3 math required, 3 science required, 2 science lab recommended, 2 foreign language recommended, 3 social studies required, 7 elective required.

The Inside Word

There are few better choices than St. Mary's for better-than-average students who are not likely to get admitted to one of the top 50 or so colleges in the country. It is likely that if funding for public colleges is able to stabilize, or even grow, that this place will soon be joining the ranks of the best. Now is the time to take advantage, before the academic expectations of the admissions committee start to soar.

FINANCIAL AID

Students should submit: FAFSA. Regular filing deadline is March 1. The Princeton Review suggests that all financial aid forms be submitted as soon as possible after January 1. *Need-based scholarships/grants offered:* Pell, SEOG, state scholarships/grants, private scholarships, the school's own gift aid. *Loan aid offered:* FFEL Subsidized Stafford, FFEL Unsubsidized Stafford, FFEL PLUS, Federal Perkins. Federal Work-Study Program available. Institutional employment available. Applicants will be notified of awards on or about April 1. Off-campus job opportunities are good.

FROM THE ADMISSIONS OFFICE

"St. Mary's College of Maryland . . . occupies a distinctive niche and represents a real value in American higher education. It is a public college, dedicated to the ideal of affordable, accessible education but committed to quality teaching and excellent programs for undergraduate students. The result is that St. Mary's offers the small college experience of the same high caliber usually found at prestigious private colleges, but at public college prices. Designated by the state of Maryland as 'Its Public Honors College,' one of only two public colleges in the nation to hold that distinction, St. Mary's has become increasingly attractive to high school students. Admission is very selective."

For even more information on this school, turn to page 260 of the "Stats" section.

SAINT JOSEPH'S UNIVERSITY

5600 CITY AVENUE, PHILADELPHIA, PA 19131 • ADMISSIONS: 610-660-1300 • FAX: 610-660-1314
E-MAIL: ADMI@SJU.EDU • WEBSITE: WWW.SJU.EDU

Ratings
Quality of Life: 71   Academic: 83   Admissions: 78   Financial Aid: 73

Academics

Of Saint Joe's 4,600 undergraduate students, about 1,500 of them attend the Haub School of Business. In other words, business is one of Saint Joe's strong suits, and many students come here for

> **SURVEY SAYS . . .**
> *Students love Philadelphia*
> *Classes are small, High cost of living*
> *Great off-campus food, Students are religious*

that reason. Other students—nonbusiness students—complain that "there is an extreme bias toward the business school," and these disgruntled undergrads would like to see the playing field evened a little. With such a high-profile business program, it seems almost paradoxical that "Saint Joe's is a small, liberal arts college" with a variety of academic opportunities. Students choose from around 40 majors and must complete a core curriculum of "general requirements" that "enrich studies greatly" and foster "relationships . . . with professors from other departments." Because "class sizes are small," students can rest assured that they'll work closely with their professors. And at Saint Joe's, "there is no such thing as a teaching assistant," which ensures more student/faculty interaction than you'd typically find at a larger university. Overall, students' opinions about their profs run the gamut, from "dedicated," "brilliant," and "always willing to help, encourage, and motivate," to "not the greatest." Student complaints focus on the "very, very bad and frustrating" "organizational structure" of the campus and the "out-of-touch" administration that oversees it all.

Life

Saint Joe's has the privilege of an enviable location: it sits on a "beautiful campus," near the hip neighborhood of Manayunk, just outside of Philadelphia. Students are city regulars, hopping from "museums to nightclubs," turning up to watch "professional sports teams," attending "concerts and shows," joining in the bohemian extravaganza on "amazing" South Street, or enjoying the first-class restaurants of Philly. They also mix with students from other institutions in this university-laden city. Campus life, for better or worse, is integral to the SJU experience. A recent innovation in SJU campus life that's caused plenty of comment is the "SJU 'til 2," a program that "plans activities on the weekends for nondrinkers." As the name suggests, SJU 'til 2ers have the option of socializing until 2 A.M. while watching "movies," playing "games," and enjoying "free food." But according to most SJU students, there is little interest in nonalcoholic functions—unless, of course, those events are Hawks basketball games. Despite recent administrative crackdowns, drinking and partying are alive and well at Saint Joe's. With only a handful of Greek organizations and no on-campus frat houses, students often end up "huddled in someone's dorm room" with a case of beer or hanging out at an "upperclassman's apartment, drinking beer and playing drinking games." Some students complain that at "a lot of parties, people won't let you in unless you know someone." Road trips to Atlantic City, the Jersey Shore, and the sprawling King of Prussia Mall are also common.

Student Body

Because of its location, its price tag, and its high regional reputation, Saint Joe's tends to attract "very wealthy" students from southeast Pennsylvania and neighboring states, such as

New Jersey and Delaware. Students are the first to admit the "socioeconomic limitations of the student body," as one business student puts it. Some students simply shrug and say that if you look hard enough, you'll find "very different attitudes and mentalities" and many "amazing students." One minority student, while lamenting the lack of diversity on campus, quickly adds, "I am not implying that SJU is necessarily a bad environment for someone who is not white." With a renewed appreciation for "individualism" spreading across campus, students are starting to break away from the "cliquey-ness" and homogeneity that have defined the student body in recent years. One student advises, "Be yourself, do not conform, and you will meet people you like."

ADMISSIONS

Very important factors considered by the admissions committee include: secondary school record. *Important factors considered include:* class rank, essays, recommendations, and standardized test scores. *Other factors considered include:* character/personal qualities, extracurricular activities, interview, volunteer work, and work experience. SAT I or ACT required; SAT II recommended. TOEFL required of all international applicants. High school diploma is required and GED is not accepted. *High school units required/recommended:* 15 total required; 17 total recommended; 4 English required, 3 math required, 2 science required, 3 science recommended, 1 science lab required, 2 foreign language required, 1 social studies recommended, 1 history required, 2 elective required.

The Inside Word

Good thing the campus lies within walking distance of the Hartford scene, as on-campus students still need off-campus mobility to pursue all the school's academic and extracurricular avenues. St. Joseph is a visually beautiful school unless you find a dearth of boys aesthetically displeasing.

FINANCIAL AID

Students should submit: FAFSA. Regular filing deadline is May 1. The Princeton Review suggests that all financial aid forms be submitted as soon as possible after January 1. *Need-based scholarships/grants offered:* Pell, SEOG, state scholarships/grants, private scholarships, and the school's own gift aid. *Loan aid offered:* Direct Subsidized Stafford, Direct Unsubsidized Stafford, FFEL Subsidized Stafford, FFEL Unsubsidized Stafford, FFEL PLUS, and Federal Perkins. Federal Work-Study Program available. Institutional employment available. Applicants will be notified of awards on a rolling basis beginning on or about March 15. Off-campus job opportunities are good.

FROM THE ADMISSIONS OFFICE

"Founded by the Society of Jesus in 1851, Saint Joseph's University is celebrating more than 150 years of academic excellence. Saint Joseph's is home to 3,750 full-time undergraduates and 3,000 graduate, executive, and doctoral students. The university's strong liberal arts tradition is marked by rigorous and open-minded inquiry, high academic standards, and a love of learning and the development of the whole person.

"Potential students are urged to visit the campus, schedule a tour, attend classes, meet students and faculty, and speak with an admissions counselor. Please contact the Office of Admissions at 1-888-BE-A-HAWK to make arrangements for a campus visit.

"Saint Joseph's University adheres to a 'rolling admission' policy. Once the maximum number of acceptances has been reached, acceptable candidates are placed on a waiting list for admission. It is for this reason that we strongly encourage students to submit the admission application early in the senior year."

For even more information on this school, turn to page 261 of the "Stats" section.

SAINT VINCENT COLLEGE

OFFICE OF ADMISSION & FINANCIAL AID, 300 FRASER PURCHASE ROAD, LATROBE, PA 15650-2690
ADMISSIONS: 800-782-5549 • FAX: 724-532-5069 • E-MAIL: ADMISSION@STVINCENT.EDU
WEBSITE: WWW.STVINCENT.EDU

Ratings
Quality of Life: 77   Academic: 73   Admissions: 70   Financial Aid: 75

Academics

Students at Saint Vincent College, a Benedictine school in the mountains of western Pennsylvania, enjoy a solid mixture of secular academics and spiritual guidance. The latter is facilitated by the on-campus presence of a monastery

> **SURVEY SAYS . . .**
> *Students are religious, School is well run*
> *Student publications are popular*
> *Very little beer drinking, Classes are small*
> *No one cheats, Diversity lacking on campus*

and seminary. Explains one student, "The monastery and seminary are both important. There are so many college students that think only about material objects, it is nice to have monks and seminarians to talk to about the larger issues of life. They can act as mentors and friends that can really help out." Most undergrads here agree that "the faculty is the best feature of the SVC. Many of them spend a good deal of their personal time with the students." Notes one student, "They do not merely lecture for 45 minutes of a 50-minute class, but take time to answer questions and encourage discussion and debate. I've taken some very tough classes, and the professors will work extra hard with an individual, if that person seeks help." For others, Saint Vincent's intimate size is its chief selling point; writes a senior, "I feel that by going to a small high-caliber school like St. Vincent, I have had the opportunity to participate in activities and events that may have been out of reach at a larger school. I have had the opportunity to take charge of clubs and organizations and actually feel like I am making a difference in a group's well-being. I'm glad I chose St. Vincent and would recommend it to anyone!"

Life

Saint Vincent's undergraduates warn that "our campus is beautiful but boring, and so is the town [of Latrobe]. It is not geared to a college lifestyle. Everything closes up tight after 9:30 or 10 P.M., even on weekends." Adds one student, "Since the school is relatively secluded, students occupy their time, particularly on the weekends, by partying. There are some students under 21 who do drink but not as much as you would find on other campuses." Come Friday afternoon, "perhaps as much as 40 percent of the students that live on campus" go home. Saint Vincent has no Greek system; according to students, athletic teams serve the same function on their campus. "The lacrosse team is like a frat in itself," notes one student. "Sports are the main social elite," adds another. During the week, "student clubs are very popular," and sponsored activities include "anything from day trips to watching movies and eating pizza." The Student Government Association provides leisure-time alternatives, and for the school's religious students, "there are some small groups that form prayer groups, Bible study, and religious discussion."

Student Body

The Saint Vincent student body is predominantly white, Catholic, and local. Notes one student, "I have found that the majority of people are friendly, and everyone seems to get along with everyone. The typical St. Vincent student is one who is dressed fairly conservatively, but always looking their best." One student describes the attitude on campus: "Whether I am friends with other students or not, I always try to say 'hello' and give a polite smile or a wave. It never hurts to be nice, and I would say that most students on campus share my view!"

ADMISSIONS

Very important factors considered by the admissions committee include: class rank and secondary school record. *Important factors considered include:* character/personal qualities, essays, and standardized test scores. *Other factors considered include:* alumni/ae relation, extracurricular activities, interview, recommendations, talent/ability, and volunteer work. SAT I or ACT required, SAT I preferred. TOEFL required of all international applicants. High school diploma is required and GED is accepted. *High school units required/recommended:* 16 total required; 20 total recommended; 4 English required, 4 English recommended, 3 math required, 3 math recommended, 1 science required, 3 science recommended, 1 science lab required, 1 science lab recommended, 2 foreign language recommended, 3 social studies required, 3 social studies recommended, 5 elective required, 5 elective recommended.

The Inside Word

Saint Vincent's crunchy liberal arts structure might make you forget that its student body is predominantly white. Thousands descend on the Westmoreland Fairgrounds each summer for the rollicking Rolling Rock–sponsored town fair, so consider sticking around after classes end.

FINANCIAL AID

Students should submit: FAFSA. No regular filing deadline. The Princeton Review suggests that all financial aid forms be submitted as soon as possible after January 1. *Need-based scholarships/grants offered:* Pell, SEOG, state scholarships/grants, private scholarships, and the school's own gift aid. *Loan aid offered:* FFEL Subsidized Stafford, FFEL Unsubsidized Stafford, FFEL PLUS, and Federal Perkins. Federal Work-Study Program available. Institution employment available. Applicants will be notified of awards on a rolling basis beginning on or about March 1. Off-campus job opportunities are good.

FROM THE ADMISSIONS OFFICE

"A coeducational, Catholic, liberal arts college sponsored by the Benedictine monks of Saint Vincent Arch abbey, Saint Vincent College is the first Benedictine foundation in the United States, founded in 1846. Saint Vincent is accredited by the Middle States Association of Colleges and Schools and occupies a 200-acre suburban campus 35 miles east of Pittsburgh on U.S. Route 30 East. The diverse student population of more than 1,300 hails from 23 U.S. states/territories and 9 foreign countries. Nearly 80 percent of full-time students reside on campus in five residence halls that include a new facility for freshmen.

"Undergraduate majors are offered in accounting, anthropology, art history, studio arts, biochemistry, biology, chemistry, communication, computing and information services, economics, engineering 3/2, English, environmental administration, environmental chemistry, finance, history, international business, liberal arts, management, marketing, mathematics, music, music performance, philosophy, physics, political science, psychology, public policy, religion education, religious studies/Catholic theology, sociology, Spanish, and theater. In collaboration with Duquesne University, programs in occupational therapy, physical therapy, physician assistant, and pharmacy are also available. Education certification is offered in early childhood, elementary, and secondary education. Pre-professional programs are offered in pre-chiropractic pre-dental, pre-law, pre-medicine, pre-optometry, pre-osteopathy, and pre-veterinary.

"Saint Vincent College's approach to education is rooted in a core curriculum that provides students with a broad-based education that provides a general body of knowledge in humanities, social sciences, natural sciences, and mathematics as well as an interdisciplinary view of that knowledge base and the skills to increase that general body of knowledge throughout their lives."

For even more information on this school, turn to page 262 of the "Stats" section.

SALISBURY UNIVERSITY

ADMISSIONS OFFICE, 1101 CAMDEN AVENUE, SALISBURY, MD 21801 • ADMISSIONS: 410-543-6161
FAX: 410-546-6016 • FINANCIAL AID: 410-543-6165 • E-MAIL: ADMISSIONS@SALISBURY.EDU
WEBSITE: WWW.SALISBURY.EDU

Ratings
Quality of Life: 77   Academic: 77   Admissions: 84   Financial Aid: 84

Academics

Career-minded students on and around the Delmarva Peninsula would be hard pressed to find a better bargain than Salisbury University. The school's super-low tuition is further discounted by an unusually large endowment, funded by such business magnates as Frank Perdue (for

> **SURVEY SAYS . . .**
> *Classes are small, (Almost) everyone smokes*
> *Musical organizations aren't popular*
> *Lots of conservatives on campus*
> *Computer facilities need improving*
> *Library needs improving, Lab facilities are great*
> *Student government is unpopular*

whom the business school is named). Salisbury's greatest strengths are in education, business administration, accounting, engineering, communications, and, of course, its proximity to beachfront property. Writes one student, "We're close to the beach and have great weather, challenging courses, great people: what more could a person ask for?" Students appreciate the fact that they receive an exceptional amount of attention in return for their low tuition; reports one undergrad, "What I like most about this school is how much the professor's are willing to help students both inside and outside of class. There are also study groups and tutors available for many different subjects." Adds another, "Many of the professors try to actually teach the material instead of just lecturing about it and make time available outside of class for any problems. The class sizes are usually about the same size as most high school classes, except for lecture hall classes." Although nearly all students are satisfied at Salisbury, a few echo this sentiment: "This school is decent without being excellent in any one area. It's like driving a Ford Escort. It will get you from A to B, but not particularly fast or in good style."

Life

Students describe a sedate life on Salisbury's "absolutely gorgeous and very well-kept" campus; explains one, "For fun a bunch of us will rent a movie during the weeknights, then on weekends go out to several different parties, usually ending up at one of the apartments nearby to play drinking games and hang out. The only real place to go and hang out on weekends is the mall. Salisbury is not a college town at all." Nearby resort town Ocean City, on the other hand, is lots of fun, especially during warmer months. "Ocean City (the beach) is only about a half hour away, so when you can get a free afternoon, it is wonderful!" notes one student; adds another, "The beach being so close is a definite plus." Still, many say that "[Ocean City] is nice, but certainly not a New York; or a Washington, D.C.; or even a Cleveland. There are things to do that are entertaining, but most of the time you've got to find stuff to do on your own." Students report a large contingent of beer drinkers among their midst but warn that "the town has begin to cut down on underage drinking, which has resulted in lots of citations. If you party smart, you can keep out of trouble." Athletic activities "are very important here. There is always some physical activity going on. Whether it's playing an intercollegiate, club, or intramural sport, or watching someone else play, there's always something."

Student Body

Salisbury undergrads "are some of the nicest and most wholesome X'ers you will ever meet.

There are several types of students on campus: the idealistic activists, the apathetic me-firster business majors, the evangelical Christians, the Christian lefties, the Euro-Buddhists, the ethnic minorities, and the moderates." Another student fond of dividing classmates up by type adds that "there are those who are here to learn academically, those who are here to party and skate through classes, and those who are here to develop academically, socially and individually. Within each group the students get along." Notes one student, "The only problem is that there is not a great deal of [racial] diversity. The university tries to bring in more diversity, but it is very difficult." Quality academic programs combined with the low out-of-state tuition attract an unusually large number of students from Delaware, New Jersey, Pennsylvania, and Virginia.

ADMISSIONS

Very important factors considered by the admissions committee include: secondary school record. *Important factors considered include:* class rank, standardized test scores. *Other factors considered include:* alumni/ae relation, character/personal qualities, essays, extracurricular activities, geographical residence, minority status, recommendations, state residency, talent/ability, volunteer work, work experience. SAT I or ACT required; SAT I preferred. TOEFL required of all international applicants. High school diploma or GED is required. *High school units required/recommended:* 14 total required; 18 total recommended; 4 English required, 3 math required, 4 math recommended, 3 science required, 4 science recommended, 2 science lab required, 3 science lab recommended, 2 foreign language required, 3 foreign language recommended, 3 social studies required.

The Inside Word

As a part of the new wave of public institutions of higher learning focusing their energies on undergraduate research, Salisbury State has seen its admissions standards and the quality of its freshman class steadily improve over the past few years. As a result, candidate review is also more personalized than the formula-driven approaches of most public colleges. The admissions committee will pay close attention to the match you make with the University, evaluating your entire background instead of simply your numbers—though most students are strong academically to begin with.

FINANCIAL AID

Students should submit: FAFSA. Regular filing deadline is December 31. The Princeton Review suggests that all financial aid forms be submitted as soon as possible after January 1. *Need-based scholarships/grants offered:* Pell, SEOG, state scholarships/grants, the school's own gift aid. *Loan aid offered:* Direct Subsidized Stafford, Direct Unsubsidized Stafford, Direct PLUS, Federal Perkins. Federal Work-Study Program available. Institutional employment available. Applicants will be notified of awards on a rolling basis beginning on or about April 1. Off-campus job opportunities are good.

FROM THE ADMISSIONS OFFICE

"Friendly, convenient, safe, and beautiful are just a few of the words used to describe the campus of Salisbury University. The campus is a compact, self-contained community that offers the full range of student services. Beautiful, traditional-style architecture and impeccably landscaped grounds combine to create an atmosphere that inspires learning and fosters student pride. Located just 30 minutes from the beaches of Ocean City, Maryland, SU students enjoy a year-round resort social life as well as an inside track on summer jobs. Situated less than two hours from the urban excitement of Baltimore and Washington, D.C., greater Salisbury makes up for its lack of size—its population is about 80,000—by being strategically located. Within easy driving distance of a number of other major cities, including New York City, Philadelphia, and Norfolk, Salisbury is the hub of the Delmarva Peninsula, a mostly rural region flavored by the salty air of the Chesapeake Bay and Atlantic Ocean."

For even more information on this school, turn to page 262 of the "Stats" section.

SHENANDOAH UNIVERSITY

1460 UNIVERSITY DRIVE, WINCHESTER, VA 22601-5195 • ADMISSIONS: 540-665-4581 • FAX: 540-665-4627
E-MAIL: ADMIT@SU.EDU • WEBSITE: WWW.SU.EDU

Ratings
Quality of Life: 78   Academic: 73   Admissions: 70   Financial Aid: 83

Academics

Well known for its conservatory, Shenandoah University is called a "very personal school" where the faculty and staff "want to know you and help you reach your career goals." Students say of professors, "They are all wonderful and have strong backgrounds in their respective areas." Reportedly, teachers are "always in their office for consultation" and more than "willing to start study groups." In short, they'll do "anything to help their students," and they manage keep their wards interested with lectures that are considered "very productive." Administrators are also rumored to be "pretty much available whenever necessary." One undergraduate tells us, "The school is always trying to work with you, and if you have any problems, they help you to solve them." Every once in a while, students question expenditures: "The conservatory brings in a majority of the students, so why not give us more money for the equipment we need instead of funding our two-year-old football team?" However, overall academic satisfaction is high among this motivated crew. A common sentiment is expressed in the statement, "My experience as a performing arts major has been very challenging but very rewarding. It is definitely not a program one can easily breeze through. This school requires hard work and dedication, which is fine by me!"

> **SURVEY SAYS . . .**
> *No one watches intercollegiate sports*
> *Very little hard liquor*
> *No one plays intramural sports*
> *Students don't get along with local community*
> *Very little beer drinking*
> *Students are religious*
> *Classes are small*

Life

Social life typically mirrors academic life at Shenandoah: "If you aren't in a concert, recital, or performance of some sort, you are probably attending one." For a break from the conservatory scene, "sometimes we have parties on campus, but mostly it's movie nights and hanging out with friends." Though students often complain about the school's athletic facilities, they still "like to get together for pick-up basketball or football games." Other noted pastimes include browsing at the local Wal-Mart, chowing down at "the Japanese steak house," or "playing beer pong and other various drinking games at the on-campus 'apartments.'" The university's hometown of Winchester is called "pretty bleak"; because "there's not a whole lot to do," many people head directly for nearby Washington, D.C., once the weekend rolls around.

Student Body

As a small and accepting community of less than 1,500 undergrads, the Shenandoah student body couldn't be "more friendly or welcoming." Considering the small size, "news does travel fast," and "everyone knows everyone." One student comments that "if you aren't known then you must have tried really hard" to go unnoticed. Students do characterize their campus as diverse and claim, "There is such a wide variety of people at Shenandoah that it is impossible to feel out of place. There are no cliques and everyone seems to get along." Others perceive more division. "Because Shenandoah University is a very diverse place, it seems that groups tend to form around athletics, musical talent, or sexual orientation. But at times there are events that bring all of the students together, and when this happens everything goes smoothly." One evidently heterosexual student adds the mixed message, "There are a lot of homosexuals here, but we do not discriminate against them very much." But overall at SU, "people care about you here, not only the adults, but the students as well."

ADMISSIONS

Very important factors considered by the admissions committee include: interview, secondary school record, and talent/ability. *Important factors considered include:* extracurricular activities, standardized test scores, and volunteer work. *Other factors considered include:* alumni/ae relation, character/personal qualities, essays, recommendations, and work experience. SAT I or ACT required. TOEFL required of all international applicants. High school diploma is required and GED is accepted. *High school units required/recommended:* 15 total are required; 4 English required, 3 math required, 4 math recommended, 2 science required, 4 science recommended, 1 science lab required, 2 foreign language required, 3 foreign language recommended, 2 elective required, 4 elective recommended.

The Inside Word

Its name and address suggest a location buried in the backwoods, but D.C.—just a short car ride from campus—offers students urban advantages. A good choice for candidates looking for a diverse, arts-intensive environment, Shenandoah will often provide generous financial aid if you show the merit and sincere intention to attend.

FINANCIAL AID

Students should submit: FAFSA and state aid form. The Princeton Review suggests that all financial aid forms be submitted as soon as possible after January 1. *Need-based scholarships/grants offered:* Pell, SEOG, state scholarships/grants, private scholarships, and the school's own gift aid. *Loan aid offered:* Direct Subsidized Stafford, Direct Unsubsidized Stafford, Direct PLUS, Federal Perkins, and Federal Nursing. Federal Work-Study Program available. Institution employment available. Applicants will be notified of awards on a rolling basis beginning on or about March 1. Off-campus job opportunities are good.

For even more information on this school, turn to page 263 of the "Stats" section.

SHEPHERD COLLEGE

Office of Admissions, POBox 3210, Shepherdstown, WV 25443-3210 • Admissions: 304-876-5212
Fax: 304-876-5165 • E-mail: admoff@shepherd.edu • Website: www.shepherd.edu

Ratings
Quality of Life: 74   Academic: 77   Admissions: 79   Financial Aid: 71

Academics

Shepherd College, a state liberal arts school on the south banks of the Potomac River, is "a small college so it's like a very small committee, which is very nice because we know what is going on all around the campus." Many feel the school's location is key; writes one student, "We are in West Virginia, but we overlook

> **SURVEY SAYS . . .**
> *Classes are small*
> *School is well run*
> *No one watches intercollegiate sports*
> *Students get along with local community*
> *Very little hard liquor*
> *Student publications are popular*
> *Very little beer drinking*

Maryland. Virginia is one county to the south. We are an hour from Pennsylvania, and an hour and a half from D.C. and Baltimore. It's a great place to be." This prime location allowed the school to create the Washington Gateway Program, availing Shepherd undergrads of seminars, internships, and cooperative education opportunities in Baltimore and the nation's capital. Students here sing the praises of the music department; theatre (abetted by the presence of the annual Contemporary American Theater Festival), education, and physical education and recreation also earn plaudits. Notes one undergrad, "The general studies overall are very challenging. Freshman English weeds a lot of people out of Shepherd." Students report that "80 percent of the faculty really knows their stuff and about 70 percent can actually teach it. The teachers . . . are always there to help when you have problems and are there for guidance also. A lot of the professors have a sense of humor, which keeps you coming to class." Another windfall of attending public school in West Virginia is having "the best senator for bringing home the pork, Robert C. Byrd." Byrd not only "managed to get a number of government facilities in the area including the U.S. Fish & Wildlife's National Conservation Training Center and the U.S. Office of Personnel Management's Eastern Management Development Center," but also secured HUD grants for "extensions on our science building and our library."

Life

Hometown Shepherdstown "is a small town and most people at the school don't really go into town. But for those who do, the coffee shop, called The Lost Dog, is a place where students hang out. There are also poetry readings at a place called the Blue Moon Cafe and open mic nights at the local bars. Most students end up hanging out in their dorms to party." Greek life exists but just barely. Folks turn out to see the Rams, Shepherd's excellent football team, but most other varsity sports are poorly supported. Shepherd is "right on the Potomac River, 10 miles from Harpers Ferry and only 5 miles from Antietam Battlefield. We have lots of historic areas nearby, and the beauty of West Virginia is unending."

Student Body

Writes one Shepherd student, "Since my school is small, pretty much everyone knows everyone and we all get along well with each other." Well, mostly: writes one African American undergrad, "Race relations on campus have improved over the years, but they're still not great. The college still uses athletics as a major means of recruiting black students (mainly from Baltimore and D.C.). Because of this there are many more black male students than black female students, even though the overall population of the school is more female than male. This is part of the reason why retention of minority students is not very good." Observes another undergrad, "Students here are friendly, but they are very apathetic and have low self expectations. We have too many commuter students who just come to school, take classes, and leave. A very large percentage of the active students are out-of-state students."

ADMISSIONS

Very important factors considered by the admissions committee include: secondary school record and standardized test scores. *Other factors considered include:* alumni/ae relation, character/personal qualities, extracurricular activities, recommendations, talent/ability, and volunteer work. SAT I or ACT required. TOEFL required of all international applicants. High school diploma is required and GED is accepted. *High school units required/recommended:* 21 total required; 4 English required, 3 math required, 3 lab science required, 2 foreign language recommended, 3 social studies required, 2 history required, 10 elective required.

The Inside Word

It's not the academics, but the quality of life outside the classroom that determines happiness at Shepherd. Conventional wisdom says that four wheels are the ticket to getting the most out of your four years at this school.

FINANCIAL AID

The Princeton Review suggests that all financial aid forms be submitted as soon as possible after January 1. Institutional employment available. Applicants will be notified of awards on or about March 30. Off-campus job opportunities are good.

For even more information on this school, turn to page 264 of the "Stats" section.

SHIPPENSBURG UNIVERSITY OF PENNSYLVANIA

OLD MAIN 105, 1871 OLD MAIN DRIVE SHIPPENSBURG UNIVERSITY, SHIPPENSBURG, PA 17257-2299
ADMISSIONS: 717-477-1231 • FAX: 717-477-4016 • E-MAIL: ADMISS@SHIP.EDU • WEBSITE: WWW.SHIP.EDU

Ratings
Quality of Life: 76   Academic: 76   Admissions: 72   Financial Aid: 70

Academics

The down-to-earth, practical undergraduates of Shippensburg University are drawn by the school's fine academic reputation, especially in elementary education and criminal justice. They also appreciate Ship's small-school

> SURVEY SAYS . . .
> *Registration is a breeze*
> *Very little beer drinking*
> *Very little hard liquor*
> *Classes are small*

feel; as one student explains, "I love how personal my school is. It is very easy to get in touch with people that can help you. Professors, the administration, advisors, and tutors are all happy that you come and ask for help when you need it." Another adds: "The greatest strengths of Ship are the small classes, so there is a lot of one-on-one activity." Undergrads are extremely happy with the school's administration, complimenting the "friendly campus staff," and observing that "classes are generally offered at very convenient times, especially if you want to go home on weekends . . . . Scheduling online is also very convenient, although courses fill up if you're not an upperclassman." Students warn that "Ship is a challenging and tough school to study at. I've seen top-notch students (friends of mine with SAT scores over 1100) struggle in this university. Students at Shippensburg are required to do a lot of writing and independent research with faculty." Still, when all is said and done, it's the warm-and-fuzzy feeling they get here—and not the all-nighters—that students remember. As one under-grad put it: "It's a good feeling when you see your professor out of the classroom or even from the previous semester and they recognize you and still remember your name."

Life

No doubt about it, Ship's social life has some key proponents: "Shippensburg University is a hard school academically but socially offers a fun campus and off-campus life. On campus students have a lot of athletic, recreational, and academic opportunities for diversion. Off campus is a wonderful and quaint town that thrives due to the university's presence." On nightlife, one undergrad notes, "I usually party from Thirsty Thursday to Saturday and then catch up on my work on Sunday." Many tout the "strong and active student government" and "great football games on campus!" Adds another, "Most people live off campus after their freshman or sophomore (or junior) year, so this (coupled with the fact that it's a suitcase school to begin with) makes for less interaction and not much activity around here." Hometown Shippensburg "is very small. We have a horse-and-buggy tie-up at the Kmart, which is pretty much the only thing in town." Says one student succinctly, "The town here sucks. It's Kmart, Sheetz, and us. I never knew that Pennsylvania had hicks until I came here." To escape, "We go to Chambersburg, which is a town that is about 20 minutes away from here. There is a mall there and other things like the movie theatre, restaurants, and places to rent movies."

Student Body

Though the administration is commited to improving diversity, many students tell us the 6,000-plus students of Shippensburg are "not very diverse" but in the words of one student, "what I would consider to be all-around nondescript, nonquirky—average in mindset, habits, social standing, and intelligence." Writes one undergrad, "Most people are okay. There are two types of people here: those that go home on weekends and those that party." Although the Greeks have a considerable presence on campus, "unlike other campuses, all the sororities get along great as well as the fraternities. We are all involved in the community and campus." One student sums up his classmates this way: "Some of the people seem to be rather snobby. Others are quite easy to get along with. It is up to what you make of them."

ADMISSIONS

Very important factors considered by the admissions committee include: class rank, secondary school record, and standardized test scores. *Other factors considered include:* character/personal qualities, essays, extracurricular activities, interview, minority status, recommendations, and volunteer work. SAT I or ACT required. *High school units required/recommended:* 15 total are recommended; 4 English recommended, 3 math recommended, 3 science lab recommended, 2 foreign language recommended.

The Inside Word

It's a university with small-college access to people and resources, giving you more opportunity than you need to succeed. But if your turnoffs include a strong Greek system and a sizable commuter population, Shippensburg might not shape up . . . and you may end up shipping out.

FINANCIAL AID

Students should submit: FAFSA. Regular filing deadline is May 1. The Princeton Review suggests that all financial aid forms be submitted as soon as possible after January 1. *Need-based scholarships/grants offered:* Pell, SEOG, state scholarships/grants, private scholarships, and the school's own gift aid. *Loan aid offered:* FFEL Subsidized Stafford, FFEL Unsubsidized Stafford, FFEL PLUS, Federal Perkins, state loans, college/university loans from institutional funds, FFEL consolidation loans, and alternative loans. Federal Work-Study Program available. Institution employment available. Applicants will be notified of awards on a rolling basis. Off-campus job opportunities are fair.

FROM THE ADMISSIONS OFFICE

"Shippensburg University's student-focused philosophy remains its hallmark and its strength. That philosophy has enabled the university to be ranked among the best universities in the region for more than a decade by national publications. By maintaining a student focus, the university has been able to achieve some notable goals, including an increase in minority enrollment over the past five years, results of efforts to recruit and retain students of color from throughout the region, including Philadelphia.

"The university has also taken the lead in providing students with alternatives to drinking, including cultural and social programming that offers concerts, films, and internationally known guest speakers such as Danny Glover, Bob Ballard, and James Earl Jones. The university hosts the University-Community Alcohol Coalition Project. Through the Project, representatives from various local, state, and regional agencies and organizations work together to reduce illegal use and abuse of alcohol and drugs. That coalition, which includes students, provides guidance on programming to inform and educate students about drinking, including surveys that show that the number of students who drink is far less than students think. Other efforts include expansion of weekend programming and late-night programming throughout the week. The student-run Activities Program Board also regularly sponsors cultural trips to various major cities on the East Coast. "

For even more information on this school, turn to page 265 of the "Stats" section.

SLIPPERY ROCK UNIVERSITY OF PENNSYLVANIA

OFFICE OF ADMISSIONS, MALTBY CENTER, SLIPPERY ROCK, PA 16057 • ADMISSIONS: 724-738-2015
FAX: 724-738-2913 • E-MAIL: APPLY@SRU.EDU • WEBSITE: WWW.SRU.EDU

Ratings

Quality of Life: 74   Academic: 68   Admissions: 64   Financial Aid: 72

Academics

The environs of Slippery Rock reportedly "provide an academic setting for those serious about learning." In support of that statement, students praise the small class sizes and "excellent tutoring

> **SURVEY SAYS . . .**
> *Students are happy*
> *Lots of beer drinking*
> *Classes are small*

center provided free to students," as well as the "writing center and resident hall study groups." One undergraduate writes, "So far I have noticed that most of the professors here are really cool and laid back." Our sources also make claims such as, "My professors (at least in my major) all know me by name, are very approachable, and help in any way they can so that you will succeed." Students across disciplines benefit from strong programs, noting that "the reputation for many majors is extremely well known." The administration is considered "very helpful" and "takes a personal interest in us as people, not just students." Most agree that Slippery Rock stands as a "generally well-operated facility" where "problems are worked out efficiently."

Life

Slippery Rock existence can be summarized by the following comment: "I think most students try to focus on their school work as much as possible but also want to have a good time." Campus life offers not only "a wide range of activities to participate in to get to meet new people," but also a convenient location "close to a city where there is a lot to do." In terms of athletics, many students take advantage of the luxurious gym, "which includes an indoor rock-climbing wall." Additionally, intramural programs are popular and competitive. Students maintain an appetite for traditional parties, but one student assures potential attendees, "It's a pretty good party school if that's what you're going to school for, but if you want to get a good education, the parties won't get in your way." One damper on social life is the fact that "a lot of people go home on weekends," which can make mixers "kind of boring." However, the consensus remains that the campus provides "a lot of opportunities," to the extent that students are moved to say, "You name it, we do it. It's a great time at the Rock."

Student Body

Described as "everyday people," a marked friendliness pervades the Slippery Rock atmosphere. One student observes, "Even in classes where I don't know anyone, people are friendly. It's a breath of fresh air." Another respondent expands on the characterization by saying, "The students here are very open. They like to get loud at times, but they are serious about their classes and getting their work finished." To dispel concerns for new students, one woman recollects, "I like my fellow students. Being a new freshman worried me, but . . . I've had classes with freshmen, sophomores, juniors, and seniors, and everyone treats everyone [as an] equal." Though some people report that "you see many cliques on this campus," others claim that "mostly everyone on campus gets along." Several students share the opinion that "the school could find a way to make the student body more diverse in terms of culture and race." Overall, many feel that Slippery Rock attendees are bonded by the fact that they "are very motivated to see things get done and to change things that they feel are not right."

ADMISSIONS

Very important factors considered by the admissions committee include: secondary school record. *Important factors considered include:* class rank and standardized test scores. *Other factors considered include:* alumni/ae relation, extracurricular activities, interview, recommendations, and talent/ability. SAT I or ACT required. TOEFL required of all international applicants. High school diploma or GED is required. *High school units required/recommended:* 16 total recommended; 4 English recommended, 3 math recommended, 3 science recommended, 2 foreign language recommended, 4 social studies recommended.

The Inside Word

The sameness of the students' socio-economic/ethnic makeup may give you pause as an applicant, but the undergrads' collective will and involvement in school activities in and out of class are factors that fall solidly in Slippery Rock's favor.

FINANCIAL AID

Students should submit: FAFSA. The Princeton Review suggests that all financial aid forms be submitted as soon as possible after January 1. *Need-based scholarships/grants offered:* Pell, SEOG, state scholarships/grants, private scholarships, and the school's own gift aid. *Loan aid offered:* FFEL Subsidized Stafford, FFEL Unsubsidized Stafford, FFEL PLUS, and Federal Perkins. Federal Work-Study Program available. Institutional employment available. Applicants will be notified of awards on a rolling basis beginning on or about March 15. Off-campus job opportunities are excellent.

FROM THE ADMISSIONS OFFICE

"A rock solid education. A classic residential campus. A safe, small-town setting. An affordable life-long value. Committed, caring faculty. A once-in-a-lifetime experience.

"Slippery Rock University is a comprehensive university of 7,500 students and a member of the State System of Higher Education of Pennsylvania. It is comprised of the following colleges: Education; Humanities, Fine and Performing Arts; Business, Information, and Behavioral Sciences; Health, Environment, and Science; and Graduate Studies and Research. The 600-acre campus is located in western Pennsylvania less than an hour north of Pittsburgh in a safe, relaxed, small-town community. An honors program, academic support services, and learning communities are available to foster student success in a learner-centered environment. Students participate in over 100 co-curricular and extracurricular activities. Intercollegiate and intramural sports, concerts, plays, lectures, and other cultural activities are popular.

"Slippery Rock University offers many bachelor's and master's degrees in numerous majors, minors, and program tracks in a plethora of academic disciplines. The university also offers a Doctor of Physical Therapy degree.

"For additional information regarding admission, scheduling a campus visit, or any other aspect of the University, visit our website at www.sru.edu."

For even more information on this school, turn to page 265 of the "Stats" section.

SUSQUEHANNA UNIVERSITY

514 UNIVERSITY AVENUE, SELINSGROVE, PA 17870 • ADMISSIONS: 570-372-4260 • FAX: 570-372-2722
FINANCIAL AID: 570-372-4450 • E-MAIL: SUADMISS@SUSQU.EDU • WEBSITE: WWW.SUSQU.EDU

Ratings

Quality of Life: 94   Academic: 91   Admissions: 81   Financial Aid: 94

Academics

Professors and the administration at Susquehanna University get "two thumbs up" from students, considering that they "over-exert themselves and work above and beyond the expected." According to a psychology student, "The academic and administrative departments are very well run," and the faculty is described as

> **SURVEY SAYS . . .**
> *Lots of beer drinking*
> *Athletic facilities are great*
> *Students don't get along with local community*
> *Ethnic diversity lacking on campus*
> *Campus easy to get around*
> *Classes are small*
> *Low cost of living*

"kind and knowledgeable" as well as "pretty cool and very interesting." Small-school personal attention is readily available: "Everyone so far has taken an interest in me," writes an English major. Others tell us they visit "professors at home and have very close relationships with them." About ten percent of the student body are members of the Honors program, and over half of Susquehanna undergraduates receive some form of financial aid, often merit-based. The university prides itself on its writing program, part of the English major, which features small workshop classes and frequent student readings of fiction, creative non-fiction, poetry, screenplays, and plays.

Life

Stranded in rural Pennsylvania, surrounded by "too many Amish," Susquehanna students report that there's "not much to do except go to the one bar in town" or "paint your toenails" for fun. A junior qualifies these opinions, reporting that "Selinsgrove is a small town, but a nice small town." The Pocono ski area is nearby for those itching to hit the slopes, but the closest urban life rafts lie at least three hours away in Philadelphia or Pittsburgh. The on-campus social scene "is decent the first year, but after that, if you aren't Greek, it gets old fast," reports a sophomore, and it can be tough to find "somewhere to go to do something besides drink." School-sponsored activities exist, but a senior music major wishes there were "more activities that students would actually go to." A more optimistic student writes, "We go to the campus coffee house, rent movies, and take trips to Wal-Mart. There are so many things to get involved in or do." Many undergraduates praise "the look" of the "beautiful campus," which is home to 80 percent of the student population.

Student Body

One undergrad writes, "SU definitely lacks diversity. It's mostly rich, over-achieving white kids, and the few minorities here tend to only socialize with each other. However, everyone is friendly and gets along." Other students agree that there's "not much discrimination" but that "it's hard to differentiate" between individual members of the "well-dressed," "peaceful," and "really white" student body. A freshman also notes a need to increase "diversity, not just culturally, but in every aspect of the word," seeing as only about 8 percent are international or students of color. Seemingly, "Everyone is from a hick town. They are (many times) small-minded geeks plastered with Greek letters which now make them cool." The advantages of a small school include a public relations major's view that it's possible to "get to know so many people on a personal level." Everyone "smiles all the time," making it "quite easy to make friends," in the experience of one freshman. "I am surprised how people can fool around so much and still do so well," comments an RA.

ADMISSIONS

Very important factors considered by the admissions committee include: class rank, secondary school record, standardized test scores. *Important factors considered include:* character/personal qualities, essays, interview, minority status, recommendations, talent/ability. *Other factors considered include:* alumni/ae relation, extracurricular activities, geographical residence, religious affiliation/commitment, state residency, volunteer work, work experience. SAT II recommended. TOEFL required of all international applicants. High school diploma or GED is required. *High school units required/recommended:* 18 total required; 22 total recommended; 4 English required, 3 math required, 4 math recommended, 3 science required, 4 science recommended, 2 science lab required, 3 science lab recommended, 2 foreign language required, 3 foreign language recommended, 1 social studies required, 2 social studies recommended, 1 history required, 2 elective required.

The Inside Word

Susquehanna is about as low profile as universities come in the age of MTV. Getting in is made easier by the serious competition the university faces from numerous like institutions in the region, some with significantly better reputations.

FINANCIAL AID

Students should submit: FAFSA, CSS/Financial Aid PROFILE, state aid form, business/farm supplement. Regular filing deadline is May 1. The Princeton Review suggests that all financial aid forms be submitted as soon as possible after January 1. *Need-based scholarships/grants offered:* Pell, SEOG, state scholarships/grants, private scholarships, the school's own gift aid. *Loan aid offered:* FFEL Subsidized Stafford, FFEL Unsubsidized Stafford, FFEL PLUS, Federal Perkins, college/university loans from institutional funds. Federal Work-Study Program available. Institutional employment available. Applicants will be notified of awards on a rolling basis beginning on or about January 15. Off-campus job opportunities are good.

FROM THE ADMISSIONS OFFICE

"Students tell us they are getting both a first-rate education and practical experience to help them be competitive upon graduation. Faculty, especially in psychology, marketing, and the sciences, regularly encourage students in their research. Students also do internships at such sites as the White House, Continental Insurance, Estee Lauder, State Street Global Advisors, and Cable News Network. About 90 percent of our graduates go on for advanced degrees or get jobs in their chosen field within six months of graduation. Keeping up with the latest in information technology is easy for our students now that all residence hall rooms have connections to the computer network. Even though the university has six micro-computing laboratories, including one open 24 hours a day, many students find it convenient to use their own PCs to 'surf the 'Net' from their rooms. . . . Small classes, the opportunity to work closely with professors, and the sense of campus community all contribute to the educational experience here. . . . More than 100 student organizations provide lots of opportunity for leadership and involvement in campus life."

For even more information on this school, turn to page 266 of the "Stats" section.

SWARTHMORE COLLEGE

500 COLLEGE AVENUE, SWARTHMORE, PA 19081 • ADMISSIONS: 610-328-8300 • FAX: 610-328-8580
FINANCIAL AID: 610-328-8358 • E-MAIL: ADMISSIONS@SWARTHMORE.EDU • WEBSITE: WWW.SWARTHMORE.EDU

Ratings
Quality of Life: 85   **Academic:** 98   **Admissions:** 98   **Financial Aid:** 83

Academics

"A Swarthmore day is a 28-hour day," notes one student, reflecting on the notoriously heavy workload at this elite liberal arts school. Don't let the reputation scare you off, though; as one student explained, "Academics at Swat are hard; everyone knows that coming in. But that doesn't mean they aren't enjoyable." Furthermore, "Swarthmore has a tremendous

> **SURVEY SAYS . . .**
> *Campus is beautiful*
> *Campus easy to get around*
> *Political activism is hot*
> *Ethnic diversity on campus*
> *Great library*
> *No one cheats*
> *Musical organizations are hot*
> *Great computer facilities*

support network anchored by the professors and administration (as well as other students). When help is needed, there is always someone to turn to." The support is essential, since "the overall stress level here is high from balancing classes, activities, and social life." What do students get in return for their fretting and sweating? Academic freedom, for one; "students at Swarthmore manage to study anything and everything that interests them and may do so [to] whatever depth they choose." They also get "campus resources, including many public computers, electronics in the classroom, and free transportation to nearby campuses and Philadelphia to name a few." And let's not forget professors who "love to really get to know their students. They email you back within an hour, invite you to their homes for dinner, ask you to baby-sit for their kids, and always schedule appointments out of their office hours." Finally, students here enjoy an environment in which "learning is the goal, not the means." One thing they don't get, though, is great grades; as one student told us, "As one of our T-shirts says: 'Anywhere else it would have been an A.'"

Life

Life at Swarthmore, most here agree, is "intense. Between the challenging classes, extracurricular commitments, and small community, people here tend to stress a lot and complain frequently. However, just about everybody who makes it through to graduation looks back on their four (or five or six) years as the most incredible time in their life." On top of their mountain of schoolwork, students "tend to be very involved in campus life and in a wide range of activities. People can be in student government and active in a minority organization and in a play, all at the same time." Accordingly, students have to get their fun on the run and learn to enjoy little pleasures. "Swatties love to have discussions," writes one student. "They will talk about a subject, everything from the gender politics of Wuthering Heights to the imagery of Lord of the Rings, for hours on end." They also "love walking around the gorgeous campus and taking walks in the acres of [the] well-kept arboretum around us." When it's time to party, Swatties do it for free: all on-campus activities are paid for out of the student activity fund. Notes one student, "It's quite possible to go months without spending money on things to do." Others, however, warn that "campus events are enjoyable for the first two years, but after that get a little old." That's when students head off campus, not to surrounding

Swarthmore, which is "a pretty small suburb," but to Philadelphia. There's a train stop "at the foot of campus" that runs kids straight downtown.

Student Body

The "brilliant, creative, engaging, and always ready for a discussion on anything and everything" students of Swarthmore maintain "a very high level of intellectual and social idealism." This social idealism manifests itself in a pervasive political leftism; "almost everyone is so far left politically/ideologically that the Democratic party seems right-wing," explains one undergrad. Many here are "over-involved. A typical Swattie is involved in a ludicrous number of extracurriculars: clubs, sports, volunteering, committees (besides all the work for class!)." Also, "whether a jock or a partygoer, a published writer or world traveler, everyone at Swarthmore has a little bit of dork deep down inside of them, and it's the common bond between us all." As one student put it, "People are unconcerned with matters of fashion, pop culture, and sometimes hygiene." Most Swatties "come from an upper-middle-class background."

ADMISSIONS

Very important factors considered by the admissions committee include: character/personal qualities, class rank, essays, recommendations, secondary school record, standardized test scores. *Important factors considered include:* extracurricular activities. *Other factors considered include:* alumni/ae relation, geographical residence, interview, minority status, talent/ability, volunteer work, work experience. SAT I or ACT required; SAT II also required.

The Inside Word

Swarthmore is as good as they come; among liberal arts colleges there is none better. Candidates face an admissions process that is appropriately demanding and thorough. Even the best qualified of students need to complete their applications with a meticulous approach—during candidate evaluation, serious competition is just another file away. Those who are fortunate enough to be offered admission usually have shown the committee that they have a high level of intellectual curiosity, self-confidence, and motivation.

FINANCIAL AID

Students should submit: FAFSA, institution's own financial aid form, CSS/Financial Aid PROFILE, state aid form, noncustodial (divorced/separated) parent's statement, business/farm supplement, federal tax return, W-2 statements, year-end paycheck stub. Regular filing deadline is mid-February. The Princeton Review suggests that all financial aid forms be submitted as soon as possible after January 1. *Need-based scholarships/grants offered:* Pell, SEOG, state scholarships/grants, private scholarships, the school's own gift aid. *Loan aid offered:* FFEL Subsidized Stafford, FFEL Unsubsidized Stafford, FFEL PLUS, Federal Perkins, state loans, college/university loans from institutional funds. Federal Work-Study Program available. Institutional employment available. Applicants will be notified of awards on or about April 1. Off-campus job opportunities are poor.

FROM THE ADMISSIONS OFFICE

"Swarthmore is a highly selective college of liberal arts and engineering, located 11 miles southwest of Philadelphia. Founded as a coeducational institution in 1864, it is nonsectarian but reflects many traditions and values of its Quaker founders and attracts students who are engaged in the community as well as the classroom. Swarthmore's Honors Program provides an option to study in small seminars during the junior and senior years. A small school by deliberate policy, Swarthmore has an enrollment of about 1,450, with a student/faculty ratio of 8:1. It attracts students from 50 states and 42 countries."

For even more information on this school, turn to page 267 of the "Stats" section.

SWEET BRIAR COLLEGE

PO Box B, Sweet Briar, VA 24595 • Admissions: 434-381-6142 • Fax: 434-381-6152
Financial Aid: 434-381-6156 • E-mail: admissions@sbc.edu • Website: www.sbc.edu

Ratings
Quality of Life: 94   **Academic:** 91   **Admissions:** 81   **Financial Aid:** 94

Academics

Nestled in the foothills of Virginia's Blue Ridge Mountains, Sweet Briar's romantic name and distinctly southern location might lead the uninitiated to think its ladies are receiving instruction in the fine arts of swooning, eyelash batting, and fork placement. Not

> **SURVEY SAYS . . .**
> *Great food on campus, No one cheats*
> *Student government is popular*
> *Campus feels safe, Dorms are like palaces*
> *Class discussions encouraged*
> *Students get along with local community*

so. SBC has "cutting-edge" programs like Law & Society, the Center for Civic Renewal, and an environmental science program that includes, as one junior puts it, "3,250 acres of outdoor campus—woods, lakes, mountains—like having your own personal ecology laboratory." Sweet Briar's strengths also include highly focused instruction, a well-designed advisor program, and excellent professor-student dynamics: "Sweet Briar prides itself on small classes, individual attention, and a supportive environment," writes one student. "In a class of seven people, the professors won't let you fail." One sophomore remarks, "It's not just easy to find your professors here, it's hard to avoid them." Plus, everyone could use a little protection once they get out into the big bad world. Notes a sophomore: "The alumnae network is incredible."

Life

While there's certainly no shortage of enthusiasm for life at Sweet Briar (one student warns, "if I loved it any more than I already do, I would buy it up and keep it")—there are varying opinions about the ups and downs of socializing on and off campus. Writes a senior, "Life at Sweet Briar can get pretty dull with no men around, and the college has been characterized as a 'suitcase school' as many leave during the weekend to visit neighboring colleges"—which include Hampden-Sydney College, University of Virginia, and Washington and Lee. Fairly strict alcohol policies also "force people to go off campus to have fun," though there have been concerted efforts by the administration in the last few years to improve SBC's social programming, which now includes "feature films, musicians, lectures, theater, 'Dell Parties,' casino nights, and formals throughout the year." Though there are the occasional trips to movies, the Wal-Mart, and a local country-and-western bar, a junior complains that "the town is much like Deliverance, and I just want to escape." Despite the negatives, SBC women manage to make the best of the situation, citing the school's stunning location on "a really beautiful campus with lots of great trails for running, hiking, mountain biking, and horseback riding."

Student Body

Sweet Briar women are, in general, happy, active, involved, and mutually supportive. As one sophomore puts it, "The goals they have set for themselves are high and challenging." Adds another, "Living with 600 women changes the way you interact with women overall. Women respect women here." Of course, there are always your slightly irritating overachievers (e.g., "I sing in choir, am a class officer, am the chair of the Saturday Enrichment Program, ride on the fall team, have two campus jobs and a boyfriend!"), but on the whole SBC seems to offer students a noncompetitive, friendly atmosphere in which to pursue their studies. One student lauds "the encouragement of the women here to be all they can and to do whatever [they] want [with their] futures." And though a few students remarked on the ethnic and economic homogeneity of the student body, others disagreed. "Some people think we're a lily-white country club," writes a junior. "They've never been here. I have made friends from a wide variety of countries, cultures, races, and lifestyles. We're friends not because of some phony diversity movement, but because we're united by our academic pursuits." You go girl!

ADMISSIONS

Very important factors considered by the admissions committee include: secondary school record. *Important factors considered include:* class rank, essays, extracurricular activities, recommendations, standardized test scores. *Other factors considered include:* alumni/ae relation, character/personal qualities, interview, minority status, talent/ability, volunteer work, work experience. SAT I or ACT required. TOEFL required of all international applicants. High school diploma or GED is required. *High school units required/recommended:* 16 total required; 20 total recommended; 4 English required, 3 math required, 4 math recommended, 3 science required, 4 science recommended, 2 science lab required, 3 foreign language required, 4 foreign language recommended, 1 social studies required, 2 social studies recommended, 2 history required.

The Inside Word

A small applicant pool tempers selectivity greatly but also allows the admissions committee to take a longer look at most candidates than is typical in college admission. Despite the small applicant pool, candidates are usually well-qualified academically.

FINANCIAL AID

Students should submit: FAFSA, noncustodial (divorced/separated) parent's statement, business/farm supplement. The Princeton Review suggests that all financial aid forms be submitted as soon as possible after January 1. *Need-based scholarships/grants offered:* Pell, SEOG, state scholarships/grants, private scholarships, the school's own gift aid. *Loan aid offered:* Direct Subsidized Stafford, Direct Unsubsidized Stafford, Direct PLUS, Federal Perkins, college/university loans from institutional funds. Federal Work-Study Program available. Institutional employment available. Applicants will be notified of awards on a rolling basis beginning on or about March 1. Off-campus job opportunities are good.

FROM THE ADMISSIONS OFFICE

"The woman who applies to Sweet Briar is mature and far-sighted enough to know what she wants from her college experience. She is intellectually adventuresome, more willing to explore new fields, and more open to challenging her boundaries. Sweet Briar attracts the ambitious, confident woman who enjoys being immersed not only in a first-rate academic program, but in a variety of meaningful activities outside the classroom. Our students take charge and revel in their accomplishments. This attitude follows graduates, enabling them to compete confidently in the corporate world and in graduate school."

For even more information on this school, turn to page 267 of the "Stats" section.

TEMPLE UNIVERSITY

1801 North Broad Street, Philadelphia, PA 19122-6096 • Admissions: 215-204-7200
Fax: 215-204-5694 • Financial Aid: 215-204-8760 • E-mail: tuadm@mail.temple.edu
Website: www.temple.edu

Ratings

Quality of Life: 81   **Academic:** 72   **Admissions:** 79   **Financial Aid:** 75

Academics

Temple students love their school for its ability to integrate "a good education with significant life experiences." The school has earned a "great scholastic reputation" while prioritizing "real-life, hands-on experience with internships, co-ops, and experiential learning that prepare you for life beyond college." Many students agree that Temple helps students "develop thinking skills, ask questions, and wake up to see what the reality is." Professors are praised for "incorporating things from outside of the classroom into the lectures and discussions." Instructors both "know their material" and find "effective ways to relate it to the students." The University's heterogeneous student body is reflected in the faculty, "a diverse, intelligent group" that "finds delight in sharing their knowledge with us." Students gush about the honors program: honors classes "tend to be smaller, more interesting, and contain people who seem to actually enjoy learning." The "extremely supportive" honors professors also "go out of their way to keep in contact with the students." One student values that Temple "can also be very interesting and experimental with its class offerings." As far as logistics go, one respondent writes, " I have had no problem contacting [the] administration when I need help with a problem." Though a few students say, "The bureaucracy sucks," most agree that "the education can be magic." Not to mention affordable.

> **SURVEY SAYS . . .**
> *Ethnic diversity on campus*
> *(Almost) everyone smokes*
> *Athletic facilities are great*
> *Everyone loves the Owls*
> *Lots of beer drinking*
> *Great computer facilities*
> *Great library*
> *Great off-campus food*
> *Hard liquor is popular*

Life

Temple's urban location largely defines the campus' feel. Though the school organizes "free good food, movies, guest speakers, parties, festivals, and cultural bus trips," most students choose to make their own fun in surrounding Philadelphia, "which is easy because we are directly connected to public transportation." Undergraduates agree, "From theatre and museums to shops, clubs, and cafés, Philly has a lot to do." Students just have to "be able to take care of themselves in the city" since the surrounding area is described as "dodgy." One respondent articulates both sides of the issue: "Temple's main strength is the fact that it is in Philadelphia, but this takes away much of the close-knit campus feel." Certain issues do bring people together: "Political activism has become more popular recently, especially concerns over the government and foreign affairs." Fraternities pitch in on the weekend social scene, throwing parties attended mainly by underclassmen and those who live on campus.

Student Body

One student sums it up when she writes, "We call it Diversity University." Repeatedly, surveys emphasize that the undergraduate population comprises students from every imaginable racial, ethnic, religious, and class background. A few unifying factors do emerge: "A typical student is a fairly hardworking, goal-oriented, middle-class American looking to carve out a future for his or herself." But as soon as you think you have a beat on it, someone says, "It is impossible to define a typical student because Temple is full of every different type of person." Students appreciate the diversity, claiming that the mix of "various backgrounds challenges opinions and feeds into active class discussions." In this "huge melting pot," respondents claim, "everyone's differences become their connection to other people." Still, some share, "Most people seem to stick to their own groups, dictated by either major, race, [or] economic status." Others call the campus "annoyingly anonymous" because it is "very much a commuter school." Despite these minor grumbles, Temple students predominantly "look past the stereotypes" and accept their peers "for whom they are and what they are trying to achieve."

ADMISSIONS

Very important factors considered by the admissions committee include: class rank, secondary school record. *Important factors considered include:* standardized test scores. *Other factors considered include:* alumni/ae relation, character/personal qualities, essays, extracurricular activities, recommendations, talent/ability, volunteer work, work experience. SAT I or ACT required. TOEFL required of all international applicants. High school diploma or GED is required. *High school units required/recommended:* 16 total required; 22 total recommended; 4 English required, 3 math required, 4 math recommended, 2 science required, 3 science recommended, 1 science lab required, 2 science lab recommended, 2 foreign language required, 2 social studies required, 1 history required, 2 history recommended, 1 elective required, 3 elective recommended.

The Inside Word

Nearly 50 percent of Temple's applicants are from out of state; 25 percent are from the Philadelphia area, and 25 percent from elsewhere in Pennsylvania. Admissions standards are moderately selective in general, but candidates for the College of Music, in particular, face a rigorous review.

FINANCIAL AID

Students should submit: FAFSA. The Princeton Review suggests that all financial aid forms be submitted as soon as possible after January 1. *Need-based scholarships/grants offered:* Pell, SEOG, state scholarships/grants, private scholarships, the school's own gift aid, Federal Nursing. *Loan aid offered:* FFEL Subsidized Stafford, FFEL Unsubsidized Stafford, FFEL PLUS, Federal Perkins, Federal Nursing, college/university loans from institutional funds. Federal Work-Study Program available. Institutional employment available. Applicants will be notified of awards on a rolling basis beginning on or about February 15. Off-campus job opportunities are excellent.

FROM THE ADMISSIONS OFFICE

"Temple combines the academic resources and intellectual stimulation of a large research university with the intimacy of a small college. The university experienced record growth in attracting new students from all 50 states and over 125 countries: up 60 percent in three years. Students choose from 119 undergraduate majors. Special academic programs include honors, learning communities for first-year undergraduates, co-op education, and study abroad. Temple has seven regional campuses, including Main Campus and the Health Sciences Center in historic Philadelphia, suburban Temple University, Ambler, and overseas campuses in Tokyo and Rome. Main Campus is home to the Tuttleman Learning Center, with 1,000 computer stations linked to Paley Library. The Center is a hub for emerging learning technologies, and is designed for the high-tech students of today and tomorrow. The Liacouras Center is a state-of-the-art entertainment, recreation, and sports complex that hosts concerts, plays, trade shows, and college and professional athletics. It also includes the Independence Blue Cross Student Recreation Center, a major fitness facility for students now and in the future. Students can also take advantage of the new Student Fieldhouse. The university has constructed two new dorms, built to meet an unprecedented demand for main campus housing."

For even more information on this school, turn to page 268 of the "Stats" section.

THIEL COLLEGE

75 COLLEGE AVENUE, GREENVILLE, PA 16125 • ADMISSIONS: 724-589-2345 • FAX: 724-589-2013
E-MAIL: ADMISSION@THIEL.EDU • WEBSITE: WWW.THIEL.EDU

Ratings
Quality of Life: 73   Academic: 71   Admissions: 64   Financial Aid: 85

Academics

Thiel College, a small Lutheran liberal arts school in Western Pennsylvania, boasts small class sizes and accessible professors. One student beams of his professors, "If they had no answers to my

questions (not very often, as their teachings are so thorough, questions are answered as they form in your head), they would not stop until they had found the information to answer those questions." Another writes that the school's biggest strength is "the size. I had a class freshman year with five students. There are seminar classes, discussion courses, and other nontraditional classes open to all students, not just upperclassmen." Profs are hailed as both "top of the line" and "friendly and knowledgeable"—"many would go a great distance to see that their students succeed." One student shares a different perspective: "I have had a few amazing professors that taught me more than I could have dreamed of in a semester. . . . I have also had teachers here who belonged teaching high school and some who belonged in a nursing home rambling on to themselves instead of to a class." Students categorize biology, chemistry, psychology, and theatre as strong programs at their school.

Life

Thiel College is located in Greenville, Pennsylvania, a "pretty boring" town that is only 90 minutes from both Pittsburgh and Cleveland. Writes one, "It is really hard to find something to do in Greenville. You have to have a car to go anywhere because everything that isn't related to alcohol is 20 minutes away. We have Wal-mart, a bowling alley, and about as many bars as we have churches!" "Here people hang out, drink, and go to Wal-Mart," agrees one student who then adds, "For a Lutheran school, they have very little to do with the church." Despite Thiel's "dry campus rules . . . drinking is quite popular," but students seek out other forms of entertainment in nearby towns: "movies, shopping, some people go to clubs, and there is roller-skating and ice-skating." On-campus life has merits, though; insists one, "Even though we live in a small town we have a lot of fun. There are also a lot of school sponsored activities." For some (currently about 45 percent), participation in one of the nine frats and sororities is the way to go; meanwhile, some of the non-Greeks have dubbed themselves "the IDPs (Independent Proud)." An active student lodges the complaint that "student apathy is extremely high . . . . We recently held student government elections, and no candidates ran for the senior class. Five empty spots."

Student Body

A small liberal arts college, "Thiel College is like Thiel High School," according to many, due to its intimate size and social vibe. "Many immature cliques exist here," writes one undergrad, "and the students are not open to meeting people different from themselves." A case in point, one woman states, "I think there are too many minorities. As a white female, I feel like the minority." Yet the student body is 77 percent white, and as one student observes, Thiel "is not nearly diverse enough." There is also "a lot of separation between the Greek and the non-

Greek people," according to one. Despite these issues, most students find that it "is easy to make friends and get involved with activities" at Thiel. One student testifies: "No other place I visited affected me quite the way Thiel did. Even if you don't know someone, there is always a smile and a hello from the people you pass on the sidewalks, rain or shine."

ADMISSIONS

Very important factors considered by the admissions committee include: secondary school record. *Important factors considered include:* character/personal qualities, class rank, extracurricular activities, interview, recommendations, standardized test scores, and talent/ability. *Other factors considered include:* alumni/ae relation, essays, volunteer work, and work experience. SAT I or ACT required. TOEFL required of all international applicants. High school diploma or GED is required. *High school units required/recommended:* 13 total recommended; 4 English recommended, 2 math recommended, 2 science recommended, 2 science lab recommended, 2 foreign language recommended, 3 social studies recommended.

The Inside Word

Opportunities to get involved are ripe for the taking here, especially for students looking to kick-start the campus's interest in politics and diversity. If your interests match Thiel's strong, if unorthodox, structure, this Ohio Valley school is worth serious consideration.

FINANCIAL AID

Students should submit: FAFSA and state aid form. No deadline for regular filing. The Princeton Review suggests that all financial aid forms be submitted as soon as possible after January 1. *Need-based scholarships/grants offered:* Pell, SEOG, state scholarships/grants, private scholarships, and the school's own gift aid. *Loan aid offered:* FFEL Subsidized Stafford, FFEL Unsubsidized Stafford, FFEL PLUS, Federal Perkins, and college/university loans from institutional funds. Federal Work-Study Program available. Institutional employment available. Applicants will be notified of awards on a rolling basis beginning on or about February 1. Off-campus job opportunities are fair.

FROM THE ADMISSIONS OFFICE

"Exclusively ranked by *U.S. News & World Report* as a top-five Best Value among northeastern comprehensive colleges, Thiel is a place where classes are smaller, personal attention is given in and out of the classroom, and friendships are easily formed—all at a fraction of the cost of other private liberal arts schools. Our professors and administrators are easily accessible and involved in students' development academically and personally, one of the reasons why Thiel graduates are so successful. In fact, 98 percent of graduates have a job or are enrolled in graduate school within eight months of graduation. Faculty and administration help new students successfully adapt to college life through Thiel's First-Year Experience program. Thiel's enrollment is growing, as are facilities and resources such as the Mouganis Instructional Media Center. The recently constructed Howard Miller Student Center is the hub of campus life, with lounges, support services offices, an engaging bookstore, art galleries, the Options convenience store, Starbucks bistro, and a world-class dining hall. Also new to campus are a unique Center for Excellence in Greek Life, a multi-sport athletic complex, the state-of-the-art fitness center, and new townhouse-style apartments. Thiel's "everywhere" campuswide networking features high-speed Internet access, cable television, and enhanced telephones with voice-mail. Thiel's students become leaders and active participants in more than 50 organizations, and more than half our students take advantage of study abroad and internship opportunities. Personalized financial aid benefits more than 95 percent of Thiel students, making Thiel's values-based education an affordable investment in your future. Apply free online at www.thiel.edu."

For even more information on this school, turn to page 269 of the "Stats" section.

TOWSON UNIVERSITY

8000 YORK ROAD, TOWSON, MD 21252-0001 • ADMISSIONS: 1-888-4TOWSON • FAX: 410-704-3030
E-MAIL: ADMISSIONS@TOWSON.EDU • WEBSITE: WWW.DISCOVER.TOWSON.EDU

Ratings
Quality of Life: 78   **Academic:** 70   **Admissions:** 63   **Financial Aid:** 68

Academics

Towson University's location—just outside of Baltimore and a quick drive to Washington, D.C.—is one of its chief benefits, allowing students to supplement their

> **SURVEY SAYS . . .**
> *Classes are small*
> *Instructors are good teachers*

education with a wide range of internships, professional observation opportunities, and cultural interactions. Towson is the academic home of around 12,000 full-time undergrads, as well as nearly 2,000 part-timers. Despite these substantial numbers, this public university manages to provide "individualized attention right from the start." One student boasts that professors "know me by name and are willing at the drop of a hat to assist me in any problem that comes my way." Most class sizes remain small, and according to one satisfied undergrad, "the majority of my professors involve the students in [their] lectures by asking thought-provoking questions and letting us pretty much determine the structure of the class." The most popular majors at Towson are business administration, elementary education, mass communication, psychology, and biology; students have also urged us to point out the strong programs in art, English, health, and theatre and vocal performance. Most complaints lodged by Towson students are in regards to the measly funding that the state of Maryland offers to its second-largest institution and the fact that Towson is temporarily without a president. One student assures, "While we do not have a president, the faculty and student body still run smoothly."

Life

At Towson University, "if you want to drink and party, you can; if you want to study all night, you can; if you like to just relax with your friends, you can." After all, Towson is a sizable university at the edge of a major metropolitan area. On campus, Greek life is reportedly popular, and "there's a lot to get involved in as far as extracurricular activities" are concerned. And while some go home on the weekends, students tell us that "anything you could be interested in is probably just a few blocks away" from campus, including a mall, a movie theater, and places to eat. And for a taste of urban life, Baltimore is just down the road. "Almost everyone goes into Baltimore at least once a week for something," says a student. One of the biggest Baltimore draws is the club scene. "There's a different Baltimore club to go to each night of the week" and "they all have 'college nights' on different days." To ensure safe travel, "free buses are available every weekend to and from the clubs." Other students take to the city for the museums, the shopping, the sporting events, and the restaurants. "There is ALWAYS something to do in Towson and Baltimore," one student reports.

Student Body

Towson pulls a substantial portion of its student population from its northern neighbors, New Jersey and New York, but Maryland natives make up the majority of the student body. "Many people here have their own groups of friends even before they start attending" college, so cliques are somewhat prevalent. But "whether students live on campus and work part time or commute from home [or] work full-time attending classes at night or join a sorority on campus, all kinds of students mix here." When asked about diversity, students assure us that "there are many different kinds of people," while the student body is nonetheless a "majority white population." Just add to that mix the more than 800 international students from 96 countries that Towson enrolls and you'll find that a multitude of experiences are possible here.

ADMISSIONS

Very important factors considered by the admissions committee include: secondary school record. *Important factors considered include:* class rank and standardized test scores. *Other factors considered include:* essays, recommendations, state residency, and talent/ability.

The Inside Word

Towson's large size doesn't seem to present a problem for students; solid facilities and resources within walking and driving distance make TU and its 30 undergrad majors a great option.

FINANCIAL AID

Students should submit: FAFSA. No deadline for regular filing. The Princeton Review suggests that all financial aid forms be submitted as soon as possible after January 1. *Need-based scholarships/grants offered:* Pell, SEOG, state scholarships/grants, private scholarships, and the school's own gift aid. *Loan aid offered:* Direct Subsidized Stafford, Direct Unsubsidized Stafford, Direct PLUS, and Federal Perkins. Federal Work-Study Program available. Institutional employment available. Applicants will be notified of awards on a rolling basis beginning on or about March 15. Off-campus job opportunities are good.

FROM THE ADMISSIONS OFFICE

"Towson University is one of the most dynamic college communities in the country, offering academic programs that provide a solid liberal arts foundation and preparation for jobs and graduate school. Founded in 1866, Towson University today is nationally recognized for programs in the arts, sciences, business, communications, health professions, and education and computer science. *U.S. News & World Report* names Towson as one of the best regional public universities in the United States and Kiplinger's magazine counts us among America's great schools with reasonable cost. Students choose from more than 60 undergraduate majors and 37 graduate programs. Towson offers a student-centered learning environment with big-school choices and small-school personal attention. We encourage students to pursue learning inside and outside the classroom—through internships, student organizations, extracurricular activities, and research projects with faculty.

"An NCAA Division I program, Towson fields intercollegiate athletic teams in 23 sports. Our 24-acre sports complex includes University Stadium, home of Tiger football, field hockey, track, and lacrosse. The Tiger basketball, volleyball, and gymnastics teams compete at the 5,000-seat Towson Center. Athletic facilities include an NCAA-regulation swimming pool, gymnasiums, a sand volleyball court, tennis courts, a fitness center, and racquetball and squash courts.

"A member of the University System of Maryland, we enroll more than 17,000 students on our 328-acre campus located just eight miles north of downtown Baltimore. Local attractions include the National Aquarium, Oriole Park at Camden Yards, the Maryland Science Center, the Walters Art Museum, and historic Fells Point. The campus is a 10-minute walk to suburban shops, restaurants, movie theaters, and bookstores."

For even more information on this school, turn to page 269 of the "Stats" section.

UNITED STATES NAVAL ACADEMY

117 DECATUR ROAD, ANNAPOLIS, MD 21402 • ADMISSIONS: 410-293-4361 • FAX: 410-295-1815
E-MAIL: WEBMAIL@GWMAIL.USNA.COM • WEBSITE: WWW.USNA.EDU

Ratings
Quality of Life: 84   **Academic:** 99   **Admissions:** 99   **Financial Aid:** 99

Academics

Future Naval and Marine officers at the USNA—known as "midshipmen" or just "mids"—enter an academic world distinct from that their civilian counterparts do. First of all, the academy dictates all freshman-year classes and virtually all courses outside of a student's major in subsequent years. Professors differ in that "the only research [they] run is as a secondary researcher to an undergraduate project." Focussed on teaching, the mix of civilian and military professors couldn't be more accessible: "On several occasions my chemistry professor has come up to my company area and gone room to room helping people in first-year chemistry." The administration is less popular, characterized as "ridiculously overbearing and intrusive" and accused of "micromanaging every aspect of our life." Some students praise the efficiency born of the military chain of command, but others whine, "The administration runs things so well because we have little choice and no way to disagree." The "outrageous punishments" are said to "only make people cynical and unhappy." Deep-seated traditions and mounds of paperwork ensure that "you cannot change a thing, no matter how ridiculous it is." The free tuition, room, and board, along with a guaranteed job at graduation, make the hassles easier to swallow.

> **SURVEY SAYS . . .**
> *Very little drug use*
> *Everyone loves the Midshipmen*
> *(Almost) everyone plays intramural sports*
> *Classes are small*
> *Popular college radio*
> *Unattractive campus*
> *Campus difficult to get around*
> *Library needs improving*
> *Lab facilities are great*
> *Computer facilities need improving*

Life

A common refrain is that the academy is "a good place to be from but not to be at." One midshipman admits, "People don't pick this place for the lifestyle." But others state that the atmosphere can be "wonderful and challenging." However, incarceration analogies are alarmingly common: one student writes, "You are in jail for four years." Plebes (freshmen) are given only 12 hours of freedom per week, from 10 a.m. to 10 p.m. on Saturdays; the rest of the time they are on campus and in uniform, prohibited from driving or wearing civilian clothes until they are juniors. Though life is "very restricted," one student claims, "It is for a purpose and has worth." Drinking laws are strictly enforced, and no alcohol is allowed on campus. Thus, "for fun, we get the hell away from the academy," which generally means getting plowed in Annapolis, visiting nearby colleges such as UVA and Georgetown, or seeing a movie at the mall. Local sponsor families provide relief for students, mostly in the form of home-cooked meals.

Student Body

Not many colleges have students who say, "We must be prepared to die for one another." As part of "the biggest fraternity in the world," mids take camaraderie to a new level while fiercely "competing against each other to be the best." There is a fair share of ruthless climbers, "who don't mind who they have to step on to get one rung higher up the ladder." It's still tough to be female at this historically male institution; "strained male-female relationships" are commonly noted. But though "girls aren't treated too well, minorities are treated great" because "we share a common thread which lowers the traditional racial boundaries." Being in uniform also means that "you can't tell who comes from money and who doesn't." Amid this "type A," "moral, intelligent," "goal-oriented," and "aloof" student body, "liberal opinions are hard to find." One student observes a split between "those who buy into the indoctrination system and those who rebel." A student from the latter group warns against "group-think syndrome," concluding that "being an individual can be a good thing."

ADMISSIONS

Very important factors considered by the admissions committee include: character/personal qualities, class rank, essays, extracurricular activities, interview, recommendations, secondary school record, standardized test scores. *Important factors considered include:* talent/ability. *Other factors considered include:* alumni/ae relation, geographical residence, volunteer work, work experience. SAT I or ACT required. TOEFL required of all international applicants. *High school units required/recommended:* 4 English recommended, 4 math recommended, 2 science recommended, 1 science lab recommended, 2 foreign language recommended, 2 history recommended.

The Inside Word

It doesn't take a genius to recognize that getting admitted to Annapolis requires true strength of character; simply completing the arduous admissions process is an accomplishment worthy of remembrance. Those who have successful candidacies are strong, motivated students, and leaders in both school and community. Perseverance is an important character trait for anyone considering the life of a midshipman—the application process is only the beginning of a truly challenging and demanding experience.

FINANCIAL AID

The Princeton Review suggests that all financial aid forms be submitted as soon as possible after January 1.

FROM THE ADMISSIONS OFFICE

"The Naval Academy offers you a unique opportunity to associate with a broad cross-section of the country's finest young men and women. You will have the opportunity to pursue a four-year program that develops you mentally, morally, and physically as no civilian college can. As you might expect, this program is demanding, but the opportunities are limitless and more than worth the effort. To receive an appointment to the academy, you need four years of high school preparation to develop the strong academic, athletic, and extracurricular background required to compete successfully for admission. You should begin preparing in your freshman year and apply for admission at the end of your junior year. Selection for appointment to the academy comes as a result of a complete evaluation of your admissions package and completion of the nomination process. Complete admissions guidance may be found at www.usna.edu."

For even more information on this school, turn to page 270 of the "Stats" section.

UNIVERSITY OF DELAWARE

116 HULLIHEN HALL, NEWARK, DE 19716 • ADMISSIONS: 302-831-8123 • FAX: 302-831-6905
FINANCIAL AID: 302-831-8761 • E-MAIL: ADMISSIONS@UDEL.EDU • WEBSITE: WWW.UDEL.EDU/VIEWBOOK

Ratings
Quality of Life: 84   Academic: 79   Admissions: 83   Financial Aid: 83

Academics

Located at the very center of an urban corridor that stretches from New York City to Washington, D.C., the University of Delaware manages to provide its undergrads with a traditional university education and the opportunity to engage in a meaningful way in today's global society. Besides the old-school virtues of "a beautiful campus, strong academic reputa-

> **SURVEY SAYS . . .**
> *Frats and sororities dominate social scene*
> *Class discussions are rare*
> *Hard liquor is popular*
> *(Almost) everyone smokes, Great library*
> *Large classes, Campus difficult to get around*
> *Student government is unpopular*
> *Dorms are like dungeons*
> *Lots of TAs teach upper-level courses*

tion, and wonderful people," UD was one of the first universities to offer study abroad programs on every continent (as one senior points out, "Who could pass up learning French in Martinique—or economics in Australia—during the winter?"). Additionally, besides being the recipient of a huge influx of funds during the last few years to upgrade their technological capabilities and connectivity, it's also one of the only schools in the country designated a land-grant, sea-grant, urban-grant, and space-grant institution. All that and professors who are "excellent, accessible" and remember students' names too? Yes, writes a junior, "especially when they sense you have a question or concern, or haven't completed an assignment." A top-notch, selective Honors Program and opportunities for undergraduate research "allow for a rigorous academic career," notes one upperclassman—so do the "demanding but fun" classes. And though there are some complaints about "poor teaching style" and an administration that cares more about prospective, rather than currently enrolled, students ("All the construction makes it hard to drive around!" gripes a junior), undergrads realize that the school's many excellent resources, a fairly good financial aid program, and an administration and faculty that are "genuinely interested in students" generally make for a "positive" university experience.

Life

A UD sophomore waxes philosophical: "Life at the University of Delaware is just that, life! There are tough times and easy times, and all along the way you have so many avenues of help available." In keeping with their take on academics, UD students seem to favor a positive approach to life on this large, "fun," and always interesting college campus. "There is always something to do," claims a junior. Whether it be partying at the residence halls at one of the many different schools that make up the university, going to see an a capella concert, a student play, or an athletic event, or just hanging out at one of the local watering holes, undergrads seem to agree that at UD "there's too much to do and not enough time to do it." (Even "seasonal events like hayrides" get a mention.) As for partying, though one senior makes the case that "instead of using the school to broaden their horizons and think, students use it to get drunk every weekend," another points out that at UD, "you have plenty of options if drinking is not your thing." Newark is a "nice, small" town, after all, and if that's not enough, well, there's always a hayride.

Student Body

"Extremely friendly" peeps who "say 'hi' just because they're crossing the street towards each other" are just one reason why students love UD. Its "warm environment" and "easygoing atmosphere" are a couple more. "The overall student body is a very accepting group of individuals," adds a sophomore. "It makes such a large school more welcoming and inviting." Some would argue that these "individuals" are really one big "white, Abercrombie, upper-middle-class yuppie." There is also the sense that many students are apolitical, self-segregated, and a tad "stuck up." Notes a self-identified "left-wing" senior, "I like my friends, but it took me a while to find progressive activist students on a conservative, apathetic campus like this one."

ADMISSIONS

Very important factors considered by the admissions committee include: essays, secondary school record. *Important factors considered include:* character/personal qualities, class rank, extracurricular activities, geographical residence, recommendations, standardized test scores, state residency, talent/ability. *Other factors considered include:* alumni/ae relation, minority status, volunteer work, work experience. SAT I or ACT required; SAT II recommended. TOEFL required of all international applicants. High school diploma or GED is required. *High school units required/recommended:* 16 total required; 4 English required, 2 math required, 4 math recommended, 2 science required, 3 science recommended, 1 science lab required, 2 foreign language required, 4 foreign language recommended, 1 social studies required, 2 social studies recommended, 2 history required, 3 history required.

Inside Word

Most students applying to Delaware face a moderately selective admissions process focused mainly on grades and tests with some focus on nonacademic characteristics. Those who seek to enter the university's honors program need to be far more thorough in completing their applications and much better prepared academically in order to gain admission. The honors program has high expectations; from what we know, it appears to be well worth it.

FINANCIAL AID

Students should submit: FAFSA. Regular filing deadline is March 15. The Princeton Review suggests that all financial aid forms be submitted as soon as possible after January 1. *Need-based scholarships/grants offered:* Pell, SEOG, state scholarships/grants, private scholarships, the school's own gift aid. *Loan aid offered:* Direct Subsidized Stafford, Direct Unsubsidized Stafford, Direct PLUS, Federal Perkins, Federal Nursing. Federal Work-Study Program available. Institutional employment available. Applicants will be notified of awards on a rolling basis beginning on or about March 15. Off-campus job opportunities are good.

FROM THE ADMISSIONS OFFICE

"The University of Delaware is a major national research university with a long-standing commitment to teaching and serving undergraduates. It is one of only a few universities in the country designated as a land-grant, sea-grant, urban-grant, and space-grant institution. The academic strength of this university is found in its highly selective Honors Program, nationally recognized Undergraduate Research Program, and its successful alumni, including three Rhodes Scholars since 1998. The University of Delaware offers the wide range of majors and course offerings expected of a university, but in spirit remains a small place where you can interact with your professors and feel at home. The beautiful green campus is ideally located at the very center of the East Coast 'megacity' that stretches from New York City to Washington, D.C. All of these elements, combined with an endowment approaching $1 billion and a spirited Division I athletics program make the University of Delaware a tremendous value."

For even more information on this school, turn to page 270 of the "Stats" section.

UNIVERSITY OF MARYLAND, BALTIMORE COUNTY

1000 HILLTOP CIRCLE, BALTIMORE, MD 21250 • ADMISSIONS: 410-455-2291 • FAX: 410-455-1094
FINANCIAL AID: 410-455-2387 • E-MAIL: ADMISSIONS@UMBC.EDU • WEBSITE: WWW.UMBC.EDU

Ratings
Quality of Life: 76   **Academic:** 74   **Admissions:** 80   **Financial Aid:** 83

Academics

The University of Maryland, Baltimore County has prospered over the last few years, and its bragging rights echoed in the comments of their students. In the not-so-distant past, UMBC primarily served a student body of bright Marylanders who had underachieved in high school. UMBC offered them a chance to

> **SURVEY SAYS . . .**
> Very little drug use, (Almost) everyone smokes
> Class discussions are rare, Popular college radio
> High cost of living, Large classes
> Unattractive campus
> Ethnic diversity on campus
> Campus difficult to get around
> Students are not very happy

prove their academic worth, and so they'd come, bust their humps for good grades, and then transfer out to "better" schools. In the process, UMBC developed a reputation as a solid, no-nonsense school that pushed students to their limits. A UMBC degree began to carry greater cachet, and, consequently, more and more kids started to stick around for the full four years. Out-of-state students started arriving, and today Baltimore's commuter campus is well on the way to transforming itself into a residential school with a strong regional reputation. Students here report that "the focus of UMBC's academia lies in scientific research," and while professors "are very accessible and willing to make time for students outside of office hours and class," undergrads also warn that "the quality of professors varies quite widely, especially at the intro level. In the upper-level courses, however, I have taken, the professors are generally very knowledgeable and courteous." UMBC is a "very competitive, very academic school" that is "not for slackers," but students note that "there are many programs here to help those who have trouble academically." Students warn that UMBC's administration requires "far too many procedures . . . complications, and hassles."

Life

Although more and more a residential campus, UMBC is still growing into the shoes of a full-to-capacity residential college. Significant growth is especially true for this year's freshman class with nearly 80 percent living on campus. "The on-campus community isn't as large as most schools," explains one student, "but the school is building, and building, and keeping on building new dorms, so the on-campus community is growing. There are a lot more things to do on campus now then there was when I was a freshman." Most sponsored activities take place in The Commons, UMBC's new center for campus life. During the week there are "tons of school-sponsored social events (which can be lame sometimes but are usually pretty cool). The only times there aren't many people around are weekends. They [weekends, not students] can be absolutely dead." Campus life is further dampened by school drinking policies: "The campus is very strict about drinking and noise. People having fun in the dorms or apartment areas quickly arouses attention from the authorities because it is so unusual." Accordingly, "most people leave campus for fun. The average UMBC student spends his Friday night in Baltimore at a club. Otherwise he's sitting in his dorm room playing Counter-Strike." Adds one student, "Fun is going to Baltimore's Inner Harbor (you better have money because it's expensive). There is also Fells Point for the drinkers among us (very dirty). If not that, D.C. isn't that far away, and it's cleaner anyway."

Student Body

"There is a lot of diversity at UMBC, which is good," students tell us, although many feel that "there are some serious problems with ethnic cliques." "Most of my friends here are white," explains one white student, "for the simple reason that the different races just don't seem to interact as much." Most communication among different groups occurs in the classroom, allowing students to "learn so much about other cultures and ethnicities. It's an experience and understanding I could not have gotten elsewhere."

ADMISSIONS

Very important factors considered by the admissions committee include: secondary school record, standardized test scores. *Important factors considered include:* class rank, essays, recommendations. *Other factors considered include:* character/personal qualities, extracurricular activities, interview, talent/ability, volunteer work, work experience. SAT I or ACT required. TOEFL required of all international applicants. High school diploma or GED is required. *High school units required/recommended:* 22 total required; 23 total recommended; 4 English required, 3 math required, 4 math recommended, 3 science required, 2 science lab required, 2 foreign language required, 2 social studies required, 2 history required, 4 elective required.

The Inside Word

The State of Maryland seems blessed with several strong, small, public universities in addition to its flagship campus at College Park. UMBC is one of those to watch; its national visibility and admissions standards are on the rise. Strong students are attracted by UMBC's emphasis on academic achievement. As a result, the admissions committee has grown to expect evidence of challenging academic course work throughout high school from its candidates, preferably at the honors or AP level. This competitive path will give you the best shot for admission if you're an eager learner looking for a campus where the academic experience is engaging.

FINANCIAL AID

Students should submit: FAFSA. No deadline for regular filing. The Princeton Review suggests that all financial aid forms be submitted as soon as possible after January 1. *Need-based scholarships/grants offered:* Pell, SEOG, state scholarships/grants, private scholarships, the school's own gift aid. *Loan aid offered:* FFEL Subsidized Stafford, FFEL Unsubsidized Stafford, FFEL PLUS, Federal Perkins. Federal Work-Study Program available. Institutional employment available. Applicants will be notified of awards on a rolling basis beginning on or about March 15. Off-campus job opportunities are excellent.

FROM THE ADMISSIONS OFFICE

"UMBC students find out quickly that learning at an honors university takes place in many different ways and in a variety of settings. Students discover an environment with a strong undergraduate liberal arts and sciences focus. A midsize public research university, UMBC provides students with opportunities to work with nationally recognized faculty on research ranging from AIDS prevention and environmental issues affecting Chesapeake Bay to computer graphics and animation. The 2003 Kaplan/Newsweek 'How to Get Into College' guide names UMBC as one of 'America's Hot Schools.' UMBC's academic reputation and industry partnerships help to place students in promising careers and leading graduate programs. In fact, one-third of UMBC students immediately go on to many of the nation's finest graduate or professional schools including Harvard, Johns Hopkins, Yale, and Stanford."

For even more information on this school, turn to page 271 of the "Stats" section.

UNIVERSITY OF MARYLAND, COLLEGE PARK

MITCHELL BUILDING, COLLEGE PARK, MD 20742-5235 • ADMISSIONS: 301-314-8385 • FAX: 301-314-9693
FINANCIAL AID: 301-314-9000 • E-MAIL: UM-ADMIT@UGA.UMD.EDU • WEBSITE: WWW.MARYLAND.EDU

Ratings
Quality of Life: 69 **Academic:** 75 **Admissions:** 81 **Financial Aid:** 82

Academics

The very affordable University of Maryland is a major research university that offers a "professional atmosphere" and, for those who qualify, an exemplary Honors Program with small classes and lots of personal attention. As at many of the behemoth state universities, though, large lecture classes are the norm for the typical student. Excellent engineering, physics, economics, and business departments provide just a few of

> **SURVEY SAYS . . .**
> *Student publications are popular*
> *Ethnic diversity on campus*
> *Everyone loves the Terrapins*
> *Frats and sororities dominate social scene*
> *Great on-campus food*
> *Campus difficult to get around*
> *Students are not very happy*
> *Students are cliquish*
> *Students don't like College Park, MD*
> *(Almost) no one listens to college radio*

the near-limitless choices awaiting the self-starter here. Writes one student, "To the self-directed, enterprising student, Maryland affords immense opportunity. To those with no talent for getting through endless bureaucracy, go somewhere else!" Maryland's core curriculum, usually completed during the first two years, requires students to fulfill a wide range of distribution requirements. During their senior year, undergrads must complete two seminars designed to help integrate these disparate core courses into their major fields of study. Students write that their final two years here are better and more enjoyable than the first two. As one junior explains, "At first you feel like a number, but as you get into your upper-level classes and classes for your major, teachers become more available and there is more individual attention." Professors vary from those who are "interesting, provide humor, and keep me relatively awake" to those who "teach just so they can do research." Of the latter type, one biology major reports that "if you learn to be assertive, professors and staff are more than willing to give you some of their precious time." Students complain that "advising is horrible. There should be someone to advise you not to be advised by an advisor." As for administration, "for a big campus, it runs pretty smoothly."

Life

Maryland's "huge, largely diverse," and "great campus" has "something for everyone." To some, it's "Party Park," with "lotsa parties and cool bars. You can walk down the street and always find a good party." Others focus on the immensely popular intercollegiate sports teams. Gushes one student, "Men's basketball is huge. Games are so much fun!" Football and lacrosse also pull in big crowds. Intramural sports are big, as are the literally hundreds of clubs and extracurricular activities housed on campus. Fraternities and sororities also exert a "pretty strong" influence on campus life and provide numerous social activities. Writes one undergrad, "There is always something going on on campus and off campus, and if it doesn't suit you, D.C. is only a Metro ride away." The nation's capital has "plenty to do . . . lots of concerts," clubs, and restaurants, while Baltimore, "only 30 minutes away by car," boasts an ever-expanding downtown nightlife. College Park's choice location also provides abundant opportunities for work and "great internships," not only in the two major cities but also in nearby Annapolis, Maryland's capital. Students complain that their hometown, College Park, does not live "up to its potential" and caution that having your own wheels makes city jaunts much easier. Beware though: "We really need more parking spaces. And we need to build more dorms. No one should have to live in a double room with two other roommates. That is torture."

Student Body

Maryland students are, by and large, a pleasant group. Writes one undergrad, "If you smile at someone, they'll be sure to smile back. Even with a campus of 30,000, you're bound to run into someone you know." Most consider themselves "easy-going" and "apathetic" but "decent people who wish to hold on to their beliefs without criticism." By Maryland state law, "70 percent come from Maryland. Some are nice, some aren't." The majority are "suburban white kids from public schools," but a substantial student-of-color population means that "the diversity at UMCP is great; however, there is little interaction between groups of different cultures."

ADMISSIONS

Very important factors considered by the admissions committee include: secondary school record, standardized test scores. *Important factors considered include:* class rank, essays, recommendations, state residency, talent/ability. *Other factors considered include:* alumni/ae relation, character/personal qualities, extracurricular activities, geographical residence, minority status, volunteer work, work experience. SAT I or ACT required; SAT I preferred. TOEFL required of all international applicants. High school diploma or GED is required. *High school units required/recommended:* 16 total required; 17 total recommended; 4 English required, 3 math required, 4 math recommended, 2 science required, 2 science lab required, 2 foreign language required, 3 social studies required.

The Inside Word

Maryland's initial candidate review process emphasizes academic credentials and preparedness. Through this first review, roughly 20 percent of the applicant pool is either admitted or denied. The remaining 80 percent are then evaluated in depth by admissions officers and reviewed by an admissions committee of seven, who collectively decide upon each candidate. Don't take essays and the compilation of other personal material that is required of applicants lightly. It's uncommon for a large university to devote this kind of attention to candidate selection. Perhaps this explains why so many students here made Maryland their first choice.

FINANCIAL AID

Students should submit: FAFSA. Regular filing deadline is June 30. The Princeton Review suggests that all financial aid forms be submitted as soon as possible after January 1. *Need-based scholarships/grants offered:* Pell, SEOG, state scholarships/grants, private scholarships, the school's own gift aid. *Loan aid offered:* FFEL Subsidized Stafford, FFEL Unsubsidized Stafford, FFEL PLUS, Federal Perkins. Federal Work-Study Program available. Institutional employment available. Applicants will be notified of awards on or about April 1. Off-campus job opportunities are excellent.

FROM THE ADMISSIONS OFFICE

"Commitment to excellence, to diversity, to learning—these are the hallmarks of a Maryland education. As the state's flagship campus and one of the nation's leading public universities, Maryland offers students and faculty the opportunity to come together to explore and create knowledge, to debate and discover our similarities and our differences, and to serve as a model of intellectual and cultural excellence for the state and the nation's capital. With leading programs in engineering, business, journalism, architecture, and the sciences, the university offers an outstanding educational value."

For even more information on this school, turn to page 272 of the "Stats" section.

UNIVERSITY OF PENNSYLVANIA

1 COLLEGE HALL, PHILADELPHIA, PA 19104 • ADMISSIONS: 215-898-7507 • FAX: 215-898-9670
FINANCIAL AID: 215-898-1988 • E-MAIL: INFO@ADMISSIONS.UGAO.UPENN.EDU • WEBSITE: WWW.UPENN.EDU

Ratings

Quality of Life: 85   **Academic:** 97   **Admissions:** 99   **Financial Aid:** 83

Academics

Penn is one of the hottest names in American higher education, and students here tell us that its reputation is well deserved. First of all, there's the top-notch faculty. Writes one giddy freshman, "I mean, I've already had profs who are world famous." And while

> **SURVEY SAYS . . .**
> *Registration is a breeze*
> *Great library, Theater is hot*
> *Student publications are popular*
> *(Almost) no one listens to college radio*
> *Musical organizations are hot, Large classes*

"professors expect students to think for themselves," they're usually open to "one-on-one instruction during office hours if lectures are not sufficient." In addition to office hours, undergraduates can access professors through freshman seminar classes, and many profs live right on campus. Many students agree, however, that some of their professors are most interested in their research and "only teach because they have to." With so many professors involved in academic inquiry, however, "research opportunities [for undergraduates] abound." Regardless of professorial focus, Penn students across the board tell us they're challenged and satisfied. A few complain, however, that a pervasive business-like mentality among students, faculty, and administrators sometimes makes Penn seem "more practical than intellectual." Other complaints involve the large "intro and lecture courses" and the hit-or-miss quality of TAs.

Life

"This is the only Ivy where you can have a normal college experience in terms of social life," declares one Penn student. "People study during the week, and then know how to party on the weekends." Whether the partying occurs in the main hall of a frat house, in the living room of an off-campus apartment, or on the dance floor of an Old City club, you can be sure that parties here are "frequent, loud, and a lot of fun." The university offers "a wealth of various cultural shows every weekend—comedy, musical, dramatic, and ethnic. And people also find time to go to movies and, of course, to athletic events." While not all sports are widely supported by the student body, "football and basketball games are huge events, especially the Princeton rivalry games." Penn students also take advantage of the city surrounding them. From "downtown Philly," campus is only "a 5-minute bus or cab ride, or a 15-minute walk." The part-bohemian/part-commercial South Street is favorite spot for students and native Philadelphians alike. "West Philadelphia, where the university is located, is not the greatest place in the world," admits one student. "But there are wonderful places to eat and the campus is very safe."

Student Body

Penn is often referred to as "The Social Ivy" because its students are rumored to be the hardest partiers in the Ivy League. Many students wear this badge proudly. One student notes that because many students come from families at "the higher end" of the financial ladder, it can sometimes seem that Penn students "were all born with silver spoons in" an unprintable part of their anatomies. For a significant portion of the Penn population, fashion savvy and "designer labels" seem to be social denominators. But Penn is too large a university to let generalities tell the whole story, and despite the stereotypes, the university boasts an admirably diverse student body.

ADMISSIONS

Very important factors considered by the admissions committee include: character/personal qualities, essays, recommendations, secondary school record. *Important factors considered include:* alumni/ae relation, extracurricular activities, standardized test scores. *Other factors considered include:* class rank, geographical residence, interview, minority status, talent/ability, volunteer work, work experience. TOEFL required of all international applicants. High school diploma or GED is required. *High school units required/recommended:* 17 total required; 4 English required, 4 math required, 3 science required, 3 foreign language required, 3 social studies required, 2 history required.

The Inside Word

After a small decline a few cycles ago, applications are once again climbing at Penn. The competition in the applicant pool is formidable. Applicants can safely assume that they need to be one of the strongest students in their graduating class in order to be successful.

FINANCIAL AID

Students should submit: FAFSA, institution's own financial aid form, CSS/Financial Aid PROFILE, parent's and student's federal income tax returns (for verification). The Princeton Review suggests that all financial aid forms be submitted as soon as possible after January 1. *Need-based scholarships/grants offered:* Pell, SEOG, state scholarships/grants, private scholarships, the school's own gift aid. *Loan aid offered:* FFEL Subsidized Stafford, FFEL Unsubsidized Stafford, FFEL PLUS, Federal Perkins, Federal Nursing, college/university loans from institutional funds, Penn Guaranteed Loan. Federal Work-Study Program available. Institutional employment available. Applicants will be notified of awards on or about April 1. Off-campus job opportunities are excellent.

FROM THE ADMISSIONS OFFICE

"The nation's first university, the University of Pennsylvania had its beginnings in 1740, some 36 years before Thomas Jefferson, Benjamin Franklin (Penn's founder), and their fellow revolutionaries went public in Philadelphia with incendiary notions about life, liberty and the pursuit of happiness. Today, Penn continues in the spirit of the Founding Fathers, developing the intellectual, discussion-oriented seminars that comprise the majority of our course offerings, shaping innovative new courses of study, and allowing a remarkable degree of academic flexibility to its undergraduate students.

"Penn is situated on a green, tree-lined, 260-acre, urban campus, four blocks west of the Schuylkill River in Philadelphia. The broad lawns that connect Penn's stately halls embody a philosophy of academic freedom within our undergraduate schools. Newly developed interdisciplinary programs fusing classical disciplines with practical, professional options enable Penn to define cutting-edge academia in and out of the classroom. Students are encouraged to partake in study and research that may extend into many of the graduate and professional schools. As part of our College House system, Penn's Faculty Masters engage students in academic and civic experience while leading residential programs that promote an environment where living and learning intersect around the clock.

"Penn students are part of a dynamic community that includes a traditional campus, a lively neighborhood, and a city rich in culture and diversity. Whether your interests include artistic performance, community involvement, student government, athletics, fraternities and sororities, or cultural and religious organizations, you'll find many different options. Most importantly, students at Penn find that their lives in and out of the classroom compliment each other and are full, interesting and busy. We invite you to visit Penn in Philadelphia. You'll enjoy the revolutionary spirit of the campus and city."

For even more information on this school, turn to page 273 of the "Stats" section.

UNIVERSITY OF PITTSBURGH—JOHNSTOWN

450 SCHOOLHOUSE ROAD, 157 BLACKINGTON HALL, JOHNSTOWN, PA 15904 • ADMISSIONS: 814-269-7050
FAX: 814-269-7044 • E-MAIL: UPJADMIT@PITT.EDU • WEBSITE: WWW.UPJ.PITT.EDU

Ratings
Quality of Life: 72   Academic: 73   Admissions: 70   Financial Aid: 73

Academics

Student opinion of the teaching quality at the University of Pittsburgh—Johnstown is overwhelmingly positive. Avers a seasoned junior, "Every professor I have had in two years at UPJ has

> **SURVEY SAYS . . .**
> *Classes are small*
> *Diversity lacking on campus*
> *Campus feels safe*

made him/herself highly available to students outside of class. In several classes, having meetings outside class with professors is a requirement. I feel that my profs are very accessible, and I would never have a problem approaching them. Even the heads of departments do their best to be available." Agrees another, "The professors are accessible not only during the daytime, but also during weeknights and weekends." The mostly pre-professional students at UPJ—business, education, and biology are hot majors here—have only lovely things to say about administrators that "care about the students." For the most part, they're "mindful of the wants and needs of the students." And should students ever feel overwhelmed academically, they should rest in the knowledge that "the school also provides tutoring and makes it easy for anyone to get help." About the only thing students wish the people in charge would change is something they can't: "If they could take away the bitter winter wind, it would be just about perfect" at Johnstown.

Life

The undergraduates of UPJ look to strike a balance in their lives. One student has "found that the 'work hard, play hard' motto definitely applies at my school." Though UPJ students definitely know how to party—about 10 percent of the campus population is Greek—"having fun and getting the job done (hitting the books) usually carry equal importance for most students." The university reportedly does a decent job of providing different forms of entertainment, such as concerts on campus. And not only are there many clubs on campus, but "it is also easy to obtain a leadership role in the clubs that you are most interested in." Though the school is, according to students, totally self-enclosed from the municipality of Johnstown, so that "UPJ is almost a town of its own," it doesn't keep students from venturing out into the surrounding area to enjoy "skiing . . . movies, and hiking." And "when Johnstown gets too boring," Pittsburgh is only about a two-hour drive away. The quality of life is reportedly pretty high, as "all dorm rooms have a personal bathroom, so you never have to share," though "more washing machines and less mystery meat" in the dining hall would make life a little more pleasant for resident students.

Student Body

Though an ethnically homogenous crowd, the students at UPJ form a predominantly warm crowd. Writes one upperclassman, "There's a general feeling of goodwill around campus. For the most part people get along with one another, and social choices aren't criticized. Everyone is helpful and friendly, holds doors for others, and helps out when they can." First years are also happy and "enormously relieved" to report that "there isn't much heckling of freshmen!" And you'll find no battle of the sexes at UPJ; notes one undergrad, "I am a female in a predominately male major (engineering). I have never felt discriminated against by faculty, administrators, or other students. The school emphasizes teamwork and leadership, which creates strong relationships among students."

ADMISSIONS

Very important factors considered by the admissions committee include: class rank and secondary school record. *Important factors considered include:* interview and standardized test scores. *Other factors considered include:* character/personal qualities, essays, extracurricular activities, minority status, recommendations, talent/ability, volunteer work, and work experience. SAT I or ACT required. TOEFL required of all international applicants. High school diploma or GED is required. *High school units required/recommended:* 15 total required; 4 English required, 2 math required, 3 math recommended, 2 science required, 1 science lab required, 2 science lab recommended, 2 foreign language required, 4 social studies required.

The Inside Word

The University of Pittsburgh's Johnstown campus—two hours east of the Steel City—is an environment best suited for students who consider themselves hands-on learners who are willing to go the extra mile to interact with peers and professors.

FINANCIAL AID

Students should submit: FAFSA. Regular filing deadline is April 1. The Princeton Review suggests that all financial aid forms be submitted as soon as possible after January 1. *Need-based scholarships/grants offered:* Pell, SEOG, state scholarships/grants, private scholarships, and the school's own gift aid. *Loan aid offered:* FFEL Subsidized Stafford, FFEL Unsubsidized Stafford, FFEL PLUS, and Federal Perkins. Federal Work-Study Program available. Institutional employment available. Applicants will be notified of awards on a rolling basis beginning on or about March 15. Off-campus job opportunities are excellent.

For even more information on this school, turn to page 273 of the "Stats" section.

UNIVERSITY OF PITTSBURGH—PITTSBURGH

ALUMNI HALL, 4227 FIFTH AVENUE, FIRST FLOOR, PITTSBURGH, PA 15260 • ADMISSIONS: 412-624-7488
FAX: 412-648-8815 • FINANCIAL AID: 412-624-7488 • E-MAIL: OAFA@PITT.EDU • WEBSITE: WWW.PITT.EDU

Ratings
Quality of Life: 88   Academic: 78   Admissions: 84   Financial Aid: 80

Academics

Many University of Pittsburgh students feel "happy that we discovered this amazing yet quite underrated school." They cite the English and science programs as two of the strongest, and one student tells us, "The nursing program is excellent and prepares you for the real world." The university offers "tons of diverse courses in any one semester," and students are encouraged to take a term abroad, "which is the best

> **SURVEY SAYS . . .**
> *Lots of beer drinking*
> *(Almost) everyone smokes*
> *Great library*
> *Student newspaper is popular*
> *Everyone loves the Panthers*
> *Great off-campus food*
> *Great computer facilities*
> *Hard liquor is popular*
> *Students love Pittsburgh, PA*
> *Students are happy*

thing you can do." Some people see Pitt as "primarily a research school," but "it's stated university policy that professors are easy to see." The faculty "urges us to question things and provides an environment where we feel comfortable doing that." These "instructors and mentors" are known for being "passionate about what they teach" and "helpful both during lecture and during their office hours." Students appreciate that they "draw from real-world experience as a complement to their academic knowledge." Advisors provide additional academic support: "We meet one-on-one with our advisors at least twice a semester, and mine has always gotten me the classes I needed at the times I needed with the professors I want." The administration receives high marks "for advancing the university, raising money, recruiting strong applicants, and managing public affairs." Though they may "look out for our best interests," administrators are seen as "a bit detached," "extremely inaccessible," and "nearly impossible to reach." Recent tuition hikes only exacerbate this unfavorable assessment. Nonetheless, Pitt provides a scholastic climate where undergraduates "learn so much and grow as people." A senior writes, "It has been quite challenging, but I am thankful for my time here. It just goes to prove that I have a strong degree behind me."

Life

The Pitt existence can be "extremely busy with academics, extracurricular activities, internships, part-time jobs, work-study positions, and social life." With more than 300 student organizations, there's room for everyone to "do their own thing." Aside from some safety issues, students love their location in the Oakland section of Pittsburgh, "home to many restaurants and bars, making for a very social atmosphere." Students looking to enrich themselves take advantage of the "Carnegie Museums across the street" and the popular Pitt Arts program, which "provides discounted or free tickets to various cultural events around Pittsburgh." Couple that with free public transit for students, and one student writes, "What can beat free transportation, dinner, a symphony ticket, and dessert afterward?" The only better plan could be cheering on the top-notch football and basketball squads—season tickets set students back only 20 bucks. On campus, "the weekends are full of fun with activities planned through different student organizations and great parties." Though some students claim "the majority of students drink on the weekends," many people think the "novelty of fraternity parties tends to wear off pretty fast."

Student Body

The 18,000 undergarduate students attending Pitt form "a diverse group of students that, from what I have seen, interact easily and on a regular basis." One student observes, "We are amazingly diverse, and everyone is not only respectful, but also curious and excited to learn about and meet new people." Other respondents report that "people of the same ethnic group or background usually hang together." Even with approximately 14 percent of the student body members of minorities, one student points out, "Unfortunately, that is low for a city school." The minority populations organize effectively, in groups including the Black Action Society, Rainbow Alliance, and Asian Students Alliance. Amid this "wide spectrum of students" with a "broad range of interests," most are "friendly, outgoing, involved, motivated, and responsible." Most people seem to find their niche among "academically focused and open-minded" peers.

ADMISSIONS

Very important factors considered by the admissions committee include: secondary school record, standardized test scores. *Important factors considered include:* class rank. *Other factors considered include:* essays, extracurricular activities, interview, recommendations, talent/ability, volunteer work, work experience. SAT I or ACT required; SAT I preferred. TOEFL required of all international applicants. High school diploma or GED is required. *High school units required/recommended:* 15 total required; 4 English required, 3 math required, 3 science (with lab) required, 1 social science required (3 recommended), 4 elective required (of which 3 in one foreign language are recommended).

The Inside Word

Applicants to Pitt, as at most large public universities, are admitted primarily on the strength of basic qualifiers like grades and test scores. If you are serious about Pitt, rolling admissions allows you to get a decision earlier than most colleges notify their applicants.

FINANCIAL AID

Students should submit: FAFSA, institution's own financial aid form. No deadline for regular filing. The Princeton Review suggests that all financial aid forms be submitted as soon as possible after January 1. *Need-based scholarships/grants offered:* Pell, SEOG, the school's own gift aid, College Work Study Program (CWS). *Loan aid offered:* FFEL Subsidized Stafford, FFEL Unsubsidized Stafford, FFEL PLUS, Federal Perkins, Federal Nursing, VA, HEAL. Federal Work-Study Program available. Institutional employment available. Applicants will be notified of awards on a rolling basis beginning on or about March 15. Off-campus job opportunities are excellent.

FROM THE ADMISSIONS OFFICE

"The University of Pittsburgh is one of 62 members of the Association of American Universities, a prestigious group whose members include the major research universities of North America. There are nearly 400 degree programs available at the 16 Pittsburgh campus schools (two offering only undergraduate degree programs, four offering graduate degree programs, and ten offering both) and four regional campuses, allowing students a wide latitude of choices, both academically and in setting and style, size and pace of campus. Programs ranked nationally include philosophy, history and philosophy of science, chemistry, economics, English, history, physics, political science, and psychology. The University Center for International Studies is ranked one of the exemplary international programs in the country by the Council on Learning; and the Semester at Sea Program takes students to different ports of call around the world on an ocean liner."

For even more information on this school, turn to page 274 of the "Stats" section.

UNIVERSITY OF RICHMOND

28 Westhampton Way, Richmond, VA 23173 • Admissions: 804-289-8640 • Fax: 804-287-6003
Financial Aid: 804-289-8438 • E-mail: admissions@richmond.edu • Website: www.richmond.edu

Ratings
Quality of Life: 96   **Academic:** 90   **Admissions:** 91   **Financial Aid:** 83

Academics

Students at University of Richmond love the benefits of attending a small, undergraduate-oriented school. "One of the greatest positives about the University of Richmond is its small size," explains one student. "My teachers almost always know my name, even years after I had them as instructors." Adds another, "I have

> **SURVEY SAYS . . .**
> *Frats and sororities dominate social scene*
> *Students love Richmond, VA*
> *Diversity lacking on campus*
> *Great food on campus*
> *Athletic facilities are great*
> *Students get along with local community*
> *Class discussions encouraged*

some friends who have attended large state schools and they are perpetually astonished by how small my classes are, while I can't imagine a classroom with 200 to 300 people in it." A caring and committed faculty enhances the educational experience here; students sense that "professors are here to teach first and foremost," "really want you to do well, and they actually appreciate your getting to know them." They "are extremely accessible, and even offer to come to campus on weekends if you need extra help." Students also enjoy "an excellent advising system" and an administration that makes sure "everything on campus runs very smoothly." Complaints center on some restrictive administrative policies, the required first-year course ("It is like an AP English literature course: we read 10 or so books, analyze them, have discussions, and write papers. Many of us do not see the point"), and the insular nature of life on campus ("Welcome to the bubble!!! College is supposed to be the next step toward the 'real world' but Richmond is not quite close enough").

Life

For most students at UR, "social life tends to revolve around the Greek system. The place to be on Friday night is Fraternity Row." Other orbits exist, however; explains one student, "Weekend culture revolves around Fraternity Row, but I have never been to the Row and still manage to amuse myself. I attend arts performances in our arts building, which is beautiful and accommodates many different groups. There is a prominent D-Hall (dining hall) culture among more intellectual students; they sit and talk for hours after dinner or even after lunch on Fridays. Much non-Greek weekend activity revolves around religious organizations and sports teams. We take trips to Virginia Beach or Washington, D.C., or even just into Richmond. If you have a car, this is a great place to be. It's only when I can't find a friend with a car that I sometimes get bored on weekends." Students agree that "Richmond is a terrific city, with great restaurants, museums, bars, theaters, etc." and love the fact that "We're also two hours away from the ocean, two hours away from the mountains, an hour and a half from D.C., so road trips are frequent." They also appreciate that UR is "small enough that when you walk to classes you will always run into people you know, but it's big enough that you can't know everybody. There are definite groups of people; you have to find your niche, but basically, everyone is just nice."

Student Body

The students at University of Richmond are "extremely ambitious: it feels like everyone was class president in high school. But for the most part they are also very down-to-earth, friendly, and helpful." Most agree there is a sameness to the student body, and "sometimes it's easy to see where the nickname 'the University of Rich Men' came from." Observes one undergrad, "Students here are generally white and upper-middle-class to upper-class. There is not much diversity, aside from a large percentage of international students, many from Latin America and Eastern Europe." Students' commitment to religion is divided into "two different extremes: there are religious people, and there are students who have set religion aside for a while."

ADMISSIONS

Very important factors considered by the admissions committee include: secondary school record. *Important factors considered include:* character/personal qualities, class rank, essays, standardized test scores, talent/ability. *Other factors considered include:* alumni/ae relation, extracurricular activities, geographical residence, minority status, recommendations, state residency, volunteer work, work experience. TOEFL required of all international applicants. High school diploma or GED is required. *High school units required/recommended:* 16 total required; 20 total recommended; 4 English required, 3 math required, 4 math recommended, 2 science required, 4 science recommended, 2 science lab required, 4 science lab recommended, 2 foreign language required, 4 foreign language recommended, 2 history required, 4 history recommended.

The Inside Word

There may not be an admissions formula, but two SAT II: Subject Tests are an important application requirement; we'd advise candidates to prepare for them thoroughly, since they outweigh the SAT I. When used with a measure of flexibility and a willingness to consider other factors, as Richmond does, there is nothing inherently wrong with such an approach. There does appear to be an effort to look at the candidate's record carefully and thoroughly. Make no mistake: Course of study, high school performance, and test scores are the most important parts of your application, but Richmond also makes sure that all files are read at least three times before a final decision has been rendered.

FINANCIAL AID

Students should submit: FAFSA, institution's own financial aid form. Regular filing deadline is February 25. The Princeton Review suggests that all financial aid forms be submitted as soon as possible after January 1. *Need-based scholarships/grants offered:* Pell, SEOG, state scholarships/grants, private scholarships, the school's own gift aid. *Loan aid offered:* Direct Subsidized Stafford, Direct Unsubsidized Stafford, Direct PLUS, Federal Perkins. Federal Work-Study Program available. Institutional employment available. Applicants will be notified of awards on or about April 1. Off-campus job opportunities are good.

FROM THE ADMISSIONS OFFICE

"The University of Richmond combines the characteristics of a small college with the dynamics of a large university. The unique size, beautiful suburban campus, and world-class facilities offer students an extraordinary mix of opportunities for personal growth and intellectual achievement. At Richmond, students are encouraged to engage themselves in their environment. Discussion and dialogue are the forefront of the academic experience, while research, internships, and international experiences are important components of students' co-curricular lives. The university is committed to providing undergraduate students with a rigorous academic experience, while integrating these studies with opportunities for experiential learning and promoting total individual development."

For even more information on this school, turn to page 274 of the "Stats" section.

UNIVERSITY OF SCRANTON

800 LINDEN STREET, SCRANTON, PA 18510 • ADMISSIONS: 570-941-7540 • FAX: 570-941-5928
FINANCIAL AID: 570-941-7700 • E-MAIL: ADMISSIONS@SCRANTON.EDU • WEBSITE: WWW.SCRANTON.EDU

Ratings
Quality of Life: 77   Academic: 77   Admissions: 85   Financial Aid: 79

Academics

The "intimacy between faculty and students" at the University of Scranton is illustrated by one freshman's comment, "My professors are more like my friends." This buddy-buddy relationship, combined with small class sizes, allows for individual attention and

> **SURVEY SAYS . . .**
> *Lots of beer drinking*
> *Low cost of living*
> *Lots of classroom discussion*
> *Students don't like Scranton, PA*
> *Students are cliquish*

depth of study. "My teachers don't base grades on robotic regurgitation of their lectures. They evaluate my performance on original and creative thought," states a senior English major. One purist undergrad is pleased that Scranton maintains a "rigorous insistence on competency in certain 'old-school' disciplines: logic, rhetoric, and effective writing." Scranton's physical therapy, occupational therapy, and education programs are also routinely praised. A sophomore, does, however, sing the familiar small-private-school blues, characterizing Scranton academics as "average" and "not worth what we pay." Word has it that the administration "works hard to produce a socially active and learning-conducive environment." Some general complaints center around limited course availability and meager career services, though registration is reported to be "a breeze."

Life

The Jesuit environment defines much of Scranton life, from the thriving campus ministry program to a plethora of school-sponsored sober activities, including dances, bands, and a popular coffee house. "Even as a no-alcohol person, I find so much to do," claims a content freshman. Of course, booze finds its way even into this den of Catholicism. A junior theology major notes the unusual triad of activities, "Drink Coronas, pray, study," and a sophomore corroborates with, "We have a good time, mostly at the bar." As far as the city of Scranton goes, a junior tells us "it ain't Canaan" but "it's cheap to live" and the lack of Studio 54–type nightlife "keeps you focused on school work." An industrious sophomore points out, "Though hard to fathom, I've seen Carmen performed by the London City Opera, the band Moe, and David Sedaris all within minutes of the campus." So though there's not much in terms of athletics or school spirit, a sophomore philosophy major exclaims, "Scranton should be called ScranFUN!"

Student Body

The Scranton student population can generally be divided into "partiers and religious people, with no middle ground," according to a female senior. But in class on a Tuesday, it could be tough to tell the two groups apart. A freshman observes, "There is no variety when it comes to the student body," which is described as "white, Catholic, and upper-middle class" as well as "very conservative and closed-minded at times." Scranton is an insular and close-knit place: "The school is very concerned with creating a community. It worked—being at school is like forgetting about everything else," comments a senior. One student points out the benefits of living with the God squad, that the student body "exemplifies the Christian attribute of loving one's neighbor." A sophomore agrees and writes, "This was easily the friendliest, warmest, most welcoming campus I visited. My experience here has strengthened this view."

ADMISSIONS

Very important factors considered by the admissions committee include: secondary school record. *Important factors considered include:* class rank, standardized test scores. *Other factors considered include:* alumni/ae relation, character/personal qualities, essays, extracurricular activities, interview, minority status, recommendations, talent/ability, volunteer work, work experience. SAT I or ACT required. TOEFL required of all international applicants. High school diploma or GED is required. *High school units required/recommended:* 16 total required; 4 English required, 3 math required, 4 math recommended, 1 science required, 2 science recommended, 2 foreign language required, 2 social studies required, 3 social studies recommended.

The Inside Word

Admission to Scranton gets harder each year. A steady stream of smart kids from the tri-state area keeps classes full and the admit rate low. Successful applicants will need solid grades and test scores. As with many religiously affiliated schools, students should be a good match philosophically as well.

FINANCIAL AID

Students should submit: FAFSA. No deadline for regular filing. The Princeton Review suggests that all financial aid forms be submitted as soon as possible after January 1. *Need-based scholarships/grants offered:* Pell, SEOG, state scholarships/grants, private scholarships, the school's own gift aid. *Loan aid offered:* FFEL Subsidized Stafford, FFEL Unsubsidized Stafford, FFEL PLUS, Federal Perkins. Federal Work-Study Program available. Institutional employment available. Applicants will be notified of awards on a rolling basis beginning on or about March 1. Off-campus job opportunities are good.

FROM THE ADMISSIONS OFFICE

"A Jesuit institution in Pennsylvania's Pocono northeast region, The University of Scranton is known for many things, especially its outstanding academics, state-of-the art campus and technology, and exceptional sense of community. Founded in 1888, the University offers more than 80 undergraduate and graduate academic programs of study in five colleges and schools.

"For nine consecutive years, *U.S. News & World Report*'s America's Best Colleges edition has ranked the University among the ten finest master's universities in the North—fourth in the 2003 edition. The University also joined the elite colleges profiled in The Princeton Review's *The 351 Best Colleges*. The University was profiled in the 2003 edition of Kaplan Publishing's *The Unofficial, Unbiased Insider's Guide to the 320 Most Interesting Colleges*. As well, the University was rated 39th among the nation's 100 most-wired colleges in *Yahoo! Internet Life* magazine's 2001 edition and is one of only 100 schools in the nation on Templeton's Honor Roll of Character-Building Colleges.

"Scranton has a history of success in preparing students for medical school, law school, and the nation's most prestigious scholarships and fellowships. In 2002, the acceptance rate for graduating seniors from the University into medical and related schools reached an all-time high of 100 percent. Law schools accepted 72 percent of the graduating seniors who applied in 2002. In the past three years, Scranton students have earned a remarkable 12 Fulbright Fellowships, a Goldwater Scholarship, two Truman Scholarships, four Freeman Awards, a Jack Kent Cooke Scholarship, two NCAA Post-Graduate Scholarships, two Rotary Ambassadorial Scholarships, a DeRance Scholarship, and two State Farm Fellowships for Exceptional Students. In the spring of 2003, applications for admission reached an all-time high. Students are encouraged to apply early for admission and can do so online with no application fee at www.scranton.edu/apply."

For even more information on this school, turn to page 275 of the "Stats" section.

UNIVERSITY OF VIRGINIA—CHARLOTTESVILLE

OFFICE OF ADMISSION, PO BOX 400160, CHARLOTTESVILLE, VA 22906 • ADMISSIONS: 434-982-3200
FAX: 434-924-3587 • FINANCIAL AID: 804-982-6000 • E-MAIL: UNDERGRAD-ADMISSION@VIRGINIA.EDU
WEBSITE: WWW.VIRGINIA.EDU

Ratings

Quality of Life: 90   **Academic:** 93   **Admissions:** 94   **Financial Aid:** 88

Academics

Regarded as one of the country's premier state universities, University of Virginia offers an "excellent all-around college experience: great, intelligent students; wonderful intercollegiate sports; phenomenal faculty; and, of course, excellent academics." Students appreciate that "unlike other publics, there is not a tendency for

> **SURVEY SAYS . . .**
> *Great on-campus food*
> *Students are religious*
> *Popular college radio*
> *Students get along with local community*
> *Theater is hot*
> *Computer facilities need improving*
> *Athletic facilities need improving*

students at UVA to be lost in paperwork and bureaucracy. The people who work in the administrative offices are very nice and understanding; perhaps this is a product of 'southern hospitality.' Also, professors at UVA are not only accessible but hospitable." Indeed, "most professors at UVA are eager to get to know the students. Many bend over backward to help students and understand what is important to the students." Additionally, "UVA has an extraordinary number of professors who are both dedicated teachers and [at the] top of their fields." Students also tell us that "your education does not end at the classroom. There are numerous opportunities related to service in which you can learn to become part of your community and give back to people who need help. In addition, there are numerous cultural, social, and athletic organizations, all of which allow you to pursue a well-rounded education."

Life

"For all the hard-core nature of academics at UVA, it is still a really fun place to be," students here agree, especially if you love frat parties ("Greek life is very prominent at the university"). For students who "do not enjoy alcohol . . . there are many other things to do. The University of Virginia is located about 20 miles from the Blue Ridge Mountains, where you can go for a nice hike. Winter Green is about an hour away from Charlottesville (for those who enjoy skiing or playing golf). The James River is about 40 minutes away for those who enjoy tubing or rafting." Nor is travel off campus necessary, as the school itself offers a "diversity of activities! If you play sports, dance, act, like intellectual activities, [or] participate in the strong student self-governance, you can do it at UVA." The school also attracts "awesome speakers, including Isabel Allende, Ralph Nader, the Dalai Lama, and Archbishop Desmond Tutu, to name a few that have come while I've been here." Students may just choose to sit back and enjoy the beautiful campus itself; writes one student, "When I finished my last final first year, I walked out of my classroom elated. But as I passed the historical Lawn and the beautiful amphitheater, my heart dropped at the thought of having to leave such gorgeous surroundings." Virginia is a school rich in tradition, a fact appreciated by most students. Traditions include streaking across the Lawn ("The tradition is to start from the Rotunda, sprint down to Homer—located in front of Old Cabell hall—and kiss his butt, and sprint back. Then you look through the keyhole at the top of the steps of the rotunda to see if you can see Thomas Jefferson"), "dressing up to go to athletic events," and the Honor Code.

Student Body

Virginia has long had a reputation as a preppy haven, a reputation students tell us is well deserved. "UVA is quite a preppy, well-to-do school," writes one undergrad. "It's the perfect school for frat boys who like to wear Gucci shoes and sorority girls who dig Versace." Not everyone fits the mold; explains one student, "Upon closer inspection, you'll realize that the student population includes people of all walks of life." The student body has its share of "gun-toting, abortion-hating, Confederacy-loving students; insane-worker, dedicated-to-a-fault, anal-about-cleanliness students; and 'eccentric to a point that begs the question not of whether, but of when they'll be committed' students." Although fairly diverse, "UVA is very segregated. Different ethnic groups do not mix very much, and the Greek population is an entity unto [itself]." Political activism "is not big at the university at all. The student body is largely more conservative-leaning, and the flaming liberals don't have too much of an impact of student life."

ADMISSIONS

Very important factors considered by the admissions committee include: alumni/ae relation, minority status, secondary school record, state residency. *Important factors considered include:* character/personal qualities, class rank, essays, extracurricular activities, recommendations, standardized test scores, talent/ability. *Other factors considered include:* geographical residence, volunteer work, work experience. SAT I or ACT required; SAT I preferred; SAT II also required. TOEFL required of all international applicants. High school diploma or GED is required. *High school units required/recommended:* 16 total required; 4 English required, 4 math required, 2 science required, 4 science recommended, 2 foreign language required, 1 social studies required, 3 social studies recommended.

The Inside Word

Even many Virginia residents regard trying to get into UVA as a feeble attempt. The competition doesn't get much more severe, and only the most capable and impressive candidates stand to be offered admission. The volume of out-of-state applications borders on enormous when considered in conjunction with available spots in the entering class.

FINANCIAL AID

Students should submit: FAFSA, institution's own financial aid form. The Princeton Review suggests that all financial aid forms be submitted as soon as possible after January 1. *Need-based scholarships/grants offered:* Pell, SEOG, state scholarships/grants, private scholarships, the school's own gift aid. *Loan aid offered:* Direct Subsidized Stafford, Direct Unsubsidized Stafford, Direct PLUS, Federal Perkins, Federal Nursing, college/university loans from institutional funds. Federal Work-Study Program available. Institutional employment available. Applicants will be notified of awards on or about April 5. Off-campus job opportunities are fair.

FROM THE ADMISSIONS OFFICE

"Admission to competitive schools requires strong academic credentials. Students who stretch themselves and take rigorous courses (honors level and Advanced Placement courses, when offered) are significantly more competitive than those who do not. Experienced admission officers know that most students are capable of presenting superb academic credentials, and the reality is that a very high percentage of those applying do so. Other considerations, then, come into play in important ways for academically strong candidates, as they must be seen as 'selective' as well as academically competitive."

For even more information on this school, turn to page 276 of the "Stats" section.

Ursinus College

Ursinus College, Admissions Office, Collegeville, PA 19426 • Admissions: 610-409-3200
Fax: 610-409-3662 • Financial Aid: 610-409-3600 • E-mail: admissions@ursinus.edu
Website: www.ursinus.edu

Ratings
Quality of Life: 79   Academic: 81   Admissions: 80   Financial Aid: 89

Academics

"An amazing biology department" and an equally excellent chemistry department that churn out viable candidates for the nation's top medical schools are the star attractions at Ursinus College. Students here also speak highly of the political science

> **SURVEY SAYS . . .**
> *Frats and sororities dominate social scene*
> *Popular college radio, Lots of beer drinking*
> *Library needs improving*
> *Lousy off-campus food, Low cost of living*

department and the education program, but most would quickly concede that the medical sciences are king here. Pre-meds "get a lot in the way of academic advantages. Our chemistry building was recently updated, so there is a lot of availability of technology," including a fully networked campus. All freshmen receive a laptop "with the programs already on it" so that everyone can log on and tap into the information stream. At the threat of becoming too technology- and science-driven, Ursinus several years ago instituted a liberal studies curriculum encompassing English, math, science, and foreign language. Students approve, believing the core "is the reason that graduate schools enjoy leeching students away from the college." Professors "really know us due to the small size of classes, and are really there for us when we need them." They teach "courses that force you to think 'outside the box' and connect all areas of your life to help you become a fully integrated person." Students also appreciate how Ursinus provides "the opportunity to push beyond our requirements to work closely with professors and administrators in independent and honors research." The administration "is fairly accessible and willing to listen to our concerns," while the career services office "is constantly informing students of internship or job opportunities." Some students complain that it is not easy enough for upperclassmen to get into the electives of their choice.

Life

"Greek organizations are very popular" with the students of Ursinus, most of whom agree that "there's not a whole lot to do in this area," which is why "people spend most of the weekend drinking" at parties. Reports one, "The Greek system is the foundation of all of the partying that goes on here." One type of party unique to the school is a 'dated,' a semi-formal dance sponsored by a Greek organization. "Dateds are amazing fun in the fall," writes one student, "with at least two per weekend, as buses take students to a banquet hall full of alcohol and great music for four hours, only to return to campus [so students can] party some more!" Other than frat parties, activity is sparse, though "campus activities are held about once every two weeks or so, and they're usually pretty entertaining." Hometown Collegeville is "boring. Almost everything in Collegeville closes at 9 p.m. and there's very little excitement within walking distance. Having a car on campus (which many do) is an important asset [for] reaching a nearby Lazer Tag facility or the mammoth King of Prussia Mall." Philadelphia is two and a half inconvenient hours away by public transportation; grouses one student, "The college promo literature made it seem that a student could go to Philly any time they wanted without having to have a car on campus. No one really does this and I'm not even sure if it is a possibility." Many students also complain about dining hall food: "The food was really good, but this year it got really bad. If the food could go back to normal, it'd be great again."

Student Body

Undergrads at Ursinus "are friendly, but can get very cliquey." Students divide into cliques according to area of study, graduating class, and of course, Greek affiliation. "Many people play sports" here, while "others are really into politics and still others are very art- and music-inclined." The small student body lends an air of informality to the campus: "People here aren't worried about how you look all the time. You can go to class in sweatpants or you can go to class in a skirt—no one cares." Students are proud to report that "a key word at Ursinus is tolerance. We have a very active Gay-Straight Alliance, which sponsors many events."

ADMISSIONS

Very important factors considered by the admissions committee include: class rank, extracurricular activities, secondary school record. *Important factors considered include:* alumni/ae relation, essays, minority status, recommendations, standardized test scores, talent/ability, volunteer work, work experience. *Other factors considered include:* character/personal qualities, geographical residence, interview. SAT I or ACT required; SAT II recommended. TOEFL required of all international applicants. High school diploma or GED is required. *High school units required/recommended:* 16 total required; 20 total recommended; 4 English required, 3 math required, 4 math recommended, 1 science required, 3 science recommended, 1 science lab required, 2 foreign language required, 4 foreign language recommended, 1 social studies required, 3 social studies recommended, 5 elective required.

The Inside Word

The admission process at Ursinus is very straightforward; about 70 percent of those who apply get in. Grades, test scores, and class rank count for more than anything else, and unless you are academically inconsistent, you'll likely get good news.

FINANCIAL AID

Students should submit: FAFSA, institution's own financial aid form, CSS/Financial Aid PROFILE. Regular filing deadline is February 15. The Princeton Review suggests that all financial aid forms be submitted as soon as possible after January 1. *Need-based scholarships/grants offered:* Pell, SEOG, state scholarships/grants, private scholarships, the school's own gift aid. *Loan aid offered:* FFEL Subsidized Stafford, FFEL Unsubsidized Stafford, FFEL PLUS, Federal Perkins, college/university loans from institutional funds. Federal Work-Study Program available. Institutional employment available. Applicants will be notified of awards on or about April 1. Off-campus job opportunities are excellent.

FROM THE ADMISSIONS OFFICE

"Located one-half hour from center-city Philadelphia, the college boasts a beautiful 140-acre campus that includes the Residential Village (renovated Victorian-style homes that decorate the Main Street and house our students) and the nationally recognized Berman Museum of Art. Ursinus is a member of the Centennial Conference, competing both in academics and in intercollegiate athletics with institutions such as Dickinson, Franklin and Marshall, Gettysburg, and Muhlenberg. The academic environment is enhanced with such fine programs as a chapter of Phi Beta Kappa, an Early Assurance Program to medical school with the Medical College of Pennsylvania, and myriad student exchanges both at home and abroad. A heavy emphasis is placed on student research—an emphasis that can only be carried out with the one-on-one attention Ursinus students receive from their professors."

For even more information on this school, turn to page 276 of the "Stats" section.

VILLANOVA UNIVERSITY

800 Lancaster Avenue, Villanova, PA 19085-1672 • Admissions: 610-519-4000 • Fax: 610-519-6450
Financial Aid: 610-519-4010 • E-mail: gotovu@email.villanova.edu • Website: www.villanova.edu

Ratings
Quality of Life: 87   Academic: 82   Admissions: 83   Financial Aid: 79

Academics

Students at Villanova feel that their university "helps everyone to be their best on a personal and academic level." The challenging course work and Catholic environment draw young scholars eager to jump in on "great class discussions"

and work with professors who are "easy to approach." Instructors are known to "go out of their way to accommodate students," whether that means "inviting everyone who was going to be on campus over for Thanksgiving" or "giving out their cell phone numbers in case we are screwed on an assignment." This "great rapport" allows professors to "help you learn about the material and about yourself." Undergraduates see that the faculty "reaches out and wants to meet their students," which is part of what helps them all to be "good at their job and enjoy what they're doing." We get mixed reviews regarding the administration, with some students calling them "extremely helpful" and others "a big hassle." Overall, however, the campus seems to "run pretty smoothly," and students feel they are "a face with a name, not a number."

Life

The Villanova lifestyle combines academics with top-notch athletics and plenty of opportunities for fun. The typical schedule runs: "learn four days a week, get hammered two days a week, and save the world on the other day." The get-hammered portion is brought to you by your friendly neighborhood frat house. "Greeks provide a great social life, but you don't have to be a brother or a sister to have a good time." Students say, "I always manage to drink in some dorm room," but it can be "hard to have a lot of fun because of strict [alcohol] policies." Some think that "the rules are too strict," but they can still head to "the Brick Bar, which is pretty popular when the beer is cheap." For those not interested in bending the hooch regulations, "there are a lot of non-alcohol activities, too," including "late-night movies," theater performances, supporting the perennially successful basketball team, and listening to the ever-popular radio station. Some undergrads complain that "the campus is secluded," meaning they "must go to Philly for fun," but creative fun seekers claim "the town around campus has some good surprises." Student life is rounded out by "so many volunteer opportunities [that] it's overwhelming." Many people participate in the campus ministry, and many agree that "the religious presence here is completely optional but really adds to the sense of community and charity."

Student Body

A field guide to Villanova students might describe them as "white kids from different suburbs across the country," the progeny of "upper-middle-class, Catholic" families. Sometimes known as "Vanilla-nova," the university is "hurting for diversity," but also seems to be "making good progress to diversify the school." For now, the majority of students either are "pretty preppy or they're guidos." Certain plebeians call their peers "snobbish" and snipe that "being academic comes second to looking good." The "motivated, bright, and outgoing" population includes "very few atypical students." Those who deviate from the "fun-loving, studious, career-orient-ed" norm may be few in number, but they "find their own niche." Others argue that within this "family environment" of "involved, intelligent, and witty" students, they do count a "decent number of interesting/quirky people."

ADMISSIONS

Factors considered include: alumni/ae relation, character/personal qualities, class rank, essays, extracurricular activities, geographical residence, minority status, recommendations, secondary school record, standardized test scores, volunteer work, work experience. SAT I or ACT required. TOEFL required of all international applicants. High school diploma or GED is required. *High school units required/recommended:* 18 total required; 20 total recommended; 4 English required, 4 math required, 4 science required, 2 science lab required, 3 science lab rec-ommended, 2 foreign language required, 4 foreign language recommended.

The Inside Word

Villanova has a very solid and growing reputation among Catholic universities nationally, yet is less competitive for admissions than the top tier of schools like Georgetown and Notre Dame. If Villanova is your first choice, be careful. As is the case at many universities, Early Action applicants face higher academic standards than those for the regular pool. This uni-versity is a very sound option, whether high on your list of choices or as a safety school.

FINANCIAL AID

Students should submit: FAFSA, institution's own financial aid form. Regular filing deadline is February 15. The Princeton Review suggests that all financial aid forms be submitted as soon as possible after January 1. *Need-based scholarships/grants offered:* Pell, SEOG, state scholar-ships/grants, private scholarships, the school's own gift aid. *Loan aid offered:* Direct Subsidized Stafford, Direct Unsubsidized Stafford, Direct PLUS, FFEL Subsidized Stafford, FFEL Unsubsidized Stafford, FFEL PLUS, Federal Perkins, state loans. Federal Work-Study Program available. Institutional employment available. Applicants will be notified of awards on or about April 1. Off-campus job opportunities are excellent.

FROM THE ADMISSIONS OFFICE

"The University is a community of persons of diverse professional, academic, and personal interests who in a spirit of collegiality cooperate to achieve their common goals and objectives in the transmission, the pursuit, and the discovery of knowledge. . . . Villanova attempts to enroll students with diverse social, geographic, economic, and educational backgrounds. . . . Villanova welcomes students who consider it desirable to study within the philosophical framework of Christian Humanism. . . . Finally, this community seeks to reflect the spirit of St. Augustine by the cultivation of knowledge, by respect for individual differences, and by adherence to the principle that mutual love and respect should animate every aspect of University life."

—Villanova University Mission Statement

For even more information on this school, turn to page 277 of the "Stats" section.

Virginia Commonwealth University

821 West Franklin Street, PO Box 842526, Richmond, VA 23284 • Admissions: 804-828-1222
Fax: 804-828-1899 • E-mail: vcuinfo@vcu.edu • Website: www.vcu.edu

Ratings
Quality of Life: 78   **Academic:** 72   **Admissions:** 61   **Financial Aid:** 67

Academics

According to one student, Virginia Commonwealth's mission is "to not have teaching assistants teach classes. Instead, every class is taught by a professor." And the professors that are teaching are "committed to serving the

> **SURVEY SAYS . . .**
> *Students are happy*
> *Classes are small*
> *Lots of conservatives on campus*
> *Very little drug use*

students and are always available." With an undergrad population of around 17,000, personal connections with professors might not be expected, but many undergrads agree that they "do not feel like an insignificant number. The professors have made an effort to reach me individually." "The classes are challenging, but not challenging enough so that I am crying in my books everyday," or, as another student puts it, "competitive but fair." Praise for the professors, however, is countered with complaints that "professors just go through the material until class is over" and that there is "no motivation to learn." "The big lecture classes are a lot harder because the professors don't seem to try to teach us," writes one student. "They just read a bunch of notes and expect us to understand." VCU is known for its outstanding programs in the arts and in medicine, and a brand new arts facility was recently built, causing students to notice that, in comparison, "some of the equipment for labs and classrooms in general need some improvement/modernization." Although some "have not been extremely impressed with the way courses are run and how emphasis is placed on doing well on exams and not actually gaining understanding of material," others are satisfied with the "amazing professors" who "have vast knowledge in the subject being taught."

Life

Everyone at VCU seems to agree that "there is much to do here." Richmond offers off-campus action like "bands, orchestras, and theatre performances." "There is so much culture in Richmond that it blows my mind!" exclaims a particularly enthusiastic undergrad. Most students take advantage of the city, with its "tons of little restaurants and bars packed into The Fan, where many people spend their weekends." And yet, campus life has its advantages, too: "Living on campus allows you to get more involved in student activities such as movies, plays, or musical events." VCU's campus has over 150 clubs to choose from, and "we also have a river, which adds some outdoorish activities" into the mix. Another bonus for students is being able to use the Campus Connections bus system, where students get to ride to and from downtown Richmond free of charge. Even though "public transportation doesn't run late" and "parking is horrendous," most students let loose on weekends: "School is very frustrating and hard so we always look forward to the weekends to relieve the stress and anxieties from the week."

Student Body

"The diversity here makes me feel as if I am part of the real world," states one happy undergrad. "There are a wide variety of ethnic groups, social classes, etc." Not only is there cultural diversity at VCU: "There are punk kids, hippies, fraternity boys, sorority girls, drama kids, art students, the brainy med students, the hip-hop crowd—the list just goes on." Indeed, most VCU students comment that diversity is the main theme at their school and happily report that they "rarely ever see any fights." "Most people are extremely friendly and open to new ideas!" One frat brother boasts, "My fraternity alone has 11 different ethnic backgrounds within it." Interestingly enough, "most students are over 25 and hold full-time jobs." Basically, "VCU is Richmond," sums up one student. In addition, "every opinion and affiliation possible is represented," and "everyone seems to respect everyone else."

ADMISSIONS

Very important factors considered by the admissions committee include: secondary school record and talent/ability. *Important factors considered include:* standardized test scores. *Other factors considered include:* class rank, essays, extracurricular activities, interview, recommendations, volunteer work, and work experience. SAT I or ACT required, SAT I preferred. TOEFL required of all international applicants. High school diploma or GED is required. *High school units required/recommended:* 20 total required; 23 total recommended; 4 English required, 3 math required, 4 math recommended, 2 science required, 4 science recommended, 1 science lab required, 3 foreign language recommended, 1 social studies recommended, 3 history required.

The Inside Word

VCU's moderate admissions standards have some drawbacks, such as large lecture halls that may leave you feeling like a drop in a bucket. Its diverse student body and a great relationship with the Richmond community make for a vibrant atmosphere, however, one in which a variety of applicants can excel.

FINANCIAL AID

Students should submit: FAFSA. The Princeton Review suggests that all financial aid forms be submitted as soon as possible after January 1. *Need-based scholarships/grants offered:* Pell, SEOG, state scholarships/grants, private scholarships, the school's own gift aid, United Negro College Fund, and Federal Nursing. *Loan aid offered:* Direct Subsidized Stafford, Direct Unsubsidized Stafford, Direct PLUS, Federal Perkins, Federal Nursing, state loans, and college/university loans from institutional funds. Federal Work-Study Program available. Institutional employment available. Applicants will be notified of awards on or about April 1. Off-campus job opportunities are excellent.

For even more information on this school, turn to page 278 of the "Stats" section.

VIRGINIA MILITARY INSTITUTE

VMI OFFICE OF ADMISSIONS, LEXINGTON, VA 24450-0304 • ADMISSIONS: 540-464-7211 • FAX: 540-464-7746
E-MAIL: ADMISSIONS@MAIL.VMI.EDU • WEBSITE: WWW.VMI.EDU

Ratings
Quality of Life: 80   **Academic:** 79   **Admissions:** 74   **Financial Aid:** 75

Academics

Recall your history lessons about life in ancient Sparta and you'll have some idea of what to expect at the Virginia Military Institute, whose strict disciplinary approach essentially requires students to give up personal freedom. Cadets, explains one, awaken at sunrise, "go to formation, march to breakfast, and attend class at 8 A.M. At

> **SURVEY SAYS . . .**
> *Classes are small*
> *Lots of conservatives on campus*
> *Lots of classroom discussion*
> *School is well run*
> *Low cost of living*
> *No one cheats*
> *Instructors are good teachers*

12:30 P.M., I form up with my company and march to lunch. At 1:15 P.M., if I have an afternoon class, I am there. Then at 4:15 P.M., I am at military duty (practice parade, parade, or physical training). I form up and march to dinner at 6:30 P.M., and from 7 P.M. to 11 P.M. is study time. Lights out for everyone except seniors is 11 P.M." In addition, the Commandant's Office doles out mandatory duties "to make our everyday lives outside of class as difficult as possible." Freshman year is described as "one of, if not the, most difficult freshman years anywhere." As one lightly puts it, "It is a unique experience that is definitely not meant for everyone." Students benefit from "professors who are always there to help" but warn that "it's really hard to balance academics with military and physical demands." The administration reportedly "tells us one thing, the alumni another, and the press a third." A typical student explains that VMI's honor code "is everything to us. We do not lie, cheat, or steal in any way, nor do we tolerate other cadets who might. There are no shades of honor here. It is either honest or dishonest. It breeds a strong moral character that cannot be broken by the influence of society."

Life

Students warn that extracurricular fun at VMI "is nonexistent." "There isn't much to do on campus, in town, or in the county," and cadets "are restricted from leaving school grounds until Saturday afternoon or on Wednesday when we get two hours to go into town . . . . Church, besides actual study time, is the only thing that keeps my mind off of how terrible this place is!" Many students complain bitterly about "the awful food services on post, the deteriorating condition of barracks, the general filth of our living conditions, the unjust and unconstitutional treatment we receive from the administration, the unpaid work we are forced to do, the intentional deprivation of sleep, and the constant denial of requests to return home." For many, the Internet provides "our only link to our families, friends, and the general happenings of the outside world." Benefits of the VMI lifestyle, though, are apparent to many: "Life here is very structured. But that provides a framework for us and a comfort in that you know what to expect," writes one. Adds another, "VMI makes you hard, physically and mentally. You will learn to appreciate the simple things in life, which is positive." Students note that "the town of Lexington harbors VMI and Washington & Lee colleges," but "there is little to no interaction" between them.

Student Body

The cadets of VMI tell us of the "strong 'Class System' here. It emphasizes the power of the First Class (seniors) and derides the lower classes to varying degrees. The freshmen, or 'Rats,' are treated anything but well. They are yelled at, occasionally beaten and hazed, and get the brunt of the mean-spiritedness here." On account of the "bonds formed through such a hard rite of passage," "the relationships that you will form at VMI you will keep for the rest of your life." Cadets remind us that they "interact well out of necessity. If we didn't get along, or at least tolerate each other, life in the close confines of barracks would be unbearable." Students describe themselves as "confident, honorable, stern, very hardworking, clean, fit, and have a bad sense of humor." VMI underwent a court-ordered transition to coeducation in 1997; reports one cadet, "This is the fourth year VMI has been coed, and there is still some gender strain. Racial relations seem very good, though."

ADMISSIONS

Very important factors considered by the admissions committee include: character/personal qualities, class rank, secondary school record, and standardized test scores. *Important factors considered include:* extracurricular activities, interview, minority status, state residency, and volunteer work. *Other factors considered include:* alumni/ae relation, essays, geographical residence, recommendations, talent/ability, and work experience. SAT I or ACT required. TOEFL required of all international applicants. High school diploma is required and GED is not accepted. *High school units required/recommended:* 4 English required, 3 math required, 4 math recommended, 3 science required, 3 science lab required, 3 foreign language required, 4 foreign language recommended.

The Inside Word

Spontaneous students starving to take tangential trips to whatever topics tickle their fancy need not apply to VMI; students striving for discipline and structure will have the greatest success here.

FINANCIAL AID

Students should submit: FAFSA and institution's own financial aid form. Regular filing deadline is March 1. The Princeton Review suggests that all financial aid forms be submitted as soon as possible after January 1. *Need-based scholarships/grants offered:* Pell, SEOG, state scholarships/grants, private scholarships, and the school's own gift aid. *Loan aid offered:* Direct Subsidized Stafford, Direct Unsubsidized Stafford, Direct PLUS, and Federal Perkins. Federal Work-Study Program available. Institutional employment available. Applicants will be notified of awards on a rolling basis beginning on or about March 15. Off-campus job opportunities are poor.

For even more information on this school, turn to page 278 of the "Stats" section.

VIRGINIA TECH

UNDERGRADUATE ADMISSIONS, 201 BURRUSS HALL, BLACKSBURG, VA 24061 • ADMISSIONS: 540-231-6267
FAX: 540-231-3242 • FINANCIAL AID: 540-231-5179 • E-MAIL: VTADMISS@VT.EDU • WEBSITE: WWW.VT.EDU

Ratings

Quality of Life: 86   Academic: 81   Admissions: 84   Financial Aid: 82

Academics

For 20,000-plus bright, goal-oriented Virginia undergraduates, Virginia Polytechnic and State University offers the perfect mixture of academic theory and practical application (and, of course, football). As one student explains, "I feel that many schools, like University of Virginia, have excellent academics, but do not offer a real-world mentality attached to that education. Virginia Tech has

> **SURVEY SAYS . . .**
> *Everyone loves the Hokies*
> *Students are happy*
> *Class discussions are rare*
> *Political activism is hot*
> *Students are religious*
> *High cost of living*
> *(Almost) everyone smokes*
> *Hard liquor is popular*
> *Large classes*

the best of both worlds. I feel that upon graduation I will have a successful professional life that will be easily transitioned into." Tech students also appreciate how their school "is a place where people really care about learning and are proud of their studies, but they also know how to enjoy life and not just spend all their time in the books." Undergrads here speak highly of the "excellent engineering department," "the state's only veterinary school," and "solid business and computer science departments." Profs here, as at most tech schools, are a mixed bag; "some professors are great, while others are dreadful," reports one engineer. "Fortunately, there's this really useful website where you can evaluate teachers that you have had, and check up on what teachers that you may have are like." Most here agree that the quality of instruction—as well as the interest level of the material—improves as they progress through school. "All professors are helpful, but the more high-level classes you take, the even-more-helpful the professors are. I have had a very good academic experience here." Students note that VT has not been immune to the nationwide epidemic of state budget-cutting; reports one undergrad, "With the recent huge budget cuts in Virginia, students will be paying more and getting less."

Life

Students tell us that "life at VT is pretty laid-back, for the most part. Students are expected to work hard for good grades, and they generally do. Monday through Thursday is pretty academically geared. But come Thursday night, it's all about the party." Notes one student, "Most people start partying on Thursday night. They go downtown to one of the many local bars, go to a frat party, or go to an apartment party. There are so many apartments off campus that there are at least ten parties at anyone's fingertips at one time. We party hard and we love our sports." Hokie football reigns supreme on the Blacksburg campus; volleyball and women's basketball both have also fielded competitive squads in recent seasons. If you're not into partying or sports, students warn, "There's not much more available aside from the restaurants and local theatre. Since most of the things to do, like bowling or the big movie theatre, are located in the next town (about 15 minutes by car), they are somewhat uncompelling." Agrees one student, "Wal-Mart is about as much fun as it gets for the nonpartiers, as there are pretty slim pickings if you don't party." Hometown Blacksburg, most admit, "doesn't offer much." The closest city, Roanoke, is about an hour's drive from campus.

Student Body

Students at VT are bright but not necessarily intellectually curious: "We're very concerned about doing well, though not necessarily learning" is how one student puts it. While "the typical student is white, dresses in clothes from Abercrombie, Structure, Gap, American Eagle, etc. . . . and obviously comes from a white-collar family," there are "many atypical students, probably just under 50 percent of the student body. The school is big enough so that cliques are impossible." As one student put it, "The campus is really diverse, and everyone can find a place not just with people like them, but with almost anyone." As a rule, "people here are generally pretty laid-back and friendly," eschewing the cutthroat competitiveness that characterizes many engineering and tech schools.

ADMISSIONS

Very important factors considered by the admissions committee include: secondary school record, standardized test scores. *Important factors considered include:* extracurricular and after-school activities. *Other factors considered include:* alumni/ae relation, essays, extracurricular activities, geographical residence, minority status, recommendations, state residency, talent/ability, volunteer work, work experience. SAT I or ACT required; SAT I preferred; SAT II also recommended. TOEFL required of all international applicants. High school diploma or GED is required. *High school units required/recommended:* 18 total required; 4 English required, 3 math required, 2 science required, 3 science recommended, 2 science lab required, 3 foreign language recommended, 1 social studies required, 1 history required, 3 elective required.

The Inside Word

When compared to applying to UVA or William and Mary, getting into Virginia Tech is a cakewalk. Tech has a great reputation, which from a careerist point of view makes it well worth considering.

FINANCIAL AID

Students should submit: FAFSA, General Scholarship Application. Regular filing deadline is March 11. The Princeton Review suggests that all financial aid forms be submitted as soon as possible after January 1. *Need-based scholarships/grants offered:* Pell, SEOG, state scholarships/grants, private scholarships, the school's own gift aid, cadet scholarships/grants. *Loan aid offered:* Direct Subsidized Stafford, Direct Unsubsidized Stafford, Direct PLUS, FFEL PLUS, Federal Perkins, college/university loans from institutional funds. Federal Work-Study Program available. Institutional employment available. Applicants will be notified of awards on or about April 15. Off-campus job opportunities are good.

FROM THE ADMISSIONS OFFICE

"Virginia Tech offers the opportunities of a large research university in a small-town setting. Undergraduates choose from more than 75 majors in 7 colleges, including nationally ranked business, forestry, and engineering schools, as well as excellent computer science, biology, communication studies, and architecture programs. Technology is a key focus, both in classes and in general. All first-year students are required to own a personal computer, each residence hall room has Ethernet connections, and every student is provided e-mail and Internet access. Faculty incorporate a wide variety of technology into class, utilizing chat rooms, online lecture notes, and multimedia presentations. The university offers cutting-edge facilities for classes and research, abundant opportunities for advanced study in the Honors Program, undergraduate research opportunities, study abroad, internships, and cooperative education. Students enjoy more than 500 organizations, which offer something for everyone. Tech offers the best of both worlds—everything a large university can provide and a small-town atmosphere."

For even more information on this school, turn to page 279 of the "Stats" section.

WASHINGTON & JEFFERSON COLLEGE

60 SOUTH LINCOLN STREET, WASHINGTON, PA 15301 • ADMISSIONS: 724-223-6025 • FAX: 724-223-6534
E-MAIL: ADMISSION@WASHJEFF.EDU • WEBSITE: WWW.WASHJEFF.EDU

Ratings
Quality of Life: 81   **Academic:** 84   **Admissions:** 77   **Financial Aid:** 84

Academics

Nobody at Washington & Jefferson College doubts that there is a plethora of outstanding academic opportunities here. "The administrators and the profs are top notch," and the classes are "small" and "rigorous." But "the trick is actually getting into a class you want," mutters a student. "Hell, as a freshman, I didn't get ANY of the classes I wished to receive for the second semester." Once past registration, students are greeted by "accessible" professors, most of whom "promote class participation" and put an "emphasis on discussions" rather than lectures. The faculty members make themselves readily available to the students—"and not just academically. They are genuinely concerned with all aspects of students' lives and overall well-being." The students at this liberal arts school feel that they're catching the college on an upswing, as the college's young administration has recently approved "the building of a new technology center" and a new business center "was just completed." Among the curricular highlights of this "incredibly academically charged" community are the pre-law and pre-health programs; the college reports that in recent years, around 90 percent of all W&J graduates that applied to medical school, law school, or health-related graduate programs were accepted. These programs aside, students can choose from 25 majors and another dozen or so specialized and pre-professional programs. "Academically, this school has passed my expectations," nods a student.

> **SURVEY SAYS . . .**
> *Lots of classroom discussion*
> *Instructors are good teachers*
> *Classes are small*
> *Diversity lacking on campus*

Life

Weekends and weekdays are very distinct at Washington & Jefferson. "Most people drink on the weekend," explains a student, then "study their asses off during the week." A large majority of the students participate in at least one of the many activities and organizations W&J's campus affords. Sports are particularly popular, whether intercollegiate or intramural (apparently 70 percent of students here take part in the latter). Greek life is also a big hit: almost half the students "are members of a sorority or fraternity," and the ones who aren't often have little problem turning out for the frequent frat parties. But if drinking isn't your idea of a good time, there are many other options. George and Tom's Place is a nonalcoholic "pub" on campus that brings in a variety of acts and programs for the students, and a handful of annual events, like the W&J Arts Series welcomes a menu of musical, artistic, and theatrical acts as well. For students with access to a car, Pittsburgh can be reached in less than 45 minutes; in fact, many mention that having a car seriously broadens the spectrum of available options, both leisurely and functional. The campus location on the out-skirts of Washington, Pennsylvania, is a 10-minute journey from grocery stores and other areas of interest in town.

Student Body

Many of the students at this small, liberal arts college in southwestern Pennsylvania "come from similar backgrounds." W&J attracts "the cookie-cutter student," explains an undergrad: "White, preppy, good looking, overachieving, and heterosexual." Perhaps because the students are so similar, they "are easy to talk to" and "very helpful." While many of these students have quite a bit of brainpower—and like to exercise said brainpower competitively in the classroom—many of them hail from small-town communities in this part of the country and arrive at W&J with the "very closed-minded" perspectives that they grew up with. "Many students have been living in what I call a 'bubble,' in which they only know what they see or hear on television in regards to minorities," says a student. Undergrads here hope that by recruiting "a wider diversity of students" the college can help to pop those bubbles.

ADMISSIONS

Very important factors considered by the admissions committee include: secondary school record, standardized test scores, and class rank. *Important factors considered include:* essay, extracurricular activities, interview, recommendations, volunteer/work experience, and personal qualities. *Other factors considered include:* geographical residence and talent/ability. TOEFL required of all international applicants. High school diploma or GED is required. *High school units required/recommended:* 15 total required; 3 English required, 3 math required, 1 science required, 2 foreign language required, 6 elective required.

The Inside Word

WJC puts its facilities and resources within easy reach of students striving to maintain high scholastic standards, and students respond by raising the bar just a little higher when they blow off steam, as well. Minority students and those hailing from far outside the region are raising its level of diversity, too.

FINANCIAL AID

Students should submit: FAFSA. The Princeton Review suggests that all financial aid forms be submitted as soon as possible after January 1. *Need-based scholarships/grants offered:* Pell, SEOG, state and institutional grants. *Loan aid offered:* FFEL Subsidized Stafford, FFEL Unsubsidized Stafford, FFEL PLUS, Federal Perkins, and GATE. Federal Work-Study Program available. Institutional employment available. *Merit-based aid offered:* Academic scholarships, Alumni Awards, and Eagle Awards. Veterans are eligible for assistance under the G.I. Bill. Tuition payment plan available. Applicants will be notified of awards on a rolling basis beginning on or about March 1. Off-campus job opportunities are good.

FROM THE ADMISSIONS OFFICE

"An avalanche of applications has hit Washington & Jefferson College. Last year, W&J shattered the all-time school record for the number of applications for admission. This year's application numbers have already eclipsed last year's total, and the quality of the pool has not been compromised. Incoming freshmen have an average SAT score of above 1,100 and a median grade point average of 3.3. A revised curriculum and new academic programs and facilities have contributed to the influx.

"The Office of Admissions welcomes prospective students and their families. Students can schedule a personal interview, tour the campus, spend the night, and attend a class. To schedule a visit, students should contact the office directly or go to the website."

For even more information on this school, turn to page 280 of the "Stats" section.

WASHINGTON AND LEE UNIVERSITY

LETCHER AVENUE, LEXINGTON, VA 24450-0303 • ADMISSIONS: 540-463-8710 • FAX: 540-463-8062
FINANCIAL AID: 540-463-8715 • E-MAIL: ADMISSIONS@WLU.EDU • WEBSITE: WWW.WLU.EDU

Ratings
Quality of Life: 92   **Academic:** 96   **Admissions:** 99   **Financial Aid:** 86

Academics

While not the best-known small, traditional, liberal arts school on the East Coast, Washington and Lee may well be the best loved by its students. The school is not for everyone—see Student Body, below—but for those who fit the mold, W&L is a "little utopian soci-

> **SURVEY SAYS . . .**
> *Frats and sororities dominate social scene*
> *No one cheats, Diversity lacking on campus*
> *Hard liquor is popular*
> *Student publications are popular*
> *Class discussions encouraged*

ety" that offers "really small classes" and a "strong sense of community among the students, faculty, and administration." These factors help mitigate the heavy workload here. Writes one student, "Academically, W&L is very challenging, but the small classes and group discussions make it very easy to participate and learn." Students say the faculty is "extremely helpful and always accessible" and appreciate professors who "epitomize southern hospitality. They're amazing!" All classes are taught by full professors; W&L has "no TAs, which is excellent." Undergrads are equally sanguine about the administration, reporting that the "administration and departments bend over backwards to help you out. If you are serious about learning and not just willing but want to work for your education, W&L will present excellent opportunities." The school runs on an unusual academic schedule, featuring two full-length terms (fall and winter) and a mandatory six-week term in the spring, during which students participate in seminars and internships or travel abroad. W&L also has a very popular Honor System that allows students to schedule their own nonproctored exams and leave their dorm rooms unlocked. Take-home, closed-book examinations are not uncommon, and "the buildings are open 24/7" as well. Brags one student, "The Honor System dominates life on campus and is a large part of what makes this university so special."

Life

Students at W&L really, really want you to know how much they drink. More than a few, in fact, are deeply offended that they dropped in this publication's "Drinking School" ranking last year. We'll let the students set the record straight. Writes one, "W&L allows students to pursue a wide range of academics while maintaining a strong sense of drunkenness." Adds another, "W&L is Utopia, with frat parties and kegs added." Indeed, the W&L social universe revolves around the Greek scene. Comments one student, "We have the greatest fraternity scene in the country. Period. If you like bourbon and Coke or beer flowing like water, there is no place to go but here." Agrees another, "We like to get our drink on." Because "fraternity parties are open to everyone, except for special functions," W&L suffers less from Greek/independent antagonism than do many other Greek-dominated campuses. During nondrinking hours, "club and intramural sports are popular. The opportunities for satisfying extracurricular activities are excellent." Students also love to "go tubing in the river, play Frisbee in the quad, dance all night long," hang out in their "palatial dorms," or walk across their postcard-perfect, ivy-covered campus. But when it comes right down to it, "basically, students study their asses off during the week, then party their asses off on the weekend. 'Work hard, drink hard' is our motto."

Student Body

"W&L is often described as having a student body like a country club: white, well-off, Republican," explains one student. "Many students here come from families of wealth. My little Neon is parked next to a Lexus, a Saab, and a brand-new SUV—in the freshman lot!" Students concur that the "conservative, clean-cut, red-blooded American boys and girls" who attend W&L are "fun-loving, ambitious, and elitist." Writes one African American undergrad, "You can tell some of them have never even been around minority students before." Those who fit in agree that "never before have I met friendlier people. A lot of our students [approximately 10 percent] are from Texas, so friendliness is an inherent trait." Those who don't fit in either transfer out or endure a long four years.

ADMISSIONS

Very important factors considered by the admissions committee include: character/personal qualities, extracurricular activities, secondary school record, standardized test scores. *Important factors considered include:* class rank, recommendations. *Other factors considered include:* alumni/ae relation, essays, geographical residence, minority status, state residency, talent/ability, volunteer work, work experience. SAT I or ACT required; SAT II also required. High school diploma is required and GED is not accepted. *High school units required/recommended:* 16 total required; 4 English required, 3 math required, 4 math recommended, 1 science required, 3 science recommended, 1 science lab required, 2 foreign language required, 3 foreign language recommended, 1 social studies required, 1 history required, 2 history recommended, 4 elective required.

The Inside Word

If you're looking for a bastion of southern tradition, Washington and Lee is one of the foremost. Its admissions process is appropriately traditional, and highly selective. Under these circumstances, it is always best to take a cautious and conservative approach to preparing your candidacy. Smart applicants have taken the toughest courses available to them in high school—the minimum requirements aren't likely to help you gain admission. Neither will a glib approach to the personal side of the application; a well-written essay is what they're after.

FINANCIAL AID

Students should submit: FAFSA, CSS/Financial Aid PROFILE, noncustodial (divorced/separated) parent's statement, business/farm supplement. The Princeton Review suggests that all financial aid forms be submitted as soon as possible after January 1. *Need-based scholarships/grants offered:* Pell, SEOG, state scholarships/grants, private scholarships, the school's own gift aid. *Loan aid offered:* FFEL Subsidized Stafford, FFEL Unsubsidized Stafford, FFEL PLUS, Federal Perkins, college/university loans from institutional funds. Federal Work-Study Program available. Institutional employment available. Applicants will be notified of awards on or about April 3. Off-campus job opportunities are fair.

FROM THE ADMISSIONS OFFICE

"W&L, the nation's ninth oldest college, is a small, private, liberal arts school located in the heart of the beautiful Shenandoah Valley. As one might expect, W&L possesses an inordinate amount of history. Quality teaching both in and out of the classroom, and the development of students into well-rounded leaders, summarize the school's primary goals. An average W&L class contains 15 students, and courses are taught by the school's full-time faculty members; no graduate students or teacher assistants are on the faculty. W&L possesses a uniquely broad and deep curriculum, as well as a time-honored, student-run Honor System that allows students a wide range of freedoms. W&L is a highly competitive school, where students will receive a first-rate, personalized education, develop leadership skills, enjoy life outside of the classroom, and reap the innumerable postgraduation benefits of a W&L education."

For even more information on this school, turn to page 281 of the "Stats" section.

WASHINGTON COLLEGE

300 WASHINGTON AVENUE, CHESTERTOWN, MD 21620 • ADMISSIONS: 410-778-7700 • FAX: 410-778-7287
E-MAIL: ADM.OFF@WASHCOLL.EDU • WEBSITE: WWW.WASHCOLL.EDU

Ratings
Quality of Life: 77   Academic: 85   Admissions: 75   Financial Aid: 75

Academics

According to its undergrads, Washington College "has many wonderful professors who are eager to help the students learn what they teach, not just get high marks." One student avers "each professor cares deeply about each

> **SURVEY SAYS . . .**
> *Profs teach upper levels*
> *Instructors are good teachers*
> *Very little drug use*
> *Classes are small*

individual student," while another gushes that WC professors have "encouraged me to push my limits and try new things." Personal attention can really pay off, as it did for one WC student who was able to "develop an independent studies major in digital media," or for another who praises "one professor who will call me in the morning to make sure I wake up for class." Though eager to applaud their professors, students are split when it comes to the administration. Some WC students worry that the "administration is unresponsive to student needs. It awards tenure on the basis of published research, not the ability to teach." Others describe administrators as "excellent," "awesome," or "very helpful," adding that "the dean is a very social person and is always there to help students out. Overall, [my] academic experience is good."

Life

Though students say Washington College is something of a "suitcase campus," "characterized by the majority of students packing up and leaving every weekend," during the week, "big-name bands come and play, comedians and musicians perform, and celebrity scholars give lectures." In addition, students keep busy with clubs and student government, the Greek system is popular, and creative writers "publish three or four independent literary magazines every year." Exclaims one student, "There's almost always something to do here—you just need to find it!" Many students cite drinking as a popular weekend activity; others say "people are more concerned with doing well in class and less concerned with partying. For fun I play intramural sports, go to movies, and go out with friends." Since hometown Chesterton is pretty rural ("in the middle of nowhere," according to one student) students can escape the small-town blues with trips to Annapolis, Baltimore, or Newark.

Student Body

Washington College has strong ties with many international universities, drawing a "high percentage of international students" to the campus. Students site the global diversity as a real strength of the school, remarking, "Students attend from all over: Pakistan, South Africa, France, Australia, to name just a few countries." Don't expect much of a multicultural environment at WC, though. Despite international influences, "there is a very small minority population, allowing for little counterbalance against the large white majority." In addition, students claim that the student body has a tendency to be cliquey, prohibiting students from different backgrounds from getting to know one another. One student describes the situation: "It's to the point where, honest to goodness, tables in the cafeteria are certain tables for certain people, and you don't dare sit there if you're not part of that group." A majority of students, however, get along well with their fellow students and describe Washington College as a "close-knit environment" in which most people are "open and friendly."

ADMISSIONS

Very important factors considered by the admissions committee include: interview and secondary school record. *Important factors considered include:* character/personal qualities, class rank, essays, recommendations, and standardized test scores. *Other factors considered include:* alumni/ae relation, extracurricular activities, minority status, talent/ability, volunteer work, and work experience. SAT I or ACT required. TOEFL required of all international applicants. High school diploma or GED is required. *High school units required/recommended:* 16 total required; 20 total recommended; 4 English required, 3 math required, 4 math recommended, 3 science required, 4 science recommended, 2 science lab required, 3 science lab recommended, 2 foreign language required, 4 foreign language recommended, 4 social studies required, 4 social studies recommended.

The Inside Word

Admissions standards are moderately selective at Washington College, the 10th oldest college in the nation, where nearly half of all applicants are from out of state. A strong B student should not encounter many obstacles to admission, but applicants should note that interviews are considered very important factors in the selection process.

FINANCIAL AID

Students should submit: FAFSA. Regular filing deadline is February 15. The Princeton Review suggests that all financial aid forms be submitted as soon as possible after January 1. *Need-based scholarships/grants offered:* Pell, SEOG, state scholarships/grants, private scholarships, and the school's own gift aid. *Loan aid offered:* FFEL Subsidized Stafford, FFEL Unsubsidized Stafford, FFEL PLUS, Federal Perkins, and college/university loans from institutional funds. Federal Work-Study Program available. Institutional employment available. Applicants will be notified of awards on a rolling basis beginning on or about March 1. Off-campus job opportunities are excellent.

FROM THE ADMISSIONS OFFICE

"Founded in 1782, Washington College is the 10th oldest college in America. George Washington, in whose honor the college was named, served as a trustee from 1784 until 1789 and was awarded the college's first honorary degree. From its inception, Washington College has maintained an unwavering commitment to the liberal arts and sciences. Through diverse curricular offerings, excellent teaching, and engaged learning we develop in our students the habits of analytic thought, aesthetic insight, imagination, ethical sensitivity, and clarity of expression. We choose to maintain an enrollment of approximately 1,250 students and a 12:1 student/faculty ratio. Two-thirds of all WC classes have 20 or fewer students, making it easy for undergrads and their professors to engage in the exchange of information and ideas. Our graduates leave us prepared for admission to graduate and professional schools, able to pursue a wide variety of career options, and ready for lives of responsible citizenship and personal fulfillment.

"Our 112-acre campus is in historic Chestertown on Maryland's Eastern Shore. We are situated in a county with more than 200 miles of waterfront including a beautiful stretch along the Chester River just a short walk from campus. Location is everything and ours is in the very heart of the Chesapeake Bay region, 45 minutes from Annapolis and 90 minutes from Baltimore, Philadelphia, and Washington, D.C.

"More than 50 percent of Washington College students are National Honor Society members. The college offers $40,000 scholarships to all NHS members who qualify for admission."

For even more information on this school, turn to page 281 of the "Stats" section.

WEST CHESTER UNIVERSITY OF PENNSYLVANIA

MESSIKOMER HALL, 100 W. ROSEDALE AVENUE, WEST CHESTER, PA 19383 • ADMISSIONS: 610-436-3411
FAX: 610-436-2907 • E-MAIL: UGADMISS@WCUPA.EDU • WEBSITE: WWW.WCUPA.EDU

Ratings

Quality of Life: 73   **Academic:** 62   **Admissions:** 60   **Financial Aid:** 70

Academics

Students at West Chester University of Pennsylvania, a midsize state school located outside Philadelphia, want you to know that "the education department is very good" here, as are the departments of science, criminal justice, and psychology. If you ask,

> **SURVEY SAYS . . .**
> *Classes are small*
> *Very little beer drinking*
> *Students don't get along with local community*
> *School is well run*
> *Very little hard liquor*

students will tell you that they "also like that our school is small [relative to other state universities], because it seems safer and more like home." As at many state schools, professors here get mixed grades. A typical undergrad opines, "The professors are pretty much the same as they are at every university or college; some are wonderful," but there are a few who are not helpful." Administrative duties, students warn, are also occasionally perplexing: "Often I am confused with my requirements for graduation," notes a typical student. There are those here, however, who think the fault lies primarily with the students rather than the institution. Explains one such undergrad, "Of course, there are some rough spots, but every school is going to be criticized by some of its students. A lot of students from here go home every weekend, so it doesn't really matter anyway."

Life

One student summarizes, "my life at school exists studying every spare minute I have during the week, working to help pay rent, and then going out on the weekends." Students also enjoy trips to Philadelphia and New York City and events sponsored by the student activities board. Reports one student, "On certain weekends, they show movies that were recently out in the theatres. They offer a lot of different things for us to do. In the first two weeks of school we had a hypnotist and a comedy show featuring comedians that have been on Comedy Central. There's always something to do at WCU." Undergrads also note that there are "tons of places to hang out and go out to eat" scattered throughout the upscale suburban enclave surrounding campus.

Student Body

The 10,000-plus strong undergraduates of WCU include "diverse . . . groups floating around campus. . . . Everyone seems to find their niche. It just takes awhile." Other students agree: "The students here are pretty diverse. Every year the Homecoming court has the most different group of people imaginable! There are students represented in the lesbian, gay, and bisexual organization; there are students represented from the black student union; there're students from Greek organizations; and many others. I would say, for the most part, everyone gets along well!" Many warn, "A lot of students go home for weekends . . . . Resident students and off-campus students do not interact as much. Many off-campus students do not feel connected to the campus at all." As one student tells us, "If you do not live in the dorms the first year you are here, it is very difficult to meet people."

ADMISSIONS

Very important factors considered by the admissions committee include: level of difficulty of high school curriculum, class rank, grade point average, and standardized test scores. High school diploma or GED, personal essay, SAT or ACT required. TOEFL required of all international applicants. *High school units required/recommended:* 4 English required, 4 social studies/history required, 3 math required, 4 math recommended, 2 science required, 3 science recommended, 2 foreign language recommended, 4 elective recommended.

The Inside Word

Students from up and down the Northeast Corridor converge on WCU as much for its campus energy as for its strength in the social sciences. Its proximity to Philly and The Big Apple make it attractive for both homebodies and those with wanderlust.

FINANCIAL AID

Students should submit: FAFSA. Priority filing deadline is March 1. The Princeton Review suggests that all financial aid forms be submitted as soon as possible after January 1. *Need-based scholarships/grants offered:* Pell, SEOG, state scholarships/grants, private scholarships, and the school's own gift aid. *Loan aid offered:* Federal Perkins, Federal Nursing, and state loans. Federal Work-Study Program available. Institutional employment available. Applicants will be notified of awards on a rolling basis beginning on or about April 15. Off-campus job opportunities are excellent.

FROM THE ADMISSIONS OFFICE

"West Chester University (WCU) has an enrollment of more than 12,000 and is the second largest of the 14 institutions in the Pennsylvania State System of Higher Education as well as the fourth-largest university in the Philadelphia metropolitan area. While the university attracts the majority of its students from Pennsylvania, New Jersey, and Delaware, it also enrolls many students from other areas across the United States and from more than 50 countries. It has become increasingly selective; WCU received more than 9,000 applications for the 1,700 spaces in the fall 2002 freshman class.

"The College of Arts and Sciences offers 40 different undergraduate degree programs, including its celebrated pre-medical program, which has placed 95 percent of its graduates in medical schools over the past 24 years. The School of Business and Public Affairs is recognized locally for its frequent assistance to the business community. WCU had the second-best pass rate in the state for first-time candidates of the CPA exam in 1999 and has been number two for seven of the past 13 years. The School of Music offers students the opportunity to learn from, and play with, award-winning faculty as well as the opportunity to experiment in the Center for Music Technology, where computers offer yet another aspect of music education. The School of Health Sciences offers a wide range of programs, from public health and nursing to sports medicine. The School of Education prepares more teachers than any other institution in southeastern Pennsylvania.

"Numerous campus groups in music, theater, athletics, and other activities as well as clubs, fraternities, sororities, service organizations, and honor societies provide students with the opportunity to participate in a full range of programs. The university offers 23 intercollegiate sports and 11 club sports for men and women. WCU offers other innovations, as well, including free room and board during summer sessions for those who take a minimum number of credits. The program, in its fifth year, was proclaimed a 'Great Deal' by *Time* magazine."

For even more information on this school, turn to page 282 of the "Stats" section.

WEST VIRGINIA UNIVERSITY

ADMISSIONS OFFICE, PO BOX 6009, MORGANTOWN, WV 26506-6009 • ADMISSIONS: 800-344-9881
FAX: 304-293-3080 • FINANCIAL AID: 304-293-5242 • E-MAIL: WVUADMISSIONS@ARC.WVU.EDU
WEBSITE: WWW.WVU.EDU

Ratings
Quality of Life: 73   **Academic:** 64   **Admissions:** 75   **Financial Aid:** 82

Academics

Spread out across three campuses in Morgantown (and several smaller regional campuses), West Virginia University works hard to overcome the usual shortcomings of mammoth undergraduate programs. Operation Jump-Start typifies WVU's efforts to personalize the university. The program groups freshmen in nine residential houses according to academic

> **SURVEY SAYS . . .**
> *Everyone loves the Mountaineers*
> *Frats and sororities dominate social scene*
> *Class discussions are rare*
> *(Almost) everyone smokes, High cost of living*
> *Campus difficult to get around, Large classes*
> *Theater is unpopular*
> *Student publications are popular*
> *Ethnic diversity on campus*

interest. Faculty couples live close by and serve as mentors for the incoming students, helping them acclimate to the university and quickly achieve a sense of community. Some Jump-Start groups have taken on community service projects, and others have taken trips together. Similarly, "the university Honors Program allows students to have a fulfilling and challenging undergraduate experience" that includes smaller classes and more seminar-style teaching. Professors at WVU run the gamut from wonderful to awful, depending on the department and the individual. Several students in the biological sciences voice such complaints as "I find myself teaching myself through learning centers and excessive studying." Professors in the popular Division of Agriculture and Forestry, however, "run in the good-to-excellent range." The College of Engineering and the College of Human Resources and Education are among the popular and well-regarded options here. According to one dissatisfied student, "Because of problems with the PRT [personnel rapid transit], it usually takes me half an hour to get to class! My advisor has also continually told me wrong information on the classes I need to take."

Life

Many students love the Morgantown area for its quiet vibe. Explains one, "The town moves at a slow pace when you compare it to some of the larger cities in proximity to Morgantown (i.e., D.C., Pittsburgh, Baltimore, etc.), but that's not a problem. There is always something to do, everything from hiking up to Coopers Rock and taking in the magnificent view from the top, or taking a walk/run along the Monongahela River." They also like its proximity to Pittsburgh, only an hour-and-a-half away by car. Students warn, however, that town-gown relations are extremely strained, except during football games. "WVU students are avid sports fans. Thousands of us go to cheer on our team at each sporting event, be [it] football or basketball." While "WVU was formerly ranked #1 party school in the nation back in 1998 or so . . . now we are nowhere near that ranking. Unfortunately, our president has seen to it that we will never achieve that ranking ever again through [stringent] policies and such." In the place of bleary-eyed beer bashes, "WVU has implemented an alcohol-free program called WVU Up All Night which takes place on Thursday, Friday, and Saturday nights. A lot of free activities and free food are provided during Up All Night. And the turn out is tremendous."

Student Body

WVU draws students largely from within the state. Maryland, New Jersey, and Pennsylvania also contribute heavily to the student population. Writes one student, "There is a 'country boy meets city boy' situation that occurs for every freshman here at WVU. By this I mean you have a solid in-state population of good ol' West Virginia boys meeting up with the Long Islanders and Jersey boys. . . . I don't want to say there is hostility between these two groups but getting along takes a little effort." About 600 African American undergrads constitute the largest non-white group; complains one black student, "I just wish there were more minorities on campus."

ADMISSIONS

Very important factors considered by the admissions committee include: secondary school record, standardized test scores. *Other factors considered include:* alumni/ae relation. SAT I or ACT required. TOEFL required of all international applicants. High school diploma or GED is required. *High school units required/recommended:* 13 total required; 4 English required, 3 math required, 3 science required, 2 science lab required, 2 foreign language recommended, 3 social studies required.

The Inside Word

West Virginia's admissions office made an excellent point about rolling admission policies in their response to us. As the admissions committee gets closer to its enrollment targets, the admissions process becomes progressively more selective. At West Virginia the early bird usually gets a worm, and there is often another one for a late bird. Still, don't hold off on rolling admission applications just because others have more pressing deadlines. Forget that there's a rolling plan, and complete your application as if it has to be in at the same time as all the rest.

FINANCIAL AID

Students should submit: FAFSA. Regular filing deadline is March 1. The Princeton Review suggests that all financial aid forms be submitted as soon as possible after January 1. *Need-based scholarships/grants offered:* Pell, SEOG, state scholarships/grants, private scholarships, the school's own gift aid. *Loan aid offered:* Direct Subsidized Stafford, Direct Unsubsidized Stafford, Direct PLUS, Federal Perkins, Federal Nursing, state loans, college/university loans from institutional funds. Federal Work-Study Program available. Institutional employment available. Applicants will be notified of awards on a rolling basis. Off-campus job opportunities are good.

FROM THE ADMISSIONS OFFICE

"From quality academic programs and outstanding, caring faculty to incredible new facilities and a campus environment that focuses on students' needs, WVU is a place where dreams can come true. The University's tradition of academic excellence attracts some of the region's best high school seniors. WVU has produced 25 Rhodes Scholars, 24 Goldwater Scholars, 14 Truman Scholars, 5 members of *USA Today*'s All-USA College Academic First Team, and 2 Udall Scholarship winners. Whether your goal is to be an aerospace engineer, reporter, physicist, athletic trainer, opera singer, forensic investigator, pharmacist, or CEO, WVU's 170 degree choices can make it happen. Unique student-centered initiatives include Operation Jump Start, which helps freshmen adjust to college, and WVU All Night, which provides free food and activities nearly every weekend. Resources for the parents include the Mountaineer Parents' Club and a parents' helpline (800-WVU-0096). A new Student Recreation Center includes athletic courts, pools, weight/fitness equipment, and a 50-foot indoor climbing wall. Also, a brand-new life sciences building and completely renovated library complex just opened. With programs for studying abroad, a Center for Black Culture and Research, an Office of Disability Services, and a student body from 49 states and 90 different countries, WVU encourages and nurtures diversity. More than $133 million in annual grant funding makes WVU a major research institution where undergraduates can participate. The area's natural beauty provides chances to ski, bike, hike, and go whitewater rafting."

For even more information on this school, turn to page 283 of the "Stats" section.

WEST VIRGINIA WESLEYAN COLLEGE

59 COLLEGE AVENUE, BUCKHANNON, WV 26201 • ADMISSIONS: 304-473-8510 • FAX: 304-473-8108
E-MAIL: ADMISSION@WVWC.EDU • WEBSITE: WWW.WVWC.EDU

Ratings
Quality of Life: 79   **Academic:** 80   **Admissions:** 71   **Financial Aid:** 77

Academics

"The professors and overall academic experience at Wesleyan are phenomenal," says a seasoned West Virginia Wesleyan College student. This school has all of the charms of a small college, especially "encouraging and personable professors." One student writes, "The professors are some of the best I know of. As at all schools, you have some that couldn't find their way out of a paper bag, but they are excellent resources." Some point out the downfalls that accompany the benefits of a small school; according to one student, the college doesn't "offer very many courses in each of the majors." Another informs us that "many departments and professors are too concerned with the lives of the students. In the music department, for example, students are chastised for joining social fraternities or sororities." Other major complaints are aimed at an administration that "seems out of touch with what goes on at the heart of the campus." Surprisingly, one thing that students don't gripe about is the string of "challenging" general studies courses they must complete; one mature student writes, "You may not like to admit it, but in the end you learn a lot from those classes." While some students wish that the cost of an education at WVWC wasn't so steep, they offer incomers this piece of good news: "They offer tons of scholarships." Still not sure if West Virginia Wesleyan is right for you? "You simply must drop in and see for yourself!"

> **SURVEY SAYS . . .**
> *School is well run*
> *Classes are small*
> *Students are religious*
> *Students are happy*

Life

"You have to get involved" in student activities at this "small" campus "in the middle of nowhere" or else "you will be bored forever." The "wide variety of clubs" here includes "Students for a Free Tibet, self-defense clubs, Ultimate Frisbee, dance and music clubs, Students in Free Enterprise," and many more. Student organizations like CAB (the campus activities board) work hard to provide entertainment—music, performances, or interactive games. Greek life, too, breathes life into the campus, as "35 percent of the students at Wesleyan are involved in social fraternities/sororities," according to one. "Most people spend a great deal of time drinking," reports one student, whether they "go to frat houses" looking for "a party" or hang tough with a few good friends in the dorms. West Virginia Wesleyan also offers "lots of really awesome outdoor opportunities," and it's "a haven for mountain bikers, kayakers, rock climbers, snowboarders, and avid hikers." And the "outdoor rec department" actually "covers two-thirds of the cost of every outdoor rec trip." It may be difficult to locate a decent meal upon your return, though: "No one likes the cafeteria food," warns one student, while another groans, "They either need to be more inventive or change the food schedule. Mondays are always chicken nugget day." Hometown Buckhannon is "basically bare"—it's "in this little tiny town in the ass crack of West Virginia" where "there is nothing to do." If local branches of Wal-Mart and Sheetz don't satiate students' appetite for fun, Pittsburgh is pretty close by. If all else fails, there's always the Internet; it's a popular destination, considering the "laptops that are provided to each student" upon arrival at WVWC.

Student Body

The 1,500 or so students at this "private, religious school" in Buckhannon are "friendly, but there is no diversity." As a result of the homogeneity, you may find that some students "just need to learn that others may think and act differently than them, and they need to accept that." But with students "from all over the country and the world," WVWC isn't completely absent of diversity, either, and student personalities range from "the pseudo-political egomaniacs to the Johnny-football-hero frat boys to the eccentric hippie-anarchists." There are "many cliques" within the student community, which leads one to comment, "Wesleyan is a lot like high school." If you keep an open mind, though, you can meet "many different people of different backgrounds, different experiences, different interests, different sexual orientations, and different lifestyles."

ADMISSIONS

Very important factors considered by the admissions committee include: secondary school record and standardized test scores. *Important factors considered include:* character/personal qualities, class rank, essays, and interview. *Other factors considered include:* alumni/ae relation, extracurricular activities, recommendations, talent/ability, volunteer work, and work experience. SAT I or ACT required. TOEFL required of all international applicants. High school diploma or GED is required. *High school units required/recommended:* 4 English required, 3 math required, 3 science required, 2 science lab required, 2 foreign language recommended, 2 social studies required, 3 social studies recommended, 2 history required, 3 elective required.

The Inside Word

High academic expectations set the stage for an experience at WVWC, which is best suited for students who want personal attention and won't be dismayed by the modest number of classes offered for each major.

FINANCIAL AID

Students should submit: FAFSA. No deadline for regular filing. The Princeton Review suggests that all financial aid forms be submitted as soon as possible after January 1. *Need-based scholarships/grants offered:* Pell, SEOG, state scholarships/grants, private scholarships, the school's own gift aid, and Federal Nursing. *Loan aid offered:* Direct Subsidized Stafford, Direct Unsubsidized Stafford, Direct PLUS, Federal Perkins, Federal Nursing, and college/university loans from institutional funds. Federal Work-Study Program available. Institutional employment available. Applicants will be notified of awards on a rolling basis beginning on or about March 30. Off-campus job opportunities are poor.

FROM THE ADMISSIONS OFFICE

"West Virginia Wesleyan has expanded its academic programs with several new majors and degree offerings. Wesleyan students can now elect to complete the Five-Year Undergraduate/Master of Business Administration Program with available majors in accounting, business administration, economics, finance, international business, management, and marketing. Wesleyan now offers a Bachelor of Fine Arts in theatre arts and musical theatre, as well as a minor in dance. Finally, the college now offers a Bachelor of Arts in criminal justice."

For even more information on this school, turn to page 283 of the "Stats" section.

WESTMINSTER COLLEGE

319 SOUTH MARKET STREET, NEW WILMINGTON, PA 16172 • ADMISSIONS: 800-942-8033
FAX: 724-946-7171 • FINANCIAL AID: 724-946-7102 • E-MAIL: ADMIS@WESTMINSTER.EDU
WEBSITE: WWW.WESTMINSTER.EDU

Ratings
Quality of Life: 79   **Academic:** 77   **Admissions:** 75   **Financial Aid:** 88

Academics

Westminster College, a small Presbyterian school in Western Pennsylvania where "professors have a genuine passion to teach," enjoys an excellent reputation for combining "tough academics" with "real-world preparation." The largely professional-minded student body here is inundated with the essentials of a solid liberal arts education through "the Westminster Plan," a thorough core curriculum in the sciences, humanities, mathematics, computer science, and religion. As a result of the program, every student graduates with at least two majors: a "common" major in the western liberal arts tradition and a specialized major of the student's choosing. While some students complain that these "introductory courses could use some help" and feel that the school "is a slave to tradition" and so refuses to change the program, others feel that the Westminster Plan forms the bedrock of their educational experience. Students happily report that "professors make you welcome to talk with them outside of class, visit their homes, and even eat meals with them." More than a few undergrads bemoan the fact that "the professors teach the classes like you've already had it and fly through the material . . . . They also act like a C is a good grade." Students appreciate the school's president, who "leaves his door open and encourages the students to stop in and say hello."

> **SURVEY SAYS . . .**
> *Frats and sororities dominate social scene*
> *Diversity lacking on campus*
> *Classes are small*
> *(Almost) everyone smokes*
> *Very little drug use*
> *Lousy food on campus*
> *Political activism is (almost) nonexistent*
> *Lousy off-campus food*
> *Students don't like New Wilmington, PA*
> *Theater is unpopular*

Life

According to many Westminster students we heard from, students' social life follows a predictable arc during their four-year tenure here. Explains one, "As a freshman you love the fraternity houses! They're . . . a great way to meet new people. Then things tend to get old as you make it to being a senior. It's a dry town so there aren't any bars; it actually kinda sucks!" Indeed, by senior year, most students find themselves either going home on weekends or heading to nearby Sharon, Youngstown, or Pittsburgh (a little further down the road but with much more to offer) for fun. Until then, most students enjoy a Greek-centered scene. Reports one underclassman, "Greek life is a great way to spend your college experience at school. You get to meet a lot of different people and for the most part they all have your back." Adds another, "Life at Westminster is double-sided. During the day, students are involved in campus organizations, get good grades, go to church. . . . If we are involved, do well in classes, and have faith in God, why not party a little?" Hometown New Wilmington "has one traffic light, so as you can imagine, there's not much to [it], except a significant Amish population." The town does boast "$3 movie theatres that are 10 minutes away, as well as Perkins and Wal-

Mart. We couldn't live without 2 a.m. Wal-Mart runs!" While many feel that "besides frat parties, there is nothing to do," they have faith that "the new campus center being built should help things."

Student Body

Westminster's "very conservative" students, "the majority of whom come from upper-middle-class, white suburban homes," are the type of people who open doors for each other, smile and say 'hi' even to those they don't know, and immerse themselves in extracurriculars and community service. According to many, however, their friendliness "doesn't go beyond the superficial level. Most students form their groups early on in freshman and sophomore year and don't seem to expand those groups much throughout the rest of their college career." Greeks in particular "have some serious rivalries" with each other and also "cause some of the independents to feel like outsiders." Several students reported campus unrest over the issue of sexual preference. Explains one undergrad, "Westminster is a very small school, and as such there isn't a whole lot of diversity held within. Most of the students have never been outside of the area, and all typically share the same dreams and goals . . . . Only a few students break away . . . and some find it too hard to remain on campus because of it."

ADMISSIONS

Very important factors considered by the admissions committee include: interview, secondary school record, standardized test scores. *Important factors considered include:* character/personal qualities, class rank, essays, recommendations. *Other factors considered include:* alumni/ae relation, extracurricular activities, minority status, talent/ability, volunteer work, work experience. SAT I or ACT required. TOEFL required of all international applicants. High school diploma or GED is required. *High school units required/recommended:* 16 total required; 4 English required, 3 math required, 2 science required, 2 science lab required, 2 foreign language required, 2 social studies required, 1 history required, 3 elective required.

The Inside Word

The vast majority of those who apply to Westminster gain admission, but the applicant pool is strong enough to enable the college to weed out those who don't measure up to the solid entering class academic profile. Candidates who are shooting for academic scholarships should play the admissions game all the way and put a solid effort into the completion of their applications.

FINANCIAL AID

Students should submit: FAFSA, institution's own financial aid form. The Princeton Review suggests that all financial aid forms be submitted as soon as possible after January 1. *Need-based scholarships/grants offered:* Pell, SEOG, state scholarships/grants, private scholarships, the school's own gift aid. *Loan aid offered:* FFEL Subsidized Stafford, FFEL Unsubsidized Stafford, FFEL PLUS, Federal Perkins. Federal Work-Study Program available. Applicants will be notified of awards on a rolling basis. Off-campus job opportunities are good.

FROM THE ADMISSIONS OFFICE

"Since its founding, Westminster has been dedicated to a solid foundation in today's most crucial social, cultural, and ethical issues. Related to the Presbyterian Church (U.S.A.), Westminster is home to people of many faiths. Our students and faculty, tradition of campus, and small-town setting all contribute to an enlightening educational experience."

For even more information on this school, turn to page 284 of the "Stats" section.

YORK COLLEGE OF PENNSYLVANIA

COUNTRY CLUB ROAD, YORK, PA 17405-7199 • ADMISSIONS: 717-849-1600 • FAX: 717-849-1607
E-MAIL: ADMISSIONS@YCP.EDU • WEBSITE: WWW.YCP.EDU

Ratings
Quality of Life: 74   **Academic:** 70   **Admissions:** 73   **Financial Aid:** 81

Academics

What distinguishes York College of Pennsylvania from the pack, undergraduates at this central Pennsylvania liberal arts school agree, is the quality of teaching. "I feel that 'professors' [is] a misnomer for the faculty here because they are teachers rather than stereotypical professors," crows one student. Adds another, "All

> **SURVEY SAYS . . .**
> *Classes are small*
> *Very little beer drinking*
> *Intercollegiate sports are popular*
> *Student publications are popular*
> *(Almost) everyone plays intramural sports*
> *Popular college radio*
> *Diversity lacking on campus*

professors are tops in their fields and have real-world experience. Last semester I had a former army officer for my American government class, and the leader of Central Pennsylvania's largest marketing firm teach marketing. You'll run into the occasional slave driver here, but most professors try to teach you something." This high level of didactic excellence, along with "small classes that encourage discussions as opposed to lecturing all the time," "a hands-on approach to learning," and an insistence on "holding everyone to a higher standard" contribute to York students' satisfaction with their academic experience. Administrators are "easily accessible and will listen to any problems you are having in their jurisdiction," according to undergraduates, who also caution that "the work gets a little overwhelming at times, but it's never that stressful." According to survey respondents, "York's strongest departments include communications, criminal justice, education, and nursing."

Life

Students at York enjoy a "great studying atmosphere, but there are always places to relax and party when you're done." In fact, most feel that "people at this school party harder than [students at] most larger universities. Any night of the week, drinking is easily accessible on or off campus. Fraternities and sororities pretty much run the show. If someone is not in an organization, whether it's Greek or sports related, they are out of the loop." Elaborates one undergrad, at Greek parties "a cup at the door is $3, and that's good for the night. The parties are in pretty gross houses, and most of the time is spent in an even grosser basement. However, no one seems to mind this." All the partying, combined with the fact that "York is a city that combines the ritzy developments with the row houses," has given rise to poor town-gown relations, but students don't much care because they find plenty to do on and around campus. "There are over 60 clubs/organizations on campus, so everyone can have something to do," notes one student. Adds another, "The school provides many activities for students, so there is plenty to do for anyone. For example, there are comedians and bands that come and play for the students." Students complain that the "athletic program is a joke. We don't even have a football team or a gymnastics team. The 'gym' is also pathetic. It's pretty much limited to about two treadmills and a few other machines." Those desperate for some kind of physical activity will be pleased to know that "there's this humongous hill across from the college entrance. It's always fun when it snows because you see college property put to good use as sledding equipment. Cafeteria trays, mattresses—you name it, we've tried it!"

Student Body

"A great majority" of the student body at York College "is extremely friendly." "There are cliques [in the form of] frats, sports teams, and others, but in the end the groups don't really matter because everyone is friendly to everyone else." Opines another undergrad, "It's like a small town where everyone knows everyone else." Adds another member of the simile-happy undergrad population, "This school is a lot like high school was in many ways. Small classes allow students to interact and get to know each other." Many here tell us that "pretty much everyone that goes to school at York has similar backgrounds" despite the school's aggressive efforts to recruit minority students. Some undergrads also complain, "Most students here don't take their school experience seriously enough and party too much."

ADMISSIONS

Very important factors considered by the admissions committee include: secondary school record. *Important factors considered include:* character/personal qualities, class rank, and standardized test scores. *Other factors considered include:* alumni/ae relation, essays, extracurricular activities, interview, recommendations, talent/ability, volunteer work, and work experience. SAT I or ACT required. TOEFL required of all international applicants. High school diploma is required and GED is accepted. *High school units required/recommended:* 15 total are required; 4 English required, 3 math required, 4 math recommended, 3 science required, 2 foreign language required, 3 social studies required.

The Inside Word

York College can be a very satisfying experience for students who pine for a one-on-one relationship with both academicians and administrators. Joining the ranks of its 5,000 students also affords matriculants access to the impressive array of extracurricular activities on campus.

FINANCIAL AID

Students should submit: FAFSA and institution's own financial aid form. No regular filing deadline. The Princeton Review suggests that all financial aid forms be submitted as soon as possible after January 1. *Need-based scholarships/grants offered:* Pell, SEOG, state scholarships/grants, private scholarships, and the school's own gift aid. *Loan aid offered:* Direct Subsidized Stafford, Direct Unsubsidized Stafford, Direct PLUS, Federal Perkins, Federal Nursing, state loans, and college/university loans from institutional funds. Federal Work-Study Program available. Institutional employment available. Applicants will be notified of awards on a rolling basis beginning on or about February 15. Off-campus job opportunities are excellent.

For even more information on this school, turn to page 285 of the "Stats" section.

PART 3

THE STATS

ALBRIGHT COLLEGE

CAMPUS LIFE
Quality of Life Rating   **73**

Type of school	private
Affiliation	Methodist
Environment	suburban

STUDENTS

Total undergrad enrollment	1,451
% male/female	56/44
% from out of state	33
% from public high school	71
% live on campus	80
% in (# of) fraternities	28 (4)
% in (# of) sororities	32 (3)
% African American	8
% Asian	3
% Caucasian	80
% Hispanic	3
% international	4

ACADEMICS
Academic Rating   **74**

Calendar	4-1-4
Student/faculty ratio	12:1
Profs interesting rating	87
Profs accessible rating	87
% profs teaching UG courses	100
Avg lab size	10-19 students
Avg regular class size	10-19 students

MOST POPULAR MAJORS
Biology/life sciences
Business administration
Psychology

SELECTIVITY
Admissions Rating   **71**

# of applicants	2,589
% of applicants accepted	73
% of acceptees attending	24

FRESHMAN PROFILE

Range SAT Verbal	450-570
Average SAT Verbal	513
Range SAT Math	450-570
Average SAT Math	512
Range ACT Composite	18-21
Average ACT Composite	19
Minimum TOEFL	530
Average HS GPA	3.2
% graduated top 10% of class	20
% graduated top 25% of class	43
% graduated top 50% of class	73

DEADLINES

Nonfall registration?	yes

FINANCIAL FACTS
Financial Aid Rating   **79**

Tuition	$21,790
Room and board	$6,809
Books and supplies	$800
Avg frosh grant	$14,000
Avg frosh loan	$3,500

ALLEGHENY COLLEGE

CAMPUS LIFE
Quality of Life Rating   **75**

Type of school	private
Affiliation	other
Environment	rural

STUDENTS

Total undergrad enrollment	1,924
% male/female	48/52
% from out of state	32
% from public high school	85
% live on campus	73
% in (# of) fraternities	26 (5)
% in (# of) sororities	29 (4)
% African American	2
% Asian	2
% Caucasian	94
% Hispanic	1
% international	1
# of countries represented	16

ACADEMICS
Academic Rating   **83**

Calendar	semester
Student/faculty ratio	14:1
Profs interesting rating	77
Profs accessible rating	87
% profs teaching UG courses	100
Avg lab size	10-19 students
Avg reg class size	10-19 students

MOST POPULAR MAJORS
Biology/biological sciences
Psychology
Economics

SELECTIVITY
Admissions Rating	**87**
# of applicants	2,612
% of applicants accepted	80
% of acceptees attending	26
# accepting a place on wait list	62
% admitted from wait list	18
# of early decision applicants	102
% accepted early decision	97

FRESHMAN PROFILE
Range SAT Verbal	550-650
Average SAT Verbal	598
Range SAT Math	550-650
Average SAT Math	600
Range ACT Composite	23-27
Average ACT Composite	25
Minimum TOEFL	550
Average HS GPA	3.7
% graduated top 10% of class	40
% graduated top 25% of class	74
% graduated top 50% of class	94

DEADLINES
Early decision	1/15
Early decision notification	10/15
Regular admission	2/15
Regular notification	4/1
Nonfall registration?	yes

FINANCIAL FACTS
Financial Aid Rating	**85**
Tuition	$23,100
Room and board	$5,600
Books and supplies	$700
Required fees	$280
% frosh receiving aid	74
% undergrads receiving aid	71
Avg frosh grant	$14,266
Avg frosh loan	$3,062

AMERICAN UNIVERSITY

CAMPUS LIFE
Quality of Life Rating	**80**
Type of school	private
Affiliation	Methodist
Environment	urban

STUDENTS
Total undergrad enrollment	5,872
% male/female	39/61
% from out of state	93
% live on campus	68
% in (# of) fraternities	17 (10)
% in (# of) sororities	18 (12)
% African American	6
% Asian	4
% Caucasian	58
% Hispanic	5
% international	9

ACADEMICS
Academic Rating	**79**
Calendar	semester
Student/faculty ratio	15:1
Profs interesting rating	78
Profs accessible rating	77
% profs teaching UG courses	95
% classes taught by TAs	5

MOST POPULAR MAJORS
Business administration/management
International relations and affairs
Political science and government

SELECTIVITY
Admissions Rating	**83**
# of applicants	9,879
% of applicants accepted	63
% of acceptees attending	21
# of early decision applicants	397
% accepted early decision	66

FRESHMAN PROFILE
Range SAT Verbal	560-670
Average SAT Verbal	613
Range SAT Math	550-650
Average SAT Math	600
Average ACT Composite	27
Minimum TOEFL	550
Average HS GPA	3.3
% graduated top 10% of class	31
% graduated top 25% of class	66
% graduated top 50% of class	97

DEADLINES
Early decision	11/15
Early decision notification	12/31
Regular admission	2/1
Regular notification	4/1
Nonfall registration?	yes

FINANCIAL FACTS
Financial Aid Rating **84**

Tuition	$23,068
Room and board	$9,488
Books and supplies	$600
Required fees	$387
% frosh receiving aid	66
% undergrads receiving aid	62
Avg frosh grant	$13,775
Avg frosh loan	$5,791

ARCADIA UNIVERSITY

CAMPUS LIFE
Quality of Life Rating **71**

Type of school	private
Affiliation	Presbyterian
Environment	suburban

STUDENTS

Total undergrad enrollment	1,692
% male/female	30/70
% from out of state	29
% live on campus	70
% African American	12
% Asian	3
% Caucasian	80
% Hispanic	3
% international	3

ACADEMICS
Academic Rating **73**

Calendar	semester
Student/faculty ratio	12:1
Profs interesting rating	90
Profs accessible rating	90
% profs teaching UG courses	100
% classes taught by TAs	0

MOST POPULAR MAJORS
Fine/studio arts
Education
Biology/biological sciences

SELECTIVITY
Admissions Rating **71**

# of applicants	2,239
% of applicants accepted	75

FRESHMAN PROFILE

Range SAT Verbal	490-600
Average SAT Verbal	540
Range SAT Math	480-580
Average SAT Math	530
Minimum TOEFL	520
Average HS GPA	3.2
% graduated top 10% of class	25
% graduated top 25% of class	55
% graduated top 50% of class	87

DEADLINES

Early decision	10/15
Regular admission	8/1
Regular notification	rolling
Nonfall registration?	yes

FINANCIAL FACTS
Financial Aid Rating **84**

Tuition	$20,990
Room and board	$8,620
Books and supplies	$800
Avg frosh grant	$13,258
Avg frosh loan	$2,656

BLOOMSBURG UNIVERSITY OF PENNSYLVANIA

CAMPUS LIFE
Quality of Life Rating **76**

Type of school	public
Affiliation	none
Environment	rural

STUDENTS

Total undergrad enrollment	7,222
% male/female	39/61
% from out of state	10
% from public high school	91
% live on campus	43
% in (# of) fraternities	3 (10)
% in (# of) sororities	4 (12)
% African American	3
% Asian	1
% Caucasian	94
% Hispanic	2
# of countries represented	32

ACADEMICS
Academic Rating   **70**

Calendar	semester
Student/faculty ratio	20:1
Profs interesting rating	87
Profs accessible rating	84
% classes taught by TAs	0
Avg lab size	10-19 students
Avg regular class size	20-29 students

MOST POPULAR MAJORS
Speech and rhetorical studies
Business administration/management
Elementary education and teaching

SELECTIVITY
Admissions Rating   **66**

# of applicants	6,413
% of applicants accepted	51
% of acceptees attending	33
# accepting a place on wait list	30
# of early decision applicants	297
% accepted early decision	62

FRESHMAN PROFILE

Range SAT Verbal	460-550
Average SAT Verbal	506
Range SAT Math	460-560
Average SAT Math	510
Minimum TOEFL	500
Average HS GPA	3.0
% graduated top 10% of class	7
% graduated top 25% of class	31
% graduated top 50% of class	74

DEADLINES

Early decision	11/15
Nonfall registration?	yes

FINANCIAL FACTS
Financial Aid Rating   **77**

In-state tuition	$4,016
Out-of-state tuition	$10,040
Room and board	$4,442
Books and supplies	$600

BRYN MAWR COLLEGE

CAMPUS LIFE
Quality of Life Rating   **87**

Type of school	private
Environment	suburban

STUDENTS

Total undergrad enrollment	1,322
% male/female	2/98
% from out of state	80
% from public high school	56
% live on campus	98
% African American	4
% Asian	14
% Caucasian	66
% Hispanic	3
% international	8
# of countries represented	45

ACADEMICS
Academic Rating   **96**

Calendar	semester
Student/faculty ratio	8:1
Profs interesting rating	96
Profs accessible rating	98
% profs teaching UG courses	100
Avg lab size	20-29 students
Avg reg class size	10-19 students

MOST POPULAR MAJORS
English language and literature
Mathematics
Biology/biological sciences

SELECTIVITY
Admissions Rating   **93**

# of applicants	1,743
% of applicants accepted	50
% of acceptees attending	35
# accepting a place on wait list	163
% admitted from wait list	26
# of early decision applicants	157
% accepted early decision	62

FRESHMAN PROFILE

Range SAT Verbal	630-730
Average SAT Verbal	672
Range SAT Math	600-690
Average SAT Math	638
Range ACT Composite	26-30
Average ACT Composite	28
Minimum TOEFL	600

% graduated top 10% of class	57
% graduated top 25% of class	93
% graduated top 50% of class	100

DEADLINES

Early decision	11/15
Early decision notification	12/15
Regular admission	1/15
Regular notification	4/1

FINANCIAL FACTS

Financial Aid Rating **80**

Tuition	$25,550
Room and board	$8,970
Books and supplies	$1,450
Required fees	$670
% frosh receiving aid	64
% undergrads receiving aid	59
Avg frosh grant	$19,738
Avg frosh loan	$2,815

BUCKNELL UNIVERSITY

CAMPUS LIFE

Quality of Life Rating **91**

Type of school	private
Environment	rural

STUDENTS

Total undergrad enrollment	3,440
% male/female	51/49
% from out of state	68
% from public high school	76
% live on campus	89
% in (# of) fraternities	41 (13)
% in (# of) sororities	45 (7)
% African American	3
% Asian	6
% Caucasian	87
% Hispanic	2
% international	2
# of countries represented	34

ACADEMICS

Academic Rating **91**

Calendar	semester
Student/faculty ratio	12:1
Profs interesting rating	95
Profs accessible rating	99
% profs teaching UG courses	100

Avg lab size	10-19 students
Avg reg class size	10-19 students

MOST POPULAR MAJORS
Business administration/management
English language and literature
Economics

SELECTIVITY

Admissions Rating **91**

# of applicants	7,760
% of applicants accepted	39
% of acceptees attending	30
# accepting a place on wait list	740
# of early decision applicants	693
% accepted early decision	52

FRESHMAN PROFILE

Range SAT Verbal	590-670
Average SAT Verbal	631
Range SAT Math	620-700
Average SAT Math	659
Minimum TOEFL	550
% graduated top 10% of class	64
% graduated top 25% of class	94
% graduated top 50% of class	99

DEADLINES

Early decision	11/15
Early decision notification	12/15
Regular admission	1/1
Regular notification	4/1

FINANCIAL FACTS

Financial Aid Rating **82**

Tuition	$28,764
Room and board	$6,302
Books and supplies	$750
Required fees	$196
% frosh receiving aid	55
% undergrads receiving aid	48
Avg frosh grant	$19,629
Avg frosh loan	$3,937

CARNEGIE MELLON UNIVERSITY

CAMPUS LIFE

Quality of Life Rating **81**

Type of school	private
Environment	urban

STUDENTS

Total undergrad enrollment	5,475
% male/female	61/39
% from out of state	76
% live on campus	72
% in (# of) fraternities	14 (13)
% in (# of) sororities	10 (5)
% African American	5
% Asian	26
% Caucasian	48
% Hispanic	5
% international	11
# of countries represented	100

ACADEMICS
Academic Rating   94

Calendar	semester
Student/faculty ratio	11:1
Avg lab size	20-29 students
Avg reg class size	10-19 students

MOST POPULAR MAJORS
Computer science
Computer engineering
Business administration/management

ADMISSIONS
Admissions Rating   92

# of applicants	14,271
% of applicants accepted	38
% of acceptees attending	25
# accepting a place on wait list	915
% admitted from wait list	16
# of early decision applicants	273
% accepted early decision	49

FRESHMAN PROFILE

Range SAT Verbal	590-700
Average SAT Verbal	646
Range SAT Math	680-770
Average SAT Math	716
Range ACT Composite	27-32
Average ACT Composite	29
Minimum TOEFL	600
Average HS GPA	3.6
% graduated top 10% of class	72
% graduated top 25% of class	95
% graduated top 50% of class	100

DEADLINES

Early decision	11/15
Early decision notification	12/15
Regular admission	1/1
Regular notification	4/15

FINANCIAL FACTS
Financial Aid Rating   84

Tuition	$26,910
Room and board	$7,844
Books and supplies	$880
Required fees	$385
% undergrads receiving aid	49
Avg frosh grant	$19,902
Avg frosh loan	$4,021

CATHOLIC UNIVERSITY OF AMERICA

CAMPUS LIFE
Quality of Life Rating   80

Type of school	private
Affiliation	Roman Catholic
Environment	urban

STUDENTS

Total undergrad enrollment	2,668
% male/female	45/55
% from out of state	96
% from public high school	39
% live on campus	75
% in (# of) fraternities	1 (2)
% in (# of) sororities	1 (2)
% African American	6
% Asian	3
% Caucasian	79
% Hispanic	3
% international	2
# of countries represented	31

ACADEMICS
Academic Rating   82

Calendar	semester
Student/faculty ratio	8:1
Profs interesting rating	94
Profs accessible rating	92
% profs teaching UG courses	74
% classes taught by TAs	8
Avg lab size	10-19 students
Avg reg class size	10-19 students

SELECTIVITY
Admissions Rating   86

# of applicants	2,708
% of applicants accepted	82
% of acceptees attending	32

FRESHMAN PROFILE

Range SAT Verbal	530-640
Range SAT Math	520-640
Range ACT Composite	21-28
Minimum TOEFL	550
Average HS GPA	3.4
% graduated top 10% of class	33
% graduated top 25% of class	62
% graduated top 50% of class	87

DEADLINES

Early decision	12/1
Early decision notification	1/15
Regular admission	2/15
Regular notification	3/20
Nonfall registration?	yes

FINANCIAL FACTS

Financial Aid Rating	**85**
Tuition	$22,200
Room and board	$9,002
Books and supplies	$925
Required fees	$1,050
% frosh receiving aid	78
% undergrads receiving aid	78
Avg frosh grant	$13,573
Avg frosh loan	$3,460

CHATHAM COLLEGE

CAMPUS LIFE

Quality of Life Rating	**80**
Type of school	private
Affiliation	none
Environment	urban

STUDENTS

Total undergrad enrollment	589
% from out of state	23
% from public high school	96
% live on campus	63
% African American	12
% Asian	2
% Caucasian	77
% Hispanic	2
% international	6
# of countries represented	10

ACADEMICS

Academic Rating	**67**
Calendar	4-1-4

Student/faculty ratio	12:1
Profs interesting rating	78
Profs accessible rating	77
% profs teaching UG courses	100
% classes taught by TAs	0
Avg reg class size	10-19 students

MOST POPULAR MAJORS
Psychology
English language and literature
Biology/biological sciences

SELECTIVITY

Admissions Rating	**64**
# of applicants	534
% of applicants accepted	78
% of acceptees attending	32

FRESHMAN PROFILE

Range SAT Verbal	500-610
Average SAT Verbal	551
Range SAT Math	450-570
Average SAT Math	510
Range ACT Composite	20-27
Average ACT Composite	24
Minimum TOEFL	550
Average HS GPA	3.3
% graduated top 10% of class	8
% graduated top 25% of class	43
% graduated top 50% of class	70

DEADLINES

Nonfall registration?	yes

FINANCIAL FACTS

Financial Aid Rating	**79**
Tuition	$18,803
Room and board	$6,496
Books and supplies	$700
Avg frosh grant	$10,650
Avg frosh loan	$3,757

CHRISTOPHER NEWPORT UNIVERSITY

CAMPUS LIFE

Quality of Life Rating	**78**
Type of school	public
Affiliation	none
Environment	suburban

STUDENTS

Total undergrad enrollment	5,158
% male/female	39/61
% from out of state	3
% from public high school	98
% live on campus	30
% in (# of) fraternities	5 (5)
% in (# of) sororities	4 (5)
% African American	14
% Asian	3
% Caucasian	79
% Hispanic	3

ACADEMICS

Academic Rating	**65**
Calendar	semester
Student/faculty ratio	20:1
Profs interesting rating	78
Profs accessible rating	76
% profs teaching UG courses	100
% classes taught by TAs	0
Avg reg class size	20-29 students

MOST POPULAR MAJORS
Public administration
Psychology
Business administration/management

SELECTIVITY

Admissions Rating	**60**
# of applicants	4,270
% of applicants accepted	48
% of acceptees attending	51
# accepting a place on wait list	125

FRESHMAN PROFILE

Range SAT Verbal	530-610
Average SAT Verbal	567
Range SAT Math	510-595
Average SAT Math	553
Range ACT Composite	18-22
Average ACT Composite	20
Minimum TOEFL	530
Average HS GPA	3.3
% graduated top 10% of class	17
% graduated top 25% of class	54
% graduated top 50% of class	92

DEADLINES

Regular admission	3/1
Nonfall registration?	yes

FINANCIAL FACTS

Financial Aid Rating	**75**
In-state tuition	$1,888
Out-of-state tuition	$7,910
Room and board	$5,750
Books and supplies	$704
Avg frosh grant	$4,239
Avg frosh loan	$1,724

COLLEGE OF NOTRE DAME OF MARYLAND

CAMPUS LIFE

Quality of Life Rating	**79**
Type of school	private
Affiliation	Roman Catholic
Environment	suburban

STUDENTS

Total undergrad enrollment	1,930
% male/female	5/95
% from out of state	14
% from public high school	68
% live on campus	56
% African American	21
% Asian	2
% Caucasian	73
% Hispanic	2
% international	2

ACADEMICS

Academic Rating	**80**
Calendar	4-1-4
Student/faculty ratio	12:1
Profs interesting rating	80
Profs accessible rating	80
% profs teaching UG courses	100
Avg lab size	10-19 students
Avg regular class size	10-19 students

SELECTIVITY

Admissions Rating	**73**
# of applicants	383
% of applicants accepted	80
% of acceptees attending	54

FRESHMAN PROFILE

Range SAT Verbal	480-570
Average SAT Verbal	540
Range SAT Math	440-540

Average SAT Math	500
Minimum TOEFL	500
Average HS GPA	3.3
% graduated top 10% of class	16
% graduated top 25% of class	46
% graduated top 50% of class	85

DEADLINES

Regular notification	rolling
Nonfall registration?	yes

FINANCIAL FACTS

Financial Aid Rating	**73**
Tuition	$16,600
Room and board	$7,200
Books and supplies	$600
Avg frosh loan	$2,625

COLLEGE OF WILLIAM AND MARY

CAMPUS LIFE

Quality of Life Rating	**84**
Type of school	public
Environment	suburban

STUDENTS

Total undergrad enrollment	5,694
% male/female	44/56
% from out of state	34
% live on campus	75
% in (# of) fraternities	31 (15)
% in (# of) sororities	33 (12)
% African American	5
% Asian	7
% Caucasian	84
% Hispanic	3
% international	1
# of countries represented	73

ACADEMICS

Academic Rating	**92**
Calendar	semester
Student/faculty ratio	12:1
Profs interesting rating	95
Profs accessible rating	98
% profs teaching UG courses	63
% classes taught by TAs	1
Avg reg class size	10-19 students

MOST POPULAR MAJORS

Business administration/management
English language and literature
Psychology

SELECTIVITY

Admissions Rating	**94**
# of applicants	8,917
% of applicants accepted	35
% of acceptees attending	43
# accepting place on wait list	1,278
% admitted from wait list	3
# of early decision applicants	889
% accepted early decision	54

FRESHMAN PROFILE

Range SAT Verbal	620-730
Average SAT Verbal	669
Range SAT Math	630-710
Average SAT Math	666
Range ACT Composite	27-31
Average ACT Composite	29
Minimum TOEFL	600
% graduated top 10% of class	90
% graduated top 25% of class	99
% graduated top 50% of class	100

DEADLINES

Early decision	11/1
Early decision notification	12/1
Regular admission	1/15
Regular notification	4/1
Nonfall registration?	yes

FINANCIAL FACTS

Financial Aid Rating	**81**
In-state tuition	$1,880
Out-of-state tuition	$9,230
% undergrads receiving aid	26
Avg frosh grant	$8,626
Avg frosh loan	$3,202

DELAWARE VALLEY COLLEGE

CAMPUS LIFE

Quality of Life Rating	**72**
Type of school	private
Affiliation	none
Environment	suburban

STUDENTS

Total undergrad enrollment	1,925

% male/female	48/52
% from out of state	26
% live on campus	47
% in (# of) fraternities	8 (5)
% in (# of) sororities	9 (3)
% African American	3
% Asian	1
% Caucasian	94
% Hispanic	2

ACADEMICS

Academic Rating	**77**
Calendar	semester
Student/faculty ratio	15:1
% profs teaching UG courses	100
% classes taught by TAs	0
Avg lab size	10-19 students
Avg reg class size	10-19 students

MOST POPULAR MAJORS
Equestrian/equine studies
Animal sciences
Business administration/management

SELECTIVITY

Admissions Rating	**75**
# of applicants	1,273
% of applicants accepted	83
% of acceptees attending	39

FRESHMAN PROFILE

Range SAT Verbal	440-740
Average SAT Verbal	500
Range SAT Math	430-700
Average SAT Math	500
Average ACT Composite	21
Minimum TOEFL	500
Average HS GPA	3.3
% graduated top 10% of class	11
% graduated top 25% of class	32
% graduated top 50% of class	63

DEADLINES

Nonfall registration?	yes

FINANCIAL FACTS

Financial Aid Rating	**73**
Tuition	$17,680
Room and board	$6,870
Books and supplies	$1,000
Avg frosh grant	$11,770
Avg frosh loan	$3,140

DICKINSON COLLEGE

CAMPUS LIFE

Quality of Life Rating	**83**
Type of school	private
Environment	suburban

STUDENTS

Total undergrad enrollment	2,208
% male/female	42/58
% from out of state	59
% from public high school	69
% live on campus	92
% in (# of) fraternities	25 (8)
% in (# of) sororities	26 (4)
% African American	2
% Asian	2
% Caucasian	92
% Hispanic	2
% international	2

ACADEMICS

Academic Rating	**88**
Calendar	semester
Student/faculty ratio	12:1
Profs interesting rating	95
Profs accessible rating	98
% profs teaching UG courses	100
Avg lab size	20-29 students
Avg reg class size	10-19 students

MOST POPULAR MAJORS
English language and literature
Biology/biological sciences
Political science and government

SELECTIVITY

Admissions Rating	**82**
# of applicants	3,820
% of applicants accepted	64
% of acceptees attending	25
# accepting a place on wait list	190
% admitted from wait list	2
# of early decision applicants	179
% accepted early decision	74

FRESHMAN PROFILE

Range SAT Verbal	580-670
Average SAT Verbal	623
Range SAT Math	570-650
Average SAT Math	612
Average ACT Composite	27
Minimum TOEFL	550

% graduated top 10% of class	47
% graduated top 25% of class	79
% graduated top 50% of class	97

DEADLINES

Early decision	11/15
Early decision notification	12/15
Regular admission	2/1
Regular notification	3/31
Nonfall registration?	yes

FINANCIAL FACTS

Financial Aid Rating	87
Tuition	$28,380
Room and board	$7,210
Books and supplies	$750
Required fees	$260
% undergrads receiving aid	59
Avg frosh grant	$14,238
Avg frosh loan	$3,405

DREXEL UNIVERSITY

CAMPUS LIFE

Quality of Life Rating	68
Type of school	private
Environment	urban

STUDENTS

Total undergrad enrollment	11,584
% male/female	61/39
% from out of state	36
% from public high school	70
% live on campus	25
% in (# of) fraternities	12 (16)
% in (# of) sororities	8 (6)
% African American	10
% Asian	15
% Caucasian	63
% Hispanic	2
% international	5

ACADEMICS

Academic Rating	73
Calendar	differs by program
Student/faculty ratio	14:1
Profs interesting rating	90
Profs accessible rating	89
% profs teaching UG courses	100
Avg lab size	20-29 students
Avg reg class size	10-19 students

MOST POPULAR MAJORS
Computer science
Electrical, electronics, and
communications engineering
Mechanical engineering

SELECTIVITY

Admissions Rating	79
# of applicants	11,981
% of applicants accepted	61
% of acceptees attending	29
# accepting a place on wait list	66
% admitted from wait list	23

FRESHMAN PROFILE

Range SAT Verbal	520-620
Average SAT Verbal	570
Range SAT Math	550-660
Average SAT Math	600
Minimum TOEFL	550
Average HS GPA	3.3
% graduated top 10% of class	23
% graduated top 25% of class	55
% graduated top 50% of class	88

DEADLINES

Regular admission	3/1
Nonfall registration?	yes

FINANCIAL FACTS

Financial Aid Rating	78
Tuition	$17,393
Room and board	$9,090
Books and supplies	$650
Required fees	$1,020
% frosh receiving aid	73
% undergrads receiving aid	69

DUQUESNE UNIVERSITY

CAMPUS LIFE

Quality of Life Rating	70
Type of school	private
Affiliation	Roman Catholic
Environment	urban

STUDENTS

Total undergrad enrollment	5,556
% male/female	42/58
% from out of state	19
% from public high school	79
% live on campus	48

% in (# of) fraternities	21 (10)
% in (# of) sororities	15 (9)
% African American	4
% Asian	1
% Caucasian	83
% Hispanic	2
% international	3
# of countries represented	73

ACADEMICS
Academic Rating   72
Calendar	semester
Student/faculty ratio	15:1
Profs interesting rating	92
Profs accessible rating	91
Avg lab size	10-19 students
Avg reg class size	20-29 students

MOST POPULAR MAJORS
Pre-professional doctor of pharmacy
Information technology
Elementary education

SELECTIVITY
Admissions Rating   76
# of applicants	3,879
% of applicants accepted	91
% of acceptees attending	40
# accepting a place on wait list	22
% admitted from wait list	82
# of early decision applicants	184
% accepted early decision	98

FRESHMAN PROFILE
Range SAT Verbal	490-590
Average SAT Verbal	545
Range SAT Math	490-600
Average SAT Math	545
Range ACT Composite	21-26
Average ACT Composite	24
Average HS GPA	3.5
% graduated top 10% of class	22
% graduated top 25% of class	51
% graduated top 50% of class	83

DEADLINES
Early decision	11/1
Early decision notification	12/15
Priority admission	11/1
Regular admission	7/1
Nonfall registration?	yes

FINANCIAL FACTS
Financial Aid Rating   82
Tuition	$17,012
Room and board	$7,170
Books and supplies	$600
Required fees	$1,515
% frosh receiving aid	67
% undergrads receiving aid	64
Avg frosh grant	$8,960
Avg frosh loan	$5,590

EASTERN MENNONITE UNIVERSITY

CAMPUS LIFE
Quality of Life Rating   72
Type of school	private
Affiliation	Mennonite
Environment	urban

STUDENTS
Total undergrad enrollment	976
% male/female	40/60
% from out of state	59
% from public high school	64
% live on campus	68
% African American	6
% Asian	2
% Caucasian	85
% Hispanic	1
% international	4
# of countries represented	20

ACADEMICS
Academic Rating   73
Calendar	4-1-4
Student/faculty ratio	13:1
Profs interesting rating	90
Profs accessible rating	87
% profs teaching UG courses	98
% classes taught by TAs	0
Avg lab size	10-19 students
Avg reg class size	10-19 students

MOST POPULAR MAJORS
Business administration/management
Biology/biological sciences
Nursing/registered nurse training
(RN, ASN, BSN, MSN)

SELECTIVITY	
Admissions Rating	**70**
# of applicants	676
% of applicants accepted	77
% of acceptees attending	41

FRESHMAN PROFILE	
Range SAT Verbal	460-620
Average SAT Verbal	547
Range SAT Math	450-610
Average SAT Math	543
Range ACT Composite	19-28
Average ACT Composite	22
Minimum TOEFL	550
Average HS GPA	3.4

DEADLINES	
Regular admission	8/1
Nonfall registration?	yes

FINANCIAL FACTS	
Financial Aid Rating	**74**
Tuition	$16,370
Room and board	$5,350
Books and supplies	$700
Avg frosh grant	$10,026
Avg frosh loan	$5,024

ELIZABETHTOWN COLLEGE

CAMPUS LIFE	
Quality of Life Rating	**73**
Type of school	private
Affiliation	Church of Brethren
Environment	suburban

STUDENTS	
Total undergrad enrollment	1,901
% male/female	38/62
% from out of state	27
% from public high school	80
% live on campus	85
% African American	1
% Asian	1
% Caucasian	92
% Hispanic	1
% international	3
# of countries represented	17

ACADEMICS	
Academic Rating	**79**

Calendar	semester
Student/faculty ratio	12:1
Profs interesting rating	79
Profs accessible rating	75
% profs teaching UG courses	100
% classes taught by TAs	0
Avg lab size	10-19 students
Avg reg class size	10-19 students

MOST POPULAR MAJORS
Business administration
Education
Communications

SELECTIVITY	
Admissions Rating	**75**
# of applicants	2,754
% of applicants accepted	69
% of acceptees attending	28

FRESHMAN PROFILE	
Range SAT Verbal	510-610
Range SAT Math	500-610
Range ACT Composite	19-24
Minimum TOEFL	525
% graduated top 10% of class	31
% graduated top 25% of class	63
% graduated top 50% of class	90

DEADLINES	
Nonfall registration?	yes

FINANCIAL FACTS	
Financial Aid Rating	**77**
Tuition	$20,200
Room and board	$5,800
Books and supplies	$600

FRANKLIN & MARSHALL COLLEGE

CAMPUS LIFE	
Quality of Life Rating	**80**
Type of school	private
Environment	suburban

STUDENTS	
Total undergrad enrollment	1,926
% male/female	52/48
% from out of state	65
% from public high school	55

% live on campus	67
% African American	3
% Asian	4
% Caucasian	81
% Hispanic	2
% international	7

ACADEMICS
Academic Rating 92
Calendar	semester
Student/faculty ratio	11:1
Profs interesting rating	94
Profs accessible rating	99
% profs teaching UG courses	100
Avg lab size	10-19 students
Avg reg class size	10-19 students

MOST POPULAR MAJORS
Business administration/management
English language and literature
Political science and government

SELECTIVITY
Admissions Rating 89
# of applicants	3,425
% of applicants accepted	62
% of acceptees attending	25
# accepting a place on wait list	592
% admitted from wait list	11
# of early decision applicants	279
% accepted early decision	70

FRESHMAN PROFILE
Range SAT Verbal	570-660
Average SAT Verbal	615
Range SAT Math	590-680
Average SAT Math	633
Minimum TOEFL	600
% graduated top 10% of class	46
% graduated top 25% of class	70
% graduated top 50% of class	92

DEADLINES
Early decision	11/15
Early decision notification	12/15
Regular admission	2/1
Regular notification	4/1
Nonfall registration?	yes

FINANCIAL FACTS
Financial Aid Rating 81
Tuition	$27,230
Room and board	$6,580

Books and supplies	$650
Required fees	$50
% frosh receiving aid	65
% undergrads receiving aid	64
Avg frosh grant	$15,913
Avg frosh loan	$3,879

GANNON UNIVERSITY

CAMPUS LIFE
Quality of Life Rating 74
Type of school	private
Affiliation	Roman Catholic
Environment	urban

STUDENTS
Total undergrad enrollment	2,374
% male/female	42/58
% from out of state	23
% from public high school	78
% live on campus	52
% in (# of) fraternities	15 (6)
% in (# of) sororities	15 (5)
% African American	5
% Asian	1
% Caucasian	91
% Hispanic	1
% international	3

ACADEMICS
Academic Rating 79
Calendar	semester
Student/faculty ratio	13:1
Profs interesting rating	86
Profs accessible rating	83
% profs teaching UG courses	95
% classes taught by TAs	1
Avg lab size	10-19 students
Avg regular class size	10-19 students

MOST POPULAR MAJORS
Biology
Physician assistant
Psychology

SELECTIVITY
Admissions Rating 70
# of applicants	2,188
% of applicants accepted	84
% of acceptees attending	29

FRESHMAN PROFILE

Range SAT Verbal	460-570
Average SAT Verbal	513
Range SAT Math	460-570
Average SAT Math	517
Range ACT Composite	18-24
Average ACT Composite	22
Minimum TOEFL	500
Average HS GPA	3.16
% graduated top 10% of class	19
% graduated top 25% of class	44
% graduated top 50% of class	74

DEADLINES

Nonfall registration?	yes

FINANCIAL FACTS

Financial Aid Rating	**73**
Tuition	$15,780
Room and board	$6,210
Books and supplies	$800
Avg frosh grant	$6,289
Avg frosh loan	$2,415

GEORGE MASON UNIVERSITY

CAMPUS LIFE

Quality of Life Rating	**74**
Type of school	public
Environment	suburban

STUDENTS

Total undergrad enrollment	15,802
% male/female	44/56
% from out of state	10
% live on campus	19
% in (# of) fraternities	3 (18)
% in (# of) sororities	3 (10)
% African American	10
% Asian	17
% Caucasian	65
% Hispanic	8
% international	4

ACADEMICS

Academic Rating	**79**
Calendar	semester
Student/faculty ratio	16:1
Profs interesting rating	91

Profs accessible rating	89
% profs teaching UG courses	82
% classes taught by TAs	18
Avg lab size	10-19 students
Avg reg class size	20-29 students

MOST POPULAR MAJORS
Business, management, marketing, and
related support services
Political science and government
Computer science

SELECTIVITY

Admissions Rating	**85**
# of applicants	8,106
% of applicants accepted	68
% of acceptees attending	39
# accepting a place on wait list	377
% admitted from wait list	36

FRESHMAN PROFILE

Range SAT Verbal	480-580
Average SAT Verbal	534
Range SAT Math	490-590
Average SAT Math	542
Range ACT Composite	19-23
Minimum TOEFL	570
Average HS GPA	3.2

DEADLINES

Regular admission	2/1
Regular notification	4/1
Nonfall registration?	yes

FINANCIAL FACTS

Financial Aid Rating	**77**
In-state tuition	$2,376
Out-of-state tuition	$11,220
Room and board	$5,400
Books and supplies	$750
Required fees	$1,416
% frosh receiving aid	37
% undergrads receiving aid	40
Avg frosh grant	$3,756
Avg frosh loan	$6,222

GEORGE WASHINGTON UNIVERSITY

CAMPUS LIFE

Quality of Life Rating	**88**

Type of school	private
Environment	urban

STUDENTS

Total undergrad enrollment	10,063
% male/female	44/56
% from out of state	94
% from public high school	70
% live on campus	62
% in (# of) fraternities	14 (12)
% in (# of) sororities	11 (9)
% African American	6
% Asian	11
% Caucasian	68
% Hispanic	5
% international	5
# of countries represented	101

ACADEMICS

Academic Rating	**88**
Calendar	semester
Student/faculty ratio	14:1
Profs interesting rating	91
Profs accessible rating	92
% profs teaching UG courses	67
% classes taught by TAs	3
Avg lab size	20-29 students
Avg reg class size	10-19 students

SELECTIVITY

Admissions Rating	**91**
# of applicants	15,960
% of applicants accepted	48
% of acceptees attending	33
# accepting a place on wait list	709
% admitted from wait list	26
# of early decision applicants	695
% accepted early decision	61

FRESHMAN PROFILE

Range SAT Verbal	570-660
Average SAT Verbal	620
Range SAT Math	580-670
Average SAT Math	620
Range ACT Composite	24-29
Average ACT Composite	26
Minimum TOEFL	550
% graduated top 10% of class	46
% graduated top 25% of class	83
% graduated top 50% of class	99

DEADLINES

Early decision	12/1

Early decision notification	12/15
Priority admission	12/1
Regular admission	1/15
Regular notification	3/15
Nonfall registration?	yes

FINANCIAL FACTS

Financial Aid Rating	**84**
Tuition	$27,790
Room and board	$9,110
Books and supplies	$850
Required fees	$30
% frosh receiving aid	41
% undergrads receiving aid	38
Avg frosh grant	$11,800
Avg frosh loan	$3,000

GEORGETOWN UNIVERSITY

CAMPUS LIFE

Quality of Life Rating	**89**
Type of school	private
Affiliation	Roman Catholic
Environment	urban

STUDENTS

Total undergrad enrollment	6,332
% male/female	47/53
% from out of state	98
% from public high school	46
% live on campus	69
% African American	7
% Asian	10
% Caucasian	74
% Hispanic	5
% international	4

ACADEMICS

Academic Rating	**96**
Calendar	semester
Student/faculty ratio	11:1
Profs interesting rating	94
Profs accessible rating	92
% profs teaching UG courses	100
Avg lab size	10-19 students
Avg reg class size	10-19 students

MOST POPULAR MAJORS
Finance
English language and literature
International relations and affairs

SELECTIVITY

Admissions Rating	**99**
# of applicants	15,536
% of applicants accepted	21
% of acceptees attending	46
# accepting a place on wait list	822
% admitted from wait list	28

FRESHMAN PROFILE

Range SAT Verbal	640-730
Range SAT Math	640-730
Range ACT Composite	27-32
Minimum TOEFL	550
% graduated top 10% of class	80
% graduated top 25% of class	94
% graduated top 50% of class	99

DEADLINES

Regular admission	1/10
Regular notification	4/1

FINANCIAL FACTS

Financial Aid Rating	**84**
Tuition	$26,544
Room and board	$9,692
Books and supplies	$940
Required fees	$309
% frosh receiving aid	41
% undergrads receiving aid	41
Avg frosh grant	$16,300
Avg frosh loan	$2,250

GETTYSBURG COLLEGE

CAMPUS LIFE

Quality of Life Rating	**84**
Type of school	private
Affiliation	Lutheran
Environment	suburban

STUDENTS

Total undergrad enrollment	2,495
% male/female	50/50
% from out of state	72
% from public high school	70
% live on campus	91
% in (# of) fraternities	44 (10)
% in (# of) sororities	26 (5)
% African American	3
% Asian	1
% Caucasian	94

% Hispanic	1
% international	2

ACADEMICS

Academic Rating	**90**
Calendar	semester
Student/faculty ratio	11:1
Profs interesting rating	95
Profs accessible rating	99
% profs teaching UG courses	100
Avg reg class size	10-19 students

MOST POPULAR MAJORS
Psychology
Business/management
Biology

SELECTIVITY

Admissions Rating	**87**
# of applicants	4,573
% of applicants accepted	50
% of acceptees attending	30
# of early decision applicants	210
% accepted early decision	93

FRESHMAN PROFILE

Range SAT Verbal	580-650
Range SAT Math	590-660
Average ACT Composite	28
Minimum TOEFL	550
% graduated top 10% of class	62
% graduated top 25% of class	80
% graduated top 50% of class	99

DEADLINES

Early decision	2/1
Early decision notification	2/15
Priority admission	2/15
Regular notification	4/1
Nonfall registration?	yes

FINANCIAL FACTS

Financial Aid Rating	**87**
Tuition	$28,424
Room and board	$6,972
Books and supplies	$500
Required fees	$250
% frosh receiving aid	53
% undergrads receiving aid	56
Avg frosh grant	$18,600
Avg frosh loan	$3,500

Goucher College

CAMPUS LIFE
Quality of Life Rating   **80**
Type of school   private
Environment   suburban

STUDENTS
Total undergrad enrollment   1,270
% male/female   30/70
% from out of state   62
% from public high school   66
% live on campus   62
% African American   6
% Asian   3
% Caucasian   62
% Hispanic   2
% international   2

ACADEMICS
Academic Rating   **81**
Calendar   semester
Student/faculty ratio   10:1
Profs interesting rating   94
Profs accessible rating   94
% profs teaching UG courses   100
Avg reg class size   10-19 students

SELECTIVITY
Admissions Rating   **80**
# of applicants   2,596
% of applicants accepted   68
% of acceptees attending   21
# of early decision applicants   531
% accepted early decision   84

FRESHMAN PROFILE
Range SAT Verbal   540-650
Average SAT Verbal   605
Range SAT Math   520-640
Average SAT Math   575
Range ACT Composite   22-28
Average ACT Composite   26
Minimum TOEFL   550
Average HS GPA   3.2
% graduated top 10% of class   19
% graduated top 25% of class   63
% graduated top 50% of class   75

DEADLINES
Early decision   11/15
Early decision notification   12/15
Regular admission   2/1
Regular notification   4/1
Nonfall registration?   yes

FINANCIAL FACTS
Financial Aid Rating   **88**
Tuition $24,150
Room and board $8,200
Books and supplies $800
Required fees $300
Avg frosh grant $13,500
Avg frosh loan $3,500

Grove City College

CAMPUS LIFE
Quality of Life Rating   **79**
Type of school   private
Affiliation   Presbyterian
Environment   rural

STUDENTS
Total undergrad enrollment   2,288
% male/female   49/51
% from out of state   46
% from public high school   88
% live on campus   91
% in (# of) fraternities   9 (10)
% in (# of) sororities   12 (8)
% Asian   1
% Caucasian   98
% international   1
# of countries represented   11

ACADEMICS
Academic Rating   **86**
Calendar   semester
Student/faculty ratio   19:1
% profs teaching UG courses   100
Avg lab size   10-19 students
Avg reg class size   20-29 students

MOST POPULAR MAJORS
Business administration/management
Elementary education and teaching
English/language arts teacher
education

SELECTIVITY
Admissions Rating   **91**
# of applicants   2,001
% of applicants accepted   47
% of acceptees attending   62

# accepting a place on wait list	157
% admitted from wait list	15
# of early decision applicants	683
% accepted early decision	48

FRESHMAN PROFILE

Range SAT Verbal	570-692
Average SAT Verbal	633
Range SAT Math	574-690
Average SAT Math	639
Range ACT Composite	24-30
Average ACT Composite	28
Minimum TOEFL	550
Average HS GPA	3.7
% graduated top 10% of class	60
% graduated top 25% of class	87
% graduated top 50% of class	98

DEADLINES

Early decision	11/15
Early decision notification	12/15
Priority admission	11/15
Regular admission	2/1
Regular notification	3/15
Nonfall registration?	yes

FINANCIAL FACTS
Financial Aid Rating · 88

Tuition	$9,376
Room and board	$4,852
Books and supplies	$900
% frosh receiving aid	62
% undergrads receiving aid	37
Avg frosh grant	$4,623
Avg frosh loan	$6,055

HAMPDEN-SYDNEY COLLEGE

CAMPUS LIFE
Quality of Life Rating · 84

Type of school	private
Affiliation	Presbyterian
Environment	rural

STUDENTS

Total undergrad enrollment	1,026
% from out of state	37
% from public high school	62
% live on campus	94
% in (# of) fraternities	37 (11)
% African American	4

% Asian	1
% Caucasian	88
% Hispanic	1
# of countries represented	3

ACADEMICS
Academic Rating · 85

Calendar	semester
Student/faculty ratio	10:1
Profs interesting rating	96
Profs accessible rating	97
% profs teaching UG courses	100
Avg reg class size	10-19 students

MOST POPULAR MAJORS
Economics
History
Political science and government

SELECTIVITY
Admissions Rating · 78

# of applicants	925
% of applicants accepted	77
% of acceptees attending	46
# accepting a place on wait list	26
% admitted from wait list	73
# of early decision applicants	122
% accepted early decision	84

FRESHMAN PROFILE

Range SAT Verbal	500-620
Average SAT Verbal	561
Range SAT Math	510-610
Average SAT Math	562
Range ACT Composite	20-25
Average ACT Composite	22
Minimum TOEFL	570
Average HS GPA	3.1
% graduated top 10% of class	13
% graduated top 25% of class	32
% graduated top 50% of class	69

DEADLINES

Early decision	11/15
Early decision notification	12/15
Regular admission	3/1
Regular notification	4/15
Nonfall registration?	yes

FINANCIAL FACTS
Financial Aid Rating · 87

Tuition	$20,446
Room and board	$7,020

Books and supplies	$800
Required fees	$891
% frosh receiving aid	50
% undergrads receiving aid	46
Avg frosh grant	$11,589
Avg frosh loan	$3,294

HAMPTON UNIVERSITY

CAMPUS LIFE
Quality of Life Rating	**69**
Type of school	private
Environment	urban

STUDENTS
Total undergrad enrollment	4,981
% male/female	39/61
% from out of state	69
% from public high school	90
% live on campus	59
% in (# of) fraternities	5 (6)
% in (# of) sororities	4 (3)
% African American	96
% Caucasian	3
# of countries represented	33

ACADEMICS
Academic Rating	**72**
Calendar	semester
Student/faculty ratio	16:1
Profs interesting rating	89
Profs accessible rating	91
% profs teaching UG courses	100
Avg lab size	10-19 students
Avg reg class size	under 10 students

MOST POPULAR MAJORS
Business administration/management
Biology/biological sciences
Psychology

SELECTIVITY
Admissions Rating	**79**
# of applicants	5,696
% of applicants accepted	62
% of acceptees attending	30

FRESHMAN PROFILE
Range SAT Verbal	490-590
Average SAT Verbal	526
Range SAT Math	480-580
Average SAT Math	516

Range ACT Composite	20-24
Average ACT Composite	20
Minimum TOEFL	550
Average HS GPA	3.0
% graduated top 10% of class	20
% graduated top 25% of class	45
% graduated top 50% of class	90

DEADLINES
| Priority admission | 3/1 |
| Nonfall registration? | yes |

FINANCIAL FACTS
Financial Aid Rating	**73**
Tuition	$10,990
Room and board	$5,828
Books and supplies	$730
Required fees	$1,262
% frosh receiving aid	56
% undergrads receiving aid	58
Avg frosh grant	$2,885
Avg frosh loan	$2,254

HAVERFORD COLLEGE

CAMPUS LIFE
Quality of Life Rating	**87**
Type of school	private
Environment	suburban

STUDENTS
Total undergrad enrollment	1,105
% from out of state	80
% from public high school	58
% live on campus	98
% African American	5
% Asian	15
% Caucasian	72
% Hispanic	7
% international	3
# of countries represented	38

ACADEMICS
Academic Rating	**98**
Calendar	semester
Student/faculty ratio	8:1
% profs teaching UG courses	100
Avg lab size	under 10 students
Avg reg class size	10-19 students

History
Biology/biological sciences
Political science and government

SELECTIVITY
Admissions Rating	**98**
# of applicants	2,598
% of applicants accepted	32
% of acceptees attending	37
# accepting a place on wait list	208
# of early decision applicants	199
% accepted early decision	55

FRESHMAN PROFILE
Range SAT Verbal	640-740
Range SAT Math	640-720
% graduated top 10% of class	80
% graduated top 25% of class	94
% graduated top 50% of class	100

DEADLINES
Early decision	11/15
Early decision notification	12/15
Regular admission	1/15
Regular notification	4/15

FINANCIAL FACTS
Financial Aid Rating	**86**
Tuition	$28,612
Room and board	$9,020
Required fees	$268
Avg frosh grant	$22,706
Avg frosh loan	$3,459

HOLLINS UNIVERSITY

CAMPUS LIFE
Quality of Life Rating	**98**
Type of school	private
Environment	suburban

STUDENTS
Total undergrad enrollment	847
% from out of state	48
% from public high school	74
% live on campus	90
% African American	7
% Asian	1
% Caucasian	83
% Hispanic	2

% international	3
# of countries represented	12

ACADEMICS
Academic Rating	**90**
Calendar	4-1-4
Student/faculty ratio	9:1
Profs interesting rating	97
Profs accessible rating	99
% profs teaching UG courses	100
Avg lab size	under 10 students
Avg reg class size	10-19 students

MOST POPULAR MAJORS
Creative writing
Psychology
Fine/studio arts

SELECTIVITY
Admissions Rating	**79**
# of applicants	686
% of applicants accepted	80
% of acceptees attending	37
# accepting a place on wait list	9
% admitted from wait list	89
# of early decision applicants	57
% accepted early decision	79

FRESHMAN PROFILE
Range SAT Verbal	530-660
Average SAT Verbal	595
Range SAT Math	490-610
Average SAT Math	550
Range ACT Composite	21-28
Average ACT Composite	24
Minimum TOEFL	550
Average HS GPA	3.4
% graduated top 10% of class	30
% graduated top 25% of class	58
% graduated top 50% of class	89

DEADLINES
Early decision	12/1
Early decision notification	12/15
Priority admission	2/15
Nonfall registration?	yes

FINANCIAL FACTS
Financial Aid Rating	**95**
Tuition	$18,200
Room and board	$6,875
Books and supplies	$600
Required fees	$250
% frosh receiving aid	65
% undergrads receiving aid	59

| Avg frosh grant | $9,041 |
| Avg frosh loan | $3,979 |

Hood College

CAMPUS LIFE
Quality of Life Rating 71
Type of school	private
Affiliation	none
Environment	suburban

STUDENTS
Total undergrad enrollment	784
% male/female	12/88
% from out of state	23
% from public high school	74
% live on campus	52
% African American	13
% Asian	2
% Caucasian	63
% Hispanic	3
% international	5

ACADEMICS
Academic Rating 78
Calendar	semester
Student/faculty ratio	9:1
Profs interesting rating	75
Profs accessible rating	73
% profs teaching UG courses	100
% classes taught by TAs	0
Avg lab size	under 10 students
Avg reg class size	10-19 students

MOST POPULAR MAJORS
Psychology
Business administration/management
Early childhood education and teaching

SELECTIVITY
Admissions Rating 73
# of applicants	502
% of applicants accepted	74
% of acceptees attending	30

FRESHMAN PROFILE
Range SAT Verbal	520-630
Average SAT Verbal	577
Range SAT Math	520-620
Average SAT Math	557
Range ACT Composite	22-25
Average ACT Composite	23

Minimum TOEFL	530
Average HS GPA	3.5
% graduated top 10% of class	40
% graduated top 25% of class	74
% graduated top 50% of class	94

DEADLINES
Regular admission	2/15
Regular notification	3/15
Nonfall registration?	yes

FINANCIAL FACTS
Financial Aid Rating 82
Tuition	$18,795
Room and board	$6,900
Books and supplies	$600
Avg frosh grant	$14,158
Avg frosh loan	$3,925

Howard University

CAMPUS LIFE
Quality of Life Rating 77
| Type of school | private |
| Environment | urban |

STUDENTS
Total undergrad enrollment	6,892
% male/female	34/66
% from out of state	88
% from public high school	80
% live on campus	58
% African American	85
% Asian	1
% Hispanic	1
% international	12
# of countries represented	102

ACADEMICS
Academic Rating 72
Calendar	semester
Student/faculty ratio	8:1
Profs interesting rating	92
Profs accessible rating	94
Avg lab size	10-19 students
Avg reg class size	10-19 students

MOST POPULAR MAJORS
Biology
Psychology
Radio, TV, and film

SELECTIVITY
Admissions Rating	**80**
# of applicants	6,664
% of applicants accepted	56
% of acceptees attending	27

FRESHMAN PROFILE
Range SAT Verbal	440-680
Average SAT Verbal	545
Range SAT Math	430-680
Average SAT Math	534
Range ACT Composite	16-27
Minimum TOEFL	500

DEADLINES
Early decision	11/1
Early decision notification	12/24
Regular admission	2/15
Nonfall registration?	yes

FINANCIAL FACTS
Financial Aid Rating	**76**
Tuition	$10,130
Room and board	$5,570
Books and supplies	$1,020
Required fees	$405
% frosh receiving aid	68
% undergrads receiving aid	68
Avg frosh grant	$4,475
Avg frosh loan	$9,457

INDIANA UNIVERSITY OF PENNSYLVANIA

CAMPUS LIFE
Quality of Life Rating	**80**
Type of school	public
Environment	suburban

STUDENTS
Total undergrad enrollment	11,834
% male/female	44/56
% from out of state	3
% from public high school	95
% live on campus	32
% in (# of) fraternities	10 (19)

% in (# of) sororities	11 (14)
% African American	6
% Asian	1
% Caucasian	91
% Hispanic	1
% international	2
# of countries represented	71

ACADEMICS
Academic Rating	**81**
Calendar	semester
Student/faculty ratio	17:1
% profs teaching UG courses	100
Avg reg class size	20-29 students

MOST POPULAR MAJORS
Communications studies/speech communication and rhetoric
Elementary education and teaching
Criminology

ADMISSIONS
Admissions Rating	**78**
# of applicants	8,005
% of applicants accepted	54
% of acceptees attending	64

FRESHMAN PROFILE
Range SAT Verbal	480-580
Average SAT Verbal	534
Range SAT Math	480-570
Average SAT Math	528
Minimum TOEFL	500
% graduated top 10% of class	17
% graduated top 25% of class	44
% graduated top 50% of class	77

DEADLINES
Priority admission	12/31
Nonfall registration?	yes

FINANCIAL FACTS
Financial Aid Rating	**82**
In-state tuition	$4,378
Out-of-state tuition	$10,946
Room and board	$4,524
Books and supplies	$800
Required fees	$1,163
% frosh receiving aid	64
% undergrads receiving aid	64
Avg frosh grant	$3,682
Avg frosh loan	$2,573

JAMES MADISON UNIVERSITY

CAMPUS LIFE
Quality of Life Rating | **85**
Type of school | public
Environment | rural

STUDENTS
Total undergrad enrollment | 14,402
% male/female | 40/60
% from out of state | 29
% from public high school | 95
% live on campus | 40
% in (# of) fraternities | 5 (14)
% in (# of) sororities | 8 (8)
% African American | 4
% Asian | 4
% Caucasian | 84
% Hispanic | 2
% international | 2
# of countries represented | 60

ACADEMICS
Academic Rating | **81**
Calendar | semester
Student/faculty ratio | 17:1
Profs interesting rating | 92
Profs accessible rating | 88
% profs teaching UG courses | 100
% classes taught by TAs | 1
Avg lab size | 20-29 students
Avg reg class size | 20-29 students

MOST POPULAR MAJORS
Marketing/marketing management
Psychology
Integrated science and technology

SELECTIVITY
Admissions Rating | **84**
# of applicants | 15,639
% of applicants accepted | 58
% of acceptees attending | 21
# accepting a place on wait list | 902
% admitted from wait list | 21

FRESHMAN PROFILE
Range SAT Verbal | 540-620
Average SAT Verbal | 578
Range SAT Math | 540-630
Average SAT Math | 587
Minimum TOEFL | 570
Average HS GPA | 3.6
% graduated top 10% of class | 28
% graduated top 25% of class | 85
% graduated top 50% of class | 95

DEADLINES
Priority admission | 11/1
Regular admission | 1/15
Regular notification | 4/1

FINANCIAL FACTS
Financial Aid Rating | **82**
In-state tuition | $5,058
Out-of-state tuition | $13,280
Room and board | $5,736
Books and supplies | $750
% frosh receiving aid | 28
% undergrads receiving aid | 29
Avg frosh grant | $3,437
Avg frosh loan | $2,959

JOHNS HOPKINS UNIVERSITY

CAMPUS LIFE
Quality of Life Rating | **85**
Type of school | private
Environment | urban

STUDENTS
Total undergrad enrollment | 5,523
% male/female | 52/48
% from out of state | 78
% from public high school | 59
% live on campus | 54
% in (# of) fraternities | 18 (11)
% in (# of) sororities | 19 (7)
% African American | 6
% Asian | 18
% Caucasian | 72
% Hispanic | 7
% international | 6

ACADEMICS
Academic Rating | **96**
Calendar | 4-1-4
Student/faculty ratio | 8:1

Profs interesting rating	83
Profs accessible rating	80
Avg lab size	10-19 students
Avg reg class size	under 10 students

MOST POPULAR MAJORS
Biomedical/medical engineering
Biology/biological sciences
International relations and affairs

SELECTIVITY
Admissions Rating	**99**
# of applicants	8,915
% of applicants accepted	35
% of acceptees attending	36
# accepting a place on wait list	839
# of early decision applicants	507
% accepted early decision	60

FRESHMAN PROFILE
Range SAT Verbal	620-730
Average SAT Verbal	671
Range SAT Math	660-760
Average SAT Math	703
Range ACT Composite	27-31
Average ACT Composite	29
Minimum TOEFL	200 (CBT)
Average HS GPA	3.7
% graduated top 10% of class	72
% graduated top 25% of class	94
% graduated top 50% of class	100

DEADLINES
Early decision	11/15
Early decision notification	12/15
Regular admission	1/1
Regular notification	4/1

FINANCIAL FACTS
Financial Aid Rating	**86**
Tuition	$27,390
Room and board	$8,829
Books and supplies	$1,600
% frosh receiving aid	43
% undergrads receiving aid	40
Avg frosh grant	$21,375
Avg frosh loan	$2,529

JUNIATA COLLEGE

CAMPUS LIFE
Quality of Life Rating	**79**
Type of school	private
Affiliation	Church of Brethren
Environment	rural

STUDENTS
Total undergrad enrollment	1,345
% male/female	42/58
% from out of state	24
% from public high school	89
% live on campus	86
% African American	1
% Asian	1
% Caucasian	97
% Hispanic	1
% international	3
# of countries represented	27

ACADEMICS
Academic Rating	**81**
Calendar	semester
Student/faculty ratio	13:1
Profs interesting rating	81
Profs accessible rating	83
% profs teaching UG courses	100
Avg lab size	10-19 students
Avg reg class size	10-19 students

MOST POPULAR MAJORS
Business administration/management
Education
Biology/biological sciences

SELECTIVITY
Admissions Rating	**76**
# of applicants	1,346
% of applicants accepted	79
% of acceptees attending	35
# of early decision applicants	97
% accepted early decision	75

FRESHMAN PROFILE
Range SAT Verbal	520-620
Average SAT Verbal	574
Range SAT Math	530-640
Average SAT Math	583
Minimum TOEFL	550
Average HS GPA	3.7
% graduated top 10% of class	36

% graduated top 25% of class	71
% graduated top 50% of class	98

DEADLINES
Early decision	11/15
Early decision notification	12/30
Priority admission	11/15
Regular admission	3/15
Regular notification	rolling
Nonfall registration?	yes

FINANCIAL FACTS
Financial Aid Rating	**83**
Tuition	$22,240
Room and board	$6,290
Books and supplies	$450
Required fees	$550
% frosh receiving aid	100
% undergrads receiving aid	99
Avg frosh grant	$14,651
Avg frosh loan	$2,965

KUTZTOWN UNIVERSITY OF PENNSYLVANIA

CAMPUS LIFE
Quality of Life Rating	**76**
Type of school	public
Affiliation	none
Environment	rural

STUDENTS
Total undergrad enrollment	7,591
% male/female	39/61
% from out of state	8
% from public high school	96
% live on campus	41
% in (# of) fraternities	4 (5)
% in (# of) sororities	4 (6)
% African American	5
% Asian	1
% Caucasian	89
% Hispanic	3
% international	1

ACADEMICS
Academic Rating	**66**
Calendar	semester
Student/faculty ratio	21:1
Profs interesting rating	82

Profs accessible rating	80
% profs teaching UG courses	99
% classes taught by TAs	0
Avg lab size	21 students
Avg reg class size	27 students

MOST POPULAR MAJORS
Business administration
Psychology
Special education

SELECTIVITY
Admissions Rating	**63**
# of applicants	6,688
% of applicants accepted	66
% of acceptees attending	41

FRESHMAN PROFILE
Range SAT Verbal	450-540
Average SAT Verbal	495
Range SAT Math	440-540
Average SAT Math	491
Minimum TOEFL	500
% graduated top 10% of class	5
% graduated top 25% of class	18
% graduated top 50% of class	54

DEADLINES
Nonfall registration?	yes

FINANCIAL FACTS
Financial Aid Rating	**71**
In-state tuition	$4,378
Out-of-state tuition	$10,946
Room and board	$4,682
Books and supplies	$800
Avg frosh grant	$3,816
Avg frosh loan	$2,350

LAFAYETTE COLLEGE

CAMPUS LIFE
Quality of Life Rating	**80**
Type of school	private
Affiliation	Presbyterian
Environment	suburban

STUDENTS
Total undergrad enrollment	2,300
% male/female	51/49
% from out of state	70
% from public high school	68

% live on campus	96
% in (# of) fraternities	26 (7)
% in (# of) sororities	45 (6)
% African American	5
% Asian	2
% Caucasian	91
% Hispanic	2
% international	5
# of countries represented	46

ACADEMICS
Academic Rating 85
Calendar	semester
Student/faculty ratio	11:1
Profs interesting rating	94
Profs accessible rating	95
% profs teaching UG courses	100
Avg lab size	10-19 students
Avg reg class size	10-19 students

SELECTIVITY
Admissions Rating 86
# of applicants	5,504
% of applicants accepted	36
% of acceptees attending	30
# accepting a place on wait list	664
% admitted from wait list	4
# of early decision applicants	367
% accepted early decision	66

FRESHMAN PROFILE
Range SAT Verbal	560-650
Average SAT Verbal	620
Range SAT Math	610-700
Average SAT Math	665
Range ACT Composite	25-29
Average ACT Composite	28
Minimum TOEFL	550
Average HS GPA	3.8
% graduated top 10% of class	59
% graduated top 25% of class	89
% graduated top 50% of class	100

DEADLINES
Early decision	2/15
Early decision notification	12/1
Priority admission	1/1
Regular admission	1/1
Regular notification	4/1
Nonfall registration?	yes

FINANCIAL FACTS
Financial Aid Rating 82

Tuition	$25,884
Room and board	$8,069
Books and supplies	$600
Required fees	$98
% frosh receiving aid	57
% undergrads receiving aid	54
Avg frosh grant	$20,552
Avg frosh loan	$3,500

LEBANON VALLEY COLLEGE

CAMPUS LIFE
Quality of Life Rating 77
Type of school	private
Affiliation	Methodist
Environment	rural

STUDENTS
Total undergrad enrollment	1,920
% male/female	40/60
% from public high school	95
% live on campus	72
% in (# of) fraternities	14 (4)
% in (# of) sororities	10 (3)
% African American	2
% Asian	1
% Caucasian	93
% Hispanic	2
% international	1
# of countries represented	15

ACADEMICS
Academic Rating 77
Calendar	semester
Student/faculty ratio	14:1
Profs interesting rating	84
Profs accessible rating	84
% profs teaching UG courses	100
% classes taught by TAs	0
Avg lab size	10-19 students
Avg reg class size	20-29 students

MOST POPULAR MAJORS
Elementary education
Management
Psychology

SELECTIVITY
Admissions Rating 75
# of applicants	1,864
% of applicants accepted	79

% of acceptees attending	29
# accepting a place on wait list	4
% admitted from wait list	100

FRESHMAN PROFILE

Range SAT Verbal	490-600
Average SAT Verbal	544
Range SAT Math	490-610
Average SAT Math	542
Range ACT Composite	20-27
Minimum TOEFL	550
% graduated top 10% of class	33
% graduated top 25% of class	67
% graduated top 50% of class	90

DEADLINES

Nonfall registration?	yes

FINANCIAL FACTS

Financial Aid Rating	**74**
Tuition	$19,210
Room and board	$5,890
Books and supplies	$700

LEHIGH UNIVERSITY

CAMPUS LIFE

Quality of Life Rating	**85**
Type of school	private
Environment	suburban

STUDENTS

Total undergrad enrollment	4,685
% male/female	60/40
% from public high school	69
% live on campus	65
% in (# of) fraternities	33 (23)
% in (# of) sororities	43 (9)
% African American	3
% Asian	6
% Caucasian	76
% Hispanic	3
% international	3

ACADEMICS

Academic Rating	**87**
Calendar	semester
Student/faculty ratio	10:1
Profs interesting rating	77
Profs accessible rating	96
% profs teaching UG courses	100

SELECTIVITY

Admissions Rating	**88**
# of applicants	8,254
% of applicants accepted	44
% of acceptees attending	31
# accepting a place on wait list	1,319
% admitted from wait list	1
# of early decision applicants	467
% accepted early decision	80

FRESHMAN PROFILE

Range SAT Verbal	580-660
Average SAT Verbal	617
Range SAT Math	630-710
Average SAT Math	665
Minimum TOEFL	570
% graduated top 10% of class	55
% graduated top 25% of class	88
% graduated top 50% of class	99

DEADLINES

Early decision	11/15
Early decision notification	12/15
Regular admission	1/1
Regular notification	4/1
Nonfall registration?	yes

FINANCIAL FACTS

Financial Aid Rating	**85**
Tuition	$27,230
Room and board	$7,880
Required fees	$200
% frosh receiving aid	43
% undergrads receiving aid	46
Avg frosh grant	$13,676
Avg frosh loan	$4,424

LONGWOOD UNIVERSITY

CAMPUS LIFE

Quality of Life Rating	**73**
Type of school	public
Affiliation	none
Environment	small town

STUDENTS

Total undergrad enrollment	3,640
% male/female	34/66
% from out of state	10
% from public high school	92
% live on campus	77

% in (# of) fraternities	18 (8)
% in (# of) sororities	20 (12)
% African American	8
% Asian	2
% Caucasian	86
% Hispanic	2
# of countries represented	20

ACADEMICS
Academic Rating 67
Calendar	semester
Student/faculty ratio	20:1
Profs interesting rating	82
Profs accessible rating	77
% profs teaching UG courses	100
% classes taught by TAs	0
Avg lab size	20-29 students
Avg reg class size	30-40 students

MOST POPULAR MAJORS
Liberal studies/elementary education
Business administration
Psychology

SELECTIVITY
Admissions Rating 64
# of applicants	3,223
% of applicants accepted	67
% of acceptees attending	41
# accepting a place on wait list	200
% admitted from wait list	50

FRESHMAN PROFILE
Range SAT Verbal	500-570
Average SAT Verbal	550
Range SAT Math	500-560
Average SAT Math	530
Average HS GPA	3.2
% graduated top 10% of class	9
% graduated top 25% of class	38
% graduated top 50% of class	85

DEADLINES
Regular admission	3/1
Nonfall registration?	yes

FINANCIAL FACTS
Financial Aid Rating 73
In-state tuition	$4,600
Out-of-state tuition	$10,587
Room and board	$5,070
Books and supplies	$700

LOYOLA COLLEGE IN MARYLAND

CAMPUS LIFE
Quality of Life Rating 89
Type of school	private
Affiliation	Roman Catholic
Environment	suburban

STUDENTS
Total undergrad enrollment	3,488
% male/female	42/58
% from out of state	79
% live on campus	76
% African American	5
% Asian	2
% Caucasian	89
% Hispanic	2
# of countries represented	18

ACADEMICS
Academic Rating 84
Calendar	semester
Student/faculty ratio	12:1
Profs interesting rating	94
Profs accessible rating	94
Avg reg class size	20-29 students

MOST POPULAR MAJORS
Business administration/management
Communications studies/speech
communication and rhetoric
Psychology

SELECTIVITY
Admissions Rating 83
# of applicants	6,368
% of applicants accepted	61
% of acceptees attending	23
# accepting a place on wait list	670
% admitted from wait list	21

FRESHMAN PROFILE
Range SAT Verbal	560-640
Range SAT Math	570-650
Minimum TOEFL	550
Average HS GPA	3.5
% graduated top 10% of class	35
% graduated top 25% of class	76
% graduated top 50% of class	97

DEADLINES
Priority admission	1/15

Regular admission	1/15
Regular notification	4/1

FINANCIAL FACTS
Financial Aid Rating **90**

Tuition	$26,010
Room and board	$7,800
Books and supplies	$760
Required fees	$900
% frosh receiving aid	61
% undergrads receiving aid	64

LYCOMING COLLEGE

CAMPUS LIFE
Quality of Life Rating **74**

Type of school	private
Affiliation	Methodist
Environment	suburban

STUDENTS
Total undergrad enrollment	1,429
% male/female	45/55
% from out of state	21
% live on campus	80
% in (# of) fraternities	14 (4)
% in (# of) sororities	16 (4)
% African American	2
% Asian	1
% Caucasian	95
% Hispanic	1
% international	1
# of countries represented	9

ACADEMICS
Academic Rating **77**

Calendar	semester
Student/faculty ratio	13:1
Profs interesting rating	78
Profs accessible rating	74
% profs teaching UG courses	100
% classes taught by TAs	0
Avg lab size	10-19 students
Avg reg class size	10-19 students

MOST POPULAR MAJORS
Business administration/management
Biology/biological sciences
Psychology

SELECTIVITY
Admissions Rating **75**

# of applicants	1,431
% of applicants accepted	80
% of acceptees attending	36

FRESHMAN PROFILE
Range SAT Verbal	480-610
Average SAT Verbal	540
Range SAT Math	490-590
Average SAT Math	540
Range ACT Composite	21-25
Average ACT Composite	22
Minimum TOEFL	500
Average HS GPA	3.2
% graduated top 10% of class	25
% graduated top 25% of class	52
% graduated top 50% of class	81

DEADLINES
Regular admission	5/1
Nonfall registration?	yes

FINANCIAL FACTS
Financial Aid Rating **80**

Tuition	$19,104
Room and board	$5,376
Books and supplies	$800
Avg frosh grant	$9,400
Avg frosh loan	$3,200

MARSHALL UNIVERSITY

CAMPUS LIFE
Quality of Life Rating **79**

Type of school	public
Affiliation	none
Environment	suburban

STUDENTS
Total undergrad enrollment	9,653
% male/female	45/55
% from out of state	16
% African American	4
% Asian	1
% Caucasian	84
% Hispanic	1
% international	1

ACADEMICS
Academic Rating **64**

Calendar	semester
Student/faculty ratio	20:1
Profs interesting rating	83
Profs accessible rating	82
Avg reg class size	20-29 students

MOST POPULAR MAJORS
Counselor education/school counseling and
Guidance services
Elementary education and teaching

SELECTIVITY
Admissions Rating   60

# of applicants	2,416
% of applicants accepted	91
% of acceptees attending	82

FRESHMAN PROFILE

Range ACT Composite	19-23
Minimum TOEFL	500
Average HS GPA	3.3
% graduated top 25% of class	52
% graduated top 50% of class	89

DEADLINES

Nonfall registration?	yes

FINANCIAL FACTS
Financial Aid Rating   76

In-state tuition	$2,236
Out-of-state tuition	$6,806
Room and board	$5,108
Books and supplies	$800
Avg frosh grant	$3,261
Avg frosh loan	$2,320

MARY BALDWIN COLLEGE

CAMPUS LIFE
Quality of Life Rating   75

Type of school	private
Affiliation	Presbyterian
Environment	suburban

STUDENTS

Total undergrad enrollment	1,489
% male/female	4/96
% from out of state	23
% from public high school	75
% live on campus	82
% African American	19
% Asian	2

% Caucasian	73
% Hispanic	4
% international	2
# of countries represented	8

ACADEMICS
Academic Rating   75

Calendar	other
Student/faculty ratio	11:1
Profs interesting rating	78
Profs accessible rating	74
% profs teaching UG courses	100
% classes taught by TAs	0
Avg lab size	10-19 students
Avg reg class size	10-19 students

MOST POPULAR MAJORS
Psychology
Sociology
Business administration/management

SELECTIVITY
Admissions Rating   73

# of applicants	1,228
% of applicants accepted	82
% of acceptees attending	29
# of early decision applicants	49
% accepted early decision	71

FRESHMAN PROFILE

Range SAT Verbal	485-590
Average SAT Verbal	544
Range SAT Math	440-560
Average SAT Math	507
Range ACT Composite	16-23
Minimum TOEFL	500
Average HS GPA	3.2
% graduated top 10% of class	16
% graduated top 25% of class	41
% graduated top 50% of class	77

DEADLINES

Early decision	11/15
Regular notification	rolling
Nonfall registration?	yes

FINANCIAL FACTS
Financial Aid Rating   79

Tuition	$11,966
Room and board	$6,450
Books and supplies	$600
Avg frosh grant	$9,000
Avg frosh loan	$3,400

Mary Washington College

CAMPUS LIFE
Quality of Life Rating   **84**
Type of school	public
Environment	suburban

STUDENTS
Total undergrad enrollment	4,275
% male/female	32/68
% from out of state	35
% from public high school	76
% live on campus	70
% African American	4
% Asian	4
% Caucasian	88
% Hispanic	3

ACADEMICS
Academic Rating   **80**
Calendar	semester
Student/faculty ratio	17:1
Profs interesting rating	93
Profs accessible rating	94
% profs teaching UG courses	100
Avg lab size	20-29 students
Avg reg class size	20-29 students

MOST POPULAR MAJORS
Business administration/management
English language and literature
Psychology

SELECTIVITY
Admissions Rating   **91**

FRESHMAN PROFILE
Range SAT Verbal	570-660
Average SAT Verbal	613
Range SAT Math	560-640
Average SAT Math	595
Range ACT Composite	24-29
Average ACT Composite	27
Minimum TOEFL	550
Average HS GPA	3.7
% graduated top 10% of class	40
% graduated top 25% of class	85
% graduated top 50% of class	99

DEADLINES
Priority admission	1/15
Regular admission	2/1
Regular notification	4/1
Nonfall registration?	yes

FINANCIAL FACTS
Financial Aid Rating   **83**
In-state tuition	$4,089
Out-of-state tuition	$11,122
Room and board	$5,318
Books and supplies	$800
% frosh receiving aid	44
% undergrads receiving aid	39
Avg frosh grant	$2,753
Avg frosh loan	$1,894

Mercyhurst College

CAMPUS LIFE
Quality of Life Rating   **74**
Type of school	private
Affiliation	Roman Catholic
Environment	suburban

STUDENTS
Total undergrad enrollment	2,832
% male/female	43/57
% from out of state	43
% from public high school	78
% live on campus	70
% African American	4
% Asian	1
% Caucasian	91
% Hispanic	1
% international	3

ACADEMICS
Academic Rating   **77**
Calendar	trimester
Student/faculty ratio	19:1
Profs interesting rating	83
Profs accessible rating	82
% profs teaching UG courses	100
Avg reg class size	under 20 students

MOST POPULAR MAJORS
Business
Education
Music/dance

SELECTIVITY
Admissions Rating   **74**

# of applicants	2,220
% of applicants accepted	77
% of acceptees attending	39

FRESHMAN PROFILE

Range SAT Verbal	480-580
Average SAT Verbal	533
Range SAT Math	470-580
Average SAT Math	528
Range ACT Composite	20-25
Average ACT Composite	23
Minimum TOEFL	550
Average HS GPA	3.4
% graduated top 10% of class	16
% graduated top 25% of class	49
% graduated top 50% of class	82

DEADLINES

Regular notification	rolling
Nonfall registration?	yes

FINANCIAL FACTS

Financial Aid Rating	76
Tuition	$14,820
Room and board	$5,979
Books and supplies	$750
Avg frosh grant	$8,506
Avg frosh loan	$3,216

MESSIAH COLLEGE

CAMPUS LIFE

Quality of Life Rating	73
Type of school	private
Affiliation	other
Environment	suburban

STUDENTS

Total undergrad enrollment	2,858
% male/female	39/61
% from out of state	48
% from public high school	84
% live on campus	86
% African American	2
% Asian	1
% Caucasian	91
% Hispanic	2
% international	2
# of countries represented	25

ACADEMICS

Academic Rating	76
Calendar	semester
Student/faculty ratio	13:1
Profs interesting rating	80
Profs accessible rating	80
% profs teaching UG courses	100
% classes taught by TAs	0
Avg lab size	20-29 students
Avg reg class size	10-19 students

MOST POPULAR MAJORS
Nursing/registered nurse training (RN, BSN)
Engineering
Elementary education and teaching

SELECTIVITY

Admissions Rating	73
# of applicants	2,231
% of applicants accepted	78
% of acceptees attending	40
# accepting a place on wait list	20
% admitted from wait list	15

FRESHMAN PROFILE

Range SAT Verbal	540-650
Average SAT Verbal	593
Range SAT Math	540-650
Average SAT Math	593
Range ACT Composite	23-28
Average ACT Composite	25
Minimum TOEFL	550
Average HS GPA	3.7
% graduated top 10% of class	35
% graduated top 25% of class	66
% graduated top 50% of class	90

DEADLINES

Early decision	10/15
Nonfall registration?	yes

FINANCIAL FACTS

Financial Aid Rating	75
Tuition	$16,860
Room and board	$5,970
Books and supplies	$730
Avg frosh grant	$8,386
Avg frosh loan	$6,885

Moravian College

CAMPUS LIFE
Quality of Life Rating **79**

Type of school	private
Affiliation	Moravian
Environment	suburban

STUDENTS

Total undergrad enrollment	1,824
% male/female	39/61
% from out of state	39
% from public high school	86
% live on campus	73
% in (# of) fraternities	14 (2)
% in (# of) sororities	22 (4)
% African American	2
% Asian	1
% Caucasian	93
% Hispanic	4
% international	2
# of countries represented	21

ACADEMICS
Academic Rating **76**

Calendar	semester
Student/faculty ratio	12:1
Profs interesting rating	80
Profs accessible rating	85
% profs teaching UG courses	100
Avg lab size	under 10 students
Avg reg class size	10-19 students

MOST POPULAR MAJORS
Psychology
Business administration/management
Fine/studio arts

ADMISSIONS
Admissions Rating **78**

# of applicants	1,509
% of applicants accepted	77
% of acceptees attending	32
% admitted from wait list	35
# of early decision applicants	145
% accepted early decision	77

FRESHMAN PROFILE

Range SAT Verbal	490-610
Average SAT Verbal	553
Range SAT Math	500-610
Average SAT Math	556
Minimum TOEFL	550

% graduated top 10% of class	25
% graduated top 25% of class	56
% graduated top 50% of class	85

DEADLINES

Early decision	2/1
Early decision notification	12/15
Priority admission	3/1
Regular admission	3/1
Regular notification	3/15
Nonfall registration?	yes

FINANCIAL FACTS
Financial Aid Rating **83**

Tuition	$21,663
Room and board	$7,095
Books and supplies	$700
Required fees	$365
% frosh receiving aid	74
% undergrads receiving aid	78
Avg frosh grant	$11,536
Avg frosh loan	$3,265

Mount St. Mary's College

CAMPUS LIFE
Quality of Life Rating **78**

Type of school	private
Affiliation	Roman Catholic
Environment	rural

STUDENTS

Total undergrad enrollment	1,542
% male/female	41/59
% from out of state	39
% from public high school	53
% live on campus	83
% African American	5
% Asian	2
% Caucasian	88
% Hispanic	3
% international	1
# of countries represented	10

ACADEMICS
Academic Rating **72**

Calendar	semester
Student/faculty ratio	14:1
Profs interesting rating	88

Profs accessible rating	90
% profs teaching UG courses	96
% classes taught by TAs	0
Avg lab size	10-19 students
Avg reg class size	20-29 students

MOST POPULAR MAJORS
Business
Elementary education
Biology

SELECTIVITY
Admissions Rating — **67**

# of applicants	1,946
% of applicants accepted	79
% of acceptees attending	23

FRESHMAN PROFILE

Range SAT Verbal	490-590
Average SAT Verbal	540
Range SAT Math	490-580
Average SAT Math	540
Minimum TOEFL	550
Average HS GPA	3.2
% graduated top 10% of class	16
% graduated top 25% of class	41
% graduated top 50% of class	74

DEADLINES

Nonfall registration?	yes

FINANCIAL FACTS
Financial Aid Rating — **72**

Tuition	$19,500
Room and board	$7,060
Books and supplies	$600
Avg frosh grant	$11,720
Avg frosh loan	$2,372

MUHLENBERG COLLEGE

CAMPUS LIFE
Quality of Life Rating — **80**

Type of school	private
Affiliation	Lutheran
Environment	suburban

STUDENTS

Total undergrad enrollment	2,470
% male/female	44/56
% from out of state	63
% from public high school	70
% live on campus	89
% in (# of) fraternities	27 (4)
% in (# of) sororities	22 (4)
% African American	2
% Asian	3
% Caucasian	90
% Hispanic	3

ACADEMICS
Academic Rating — **82**

Calendar	semester
Student/faculty ratio	13:1
Profs interesting rating	77
Profs accessible rating	74
% profs teaching UG courses	100
Avg lab size	10-19 students
Avg reg class size	10-19 students

MOST POPULAR MAJORS
Business administration/management
Biology/biological sciences
Psychology

SELECTIVITY
Admissions Rating — **82**

# of applicants	3,822
% of applicants accepted	35
% of acceptees attending	41
# accepting a place on wait list	407
% admitted from wait list	7
# of early decision applicants	527
% accepted early decision	59

FRESHMAN PROFILE

Range SAT Verbal	550-640
Average SAT Verbal	595
Range SAT Math	560-650
Average SAT Math	606
Minimum TOEFL	550
Average HS GPA	3.7
% graduated top 10% of class	39
% graduated top 25% of class	75
% graduated top 50% of class	97

DEADLINES

Early decision	1/15
Early decision notification	2/1
Regular admission	2/15
Regular notification	3/15
Nonfall registration?	yes

FINANCIAL FACTS
Financial Aid Rating — **82**

Tuition	$23,250
Room and board	$6,295
Books and supplies	$750
Required fees	$205
% frosh receiving aid	43
% undergrads receiving aid	44
Avg frosh grant	$12,819
Avg frosh loan	$2,971

NEUMANN COLLEGE

CAMPUS LIFE
Quality of Life Rating 68

Type of school	private
Affiliation	Roman Catholic
Environment	suburban

STUDENTS
Total undergrad enrollment	1,853
% male/female	35/65
% from out of state	27
% from public high school	60
% live on campus	45
% African American	13
% Asian	1
% Caucasian	77
% Hispanic	1
# of countries represented	5

ACADEMICS
Academic Rating 68

Calendar	semester
Student/faculty ratio	16:1
Profs interesting rating	90
Profs accessible rating	90
% profs teaching UG courses	98
% classes taught by TAs	0
Avg lab size	20-29 students
Avg regular class size	20-29 students

SELECTIVITY
Admissions Rating 63

# of applicants	1,207
% of applicants accepted	95
% of acceptees attending	32

FRESHMAN PROFILE
Range SAT Verbal	400-490
Average SAT Verbal	450
Range SAT Math	390-480
Average SAT Math	440

| Minimum TOEFL | 550 |
| Average HS GPA | 3.00 |

DEADLINES
| Nonfall registration? | yes |

FINANCIAL FACTS
Financial Aid Rating 72

Tuition	$14,460
Room and board	$7,260
Books and supplies	$1,300
Avg frosh grant	$15,000
Avg frosh loan	$2,625

OLD DOMINION UNIVERSITY

CAMPUS LIFE
Quality of Life Rating 79

Type of school	public
Affiliation	none
Environment	urban

STUDENTS
Total undergrad enrollment	12,786
% male/female	43/57
% from out of state	8
% from public high school	95
% live on campus	21
% in (# of) fraternities	3 (15)
% in (# of) sororities	4 (9)
% African American	24
% Asian	7
% Caucasian	63
% Hispanic	3
% international	3

ACADEMICS
Academic Rating 71

Calendar	semester
Student/faculty ratio	16:1
Profs interesting rating	83
Profs accessible rating	79
% profs teaching UG courses	72
% classes taught by TAs	6
Avg lab size	20-29 students
Avg reg class size	10-19 students

MOST POPULAR MAJORS
Business management and administration
Health professions
Engineering and applied sciences

SELECTIVITY
Admissions Rating   **63**

# of applicants	6,500
% of applicants accepted	70
% of acceptees attending	39

FRESHMAN PROFILE

Range SAT Verbal	470-570
Average SAT Verbal	525
Range SAT Math	470-580
Average SAT Math	526
Range ACT Composite	19-25
Minimum TOEFL	550
Average HS GPA	3.2
% graduated top 10% of class	19
% graduated top 25% of class	47
% graduated top 50% of class	85

DEADLINES

Regular admission	3/15
Regular notification	ongoing
Nonfall registration?	yes

FINANCIAL FACTS
Financial Aid Rating   **68**

In-state tuition	$4,110
Out-of-state tuition	$13,140
Room and board	$5,498
Books and supplies	$700
Avg frosh grant	$1,888
Avg frosh loan	$2,545

PENNSYLVANIA STATE UNIVERSITY—UNIVERSITY PARK

CAMPUS LIFE
Quality of Life Rating   **78**

Type of school	public
Environment	suburban

STUDENTS

Total undergrad enrollment	34,829
% male/female	54/46
% from out of state	24
% live on campus	36
% in (# of) fraternities	13 (55)
% in (# of) sororities	10 (25)
% African American	4

% Asian	5
% Caucasian	87
% Hispanic	3
% international	2

ACADEMICS
Academic Rating   **87**

Calendar	semester
Student/faculty ratio	17:1

SELECTIVITY
Admissions Rating   **86**

# of applicants	27,604
% of applicants accepted	57
% of acceptees attending	38

FRESHMAN PROFILE

Range SAT Verbal	530-630
Average SAT Verbal	593
Range SAT Math	560-670
Average SAT Math	617
Minimum TOEFL	550
Average HS GPA	3.5
% graduated top 10% of class	41
% graduated top 25% of class	78
% graduated top 50% of class	96

DEADLINES

Priority admission	11/30
Nonfall registration?	yes

FINANCIAL FACTS
Financial Aid Rating   **89**

In-state tuition	$9,431
Out-of-state tuition	$18,922
Room and board	$6,000
Books and supplies	$864
Required fees	$374
% frosh receiving aid	44
% undergrads receiving aid	49
Avg frosh grant	$2,800
Avg frosh loan	$3,193

RADFORD UNIVERSITY

CAMPUS LIFE
Quality of Life Rating   **74**

Type of school	public
Affiliation	none
Environment	rural

STUDENTS

Total undergrad enrollment	8,061
% male/female	40/60
% from out of state	12
% from public high school	96
% live on campus	40
% in (# of) fraternities	13 (14)
% in (# of) sororities	14 (11)
% African American	6
% Asian	2
% Caucasian	88
% Hispanic	2
% international	1
# of countries represented	65

ACADEMICS

Academic Rating	**68**
Calendar	semester
Student/faculty ratio	20:1
Profs interesting rating	84
Profs accessible rating	81
% profs teaching UG courses	90
% classes taught by TAs	1
Avg lab size	20-29 students
Avg reg class size	20-29 students

MOST POPULAR MAJORS
Criminal justice/safety studies
Multi/interdisciplinary studies
Business administration/management

SELECTIVITY

Admissions Rating	**61**
# of applicants	6,278
% of applicants accepted	75
% of acceptees attending	40

FRESHMAN PROFILE

Range SAT Verbal	450-540
Average SAT Verbal	499
Range SAT Math	440-540
Average SAT Math	492
Range ACT Composite	18-20
Average ACT Composite	19
Minimum TOEFL	520
Average HS GPA	3.0
% graduated top 10% of class	6
% graduated top 25% of class	21
% graduated top 50% of class	77

DEADLINES

Regular admission	5/1
Nonfall registration?	yes

FINANCIAL FACTS

Financial Aid Rating	**73**
In-state tuition	$1,629
Out-of-state tuition	$7,768
Room and board	$5,233
Books and supplies	$650
Avg frosh grant	$6,356
Avg frosh loan	$3,620

RANDOLPH-MACON COLLEGE

CAMPUS LIFE

Quality of Life Rating	**87**
Type of school	private
Affiliation	Methodist
Environment	suburban

STUDENTS

Total undergrad enrollment	1,154
% male/female	50/50
% from out of state	35
% from public high school	65
% live on campus	85
% in (# of) fraternities	45 (6)
% in (# of) sororities	45 (5)
% African American	5
% Asian	1
% Caucasian	92
% Hispanic	2
% international	1
# of countries represented	16

ACADEMICS

Academic Rating	**79**
Calendar	4-1-4
Student/faculty ratio	11:1
% profs teaching UG courses	100
Avg reg class size	10-19 students

MOST POPULAR MAJORS
Business/managerial economics
English language and literature
Psychology

SELECTIVITY

Admissions Rating	**77**
# of applicants	1,689
% of applicants accepted	78
% of acceptees attending	29

# accepting a place on wait list	14
# of early decision applicants	55
% accepted early decision	73

FRESHMAN PROFILE

Range SAT Verbal	500-610
Average SAT Verbal	560
Range SAT Math	500-600
Average SAT Math	552
Minimum TOEFL	550
Average HS GPA	3.2
% graduated top 10% of class	20
% graduated top 25% of class	50
% graduated top 50% of class	81

DEADLINES

Early decision	12/1
Early decision notification	12/20
Priority admission	2/1
Regular admission	3/1
Regular notification	4/1
Nonfall registration?	yes

FINANCIAL FACTS

Financial Aid Rating	**91**
Tuition	$19,480
Room and board	$5,715
Books and supplies	$600
Required fees	$565
% frosh receiving aid	52
% undergrads receiving aid	50
Avg frosh grant	$11,491
Avg frosh loan	$3,600

RANDOLPH-MACON WOMAN'S COLLEGE

CAMPUS LIFE

Quality of Life Rating	**88**
Type of school	private
Affiliation	Methodist
Environment	suburban

STUDENTS

Total undergrad enrollment	764
% from out of state	55
% from public high school	82
% live on campus	90
% African American	8
% Asian	3
% Caucasian	85

% Hispanic	3
% international	11
# of countries represented	48

ACADEMICS

Academic Rating	**93**
Calendar	semester
Student/faculty ratio	9:1
Profs interesting rating	75
Profs accessible rating	73
% profs teaching UG courses	100
Avg lab size	10-19 students
Avg reg class size	10-19 students

MOST POPULAR MAJORS
English language and literature
Biology/biological sciences
Psychology

ADMISSIONS

Admissions Rating	**80**
# of applicants	723
% of applicants accepted	85
% of acceptees attending	33
# of early decision applicants	32
% accepted early decision	81

FRESHMAN PROFILE

Range SAT Verbal	540-640
Average SAT Verbal	592
Range SAT Math	510-620
Average SAT Math	564
Range ACT Composite	23-28
Average ACT Composite	25
Minimum TOEFL	550
Average HS GPA	3.4
% graduated top 10% of class	39
% graduated top 25% of class	65
% graduated top 50% of class	93

DEADLINES

Early decision	11/15
Early decision notification	12/15
Regular admission	3/1
Nonfall registration?	yes

FINANCIAL FACTS

Financial Aid Rating	**92**
Tuition	$18,900
Room and board	$7,560
Required fees	$380
% undergrads receiving aid	62
Avg frosh grant	$14,400
Avg frosh loan	$2,461

ROANOKE COLLEGE

CAMPUS LIFE
Quality of Life Rating **75**

Type of school	private
Affiliation	Lutheran
Environment	suburban

STUDENTS

Total undergrad enrollment	1,822
% male/female	39/61
% from out of state	41
% from public high school	80
% live on campus	57
% in (# of) fraternities	18 (3)
% in (# of) sororities	18 (4)
% African American	4
% Asian	2
% Caucasian	86
% Hispanic	2
% international	1
# of countries represented	17

ACADEMICS
Academic Rating **79**

Calendar	semester
Student/faculty ratio	14:1
Profs interesting rating	77
Profs accessible rating	78
% profs teaching UG courses	100
% classes taught by TAs	0
Avg lab size	10-19 students
Avg reg class size	10-19 students

MOST POPULAR MAJORS
Sociology
English language and literature
Business administration/management

SELECTIVITY
Admissions Rating **75**

# of applicants	2,767
% of applicants accepted	74
% of acceptees attending	25
# accepting a place on wait list	69
% admitted from wait list	36
# of early decision applicants	134
% accepted early decision	60

FRESHMAN PROFILE

Range SAT Verbal	510-600
Average SAT Verbal	559
Range SAT Math	500-610

Average SAT Math	554
Minimum TOEFL	520
Average HS GPA	3.09
% graduated top 10% of class	28
% graduated top 25% of class	60
% graduated top 50% of class	94

DEADLINES

Early decision	11/15
Regular admission	3/1
Regular notification	4/1
Nonfall registration?	yes

FINANCIAL FACTS
Financial Aid Rating **73**

Tuition	$19,186
Room and board	$6,338
Books and supplies	$850
Avg frosh grant	$12,073
Avg frosh loan	$4,533

ROSEMONT COLLEGE

CAMPUS LIFE
Quality of Life Rating **74**

Type of school	private
Affiliation	Roman Catholic
Environment	suburban

STUDENTS

Total undergrad enrollment	892
% from out of state	31
% from public high school	61
% live on campus	68
% African American	20
% Asian	3
% Caucasian	61
% Hispanic	2
% international	1

ACADEMICS
Academic Rating **82**

Calendar	semester
Student/faculty ratio	8:1
Profs interesting rating	78
Profs accessible rating	75
% profs teaching UG courses	100
% classes taught by TAs	0
Avg reg class size	10-19 students

MOST POPULAR MAJORS
Business
Psychology
English

SELECTIVITY
Admissions Rating	**80**
# of applicants	274
% of applicants accepted	97
% of acceptees attending	39

FRESHMAN PROFILE
Range SAT Verbal	450-570
Average SAT Verbal	520
Range SAT Math	420-520
Average SAT Math	500
Minimum TOEFL	500
Average HS GPA	3.1
% graduated top 10% of class	11
% graduated top 25% of class	36
% graduated top 50% of class	77

DEADLINES
Regular notification	rolling
Nonfall registration?	yes

FINANCIAL FACTS
Financial Aid Rating	**75**
Tuition	$14,580
Room and board	$7,030
Books and supplies	$800
Avg frosh grant	$8,900
Avg frosh loan	$3,625

ST. JOHN'S COLLEGE

CAMPUS LIFE
Quality of Life Rating	**87**
Type of school	private
Environment	urban

STUDENTS
Total undergrad enrollment	465
% male/female	55/45
% from out of state	85
% from public high school	67
% live on campus	66
% Asian	2
% Caucasian	92
% Hispanic	3
% international	3
# of countries represented	15

ACADEMICS
Academic Rating	**92**
Calendar	semester
Student/faculty ratio	8:1
Profs interesting rating	98
Profs accessible rating	98
% profs teaching UG courses	100
Avg reg class size	10-19 students

SELECTIVITY
Admissions Rating	**85**
# of applicants	450
% of applicants accepted	71
% of acceptees attending	39

FRESHMAN PROFILE
Range SAT Verbal	660-750
Range SAT Math	590-690
Minimum TOEFL	600
% graduated top 10% of class	46
% graduated top 25% of class	74
% graduated top 50% of class	99

DEADLINES
Priority admission	3/1
Nonfall registration?	yes

FINANCIAL FACTS
Financial Aid Rating	**91**
Tuition	$25,790
Room and board	$6,770
Books and supplies	$275
Required fees	$200
% frosh receiving aid	53
% undergrads receiving aid	56
Avg frosh grant	$14,207
Avg frosh loan	$3,125

ST. MARY'S COLLEGE OF MARYLAND

CAMPUS LIFE
Quality of Life Rating	**81**
Type of school	public
Environment	rural

STUDENTS
Total undergrad enrollment	1,823
% male/female	40/60
% from out of state	15
% from public high school	80

% live on campus	76
% African American	7
% Asian	4
% Caucasian	82
% Hispanic	3
# of countries represented	25

ACADEMICS
Academic Rating	**83**
Calendar	semester
Student/faculty ratio	12:1
Profs interesting rating	94
Profs accessible rating	95
% profs teaching UG courses	100
Avg lab size	10-19 students
Avg reg class size	10-19 students

MOST POPULAR MAJORS
Biology/biological sciences
Economics
Psychology

SELECTIVITY
Admissions Rating	**90**
# of applicants	1,884
% of applicants accepted	59
% of acceptees attending	38
# accepting a place on wait list	115
% admitted from wait list	37
# of early decision applicants	314
% accepted early decision	61

FRESHMAN PROFILE
Range SAT Verbal	570-670
Average SAT Verbal	624
Range SAT Math	560-650
Average SAT Math	608
Minimum TOEFL	550
Average HS GPA	3.5
% graduated top 10% of class	44
% graduated top 25% of class	79
% graduated top 50% of class	97

DEADLINES
Early decision	12/1
Early decision notification	1/1
Priority admission	12/1
Regular admission	1/15
Regular notification	4/1
Nonfall registration?	yes

FINANCIAL FACTS
Financial Aid Rating	**86**
In-state tuition	$6,925
Out-of-state tuition	$12,260
Room and board	$6,613
Books and supplies	$870
Required fees	$1,157
% frosh receiving aid	42
% undergrads receiving aid	45
Avg frosh grant	$4,000
Avg frosh loan	$2,625

SAINT JOSEPH'S UNIVERSITY

CAMPUS LIFE
Quality of Life Rating	**71**
Type of school	private
Affiliation	Roman Catholic
Environment	urban

STUDENTS
Total undergrad enrollment	4,590
% male/female	46/54
% from out of state	49
% from public high school	52
% live on campus	48
% in (# of) fraternities	9 (4)
% in (# of) sororities	13 (3)
% African American	7
% Asian	2
% Caucasian	82
% Hispanic	2
% international	1
# of countries represented	17

ACADEMICS
Academic Rating	**83**
Calendar	semester
Student/faculty ratio	13:1
Profs interesting rating	80
Profs accessible rating	78
% profs teaching UG courses	100
% classes taught by TAs	0
Avg lab size	10-19 students
Avg reg class size	20-29 students

MOST POPULAR MAJORS
English language and literature
Marketing
Marketing/marketing management

SELECTIVITY
Admissions Rating **78**
# of applicants 5,866
% of applicants accepted 57
% of acceptees attending 29

FRESHMAN PROFILE
Range SAT Verbal 523-642
Average SAT Verbal 607
Range SAT Math 583-681
Average SAT Math 610
Minimum TOEFL 550
Average HS GPA 3.3
% graduated top 10% of class 45
% graduated top 25% of class 91
% graduated top 50% of class 99

DEADLINES
Nonfall registration? yes

FINANCIAL FACTS
Financial Aid Rating **73**
Tuition $21,270
Room and board $8,445
Books and supplies $800
Avg frosh grant $10,940
Avg frosh loan $3,825

SAINT VINCENT COLLEGE

CAMPUS LIFE
Quality of Life Rating **77**
Type of school private
Affiliation Roman Catholic
Environment suburban

STUDENTS
Total undergrad enrollment 1,371
% male/female 50/50
% from out of state 15
% from public high school 77
% live on campus 78
% African American 3
% Asian 1
% Caucasian 92
% Hispanic 1

% international 2
# of countries represented 20

ACADEMICS
Academic Rating **73**
Calendar semester
Student/faculty ratio 14:1
Profs interesting rating 86
Profs accessible rating 84
% profs teaching UG courses 100
% classes taught by TAs 0
Avg regular class size 10-19 students

MOST POPULAR MAJORS
Psychology
Communication
Biology

SELECTIVITY
Admissions Rating **70**
# of applicants 1,013
% of applicants accepted 84
% of acceptees attending 39

FRESHMAN PROFILE
Range SAT Verbal 500-610
Range SAT Math 495-610
Range ACT Composite 22-27
Minimum TOEFL 525
Average HS GPA 3.5
% graduated top 10% of class 30
% graduated top 25% of class 60
% graduated top 50% of class 85

DEADLINES
Regular admission 5/1
Nonfall registration? yes

FINANCIAL FACTS
Financial Aid Rating **75**
Tuition $18,080
Room and board $6,100
Books and supplies $1,500
Avg frosh grant $10,654
Avg frosh loan $2,905

SALISBURY UNIVERSITY

CAMPUS LIFE
Quality of Life Rating **77**
Type of school public
Environment rural

STUDENTS

Total undergrad enrollment	6,206
% male/female	43/57
% from out of state	18
% from public high school	80
% live on campus	32
% in (# of) fraternities	5 (4)
% in (# of) sororities	7 (4)
% African American	8
% Asian	2
% Caucasian	83
% Hispanic	2
% international	1

ACADEMICS

Academic Rating	**77**
Calendar	4-1-4
Student/faculty ratio	17:1
Profs interesting rating	72
Profs accessible rating	73
% profs teaching UG courses	100
% classes taught by TAs	2
Avg lab size	20-29 students
Avg reg class size	20-29 students

MOST POPULAR MAJORS
Business administration/management
Communications studies/speech communication
and rhetoric
Elementary education and teaching

SELECTIVITY

Admissions Rating	**84**
# of applicants	5,298
% of applicants accepted	50
# accepting a place on wait list	762
% admitted from wait list	14
# of early decision applicants	575
% accepted early decision	53

FRESHMAN PROFILE

Range SAT Verbal	520-600
Average SAT Verbal	555
Range SAT Math	530-610
Average SAT Math	571
Minimum TOEFL	595
Average HS GPA	3.4
% graduated top 10% of class	22
% graduated top 25% of class	55
% graduated top 50% of class	87

DEADLINES

Early decision	12/15
Early decision notification	1/15
Regular admission	1/15
Regular notification	3/15
Nonfall registration?	yes

FINANCIAL FACTS

Financial Aid Rating	**84**
In-state tuition	$4,804
Out-of-state tuition	$10,568
Room and board	$6,530
Books and supplies	$675
Required fees	$1,430
% frosh receiving aid	43
% undergrads receiving aid	39

SHENANDOAH UNIVERSITY

CAMPUS LIFE

Quality of Life Rating	**78**
Type of school	private
Affiliation	Methodist
Environment	suburban

STUDENTS

Total undergrad enrollment	1,361
% male/female	43/57
% from out of state	35
% live on campus	54
% African American	9
% Asian	1
% Caucasian	84
% Hispanic	2
% international	4
# of countries represented	21

ACADEMICS

Academic Rating	**73**
Calendar	semester
Student/faculty ratio	10:1
Profs interesting rating	84
Profs accessible rating	81
% profs teaching UG courses	73
% classes taught by TAs	0
Avg lab size	10-19 students
Avg regular class size	under 10 students

MOST POPULAR MAJORS
Business administration/management
Drama and dramatics/theatre arts
Music teacher education

SELECTIVITY
Admissions Rating **70**

# of applicants	1,055
% of applicants accepted	100
% of acceptees attending	30

FRESHMAN PROFILE

Range SAT Verbal	450-570
Average SAT Verbal	514
Range SAT Math	430-550
Average SAT Math	490
Range ACT Composite	16-22
Average ACT Composite	22
Minimum TOEFL	450
Average HS GPA	3.09
% graduated top 10% of class	18
% graduated top 25% of class	40
% graduated top 50% of class	70

DEADLINES

Nonfall registration?	yes

FINANCIAL FACTS
Financial Aid Rating **83**

Tuition	$17,000
Room and board	$6,400
Books and supplies	$1,000
Avg frosh grant	$8,290
Avg frosh loan	$2,898

SHEPHERD COLLEGE

CAMPUS LIFE
Quality of Life Rating **74**

Type of school	public
Affiliation	none
Environment	small town

STUDENTS

Total undergrad enrollment	4,683
% male/female	42/58
% from out of state	34
% from public high school	70
% in (# of) fraternities	2 (4)
% in (# of) sororities	3 (3)
% African American	5
% Asian	1
% Caucasian	91
% Hispanic	2
% international	1
# of countries represented	27

ACADEMICS
Academic Rating **77**

Calendar	semester
Student/faculty ratio	18:1
Profs interesting rating	87
Profs accessible rating	85
% profs teaching UG courses	100
% classes taught by TAs	0
Avg regular class size	10-19 students

MOST POPULAR MAJORS
Business
Education
Recreation

SELECTIVITY
Admissions Rating **79**

# of applicants	1,800
% of applicants accepted	48
% of acceptees attending	55

FRESHMAN PROFILE

Range SAT Verbal	450-560
Average SAT Verbal	497
Range SAT Math	440-550
Average SAT Math	497
Range ACT Composite	18-23
Average ACT Composite	20
Minimum TOEFL	550
Average HS GPA	3.34
% graduated top 10% of class	20
% graduated top 25% of class	85
% graduated top 50% of class	95

DEADLINES

Regular admission	2/1
Regular notification	2/1
Nonfall registration?	yes

FINANCIAL FACTS
Financial Aid Rating **71**

In-state tuition	$2,866
Out-of-state tuition	$6,982
Room and board	$4,738
Books and supplies	$1,000
frosh grant	$3,410

Shippensburg University of Pennsylvania

CAMPUS LIFE
Quality of Life Rating | **76**
Type of school | public
Affiliation | none
Environment | rural

STUDENTS
Total undergrad enrollment | 6,238
% male/female | 46/54
% from out of state | 6
% from public high school | 90
% live on campus | 38
% in (# of) fraternities | 8 (11)
% in (# of) sororities | 9 (9)
% African American | 4
% Asian | 1
% Caucasian | 93
% Hispanic | 1
% international | 1
# of countries represented | 40

ACADEMICS
Academic Rating | **76**
Calendar | semester
Student/faculty ratio | 20:1
Profs interesting rating | 86
Profs accessible rating | 83
% profs teaching UG courses | 90
% classes taught by TAs | 0
Avg lab size | 10-19 students
Avg regular class size | 20-29 students

MOST POPULAR MAJORS
Teacher education
Criminal justice
Management

SELECTIVITY
Admissions Rating | **72**
# of applicants | 6,424
% of applicants accepted | 62
% of acceptees attending | 37

FRESHMAN PROFILE
Range SAT Verbal | 480-570
Average SAT Verbal | 526
Range SAT Math | 490-580
Average SAT Math | 533
% graduated top 10% of class | 13
% graduated top 25% of class | 41
% graduated top 50% of class | 86

DEADLINES
Nonfall registration? | yes

FINANCIAL FACTS
Financial Aid Rating | **70**
In-state tuition | $4,016
Out-of-state tuition | $10,040
Room and board | $4,642
Books and supplies | $750
Avg frosh loan | $2,400

Slippery Rock University of Pennsylvania

CAMPUS LIFE
Quality of Life Rating | **74**
Type of school | public
Affiliation | none
Environment | rural

STUDENTS
Total undergrad enrollment | 6,500
% male/female | 42/58
% from out of state | 4
% from public high school | 80
% live on campus | 40
% in (# of) fraternities | 7 (13)
% in (# of) sororities | 6 (9)
% African American | 3
% Caucasian | 89
% Hispanic | 1
% international | 3
# of countries represented | 65

ACADEMICS
Academic Rating | **68**
Calendar | semester
Student/faculty ratio | 18:1
Profs interesting rating | 82
Profs accessible rating | 80
% profs teaching UG courses | 100
% classes taught by TAs | 0
Avg lab size | 20-29 students
Avg reg class size | 20-29 students

MOST POPULAR MAJORS
Special education
Business/managerial operations
Elementary education and teaching

SELECTIVITY
Admissions Rating	**64**
# of applicants	3,429
% of applicants accepted	81
% of acceptees attending	48

FRESHMAN PROFILE
Range SAT Verbal	430-530
Average SAT Verbal	484
Range SAT Math	420-530
Average SAT Math	477
Range ACT Composite	17-22
Average ACT Composite	20
Minimum TOEFL	500
Average HS GPA	3.0
% graduated top 10% of class	6
% graduated top 25% of class	24
% graduated top 50% of class	60

DEADLINES
Nonfall registration?	yes

FINANCIAL FACTS
Financial Aid Rating	**72**
In-state tuition	$4,016
Out-of-state tuition	$10,040
Room and board	$4,210
Books and supplies	$640
Avg frosh grant	$2,430
Avg frosh loan	$2,900

SUSQUEHANNA UNIVERSITY

CAMPUS LIFE
Quality of Life Rating	**94**
Type of school	private
Affiliation	Lutheran
Environment	rural

STUDENTS
Total undergrad enrollment	1,995
% male/female	42/58
% from out of state	38
% from public high school	86
% live on campus	80
% in (# of) fraternities	25 (4)
% in (# of) sororities	28 (4)

% African American	2
% Asian	2
% Caucasian	93
% Hispanic	2
% international	1

ACADEMICS
Academic Rating	**91**
Calendar	semester
Student/faculty ratio	14:1
Profs interesting rating	93
Profs accessible rating	93
% profs teaching UG courses	100
Avg lab size	10-19 students
Avg reg class size	10-19 students

MOST POPULAR MAJORS
Business administration/management
Communications studies/speech
communication and rhetoric
Biology/biological sciences

SELECTIVITY
Admissions Rating	**81**
# of applicants	2,411
% of applicants accepted	63
% of acceptees attending	33
# accepting a place on wait list	114
% admitted from wait list	11
# of early decision applicants	184
% accepted early decision	76
% admitted from wait list	12

FRESHMAN PROFILE
Range SAT Verbal	530-620
Range SAT Math	540-630
Minimum TOEFL	550
% graduated top 10% of class	38
% graduated top 25% of class	72
% graduated top 50% of class	97

DEADLINES
Early decision	1/1
Early decision notification	1/15
Regular admission	3/1
Nonfall registration?	yes

FINANCIAL FACTS
Financial Aid Rating	**94**
Tuition	$21,930
Room and board	$6,260
Books and supplies	$600
Required fees	$320
% frosh receiving aid	65

% undergrads receiving aid	68
Avg frosh grant	$10,515
Avg frosh loan	$3,300

SWARTHMORE COLLEGE

CAMPUS LIFE
Quality of Life Rating 85
Type of school	private
Environment	suburban

STUDENTS
Total undergrad enrollment	1,479
% from out of state	83
% from public high school	55
% live on campus	93
% in (# of) fraternities	6 (2)
% African American	7
% Asian	16
% Caucasian	54
% Hispanic	9
% international	6

ACADEMICS
Academic Rating 98
Calendar	semester
Student/faculty ratio	8:1
% profs teaching UG courses	100
Avg lab size	10-19 students
Avg reg class size	10-19 students

MOST POPULAR MAJORS
Biology/biological sciences
Economics
Political science and government

SELECTIVITY
Admissions Rating 98
# of applicants	3,886
% of applicants accepted	24
% of acceptees attending	40
# of early decision applicants	360
% accepted early decision	43

FRESHMAN PROFILE
Range SAT Verbal	670-770
Average SAT Verbal	718
Range SAT Math	680-760
Average SAT Math	715
% graduated top 10% of class	90
% graduated top 25% of class	99
% graduated top 50% of class	100

DEADLINES
Early decision I	11/15
Early decision I notification	12/15
Early decision II	1/1
Early decision II notification	2/1
Regular admission	1/1
Regular notification	4/1

FINANCIAL FACTS
Financial Aid Rating 83
Tuition	$27,272
Room and board	$8,530
Books and supplies	$944
Required fees	$290
% frosh receiving aid	48
% undergrads receiving aid	49
Avg frosh grant	$21,656
Avg frosh loan	$1,989

SWEET BRIAR COLLEGE

CAMPUS LIFE
Quality of Life Rating 94
Type of school	private
Environment	rural

STUDENTS
Total undergrad enrollment	688
% male/female	3/97
% from out of state	57
% from public high school	77
% live on campus	89
% African American	4
% American Indian	1
% Asian	3
% Caucasian	86
% Hispanic	3
% international	3
# of countries represented	15

ACADEMICS
Academic Rating 91
Calendar	semester
Student/faculty ratio	8:1
Profs interesting rating	97
Profs accessible rating	99
% profs teaching UG courses	100
Avg reg class size	under 10 students

MOST POPULAR MAJORS
Psychology
English and creative writing
Biology

SELECTIVITY
Admissions Rating **81**
# of applicants 420
% of applicants accepted 86
% of acceptees attending 42
# of early decision applicants 43
% accepted early decision 93

FRESHMAN PROFILE
Range SAT Verbal 530-660
Average SAT Verbal 590
Range SAT Math 490-610
Average SAT Math 550
Range ACT Composite 22-27
Average ACT Composite 24
Minimum TOEFL 580
Average HS GPA 3.5
% graduated top 10% of class 30
% graduated top 25% of class 59
% graduated top 50% of class 90

DEADLINES
Early decision 12/1
Early decision notification 12/15
Regular admission 2/1
Nonfall registration? yes

FINANCIAL FACTS
Financial Aid Rating **94**
Tuition $19,700
Room and board $8,040
Books and supplies $600
Required fees $200
Avg frosh grant $9,093
Avg frosh loan $3,002

TEMPLE UNIVERSITY

CAMPUS LIFE
Quality of Life Rating **81**
Type of school public
Environment urban

STUDENTS
Total undergrad enrollment 21,429
% male/female 42/58

% from out of state 25
% from public high school 78
% live on campus 27
% in (# of) fraternities 1 (13)
% in (# of) sororities 1 (12)
% African American 23
% Asian 8
% Caucasian 57
% Hispanic 4
% international 4
# of countries represented 130

ACADEMICS
Academic Rating **72**
Calendar semester
Student/faculty ratio 14:1
Avg lab size 20-29 students
Avg reg class size 20-29 students

MOST POPULAR MAJORS
Elementary education and teaching
Journalism
Psychology

SELECTIVITY
Admissions Rating **79**
# of applicants 15,288
% of applicants accepted 61
% of acceptees attending 39

FRESHMAN PROFILE
Range SAT Verbal 490-590
Average SAT Verbal 536
Range SAT Math 490-590
Average SAT Math 532
Range ACT Composite 19-24
Minimum TOEFL 525
Average HS GPA 3.2
% graduated top 10% of class 20
% graduated top 25% of class 50
% graduated top 50% of class 88

DEADLINES
Regular admission 4/1
Nonfall registration? yes

FINANCIAL FACTS
Financial Aid Rating **75**
In-state tuition $7,602
Out-of-state tuition $13,856
Room and board $7,112
Books and supplies $800
Required fees $460

% frosh receiving aid	70
% undergrads receiving aid	67

THIEL COLLEGE

CAMPUS LIFE
Quality of Life Rating **73**

Type of school	private
Affiliation	Lutheran
Environment	rural

STUDENTS

Total undergrad enrollment	1,279
% male/female	50/50
% from out of state	26
% from public high school	88
% live on campus	82
% in (# of) fraternities	10 (5)
% in (# of) sororities	19 (4)
% African American	8
% Asian	1
% Caucasian	75
% Hispanic	1
% international	4
# of countries represented	13

ACADEMICS
Academic Rating **71**

Calendar	semester
Student/faculty ratio	15:1
Profs interesting rating	86
Profs accessible rating	80
% profs teaching UG courses	100
% classes taught by TAs	0
Avg lab size	10-19 students
Avg reg class size	under 10 students

MOST POPULAR MAJORS
Psychology
Math/computer science
Business administration/management

SELECTIVITY
Admissions Rating **64**

# of applicants	1,537
% of applicants accepted	81
% of acceptees attending	32

FRESHMAN PROFILE

Range SAT Verbal	420-540
Average SAT Verbal	485
Range SAT Math	420-550

Average SAT Math	488
Range ACT Composite	17-23
Average ACT Composite	20
Minimum TOEFL	500
Average HS GPA	3
% graduated top 10% of class	9
% graduated top 25% of class	27
% graduated top 50% of class	64

DEADLINES

Regular admission	8/15
Nonfall registration?	yes

FINANCIAL FACTS
Financial Aid Rating **85**

Tuition	$12,672
Room and board	$6,454
Books and supplies	$700
Avg frosh grant	$8,189
Avg frosh loan	$4,600

TOWSON UNIVERSITY

CAMPUS LIFE
Quality of Life Rating **78**

Type of school	public
Affiliation	none
Environment	urban

STUDENTS

Total undergrad enrollment	13,959
% male/female	40/60
% from out of state	18
% live on campus	25
% in (# of) fraternities	7 (13)
% in (# of) sororities	6 (11)
% African American	10
% Asian	3
% Caucasian	78
% Hispanic	2
% international	2

ACADEMICS
Academic Rating **70**

Calendar	semester
Student/faculty ratio	17:1
Profs interesting rating	83
Profs accessible rating	80
% classes taught by TAs	0
Avg lab size	under 10 students
Avg reg class size	20-29 students

MOST POPULAR MAJORS
Business administration
Mass communication
Psychology

SELECTIVITY
Admissions Rating **63**

# of applicants	9,448
% of applicants accepted	59
% of acceptees attending	35
# accepting a place on wait list	105
% admitted from wait list	48

FRESHMAN PROFILE

Range SAT Verbal	490-580
Average SAT Verbal	544
Range SAT Math	510-590
Average SAT Math	551
Average ACT Composite	22
Average HS GPA	3.4
% graduated top 10% of class	16
% graduated top 25% of class	48
% graduated top 50% of class	85

DEADLINES

Regular admission	5/1
Nonfall registration?	yes

FINANCIAL FACTS
Financial Aid Rating **68**

Room and board	$6,030
Books and supplies	$790
Avg frosh grant	$4,514
Avg frosh loan	$2,577

UNITED STATES NAVAL ACADEMY

CAMPUS LIFE
Quality of Life Rating **84**

Type of school	public
Environment	suburban

STUDENTS

Total undergrad enrollment	4,309
% from out of state	94
% from public high school	60
% live on campus	100
% African American	6
% Asian	4
% Caucasian	80

% Hispanic	8
% international	1
# of countries represented	24

ACADEMICS
Academic Rating **99**

Calendar	semester
Student/faculty ratio	7:1
Profs interesting rating	94
Profs accessible rating	100
% profs teaching UG courses	100
Avg reg class size	10-19 students

MOST POPULAR MAJORS
Systems engineering
Economics
Political science and government

SELECTIVITY
Admissions Rating **99**

# of applicants	12,331
% of applicants accepted	12
% of acceptees attending	83

FRESHMAN PROFILE

Range SAT Verbal	530-640
Average SAT Verbal	637
Range SAT Math	560-670
Average SAT Math	663
Minimum TOEFL	500
% graduated top 10% of class	57
% graduated top 25% of class	84
% graduated top 50% of class	96

DEADLINES

Regular admission	2/15

FINANCIAL FACTS
Financial Aid Rating **99**

UNIVERSITY OF DELAWARE

CAMPUS LIFE
Quality of Life Rating **84**

Type of school	public
Environment	suburban

STUDENTS

Total undergrad enrollment	17,486
% male/female	42/58
% from out of state	59
% from public high school	80

% live on campus	48
% in (# of) fraternities	15 (15)
% in (# of) sororities	15 (15)
% African American	5
% Asian	3
% Caucasian	88
% Hispanic	3
% international	1
# of countries represented	100

ACADEMICS
Academic Rating **79**

Calendar	4-1-4
Student/faculty ratio	12:1
Profs interesting rating	90
Profs accessible rating	96
% profs teaching UG courses	95
% classes taught by TAs	5
Avg lab size	20-29 students
Avg reg class size	20-29 students

SELECTIVITY
Admissions Rating **83**

# of applicants	20,365
% of applicants accepted	48
% of acceptees attending	35
# accepting a place on wait list	1,578
% admitted from wait list	3
# of early decision applicants	1,256
% accepted early decision	49

FRESHMAN PROFILE
Range SAT Verbal	530-620
Range SAT Math	550-650
Range ACT Composite	22-27
Minimum TOEFL	550
Average HS GPA	3.5
% graduated top 10% of class	34
% graduated top 25% of class	75
% graduated top 50% of class	97

DEADLINES
Early decision	11/15
Early decision notification	12/15
Priority admission	1/15
Regular admission	2/15
Regular notification	3/15
Nonfall registration?	yes

FINANCIAL FACTS
Financial Aid Rating **83**

In-state tuition	$5,190
Out-of-state tuition	$14,720

Room and board	$5,822
Books and supplies	$800
Required fees	$570
% frosh receiving aid	43
% undergrads receiving aid	37
Avg frosh grant	$4,200
Avg frosh loan	$3,500

UNIVERSITY OF MARYLAND, BALTIMORE COUNTY

CAMPUS LIFE
Quality of Life Rating **76**

Type of school	public
Environment	suburban

STUDENTS
Total undergrad enrollment	9,549
% male/female	52/48
% from out of state	8
% from public high school	84
% live on campus	33
% in (# of) fraternities	3 (11)
% in (# of) sororities	3 (10)
% African American	15
% Asian	16
% Caucasian	56
% Hispanic	3
% international	5

ACADEMICS
Academic Rating **74**

Calendar	4-1-4
Student/faculty ratio	17:1
Profs interesting rating	73
Profs accessible rating	77
% profs teaching UG courses	100
% classes taught by TAs	2
Avg lab size	10-19 students
Avg reg class size	10-19 students

MOST POPULAR MAJORS
Information technology
Psychology
Visual and performing arts

SELECTIVITY
Admissions Rating **80**

# of applicants	5,211
% of applicants accepted	63

% of acceptees attending	41	% Asian	14
# accepting a place on wait list	300	% Caucasian	59
% admitted from wait list	13	% Hispanic	5
		% international	3

FRESHMAN PROFILE

		## ACADEMICS	
Range SAT Verbal	540-640	**Academic Rating**	**75**
Average SAT Verbal	592	Calendar	semester
Range SAT Math	570-670	Student/faculty ratio	13:1
Average SAT Math	621	Profs interesting rating	89
Range ACT Composite	23-28	Profs accessible rating	90
Average ACT Composite	25	Avg lab size	20-29 students
Minimum TOEFL	220	Avg reg class size	20-29 students
Average HS GPA	3.5		
% graduated top 10% of class	30		
% graduated top 25% of class	60		
% graduated top 50% of class	90		

MOST POPULAR MAJORS
Political science and government
Criminology
Computer science

DEADLINES

		## SELECTIVITY	
Priority admission	11/1	**Admissions Rating**	**81**
Regular admission	2/1	# of applicants	23,117
Nonfall registration?	yes	% of applicants accepted	43
		% of acceptees attending	39
		# accepting a place on wait list	1,816
		% admitted from wait list	28

FINANCIAL FACTS

Financial Aid Rating	**83**	## FRESHMAN PROFILE	
In-state tuition	$4,614	Range SAT Verbal	570-670
Out-of-state tuition	$10,798	Range SAT Math	600-700
Room and board	$6,780	Minimum TOEFL	575
Books and supplies	$800	Average HS GPA	3.9
Required fees	$1,748	% graduated top 10% of class	58
% frosh receiving aid	53	% graduated top 25% of class	90
% undergrads receiving aid	54	% graduated top 50% of class	100
Avg frosh grant	$6,212		
Avg frosh loan	$2,566		

UNIVERSITY OF MARYLAND, COLLEGE PARK

DEADLINES

Priority admission	12/1
Regular admission	1/20
Nonfall registration?	yes

CAMPUS LIFE

Quality of Life Rating	**69**	## FINANCIAL FACTS	
Type of school	public	**Financial Aid Rating**	**82**
Environment	suburban	In-state tuition	$4,572
		Out-of-state tuition	$13,336

STUDENTS

Total undergrad enrollment	25,179	Room and board	$7,241
% male/female	51/49	Books and supplies	$808
% from out of state	25	Required fees	$1,098
% live on campus	39	% frosh receiving aid	40
% in (# of) fraternities	9 (27)	% undergrads receiving aid	40
% in (# of) sororities	10 (20)	Avg frosh grant	$4,858
% African American	13	Avg frosh loan	$3,301

UNIVERSITY OF PENNSYLVANIA

CAMPUS LIFE
Quality of Life Rating   **85**
Type of school   private
Environment   urban

STUDENTS
Total undergrad enrollment	9,742
% male/female	51/49
% from out of state	81
% from public high school	56
% live on campus	96
% in (# of) fraternities	11 (34)
% in (# of) sororities	8 (10)
% African American	6
% Asian	18
% Caucasian	50
% Hispanic	6
% international	9

ACADEMICS
Academic Rating	**97**
Calendar	semester
Student/faculty ratio	6:1
Profs interesting rating	91
Profs accessible rating	96
Avg reg class size	10-19 students

MOST POPULAR MAJORS
Finance
Psychology
Economics

SELECTIVITY
Admissions Rating	**99**
# of applicants	18,784
% of applicants accepted	21
% of acceptees attending	62
# accepting a place on wait list	152
% admitted from wait list	14
# of early decision applicants	3,037
% accepted early decision	39

FRESHMAN PROFILE
Range SAT Verbal	650-740
Average SAT Verbal	688
Range SAT Math	680-760
Average SAT Math	716
Range ACT Composite	28-32
Average ACT Composite	30

Minimum TOEFL	600
Average HS GPA	3.8
% graduated top 10% of class	91
% graduated top 25% of class	98
% graduated top 50% of class	100

DEADLINES
Early decision	11/1
Early decision notification	12/15
Regular admission	1/1
Regular notification	4/1

FINANCIAL FACTS
Financial Aid Rating	**83**
Tuition	$25,078
Room and board	$8,224
Books and supplies	$760
Required fees	$2,910
% frosh receiving aid	41
% undergrads receiving aid	42
Avg frosh grant	$24,285

UNIVERSITY OF PITTSBURGH—JOHNSTOWN

CAMPUS LIFE
Quality of Life Rating   **72**
Type of school   public
Affiliation   none
Environment   rural

STUDENTS
Total undergrad enrollment	3,096
% male/female	47/53
% live on campus	63
% in (# of) fraternities	10 (4)
% in (# of) sororities	9 (5)
% African American	1
% Asian	1
% Caucasian	97

ACADEMICS
Academic Rating	**73**
Calendar	semester
Student/faculty ratio	19:1
Profs interesting rating	80
Profs accessible rating	82
% profs teaching UG courses	100
% classes taught by TAs	0
Avg lab size	10-19 students
Avg reg class size	20-29 students

MOST POPULAR MAJORS
Business
Elementary education
Biology

% Asian	4
% Caucasian	82
% Hispanic	1
% international	1

SELECTIVITY
Admissions Rating	**70**
# of applicants	2,156
% of applicants accepted	85
% of acceptees attending	48

ACADEMICS
Academic Rating	**78**
Calendar	semester
Student/faculty ratio	17:1
Avg lab size	20-29 students
Avg reg class size	10-19 students

FRESHMAN PROFILE
Range SAT Verbal	460-560
Average SAT Verbal	515
Range SAT Math	450-550
Average SAT Math	506
Range ACT Composite	18-24
Minimum TOEFL	550
Average HS GPA	3.2
% graduated top 10% of class	11
% graduated top 25% of class	32
% graduated top 50% of class	72

DEADLINES
Nonfall registration?	yes

FINANCIAL FACTS
Financial Aid Rating	**73**
In-state tuition	$6,902
Out-of-state tuition	$15,160
Room and board	$5,510
Books and supplies	$900
Avg frosh grant	$2,924
Avg frosh loan	$2,921

SELECTIVITY
Admissions Rating	**84**
# of applicants	15,888
% of applicants accepted	55
% of acceptees attending	36

FRESHMAN PROFILE
Range SAT Verbal	540-640
Average SAT Verbal	595
Range SAT Math	560-650
Average SAT Math	607
Range ACT Composite	24-29
Average ACT Composite	26
Minimum TOEFL	500
% graduated top 10% of class	39
% graduated top 25% of class	74
% graduated top 50% of class	97

DEADLINES
Priority admission	3/1
Nonfall registration?	yes

FINANCIAL FACTS
Financial Aid Rating	**80**
In-state tuition	$7,868
Out-of-state tuition	$16,676
Room and board	$6,470
Books and supplies	$700
Required fees	$660
% frosh receiving aid	56
% undergrads receiving aid	55

UNIVERSITY OF PITTSBURGH—PITTSBURGH

CAMPUS LIFE
Quality of Life Rating	**88**
Type of school	public
Environment	urban

STUDENTS
Total undergrad enrollment	17,910
% male/female	48/52
% from out of state	15
% live on campus	42
% in (# of) fraternities	10 (21)
% in (# of) sororities	7 (15)
% African American	9

UNIVERSITY OF RICHMOND

CAMPUS LIFE
Quality of Life Rating	**96**
Type of school	private
Environment	suburban

STUDENTS

Total undergrad enrollment	2,998
% male/female	47/53
% from out of state	84
% from public high school	70
% live on campus	92
% in (# of) fraternities	32 (8)
% in (# of) sororities	49 (8)
% African American	5
% Asian	4
% Caucasian	89
% Hispanic	2
% international	6
# of countries represented	70

ACADEMICS

Academic Rating	**90**
Calendar	semester
Student/faculty ratio	10:1
Profs interesting rating	95
Profs accessible rating	99
% profs teaching UG courses	100
Avg reg class size	20-29 students

MOST POPULAR MAJORS
Business administration/management
Biology/biological sciences
Political science and government

SELECTIVITY

Admissions Rating	**91**
# of applicants	5,895
% of applicants accepted	41
% of acceptees attending	33
# accepting a place on wait list	961
# of early decision applicants	366
% accepted early decision	54

FRESHMAN PROFILE

Range SAT Verbal	600-690
Range SAT Math	620-700
Range ACT Composite	27-30
Minimum TOEFL	550
% graduated top 10% of class	55
% graduated top 25% of class	95
% graduated top 50% of class	99

DEADLINES

Early decision	11/15
Early decision notification	12/15
Regular admission	1/15
Regular notification	4/1

FINANCIAL FACTS

Financial Aid Rating	**83**
Tuition	$23,730
Room and board	$5,160
Books and supplies	$1,000
% frosh receiving aid	34
% undergrads receiving aid	30

UNIVERSITY OF SCRANTON

CAMPUS LIFE

Quality of Life Rating	**77**
Type of school	private
Affiliation	Roman Catholic
Environment	urban

STUDENTS

Total undergrad enrollment	4,060
% male/female	42/58
% from out of state	48
% from public high school	52
% live on campus	47
% African American	1
% Asian	2
% Caucasian	87
% Hispanic	3
% international	1

ACADEMICS

Academic Rating	**77**
Calendar	semester
Student/faculty ratio	13:1
Profs interesting rating	80
Profs accessible rating	84
% profs teaching UG courses	98
Avg lab size	10-19 students
Avg reg class size	10-19 students

ADMISSIONS

Admissions Rating	**85**
# of applicants	5,121
% of applicants accepted	70
% of acceptees attending	27
# accepting a place on wait list	430
% admitted from wait list	17

FRESHMAN PROFILE

Range SAT Verbal	510-610
Average SAT Verbal	565
Range SAT Math	520-620
Average SAT Math	562

Minimum TOEFL	500
Average HS GPA	3.4
% graduated top 10% of class	30
% graduated top 25% of class	64
% graduated top 50% of class	91

DEADLINES

Regular admission	3/1
Nonfall registration?	yes

FINANCIAL FACTS

Financial Aid Rating	**79**
Tuition	$20,248
Room and board	$8,770
Books and supplies	$900
Required fees	$200
Avg frosh grant	$10,217
Avg frosh loan	$3,300

UNIVERSITY OF VIRGINIA— CHARLOTTESVILLE

CAMPUS LIFE

Quality of Life Rating	**90**
Type of school	public
Environment	suburban

STUDENTS

Total undergrad enrollment	13,805
% male/female	46/54
% from out of state	28
% from public high school	75
% live on campus	46
% in (# of) fraternities	30 (32)
% in (# of) sororities	30 (22)
% African American	10
% Asian	11
% Caucasian	73
% Hispanic	3
% international	4
# of countries represented	97

ACADEMICS

Academic Rating	**93**
Calendar	semester
Student/faculty ratio	16:1
Profs interesting rating	77
Profs accessible rating	79
% classes taught by TAs	18
Avg lab size	10-19 students
Avg reg class size	10-19 students

MOST POPULAR MAJORS

Business/commerce
Psychology
Economics

SELECTIVITY

Admissions Rating	**94**
# of applicants	14,320
% of applicants accepted	39
% of acceptees attending	54
# accepting a place on wait list	1,157
% admitted from wait list	13
# of early decision applicants	2,384
% accepted early decision	40

FRESHMAN PROFILE

Range SAT Verbal	600-700
Average SAT Verbal	647
Range SAT Math	620-720
Average SAT Math	668
Range ACT Composite	25-31
Average ACT Composite	28
Minimum TOEFL	600
Average HS GPA	4.0
% graduated top 10% of class	84
% graduated top 25% of class	97
% graduated top 50% of class	99

DEADLINES

Early decision	11/1
Early decision notification	12/1
Regular admission	1/2
Regular notification	4/1

FINANCIAL FACTS

Financial Aid Rating	**88**
In-state tuition	$4,584
Out-of-state tuition	$20,604
Room and board	$5,591
Books and supplies	$900
Required fees	$1,565
% undergrads receiving aid	22

URSINUS COLLEGE

CAMPUS LIFE

Quality of Life Rating	**79**
Type of school	private
Environment	suburban

STUDENTS

Total undergrad enrollment	1,324

% male/female	43/57
% from out of state	36
% from public high school	68
% live on campus	91
% in (# of) fraternities	15 (9)
% in (# of) sororities	25 (5)
% African American	8
% Asian	4
% Caucasian	86
% Hispanic	2
% international	3

ACADEMICS

Academic Rating	**81**
Calendar	semester
Student/faculty ratio	11:1
Profs interesting rating	92
Profs accessible rating	91
% profs teaching UG courses	100
Avg lab size	10-19 students
Avg reg class size	under 10 students

MOST POPULAR MAJORS
Biology/biological sciences
Psychology
Economics

SELECTIVITY

Admissions Rating	**80**
# of applicants	1,547
% of applicants accepted	78
% of acceptees attending	36
# accepting a place on wait list	12
# of early decision applicants	199
% accepted early decision	80

FRESHMAN PROFILE

Range SAT Verbal	540-640
Average SAT Verbal	595
Range SAT Math	550-650
Average SAT Math	598
Minimum TOEFL	550
Average HS GPA	3.5
% graduated top 10% of class	40
% graduated top 25% of class	80
% graduated top 50% of class	94

DEADLINES

Early decision	1/15
Early decision notification	1/31
Priority admission	2/15
Regular admission	2/15
Regular notification	4/1
Nonfall registration?	yes

FINANCIAL FACTS

Financial Aid Rating	**89**
Tuition	$26,200
Room and board	$6,600
Books and supplies	$600
% frosh receiving aid	78
% undergrads receiving aid	75

VILLANOVA UNIVERSITY

CAMPUS LIFE

Quality of Life Rating	**87**
Type of school	private
Affiliation	Roman Catholic
Environment	suburban

STUDENTS

Total undergrad enrollment	7,375
% male/female	49/51
% from out of state	66
% from public high school	55
% live on campus	67
% in (# of) fraternities	6 (7)
% in (# of) sororities	25 (8)
% African American	3
% Asian	5
% Caucasian	85
% Hispanic	6
% international	2

ACADEMICS

Academic Rating	**82**
Calendar	semester
Student/faculty ratio	13:1
% profs teaching UG courses	100
Avg lab size	10-19 students
Avg reg class size	10-19 students

MOST POPULAR MAJORS
Biology/biological sciences
Psychology
Finance

SELECTIVITY

Admissions Rating	**83**
# of applicants	10,897
% of applicants accepted	47
% of acceptees attending	31
# accepting a place on wait list	2,212
% admitted from wait list	20

FRESHMAN PROFILE

Range SAT Verbal	580-650
Average SAT Verbal	605
Range SAT Math	610-680
Average SAT Math	633
Average ACT Composite	27
Minimum TOEFL	550
Average HS GPA	3.6
% graduated top 10% of class	41
% graduated top 25% of class	57
% graduated top 50% of class	96

DEADLINES

Regular admission	1/7
Regular notification	4/1

FINANCIAL FACTS

Financial Aid Rating	**79**
Tuition	$23,540
Room and board	$8,330
Required fees	$550
Books and supplies	$800

VIRGINIA COMMONWEALTH UNIVERSITY

CAMPUS LIFE

Quality of Life Rating	**78**
Type of school	public
Affiliation	none
Environment	urban

STUDENTS

Total undergrad enrollment	17,148
% male/female	41/59
% from out of state	5
% from public high school	97
% live on campus	21
% in (# of) fraternities	6 (11)
% in (# of) sororities	3 (9)
% African American	23
% Asian	8
% Caucasian	63
% Hispanic	3
% international	1
# of countries represented	62

ACADEMICS

Academic Rating	**72**
Calendar	semester
Student/faculty ratio	13:1

Profs interesting rating	84
Profs accessible rating	81
Avg lab size	10-19 students
Avg reg class size	10-19 students

MOST POPULAR MAJORS
Communications, journalism, and related fields
Psychology
Biological and physical sciences

SELECTIVITY

Admissions Rating	**61**
# of applicants	7,926
% of applicants accepted	74
% of acceptees attending	47
# of early decision applicants	166
% accepted early decision	56

FRESHMAN PROFILE

Range SAT Verbal	470-580
Average SAT Verbal	520
Range SAT Math	450-570
Average SAT Math	510
Range ACT Composite	18-23
Minimum TOEFL	550
Average HS GPA	3.1
% graduated top 10% of class	13
% graduated top 25% of class	37
% graduated top 50% of class	78

DEADLINES

Early decision	11/1
Nonfall registration?	yes

FINANCIAL FACTS

Financial Aid Rating	**67**
In-state tuition	$2,492
Out-of-state tuition	$11,946
Room and board	$4,839
Books and supplies	$800
Avg frosh grant	$4,010
Avg frosh loan	$3,122

VIRGINIA MILITARY INSTITUTE

CAMPUS LIFE

Quality of Life Rating	**80**
Type of school	public
Affiliation	none
Environment	rural

STUDENTS

Total undergrad enrollment	1,311
% from out of state	47
% from public high school	84
% live on campus	100
% African American	5
% Asian	4
% Caucasian	84
% Hispanic	3
% international	3

ACADEMICS

Academic Rating	**79**
Calendar	semester
Student/faculty ratio	11:1
Profs interesting rating	80
Profs accessible rating	74
% profs teaching UG courses	100
% classes taught by TAs	0
Avg lab size	under 10 students
Avg reg class size	10-19 students

MOST POPULAR MAJORS
History
Business/managerial economics
Mechanical engineering

SELECTIVITY

Admissions Rating	**74**
# of applicants	1,349
% of applicants accepted	63
% of acceptees attending	48
# accepting a place on wait list	73
# of early decision applicants	213
% accepted early decision	73

FRESHMAN PROFILE

Range SAT Verbal	520-610
Average SAT Verbal	570
Range SAT Math	520-610
Average SAT Math	564
Range ACT Composite	21-25
Average ACT Composite	23
Minimum TOEFL	500
Average HS GPA	3.3
% graduated top 10% of class	10
% graduated top 25% of class	44
% graduated top 50% of class	85

DEADLINES

Early decision	11/15
Regular admission	3/1

FINANCIAL FACTS

Financial Aid Rating	**75**
In-state tuition	$2,924
Out-of-state tuition	$13,993
Room and board	$4,838
Books and supplies	$650
Avg frosh grant	$10,243
Avg frosh loan	$3,012

VIRGINIA TECH

CAMPUS LIFE

Quality of Life Rating	**86**
Type of school	public
Environment	rural

STUDENTS

Total undergrad enrollment	21,468
% male/female	59/41
% from out of state	27
% from public high school	95
% live on campus	39
% in (# of) fraternities	13 (34)
% in (# of) sororities	15 (16)
% African American	6
% Asian	7
% Caucasian	82
% Hispanic	2
% international	3

ACADEMICS

Academic Rating	**81**
Calendar	semester
Student/faculty ratio	17:1
% profs teaching UG courses	75

MOST POPULAR MAJORS
Communications studies/speech
communication and rhetoric
Engineering
Biology/biological sciences

SELECTIVITY

Admissions Rating	**84**
# of applicants	18,321
% of applicants accepted	65
% of acceptees attending	41

# accepting a place on wait list	500
% admitted from wait list	0
# of early decision applicants	2,250
% accepted early decision	20

FRESHMAN PROFILE

Range SAT Verbal	540-630
Average SAT Verbal	600
Range SAT Math	570-650
Average SAT Math	650
Minimum TOEFL	550
Average HS GPA	3.6
% graduated top 10% of class	40
% graduated top 25% of class	80
% graduated top 50% of class	99

DEADLINES

Early decision	11/1
Early decision notification	12/15
Regular admission	1/15
Regular notification	4/1
Nonfall registration?	yes

FINANCIAL FACTS

Financial Aid Rating	**82**
In-state tuition	$5,095
Out-of-state tuition	$15,029
Room and board	$4,084
Books and supplies	$900
Required fees	$905
% frosh receiving aid	43
% undergrads receiving aid	45
Avg frosh grant	$9,030
Avg frosh loan	$11,625

WASHINGTON & JEFFERSON COLLEGE

CAMPUS LIFE

Quality of Life Rating	**81**
Type of school	private
Affiliation	none
Environment	suburban

STUDENTS

Total undergrad enrollment	1,209
% male/female	52/48
% from out of state	19
% from public high school	85
% live on campus	80

% in (# of) fraternities	45 (7)
% in (# of) sororities	48 (4)
% African American	2
% Asian	2
% Caucasian	91
% Hispanic	1
% international	1
# of countries represented	7

ACADEMICS

Academic Rating	**84**
Calendar	4-1-4
Student/faculty ratio	12:1
Profs interesting rating	80
Profs accessible rating	78
% profs teaching UG courses	100
% classes taught by TAs	0
Avg lab size	10-19 students
Avg reg class size	10-19 students

MOST POPULAR MAJORS
Psychology
Accounting
Business administration/management

SELECTIVITY

Admissions Rating	**77**
# of applicants	1,874
% of applicants accepted	51
% of acceptees attending	35
# of early decision applicants	52
% accepted early decision	68

FRESHMAN PROFILE

Range SAT Verbal	500-600
Average SAT Verbal	545
Range SAT Math	500-610
Average SAT Math	552
Range ACT Composite	21-26
Average ACT Composite	24
Minimum TOEFL	500
Average HS GPA	3.18
% graduated top 10% of class	28
% graduated top 25% of class	54
% graduated top 50% of class	84

DEADLINES

Early decision	12/1
Regular admission	3/1
Nonfall registration?	yes

FINANCIAL FACTS

Financial Aid Rating	**84**

Tuition	$21,258
Room and board	$5,992
Books and supplies	$600
Avg frosh grant	$18,411
Avg frosh loan	$3,534

WASHINGTON AND LEE UNIVERSITY

CAMPUS LIFE
Quality of Life Rating	**92**
Type of school	private
Environment	suburban

STUDENTS
Total undergrad enrollment	1,750
% male/female	53/47
% from out of state	82
% live on campus	64
% in (# of) fraternities	80 (15)
% in (# of) sororities	72 (5)
% African American	4
% Asian	2
% Caucasian	92
% Hispanic	1
% international	4
# of countries represented	47

ACADEMICS
Academic Rating	**96**
Calendar	differs by program
Student/faculty ratio	11:1
Profs interesting rating	98
Profs accessible rating	99
% profs teaching UG courses	100
Avg lab size	under 10 students
Avg reg class size	10-19 students

MOST POPULAR MAJORS
Business administration/management
Journalism
Economics

SELECTIVITY
Admissions Rating	**99**
# of applicants	3,188
% of applicants accepted	31
% of acceptees attending	46
# accepting a place on wait list	268
% admitted from wait list	13

# of early decision applicants	402
% accepted early decision	55

FRESHMAN PROFILE
Range SAT Verbal	640-720
Range SAT Math	640-720
Range ACT Composite	28-30
Average HS GPA	4.0
% graduated top 10% of class	80
% graduated top 25% of class	96
% graduated top 50% of class	100

DEADLINES
Early decision	12/1
Early decision notification	12/22
Regular admission	1/15
Regular notification	4/1

FINANCIAL FACTS
Financial Aid Rating	**86**
Tuition	$22,900
Room and board	$6,205
Books and supplies	$1,480
Required fees	$195
% frosh receiving aid	26
% undergrads receiving aid	27

WASHINGTON COLLEGE

CAMPUS LIFE
Quality of Life Rating	**77**
Type of school	private
Affiliation	none
Environment	rural

STUDENTS
Total undergrad enrollment	1,208
% male/female	38/62
% from out of state	51
% from public high school	67
% live on campus	80
% in (# of) fraternities	20 (3)
% in (# of) sororities	20 (3)
% African American	3
% Asian	2
% Caucasian	82
% Hispanic	1
% international	5
# of countries represented	37

ACADEMICS
Academic Rating	**85**
Calendar	semester
Student/faculty ratio	12:1
Profs interesting rating	79
Profs accessible rating	76
% profs teaching UG courses	98
% classes taught by TAs	0
Avg lab size	10-19 students
Avg reg class size	10-19 students

MOST POPULAR MAJORS
English/language arts teacher education
Environmental studies
Business administration/management

SELECTIVITY
Admissions Rating	**75**
# of applicants	1,914
% of applicants accepted	73
% of acceptees attending	24
# accepting a place on wait list	110
% admitted from wait list	4
# of early decision applicants	22
% accepted early decision	86

FRESHMAN PROFILE
Range SAT Verbal	530-630
Average SAT Verbal	578
Range SAT Math	520-620
Average SAT Math	567
Range ACT Composite	20-26
Minimum TOEFL	500
Average HS GPA	3.4
% graduated top 10% of class	42
% graduated top 25% of class	71
% graduated top 50% of class	93

DEADLINES
Early decision	11/15
Regular admission	2/15
Nonfall registration?	yes

FINANCIAL FACTS
Financial Aid Rating	**75**
Tuition	$22,740
Room and board	$5,740
Books and supplies	$1,500
Avg frosh grant	$13,892
Avg frosh loan	$2,625

WEST CHESTER UNIVERSITY OF PENNSYLVANIA

CAMPUS LIFE
Quality of Life Rating	**73**
Type of school	public
Affiliation	none
Environment	suburban

STUDENTS
Total undergrad enrollment	10,220
% male/female	40/60
% from out of state	11
% from public high school	60
% live on campus	37
% in (# of) fraternities	10 (13)
% in (# of) sororities	10 (12)
% African American	8
% Asian	2
% Caucasian	87
% Hispanic	2

ACADEMICS
Academic Rating	**62**
Calendar	semester
Student/faculty ratio	17:1
Profs interesting rating	83
Profs accessible rating	80
% profs teaching UG courses	90
% classes taught by TAs	0
Avg regular class size	20-29 students

MOST POPULAR MAJORS
Psychology
Early childhood education and teaching
Elementary education and teaching

SELECTIVITY
Admissions Rating	**60**
# of applicants	8,851
% of applicants accepted	48
% of acceptees attending	38
# accepting a place on wait list	226

FRESHMAN PROFILE
Range SAT Verbal	480-540
Average SAT Verbal	522
Range SAT Math	480-570
Average SAT Math	525
Minimum TOEFL	550
Average HS GPA	3.23

% graduated top 10% of class	10
% graduated top 25% of class	34
% graduated top 50% of class	78

DEADLINES

Regular admission	4/1
Nonfall registration?	yes

FINANCIAL FACTS
Financial Aid Rating **70**

In-state tuition	$4,378
Out-of-state tuition	$10,946
Room and board	$5,146
Books and supplies	$600
Avg frosh grant	$1,604
Avg frosh loan	$3,068

WEST VIRGINIA UNIVERSITY

CAMPUS LIFE
Quality of Life Rating **73**

Type of school	public
Environment	suburban

STUDENTS

Total undergrad enrollment	16,692
% male/female	54/46
% from out of state	38
% live on campus	21
% in (# of) fraternities	9 (17)
% in (# of) sororities	9 (14)
% African American	4
% Asian	2
% Caucasian	92
% Hispanic	1
% international	2
# of countries represented	90

ACADEMICS
Academic Rating **64**

Calendar	semester
Student/faculty ratio	19:1
Profs interesting rating	91
Profs accessible rating	94
Avg lab size	20-29 students
Avg reg class size	20-29 students

MOST POPULAR MAJORS
Engineering
Psychology
Business administration/management

SELECTIVITY
Admissions Rating **75**

# of applicants	9,147
% of applicants accepted	94
% of acceptees attending	46

FRESHMAN PROFILE

Range SAT Verbal	460-560
Average SAT Verbal	514
Range SAT Math	470-580
Average SAT Math	528
Range ACT Composite	20-25
Average ACT Composite	23
Minimum TOEFL	550
Average HS GPA	3.2
% graduated top 10% of class	19
% graduated top 25% of class	43
% graduated top 50% of class	74

DEADLINES

Priority admission	3/1
Regular admission	8/1
Nonfall registration?	yes

FINANCIAL FACTS
Financial Aid Rating **82**

In-state tuition	$3,240
Out-of-state tuition	$9,710
Room and board	$5,572
Books and supplies	$727
% frosh receiving aid	38
% undergrads receiving aid	46

WEST VIRGINIA WESLEYAN COLLEGE

CAMPUS LIFE
Quality of Life Rating **79**

Type of school	private
Affiliation	Methodist
Environment	rural

STUDENTS

Total undergrad enrollment	1,530
% male/female	45/55
% from out of state	52
% live on campus	85
% in (# of) fraternities	24 (6)
% in (# of) sororities	25 (5)
% African American	5

% Asian	1
% Caucasian	88
% Hispanic	1
% international	4

ACADEMICS
Academic Rating 80
Calendar	semester
Student/faculty ratio	14:1
Profs interesting rating	80
Profs accessible rating	77
% profs teaching UG courses	100
% classes taught by TAs	0
Avg lab size	25 students
Avg reg class size	12-23 students

MOST POPULAR MAJORS
Business
Education

SELECTIVITY
Admissions Rating 71
# of applicants	1,362
% of applicants accepted	83
% of acceptees attending	44

FRESHMAN PROFILE
Range SAT Verbal	470-580
Average SAT Verbal	526
Range SAT Math	470-590
Average SAT Math	525
Range ACT Composite	20-26
Average ACT Composite	24
Minimum TOEFL	500
Average HS GPA	3.3
% graduated top 10% of class	24
% graduated top 25% of class	57
% graduated top 50% of class	86

DEADLINES
Early decision	12/1
Regular admission	8/1
Nonfall registration?	yes

FINANCIAL FACTS
Financial Aid Rating 77
Tuition	$17,900
Room and board	$4,820
Books and supplies	$750
Avg frosh grant	$12,125
Avg frosh loan	$2,910

WESTMINSTER COLLEGE

CAMPUS LIFE
Quality of Life Rating 79
Type of school	private
Affiliation	Presbyterian
Environment	suburban

STUDENTS
Total undergrad enrollment	1,340
% male/female	34/66
% from out of state	21
% from public high school	90
% live on campus	78
% in (# of) fraternities	50 (5)
% in (# of) sororities	50 (5)
% African American	1
% Caucasian	83
% Hispanic	1

ACADEMICS
Academic Rating 77
Calendar	semester
Student/faculty ratio	13:1
Profs interesting rating	93
Profs accessible rating	90
% profs teaching UG courses	100
Avg lab size	10-19 students
Avg reg class size	10-19 students

SELECTIVITY
Admissions Rating 75
# of applicants	1,191
% of applicants accepted	78
% of acceptees attending	38

FRESHMAN PROFILE
Range SAT Verbal	480-580
Average SAT Verbal	544
Range SAT Math	480-590
Average SAT Math	543
Range ACT Composite	19-26
Average ACT Composite	24
Minimum TOEFL	500
Average HS GPA	3.3
% graduated top 10% of class	20
% graduated top 25% of class	55
% graduated top 50% of class	87

DEADLINES
Regular admission	4/15

FINANCIAL FACTS
Financial Aid Rating	**88**
Tuition	$18,100
Room and board	$5,590
Books and supplies	$1,700
Required fees	$860
% frosh receiving aid	82
% undergrads receiving aid	78
Avg frosh grant	$7,500
Avg frosh loan	$3,100

YORK COLLEGE OF PENNSYLVANIA

CAMPUS LIFE
Quality of Life Rating	**74**
Type of school	private
Affiliation	none
Environment	suburban

STUDENTS
Total undergrad enrollment	8,119
% male/female	25/75
% from out of state	45
% from public high school	82
% live on campus	45
% in (# of) fraternities	10 (10)
% in (# of) sororities	10 (7)
% African American	1
% Asian	1
% Caucasian	95
% Hispanic	1
# of countries represented	29

ACADEMICS
Academic Rating	**70**
Calendar	semester
Student/faculty ratio	15:1
Profs interesting rating	85
Profs accessible rating	80
% profs teaching UG courses	100
% classes taught by TAs	0
Avg lab size	10-19 students
Avg regular class size	20-29 students

MOST POPULAR MAJORS
Elementary education and teaching
Nursing/registered nurse
training (RN, ASN, BSN, MSN)
Criminal justice/law enforcement administration

SELECTIVITY
Admissions Rating	**73**
# of applicants	3,723
% of applicants accepted	71
% of acceptees attending	43

FRESHMAN PROFILE
Range SAT Verbal	530-610
Average SAT Verbal	548
Range SAT Math	520-590
Average SAT Math	541
Minimum TOEFL	530
Average HS GPA	3.1
% graduated top 10% of class	29
% graduated top 25% of class	64
% graduated top 50% of class	93

DEADLINES
Nonfall registration?	yes

FINANCIAL FACTS
Financial Aid Rating	**81**
Tuition	$7,000
Room and board	$5,128
Books and supplies	$500
Avg frosh grant	$3,790
Avg frosh loan	$3,379

PART 4

INDEXES

Alphabetical Index

INDEX BY STATE

ABOUT THE AUTHORS

Robert Franek is a graduate of Drew University and has been a member of The Princeton Review Staff for four years. Robert comes to The Princeton Review with an extensive admissions background, most recently at Wagner College in Staten Island, New York. In addition, he owns a walking tour business and leads historically driven, yet not boring, tours of his home town!

Tom Meltzer is a graduate of Columbia University. He has taught for The Princeton Review since 1986 and is the author or co-author of seven TPR titles, the most recent of which is *Illustrated Word Smart*, which Tom co-wrote with his wife, Lisa. He is also a professional musician and songwriter. A native of Baltimore, Tom now lives in Hillsborough, North Carolina.

Roy Opochinski is a graduate of Drew University and has been a member of The Princeton Review staff since 1990. He has taught courses for TPR for 11 years and has edited several other books for TPR, including *Word Smart II* and *Math Smart*. In addition, Roy is the executive editor at Groovevolt.com, a music website. He now lives in Toms River, New Jersey.

Tara Bray is a resident of New York City by way of Hawaii, New Hampshire, Oregon, and Chicago, and is a graduate of Dartmouth College as well as Columbia University's School of the Arts. When she's not writing, Tara likes to spend her time figuring out how to pay the rent. She is also the author of The Princeton Review's guide to life after college, *Why Won't the Landlord Take Visa?*

Christopher Maier is a graduate of Dickinson College. During the past five years, he's lived variously in New York City, coastal Maine, western Oregon, central Pennsylvania, and eastern England. Now he's at an oasis somewhere in the midwestern cornfields—the University of Illinois—where he's earning his MFA in fiction. Aside from writing for magazines, newspapers, and The Princeton Review, he's worked as a radio disc jockey, a helping hand in a bakery, and a laborer on a highway construction crew. He's trying to avoid highway construction these days.

Carson Brown graduated from Stanford University in 1998, and after getting paid too much for working for various Internet companies for several years, sold her BMW and moved to Mexico. She has now overstayed her welcome south of the border and is returning to San Francisco to be responsible and further her career working as a writer and editor.

Julie Doherty is a freelance writer, Web designer, and preschool teacher. She lives in Mexico City.

K. Nadine Kavanaugh is pursuing her Master of Fine Arts at Columbia University. Her fiction has appeared on NYCBigCityLit.com and SlackFaith.com.

Catherine Monaco—ACADEMICS: Graduated from Dickinson College and earned a master's degree from Fordham University. STUDENT BODY: Bigger hair, bushier eyebrows (but learned to pluck after junior year). LIFE: Works as NYC public school teacher, lives in Tribeca, and "always has fun quoting other people for The Princeton Review."

Dinaw Mengestu is a graduate of Georgetown University and is currently completing his MFA in fiction at Columbia University. He lives in Brooklyn, New York.

Countdown to the SAT: The Week Before the Test

Studying Tips

- Make sure that you get enough sleep every night. Try going to bed earlier and waking up earlier.
- Get up early on the weekend and take a practice test. You need to train your mind to be alert in the morning and able to think for three hours. Treat the practice test as the "real thing."
- Get into a pattern of doing 30-45 minutes' worth of SAT problems each day from now until the test day. You're probably really busy, but think of it this way: you can make this tiny sacrifice now, or go through the entire process all over again.
- When you practice at home, do so under timed conditions. You need to get the feeling of what it will be like on the day of the test. As always, don't do your homework in front of the television or with the radio playing.
- Review all of the formulas and strategies that you've learned so far.

Got What You Need?

- Make sure you have your admission ticket. If you lose it or if it hasn't arrived at least one week before the test, call ETS at (609) 771-7600.
- Put new batteries in your calculator.
- Buy some No. 2 pencils, an eraser, and a sharpener.
- Confirm the location of the test center and make sure you know exactly where it is. If you haven't been there before, take a test run. How long does it take to get there? What's traffic like on Saturdays? Where should you park?
- Make sure you have a picture ID (e.g., driver's license, school ID with photo, passport). If you don't have one, see your counselor. Have him or her write a brief physical description of you on school stationery, and then both you and your counselor should sign it.

Extra Study Tip

Get a 5" x 7" index card; write math strategies on one side and verbal strategies on the other. Keep this card with you all week. Study it whenever you have free time: in study hall, in between classes, or on the ride home.

Countdown to the SAT:
The Day Before the Test

The Morning of the Test

Studying Tips

- DON'T STUDY!!! Cramming just won't help. Put your books away on a high shelf where you can't see them.
- Take it easy and let your brain relax. Catch an early movie or have dinner with friends.

At Night

- Go to bed at a reasonable hour. However, don't try to go to sleep at 7:00 p.m. It won't work.
- Set your alarm clock.

"Don't Forget" Checklist

Prepare everything that you'll need for the morning of the test:

- Admission ticket
- Photo ID
- No. 2 pencils
- Eraser
- Sharpener
- Calculator
- Watch or clock (one that doesn't beep)
- Morning warm-up problems

Countdown to the SAT:
The Morning of the Test

At Home

- Eat a healthy breakfast. It will give you the energy you need to make it through three hours of testing. However, don't give your body what it's not used to. For example, don't eat steak and eggs if you normally have toast and a glass of juice.
- Wear comfortable clothes. Also, dress in layers. You never know whether the test center will be unusually hot or cold.
- Take everything from the "Don't Forget" Checklist with you.
- Leave yourself 20 minutes more than you think you'll need to get to the test center. Be sure to arrive at least 20 minutes before the scheduled test time.

At the Test Center

- Use the bathroom before the test starts. You'll also have a chance to go to the bathroom during the first break (after Section 2). However, you will not have a chance to go during the second break (after Section 4).
- Do your warm-up problems. A great time to work on these questions is before you're seated.
- Try to maintain your focus. Do not listen to what other people say about the test, including which section they think is the experimental one.

Classroom Courses From The Princeton Review

The Classic Way to Prep

Classrooms may remind you of school, but in Princeton Review classes, the feeling is different. You're in a friendly, supportive place where everyone has the same goal: to beat the test.

Teachers that really know their stuff.

Not only do our teachers know how to keep you interested and involved, they also know our methods inside out. And by the end of your course, so will you.

Small, focused classes.

We never put more than 12 students in any class. So you'll get the personal attention you need and work at a pace that's right for you.

Extra help when you need it.

Admit it: occasionally you might need a little bit of extra help. Your Princeton Review teacher is available to meet with you outside of class at no extra charge. (And no one else has to know.)

Online resources 24/7.

Our Online Student Center is just a click away. You can go there whenever you want to check on your class times and locations, email your teacher, review lessons, practice tough concepts, or make up a missed class.

Materials that work for you.

Ask anyone who's taken our course: our manuals are the best. They have it all. Plus, you'll take a series of full-length practice tests, so you can monitor your progress and get comfortable with the exam.

Guaranteed results.

We know our courses work. In fact, we guarantee it: your SAT score will improve by at least 100 points, or your ACT score by 4 points, or we'll work with you again for up to a year, FREE.

Classroom Courses Available: *

SAT
ACT
SAT II – Writing, Math IC and IIC,
    Biology, Chemistry, Physics
PSAT
Word Smart, Math Smart

* Availability of specific courses varies by month
  and by location.

1-2-1 Private Tutoring
From The Princeton Review

The Ultimate in Personalized Attention

If you're too busy for a classroom course, prefer learning at your own kitchen table, or simply like being the center of the universe, *1-2-1* Private Tutoring may be for you.

The focus is on you.

Forget about what some other kid doesn't understand. With *1-2-1* Private Tutoring, it really is all about you. Just you. So you'll get the best instruction in less time than you'd spend in a class.

Your tutor is your coach.

1-2-1 tutors are our best, most experienced teachers. Your tutor will work side-by-side with you, doing whatever it takes to help you get your best score. No push-ups are required.

Pick a time, any time.

We know you're very, very (very) busy. So you and your tutor will meet when it's convenient for you.

Guaranteed results.

As with our classroom and online courses, your results with a full *1-2-1* Private Tutoring program are guaranteed: your SAT score will improve by at least 100 points, or your ACT score by at least 4 points, or we'll work with you again for free.

Tutoring programs available: *

SAT
ACT
SAT II (all subject tests)
PSAT
AP tests
Academic subjects

*Availability varies by location.

Online Courses From The Princeton Review

The Best of Both Worlds

Take the newest and best in software design, combine it with our time-tested strategies, and voilà: dynamic test prep where, when, and how you want it!

Lively, engaging lessons.

Our online courses are totally different from others you may have seen. You'll never passively scroll through pages of text or watch boring, choppy video clips. These courses feature animation, audio, interactive lessons, and self-directed navigation. We put you in the driver's seat.

Customized, focused practice.

The course software will discover your personal strengths and weaknesses and will help you to prioritize. You'll get extra practice only in the areas where you need it. Of course, you'll have access to dozens of hours' worth of lessons and drills covering all areas of the test. So you can practice as much or as little as you choose. (Just don't give yourself carpal tunnel syndrome, okay?)

Real-time interaction.

Our *LiveOnline* course includes eight additional sessions that take place in a virtual classroom over the Internet. You'll interact with your specially certified teacher and your fellow students in real time, using live audio, a virtual whiteboard, and a chat interface.

Help at your fingertips.

Any time of the day or night, help is there for you: chat online with a live Coach, check our Frequently Asked Questions (FAQ) database, or talk to other students in our discussion groups.

Guaranteed results.

We stand behind our *Online* and *LiveOnline* courses with complete confidence. Your SAT score will improve by at least 100 points, or your ACT score by at least 4 points. Guaranteed.

Online Courses Available:*

SAT *Online*
SAT *LiveOnline*
SAT *ExpressOnline*
ACT *Online*
ACT *LiveOnline*
ACT *ExpressOnline*

*Available EVERYWHERE!

Hit Parade

abstract general; not concrete
aesthetic having to do with the appreciation of beauty
alleviate to ease a pain or a burden
ambivalent simultaneously feeling opposing feelings
apathetic feeling or showing little emotion
auspicious favorable; promising
benevolent well-meaning; generous
candor sincerity; openness
cogent convincing; reasonable
comprehensive large in scope or content
contemporary current, modern; from the same time
conviction a fixed or strong belief
diligent marked by painstaking effort; hard-working
dubious doubtful; of unlikely authenticity
eclectic made up of a variety of sources or styles
egregious conspicuously bad or offensive
exculpate to free from guilt or blame
florid describing flowery or elaborate speech
gratuitous given freely; unearned; unwarranted
hackneyed worn-out through overuse; trite
idealize to consider perfect
impartial not in favor of one side or the other; unbiased

imperious arrogantly domineering or overbearing
inherent inborn; built-in
innovative introducing something new
inveterate long established; deep-rooted; habitual
laudatory giving praise
maverick one who resists adherence to a group
mollify to calm or soothe
novel strikingly new or unusual
obdurate stubborn; inflexible
objectivity treating facts uninfluenced by emotion
obstinate stubbornly adhering to an opinion
ornate elaborately decorated
ostentatious describing a pretentious display
paramount of chief concern or importance
penitent expressing remorse for one's misdeeds
pervasive dispersed throughout
plausible seemingly valid or acceptable; credible
profound having great depth or seriousness
prosaic unimaginative; dull
quandary a state of uncertainty or perplexity
rancorous hateful; marked by deep-seated ill will
spurious not genuine; false; counterfeit
stoic indifferent to pleasure or pain; impassive
superfluous extra; unnecessary
tenuous having little substance or strength; unsure; weak
timorous timid; fearful about the future
transitory short-lived; temporary
vindicated freed from blame

SAT vs. ACT

	SAT	ACT
Preferred by?	Private schools, and schools on the east and west coasts.	Public schools, and schools in the middle of the country. ACT is preferred by more U.S. colleges than the SAT.
Accepted by?	Nearly all U.S. colleges and universities.	Nearly all U.S. colleges and universities.
When is it administered?	Seven times per year.	Six times per year.
Test structure	Seven-section exam: Three Verbal, three Math, and one Experimental. The Experimental section is masked to look like a regular section.	Four-section exam: English, Math, Reading, and Science Reasoning. An Experimental section is added to tests on certain dates only, and is clearly experimental.
Test content	Math: up to 9th grade basic geometry. No science section. Reading: one passage with roughly one minute to answer each question. Stresses vocabulary. A test of strategy and testmanship.	Math: up to trigonometry. Science section included. Reading: four passages with less than one minute to answer each question. Stresses grammar. A test of time management and studiousness.
Is there a penalty for wrong answers?	Yes	No
How the test is scored/highest possible score	200-800 for each subject, added together for a combined score. A 1600 is the highest possible combined score.	1-36 for each subject, averaged together for a composite score. A 36 is the highest possible composite score.
Are all scores sent to schools?	Yes. If a student requests a score report be sent to specific colleges, the report will include the scores the student received on every SAT taken.	No. There is a "score choice" option. Students can choose which schools will receive their scores AND which scores the schools will see.
Other uses for the exams	Scholarship purposes.	Scholarship purposes. Certain statewide testing programs.
When to register	At least six weeks before the test date.	At least four weeks before the test date.
For more information	Educational Testing Service (ETS) (609) 771-7600 www.ets.org The College Board www.collegeboard.com	ACT, Inc. (319) 337-1270 www.act.org

To help you decide which test is right for you, take a side-by-side glance at these important exams.

The Princeton Review Admissions Services

At The Princeton Review, we care about your ability to get accepted to the best school for you. But, we all know getting accepting involves much more than just doing well on standardized tests. That's why, in addition to our test preparation services, we also offer free admissions services to students looking to enter college or graduate school. You can find these services on our website, *www.PrincetonReview.com*, the best online resource for researching, applying to, and learning how to pay for the right school for you.

No matter what type of program you're applying to—undergraduate, graduate, law, business, or medical—**PrincetonReview.com has the free tools, services, and advice you need to navigate the admissions process.** Read on to learn more about the services we offer.

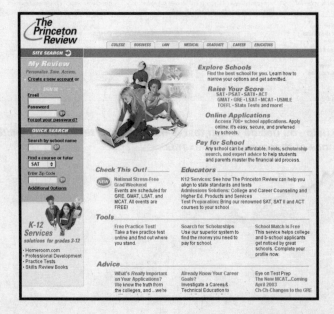

Research Schools
www.PrincetonReview.com/Research

PrincetonReview.com features an interactive tool called **Counselor-O-Matic.** When you use this tool, you enter stats and information about yourself to find a list of your best match schools, reach schools, and safety schools. From there you can read statistical and editorial information about thousands of colleges and universities. In addition, you can find out what currently enrolled college students say about their schools. Once you complete Counselor-O-Matic make sure you opt in to School Match so that colleges can come to you.

Our **College Majors Search** is one of the most popular features we offer. Here you can read profiles on hundreds of majors to find information on curriculum, salaries, careers, and the appropriate high school preparation, as well as colleges that offer it. From the Majors Search, you can investigate corresponding Careers, read **Career Profiles**, and learn what career is the best match for you by taking our **Career Quiz**.

No matter what type of school or specialized program you are considering, **PrincetonReview.com has free articles and advice, in addition to our tools, to help you make the right choice.**

Apply to School
www.PrincetonReview.com/Apply

For most students, completing the school application is the most stressful part of the admissions process. PrincetonReview.com's powerful **Online School Application Engine** makes it easy to apply.

Paper applications are mostly a thing of the past. And, our hundreds of partner schools tell us they prefer to receive your applications online.

Using our online application service is simple:

- Enter information once and the common data automatically transfers onto each application.
- Save your applications and access them at any time to edit and perfect.
- Submit electronically or print and mail in.
- Pay your application fee online, using an e-check, or mail the school a check.

Our powerful application engine is built to accommodate all your needs.

Pay for School
www.PrincetonReview.com/Finance

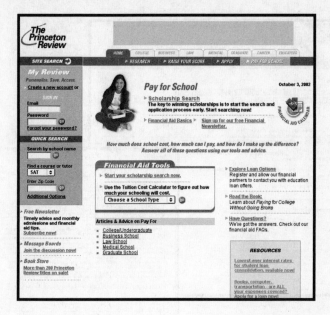

The financial aid process is confusing for everyone. But don't worry. Our free online tools, services, and advice can help you plan for the future and get the money you need to pay for school.

Our **Scholarship Search** engine will help you find free money, although often scholarships alone won't cover the cost of high tuitions. So, we offer other tools and resources to help you navigate the entire process.

Filling out the FAFSA and CSS Profile can be a daunting process, use our **Strategies for both forms** to make sure you answer the questions correctly the first time.

If scholarships and government aid aren't enough to swing the cost of tuition, we'll help you secure student loans. The Princeton Review has partnered with a select group of reputable financial institutions who will help **explore all your loans options**.

If you know how to work the financial aid process, you'll learn you don't have to **eliminate a school based on tuition.**

Be a Part of the
PrincetonReview.com Community

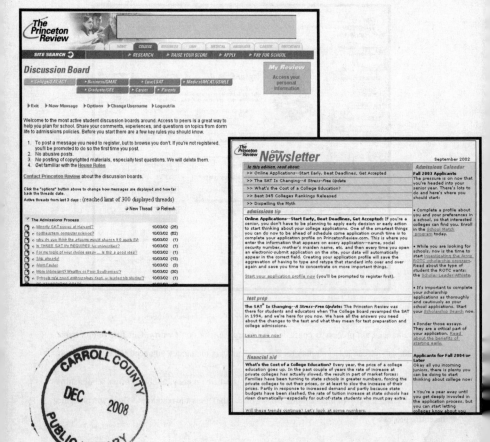

PrincetonReview.com's **Discussion Boards** and **Free Newsletters** are additional services to help you to get information about the admissions process from your peers and from The Princeton Review experts.

Book Store
www.PrincetonReview.com/college/
Bookstore.asp

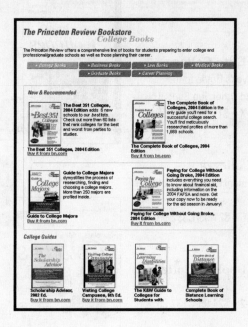

In addition to this book, we publish hundreds of other titles, including guidebooks that highlight life on campus, student opinion, and all the statistical data that you need to know about any school you are considering. Just a few of the titles that we offer are:

- Complete Book of Business Schools
- Complete Book of Law Schools
- Complete Book of Medical Schools
- The Best 351 Colleges
- The K&W Guide to Colleges for Students with Learning Disabilities or Attention Deficit Disorder
- Guide to College Majors
- Paying for College Without Going Broke

For a complete listing of all of our titles, visit our **online book store**:

www.princetonreview.com/college/bookstore.asp

MORE BOOKS FOR YOUR
COLLEGE SEARCH

America's Elite Colleges
The Smart Buyer's Guide to the
Ivy League and Other Top Schools
0-375-76206-X • $15.95/C$23.95

Best 351 Colleges
The Smart Student's Guide to Colleges
2004 Edition
0-375-76337-6 • $21.95/C$32.95

Complete Book of Colleges
2004 Edition
0-375-76339-2 • $24.95/C$37.95

Guide to College Majors
Everything You Need to Know
to Choose the Right Major
0-375-76276-0 • $21.00/C$32.00

The Internship Bible
2003 Edition
0-375-76307-4 • $25.00/C$38.00

The K&W Guide to Colleges
for Students with Learning
Disabilities or Attention
Deficit Disorder
7th Edition
0-375-76357-0 • $27.00/C$41.00

Paying for College
Without Going Broke
2004 Edition
0-375-76350-3 • $20.00/C$30.00

The Scholarship Advisor
5th Edition
0-375-76210-8 • $26.00/C$40.00

Taking Time Off
2nd Edition
0-375-76303-1 • $13.00/C$20.00

Visiting College Campuses
6th Edition
0-375-76208-6 • $20.00/C$30.00

WHEN YOU GO TO SCHOOL IN GREATER PHILADELPHIA, YOU'LL

declare every major

AND HAVE OPPORTUNITIES THAT GO WAY BEYOND THE CLASSROOM.

START EXPLORING IN A MAJOR WAY AT ONEBIGCAMPUS.COM.

major academic excellence. The Greater Philadelphia region boasts 80-plus colleges and universities. **major cultural attractions.** Art museums, The Kimmel Center, Wilma Theater, the jazz festival at Penn's Landing, First Fridays in Old City, the African American and Jewish history museums, the opera and the ballet. **major history and tradition.** From Independence Hall and the Liberty Bell, to Washington's Crossing and Valley Forge, you'll find historic sites and attractions across the entire region. **major sports action.** Nationally renowned sports franchises in every major sport — the Eagles, Flyers, Phillies and Sixers. There are also farm and minor-league teams and championship indoor soccer and lacrosse teams. **major fun.** Late-night lo mein in the heart of Chinatown at 10th and Arch. Nightclubs from Old City to Rittenhouse Square. Eat and stroll with friends on South Street. Concerts at the First Union Center and The Mann Center for the Performing Arts. **major deal.**

Visit now! For hotel packages and to discover why the Greater Philadelphia region is a major place to learn and live, visit **onebigcampus.com.**